The Great Encounter

The Great Encounter

Native Peoples and European Settlers
in the Americas, 1492–1800

Jayme A. Sokolow

M.E. Sharpe
Armonk, New York
London, England

The author gratefully acknowledges these publishers and rights holders for permission to reprint excerpts from the following works: *Popol Vuh: The Sacred Book of the Ancient Quiche Maya*. English version by Delia Goetz and Sylvanus G. Morley from the translation of Adrian Recinos. Copyright 1950 by the University of Oklahoma Press. Reprinted by permission; Johannes Wilbert and Karin Simoneau, eds., *Folk Literature of the Toba Indians*, vol. 1 (Los Angeles: UCLA Latin American Center Publications, 1982). Reproduced with permission of The Regents of the University of California; John T. Shawcross, ed., *The Complete Poetry of John Donne*, Garden City, NY: Doubleday & Company, 1967; Pablo Neruda, *Canto General. Fiftieth Anniversary Edition*. Edited/translated by Jack Schmitt. Copyright © 1991 Fundacion Pablo Neruda, Regents of the University of California; "The Myth of Tlaltecuhtli" from *The Flayed God* by Roberta H. Markman and Peter T. Markman. Copyright © 1992 by Roberta H. Markman and Peter T. Markman. Reprinted by permission of HarperCollins Publishers Inc.; *The Destruction of the Jaguar*. Copyright © 1987 by Christopher Sawyer-Larcanno. Reprinted by permission of CITY LIGHTS BOOKS; James Monney, *Myths of the Cherokees and Sacred Formulas of the Cherokees*, Nashville, TN: Charles and Randy Elder-Booksellers, 1982.

Library of Congress Cataloging-in-Publication Data

Sokolow, Jayme A., 1946–
    The great encounter : native peoples and European settlers in the Americas, 1492–1800
/ Jayme A. Sololow.
       p. cm.
    Includes bibliographical references and index.
    ISBN 0-7656-0982-7 (HC : alk. paper)
      1. Indians—First contact with Europeans. 2. Indians, Treatment of—America. 3.
Indians—Government relations. 4. America—Race relations. 5. America—Foreign
relations. 6. America—Discovery and exploration. I. Title.

E59.F53 S65 2002
970—dc21   2002023107

Printed in the United States of America

The paper used in this publication meets the minimum requirements of
American National Standard for Information Sciences
Permanence of Paper for Printed Library Materials,
ANSI Z 39.48-1984.

BM (c)   10   9   8   7   6   5   4   3   2   1

To the memory of my mother,
and to my father, Laurie, Rachel, and Sarah

If we had vision and feeling of all ordinary human life, it would be like hearing the grass grow and the squirrel's heartbeat, and we should die of that roar which lies on the other side of silence.

—George Eliot, *Middlemarch*

It is our weakness to think that distant people became civilized when we looked at them, that in their yesterdays they were brutish.

—Rebecca West, *Black Lamb and Gray Falcon*

Table of Contents

Preface

———————

This book answers a series of questions about the great encounter between native peoples and European settlers in the Americas from 1492 to 1800, including:

- What were the spiritual and material foundations of native cultures before the arrival of Europeans?
- What were the spiritual and material foundations of medieval Europe's expansion?
- Why did European countries want to conquer indigenous peoples?
- What were the similarities and differences between Spanish, Portuguese, French, and English relations with indigenous peoples?
- How did native peoples respond to the invasion of their homelands?
- What impact did native peoples have on colonial development?
- How did some native peoples survive the invasion of their homelands?
- What impact did the colonial powers have on native cultures?
- How did Europe benefit from its empires in the Western hemisphere?
- What might we learn about our own times from the colonial history of the Americas?

It is based on a simple premise: Native peoples played a crucially important role in the development of Europe's empires in the Western Hemisphere. Spain, Portugal, France, and England failed to transplant their traditional societies to the Americas because of the countless indigenous peoples and cultures they encountered. The Americas became different from Europe because of native food, native resources, free and fettered native labor, native political relations with Europeans, and the incredible mixing of Europeans, indigenous peoples, and Africans over three centuries.

The Introduction briefly explains the challenges we face in trying to understand the great encounter between native peoples and Europeans in the Americas. Chapter 1 examines the Western Hemisphere before the arrival of Christopher Columbus. It illustrates the different ways in which indigenous peoples explained their origins, expressed their most sacred beliefs in everyday life, and developed many different kinds of societies. Chapter 2 looks at the growth and expansion of medieval Europe and concludes with Columbus's first voyage to the New World. Chapter 3 describes the initial contacts between Europeans and indigenous peoples. Chapter 4 examines the attempts of European powers to build their New World empires in the sixteenth century with a focus on Spain. Chapter 5 narrates the growth of the Spanish and Portuguese empires in the seventeenth century.

Chapter 6 describes the beginnings of Britain and France's North American empires in the seventeenth century. Chapters 7 and 8 continue this story through the eighteenth century, showing how Britain, France, Portugal, and Spain's New World colonies emerged out of an unstable mixture of native defeat, accommodation, resistance, racial intermixing, and cultural borrowings. These two chapters highlight North America because the British colonies became so prosperous and powerful during this period. Finally, the concluding chapter raises some fundamental questions about our understanding of Western history.

Each chapter begins with a brief introduction followed by narrative accounts and dramatic vignettes in chronological order. The narrative accounts in Chapter 1 and Chapters 3 through 8 are grouped by geographical regions: North America, Mesoamerica (Mexico and Central America) and the Caribbean, South America, and Europe. The order of the regions will change depending on the region's centrality to each chapter.

Despite several decades of brilliant and imaginative scholarship about the Americas after 1492, many textbooks and classrooms from elementary school through college continue treating native peoples superficially. Still missing from most of our learning are thoughtful descriptions of indigenous societies and their impact on the Americas. To recover a fuller meaning of our past, we need to challenge commonly understood interpretations of the Americas before and after 1492, both for our own benefit and for the benefit of those who come after us.

As indigenous peoples have always recognized, diversity is one of the great gift of the gods and provides part of the spiritual dimension that frames our daily lives. One of our challenges at the beginning of the twenty-first century is to recognize the gift of diversity that native cultures have given us. We can begin by looking at the Americas since 1492 as if native peoples are central to our history.

The Great Encounter

Introduction

Recovering Lost Worlds

About 2,000 ago, Arawaks migrating from South America's Orinoco River basin used large dugout canoes to colonize the islands of the Caribbean. Sometime between 600 and 1,200 CE, the Taínos, as they are called, first arrived in the Bahama archipelago.

Over the next three centuries, the Taínos flourished in their new environment. Relying on a mixed diet of plants, small animals, fish, and marine mollusks, their population gradually expanded to at least 40,000 and perhaps as high as 80,000. The sandy soil of the Bahamas provided an ideal environment for growing large root and tuber crops like manioc, the mainstay of their diet.

Some Taíno villages grew to more than 3,000 inhabitants. Society was organized into a strict hierarchy of *caciques* [chiefs], *nitainos* [nobles or landlords], and *naborías* [commoners]. Regions were controlled by head chiefs; beneath them were district chiefs and village headmen.

On October 12, 1492, the Taíno world changed forever when Christopher Columbus arrived on the Bahamian island of Guanahaní, which he immediately claimed for Spain and renamed San Salvador. Within two years, Columbus and his successors began enslaving the Taínos to work in the gold mines of Hispaniola and the pearl fisheries off the coast of Venezuela.

The Spanish attitude toward the Taínos was articulated bluntly by another Italian explorer in the service of Spain, Amerigo Vespucci, who visited the Bahamas in November of 1499. "We agreed together," Vespucci wrote in his report, "to go in a northern direction, where we discovered more than a thousand islands and found many naked inhabitants. They were all timid people of small intellect; we did what we liked with them." When yet another slave expedition led by Juan Ponce de León arrived in 1513, the Bahamas were

3

deserted. In just two decades, its inhabitants had become extinct through a deadly combination of European diseases and Spanish slave expeditions.[1]

Spain's belief that Taíno land was their property and that the Taínos were an inferior human species ripe for conquest was not unusual. Whenever they could, European powers behaved in similar ways toward indigenous peoples from Alaska to the tip of South America. Neither their culture nor their sovereignty was respected. Beginning in 1492, Europe basically declared war on native peoples by treating them primarily as objects of domination or simply as obstacles to colonization.

When Columbus and the Taínos discovered each other on the beach at Guanahaní, they initiated a biological, cultural, and political encounter with profound and lasting global consequences. For the first time, Columbus brought into contact the populations of Europe, the Americas, and Africa, and he introduced new animal species, plants, and germs into these four continents. His voyages momentously changed culture, religion, and social institutions on both sides of the Atlantic. Columbus set into motion a chain of events that led to global European empires built on the talents, labor, land, and graves of indigenous peoples like the Taínos, whom Europeans called Indians.

To understand this story, we must leave our familiar surroundings and visit two strange places—the indigenous world and medieval Europe. But we can never truly understand our ancestors, despite the availability of countless documents and the brilliant work of many anthropologists, archaeologists, historians, and chroniclers over the last five centuries. No empathetic reading of documents and artifacts, no great imaginative leap can ever recover this lost world. There is too much emotional and temporal distance between ourselves and the past that cannot be overcome simply by studying documents and artifacts carefully.

Although we have ample records about the great encounter between indigenous peoples and Europeans, we will never be able to hear the tone of their conversations, or their silences; to study their facial expressions; to observe their gestures, or to feel their love, hate, regrets, envy, or pride. Important facets of human communication and understanding are forever lost to us—especially the many unrecorded voices and actions of native peoples, almost all of whom lived in cultures that did not rely on writing to store and transmit information. We cannot recover their verbal performances, the subtle cultural contexts of their conversations, and the unspoken understanding between speakers and audiences.

Almost completely missing are the voices of indigenous women. Explorers and early settlers often described the women they encountered, but they seldom quoted them directly in their narratives and letters. As a result, we will never know very much about native daily life.

Another serious problem is the source of our records. Ironically, although indigenous peoples have undertaken the bulk of language learning and translation since 1492, almost all our primary information about the encounter between Europe and the Americas comes from documents produced by Western writers for Western audiences. From the beginning of Europe's long study of the native world, indigenous people have rarely been allowed to represent themselves. Information about native societies became credible only after Europeans—who considered themselves Christians (in contrast to Moslems, their main spiritual rivals)—had recorded, edited, and published it.

While many authors found the native world incomprehensible and even grotesque, most claimed to understand it and wrote as if they had overcome any difficulties in linguistic and cultural communications. From Columbus onward, Christians admittedly did not understand indigenous languages even as they confidently and freely translated them. Despite daunting linguistic handicaps, they often acted as if sufficient rapport existed between themselves and the peoples they described to make their observations accurate.

Their accuracy, however, is very questionable. Most explorers and settlers could not understand indigenous societies because they were so alien to their own. And even when native peoples began writing about themselves, it usually had to conform to what Christians thought they should be saying. (Only in the last few decades have indigenous peoples started to use their own voice.) This is a serious problem and a seemingly insurmountable barrier to understanding the great encounter between such disparate cultures.[2]

Vitally important information about indigenous peoples comes from men who were committed to the complete transformation of the native world, or even worse, its complete demolition. From the beginning of European exploration and colonization, Christians carefully studied native peoples and produced brilliant colonial scholars, especially among the sixteenth-century Spanish. The primary aim of their studies, however, was usually political control, economic dependency, and religious conversion, for almost all of them believed that a greater knowledge of native societies would promote imperial domination.

The model for Europe's interpretation of indigenous societies was Christianity's traditional understanding of Judaism. Both Catholics and later Protestants like Martin Luther argued that they understood the Hebrew Bible far better than those who first wrote and interpreted it. Because the Jews perversely refused to acknowledge that their most sacred writings prefigured the coming of Jesus, the Hebrew Bible had to be authoritatively translated, annotated, and interpreted by Christians to be valid.

Similarly, most Christians usually wrote about indigenous cultures in what can best be described as a language of contempt. First used to describe Jews and later Moslems (medieval Europe's perpetual outsiders), Christians used the language of contempt to demonize people beyond Europe's borders and justify attempts at conversion and conquest.[3]

Although Christians confidently claimed to be writing universal history when they wrote about indigenous societies, until the last few decades the West has primarily produced historical accounts that do not take into account native experiences as Indians have perceived them. These accounts also ignore how much Europe profited and learned from contact with native peoples. The history of the Americas, especially in standard textbooks, is usually the story of European settlement and development, and little more.[4]

The native world rarely appears in all its strangeness, and it rarely poses a challenge to Christianity. The inherent estrangement between the two cultures is dissolved by either ignoring native perspectives, acknowledging them but belittling their value, denying any cultural rupture, or treating the clash among profoundly different peoples briefly and superficially. Settler history, which began with Columbus and continues triumphantly in American history textbooks today, is relentlessly progressive. The past is always rude and primitive, and the golden age is always about to appear in the near future.

Another serious problem involves the origin of many Indian sacred narratives and historical accounts. Almost all of them were first written after the defeat of indigenous peoples and were written from different political viewpoints. For example, in Peru, from 1542 to 1653, the Spanish carefully collected some forty sacred narratives about the origins of the Incas. Many of them were recounted by male Inca nobility from Cuzco, who recited their royal origins at least partly to be declared exempt from Spanish taxes and tribute. They were hardly objective storytellers because their political and social identities were at stake when they testified.

Inca sacred narratives were recorded in a highly charged political environment. Even since the mid-sixteenth century, Spanish officials had been trying to demonstrate that the Incas were a cruel and violent people who fought wars with their neighbors "without any right or title." To defend the Spanish conquest and uphold the authority of the Crown, jurists derided Inca rule and considered it an illegitimate exercise of sovereignty. When they examined Inca sacred narratives, officials were searching for evidence to dispossess Inca elites of their lands and titles of nobility.

Inca narratives passed through three stages of development that hardly clarified their meanings. First one noble told his story, then a second person translated it from Quechua, the language of the Incas, into Spanish, and finally a scribe recorded it in Spanish. Not surprisingly, this process produced many different narratives. Completely missing in the written documents was the performance aspect of the recitations—the pauses, changes in volume, alternations in pitch and tempo, silences, facial expressions, body movements, and the repetitions and parallelisms that would have accompanied the telling of any sacred narrative.

The act of translating and transcribing documents by Europeans inevitably slighted the verbal artistry that is still such an essential part of indigenous cultures. Except for a few surviving Mesoamerican documents produced before the conquest, all our native texts have been shaped in the context of colonialism. We will never know how native sacred narratives, stories, and daily conversations sounded to their original audiences or the feelings they aroused.[5]

As the Quiché Mayas of Mesoamerica wrote at the beginning of the *Popol Vuh*, their extraordinary book of creation, "We shall write about this now amid the preaching of God, in Christendom now."[6] Almost all native stories and texts have been mediated, directly or indirectly, by an alien culture that believed it could represent the indigenous world far better than itself.

Another challenge we face is narrating the histories of indigenous peoples in ways that are faithful to the narrative conventions they use to describe themselves.[7] To cite just one example among many, today Arizona's Western Apaches classify speech into three major categories: "ordinary talk," "prayer," and "narratives." Narratives are divided into four major and two minor categories. The major categories include myth ("to tell of holiness"), historical tales ("to tell of that which has happened"), sagas ("to tell of pleasantness"), and gossip. The two minor genres are Coyote stories, ("to tell Coyote's travels"), which are about a popular trickster figure among western Indians, and seduction tales ("to tell of sexual desires").

The Western Apaches divide the major narrative genres based on their time and purpose. Events that occurred "in the beginning" are classified as myths, and their purpose is to enlighten and instruct. Historic tales happened "long ago" after the Western Apache emerged from underneath the earth. Their purpose is to edify by criticizing inappropriate behavior. Sagas, which have taken place in "modern times," are designed to provide entertainment. And gossip, which occurs "now," is supposed to inform while shaming social deviants.

Myths and sagas may take hours to complete. Historic tales, in contrast, can usually be told in about five minutes. They open and conclude with the name of the places where the event occurred and are about the geographical sites as much as the event being narrated. And perhaps most importantly, historic tales describe the humiliation and punishment of those who violate Western Apache customs and norms. Although historic tales are narrated by an individual, the theme is always a collective one—the rules and values the Western Apaches use to organize their lives.[8]

We will have trouble understanding these historic tales if we do not know the names of the geographical places and their meanings, do not speak the language of the Western Apaches, and do not live in their communities or share their cultural standards. To write or speak about the past, we must adopt narrative conventions. European "realistic" narrative historical techniques may not fit the narrative historical conventions of the Western Apaches and many other indigenous peoples. There may be no master narrative that can reconcile native and European historical plots.

Despite these problems, with a large, healthy dose of social and political pluralism, we may at least partially be able to understand native cultures. We can listen to them by using whatever available evidence remains to see through their eyes, to hear through their ears, and to feel through their hearts. We must try, however inadequately, to understand native peoples in the light of their own beliefs and experiences. Even though we are greatly removed from their time and world, we can partially recover their side of the great encounter if we recognize that heterogeneity, and not homogeneity, has been the cultural and social norm in the Americas.

Without this recognition, we have neither a dialogue nor any cultural depth to the complex events that have transpired since 1492. In the words of the Aztecs, we must examine the great encounter between indigenous peoples and Europeans with a "polished eye," like a person "who is very astute in the manner of finding, of discovering, what is necessary, or who quickly sees what is difficult in an enigma."[9]

To recover a fuller meaning of our past, we need to engage in a process that constantly challenges commonly understood interpretations of the native world and the colonization process. We must be prepared to question some of our most cherished understandings of the past that comprise the core of settler history, understandings so deeply embedded in our consciousness that we rarely consider alternative ways of looking at our roots.

This is not a mysterious process that involves uncovering new sources. The building blocks for alternative interpretations have been available for the past 500 years. Until the last few decades, however, we have overlooked or undervalued most of them, and we have avoided asking unsettling questions of these sources.

This approach is a form of creative betrayal that is both radical and conservative, troubling and restorative. It is radical because alternative interpretations can overturn standard accounts of the early history of the Americas in a very simple and direct way: by making indigenous peoples central characters in a global drama called the exploration, conquest, and colonization of the New World.

In popular culture and in some American history textbooks, this is truly a betrayal of what many Americans still read and believe—that indigenous life and culture is just a brief prelude to the exploration and settlement of the

Americas. Almost completely missing from our understanding of the past is the profound impact of indigenous peoples on the development of Europe and the Americas after 1492.

This approach is also conservative because it consciously tries to salvage peoples, events, and relationships that have been discarded as part of our hemispheric heritage. It is an act of recovery that still has the power to broaden and deepen our understanding of how the Americas were created. By including native peoples in our account, we are only restoring them to the importance they had for the West from Columbus to the nineteenth century. To treat the original inhabitants of the Western Hemisphere as if they are central to the American experience is merely to give them their due.[10]

Although the story of the great encounter between native peoples and European settlers from 1492 to 1800 has in the last decade been told very well,[11] this account differs from previous ones by its combination of four thematic approaches. First, it places native peoples and their interaction with Europeans at the centerpiece of North American and South American history from 1492 through the American Revolution. Standard accounts of the period begin with a brief opening chapter about what is usually labeled "pre-Columbian America" and then in the bulk of the chapters describe colonial society as if native peoples were marginal or no longer existed. This was never the case. After the conquest, indigenous peoples remained vibrant and vitally important components of the British, French, Spanish, and Portuguese empires. In fact, their presence was the single most important factor in the development of these colonies from 1492 to 1800.

Second, this study covers the entire Western Hemisphere. Accounts of this era usually treat the British, French, Spanish, and Portuguese empires separately, as if they existed in isolation from each other. They are treated in this volume as a whole to provide a more coherent account of the colonial Americas.

Third, the historiography or scholarly controversies associated with different people, events, and issues is not discussed because they would clot this account with needless diversions and arguments that only scholars might find informative. Rather than adding to our knowledge of specialized topics, this study is designed to make the research of many talented scholars in the fields of history, anthropology, archaeology, geography, and literature available to a broader public.

And fourth, this book explicitly poses important questions about the Americas that link our past with the present. What does the history of the Western Hemisphere from Columbus through the American Revolution tell us about our own times? What can we learn from the past? And if we understand the past differently, what implications does it have for our future?

The narratives and events recounted in these chapters are part of what the poet William Wordsworth memorably called "spots of time."[12] Wordsworth understood that history is not a series of autonomous recollections that have some kind of inherent significance. What we choose to remember, record, and consider important derives its meaning from our own immediate concerns and personal experiences. As the present changes, we continuously modify our understanding of the past.

As indigenous peoples have always argued, understanding the past is impossible to separate from the ways we observe the world and interact with it. There is no natural order of things—our understandings are plural and culturally constructed. This account of native peoples and European settlers in the Americas from 1492 to 1800 is based on that perspective.

For many Americans, the past is a vague but glorious prologue to a more hopeful future. For indigenous peoples, however, memories may be very painful, and even debilitating, and reversing the legacy of the past may seem insurmountable. Although we have shared many things with them over the centuries, our understanding of the past is profoundly different from the indigenous population of this hemisphere.

Today, our challenge is to listen to stories about the great encounter without also being mutilated by them, and to remember that we are retelling something that is both saddening and ennobling: the destruction and survival of native peoples. From Columbus through the American Revolution, indigenous societies paid an extraordinarily high price to become part of Europe's overseas empires. But their histories after 1492 do not just recount resistance, defeat, and absorption.

Amid the violent transformation of the Americas, native peoples found ways to endure and maintain their identities. After Columbus, they fashioned new lives together with Europeans and Africans, and in the process they changed four continents—North America, South America, Europe, and Africa—forever. The Americas were the joint creation of many different peoples. Our past is indeed characterized by tragic conflict, but the tragedy was accompanied by the reinvention of local cultures and the creation of new ones.

➤ 1 ◄

Before the Wig and the Dress Coat

———————
————

In the words of the great Chilean poet Pablo Neruda:

> Before the wig and the dress coat
> there were rivers, arterial rivers;
> there were cordilleras, jagged waves where
> the condor and the snow seemed immutable:
> there was dampness and dense growth, the thunder
> as yet untamed, the planetary pampas.
>
> Man was dust, earthen vase, an eyelid
> of tremulous loam, the shape of clay—
> he was a Carib jug, Chibcha stone,
> imperial cup or Araucanian silica.
> Tender and bloody was he, but on the grip
> of his weapon of moist flint,
> the initials of the earth were
> written.[1]

Despite the passage of time, native peoples did remember when they were merely dust, and they handed down from generation to generation thousands of stories about their origins and emergence. Their sacred narratives explained how an orderly and balanced world developed out of chaos, confusion, and disharmony. In the beginning the world was undifferentiated and intact; later the sky and earth separated so that humans could emerge. These events occurred in primordial time, the fabled time of the beginning. They describe

11

nothing less than something momentous and miraculous—the breakthrough of the sacred into the world.

Amid the incredible variety and inventiveness of native sacred narratives and stories, amid the many deeds of the gods, spirits, tricksters, and transformers, a recurring theme emerges: all things are related. There is an old and deep kinship between humans and the rest of creation, which includes plants, animals, the heavenly bodies, and such geographic forms as mountains and stones. The past is a living part of the present, time and space are not separate dimensions, and the entire cosmos acts as a living, unified whole. Our world is a benevolent place that will nurture us if we can find our proper places in it, and only within this rootedness can we ever become complete and fulfilled.

Indigenous peoples lived in a universe where everything was inseparably connected to the spiritual because it was imbued with a sacredness established long ago when the gods created the universe. For them, the entire creation was continually involved in an elaborate spiritual exchange begun by the "Ancient Ones" or the founders. Whether they believed in life after death or in reincarnation, native societies had a deep conviction that all forms of life were indelibly and fundamentally interrelated, and they acted as if this association could be used beneficially to control the dynamic, creative forces that governed the world.

Because timelessness was a fundamental part of their world, native peoples never needed to dream of a paradise at the end of time. In their cyclical cultures, the natural and social orders replicated themselves with each new season, sacred ritual, or birth. Life was infinitely renewable because its sacred sources were so abundant and incapable of being exhausted. Diversity was built into the very structure of the cosmos.

Although everyday life was framed by ancient times, indigenous peoples knew that their existence was not predetermined by the past but shaped by their own circumstances and decisions. Since their appearance on earth, they had undergone migrations, fought other peoples, developed languages and political systems, domesticated animals and plants, modified the landscape, and learned to live in an incredibly wide variety of environments. In native societies, people understood that their lives were dynamic, not static.

Throughout the hemisphere, there were thousands of different cultures that ranged from small, highly mobile, and relatively egalitarian hunter-gatherer societies such as the Onas at the southern tip of the Americas to sedentary, highly stratified states like the Inca empire. Despite their different political and social structures, all native societies shared similar spiritual foundations. For them, subsistence was more than a means of production. It was a system for distribution and exchange that bound generations and families over time as partners with important obligations to each other. Over shared joys and hardships lasting thousands of years, indigenous peoples developed highly adaptive ways of living in varied environments throughout the hemisphere. This accomplishment stemmed from their vision of wholeness, a recognition that everything was interconnected and had meaning.[2]

South America

The Inca's Heavenly Empire

In the central Andes, indigenous peoples have always considered Lake Titicaca the center of the universe. Over 1,000 years ago, they built a temple to their supreme deity, Wiraqocha, on one of Tititaca's islands. According to the people who lived around the lake, once only darkness and chaos reigned. Then Wiraqocha appeared nearby, creating humans and all living things. But when people disobeyed Wiraqocha's moral commands, a flood destroyed the world. Wiraqocha went to Lake Titicaca again where he created the sun, moon, and stars along with the many peoples who lived in the region. Once he had finished creating the present world, Wiraqocha departed and vanished into the ocean.

In the fifteenth century, the great Inca military emperor Pachakuti Inca Yupanki ("he who overturns time and space") reorganized his state's administration and calendar and established the state worship of Wiraqocha, the celestial, androgynous creator god. According to the Incas, Wiraqocha, "lord fountainhead of the sun" and "tilted plane of the celestial sea," emerged from Lake Titicaca, created humans, made the sun rise, and then went northward to Cuzco to establish the Inca empire.

In one Inca hymn, Wiraqocha was called "*Cam cuzco capaca*" [the king of Cuzco] and "the one who measures the navel of the earth by palms." As the creator of the celestial heavens and the social order on earth, Wiraqocha was portrayed as an elderly man with a beard who wore a long robe and supported himself with a staff.

Wiraqocha had eternally ruled over the universe and created a number of benevolent gods to assist him. In the Inca's great "Temple of the Sun" at Cuzco, he was represented as a solid gold figure raising his right arm to command the heavens. Pachakuti used Wiraqocha to create a new imperial cosmology that justified Inca rule by linking the Incas to the numinous past of Lake Titicaca.

Supporting Wiraqocha were other sky and earth gods. The "Sun," a male progenitor of the Inca royal dynasty, protected crops and was the venerated object of temple devotion throughout the empire. Special stars and constellations watched over agricultural activities as did the gods of the earth. The two most important were "Pachamama," or Mother Earth, and "Mamacocha," or the Mother of Lakes and Water.

In the cities, Inca temples housed priests, oracles, and sacred objects. The most magnificent one was the Temple of the Sun, which also accommodated consecrated virgins who created ceremonial objects and beer for official festivals. Priests were powerful men in the Inca empire. They officiated over special ceremonies, interpreted oracles, performed animal and human sacrifices on important occasions, cured diseases, and heard confessions.

Wiraqocha was the official god of the Inca empire, but countless ancestor gods commanded great veneration. Throughout the Andes, people worshipped objects called *huacas* [a person or a part of the landscape associated with the sacred], which usually marked fountains, springs, hills, rocks, mountains, houses, and special viewpoints.

Huacas were also stone representations of departed Inca nobility whose mummified cadavers were attended by servants in Cuzco. The emperor and his family even had their own portable *huacas* as personal guardians. Cuzco probably contained 328 *huacas* connected by forty-one imaginary *ceques* [crooked lines] emanating from the Temple of the Sun in center of the city toward points on the horizon. The *huacas* along these *ceques* were cared for by priests representing all the different ethnic groups in the Inca empire. *Ceques* were probably drawn to correspond to the rising of certain stars, for Andean peoples have always believed that the celestial realm controlled their destiny.

The Incas also incorporated local shrines and *huacas* into the worship of Wiraqocha, whom they considered far more powerful and important than any rival community's gods. In fact, after the Incas conquered neighboring peoples, their *huacas* were chained by the feet to the statue of the Sun in his temple.

Throughout the Andes, space and time were part of a moral order maintained by the gods. Supernatural beings might bring good fortune, but they could not determine a person's life after death. The Incas believed that after good people died, they lived with the Sun under very comfortable circumstances. Bad people went to the earth's interior where they were perpetually cold and ate only stones. The Inca nobility were more fortunate, for they automatically traveled to the Sun god despite any bad deeds they might have performed.

The peoples of the Andes believed that the natural and supernatural realms were composed of complementary and cooperative halves. Whether they lived in cities or small communities, their universe was a giant web of kinship relations based on the concept of *ayni* [balance and reciprocity].

The Inca empire, with its sacred capital of Cuzco, was divided into four complimentary parts: Antisuyu in the North, Cuntisuyu in the South, Collasuyu in the East, and Chinchaysuyu in the West. Antisuyu and Chinchaysuyu, considered the upper part of the empire, were associated with the sun, masculinity, and dominance. Cuntisuyu and Collasuyu, the lower part of the empire, were associated with the moon, femininity, and subordination. Upper Cuzco was the military and administrative center while lower Cuzco focused on religion and agriculture. The Incas might have alternated rulers from each section or had two kings simultaneously rule. Even the Incas' highly rectangular buildings were constructed to be bilaterally symmetrical.

The *ayllu* [family] was the basic political and social unit of Andean society. An *ayllu* was a community composed of people claiming descent from a common ancestor. Each *ayllu*, which was ruled by a *curaca* [male chieftain], controlled such important resources as farmland, pasture, domesticated animals, and water. Heads of households had the right to use but not own land and resources. Although there were differences in wealth and power within *ayllus*, all members lived by an ethic of sharing and cooperation and were assured access to land and other community assets to meet their basic needs.

Andean *ayllus* and households were organized along parallel lines of descent based on gender. Men inherited their *ayllu* affiliation through their father's family line while women traced *ayllu* descent from their mother's family. These lines were considered complementary and entailed traditional obligations and rights that neither gender could violate. Women and their daughters, like men and their sons, had independent rights to community land, water, and other resources.

Ayllu residents probably even treated numbers and arithmetic based on gender. Counting was based on groups of five, and the fingers were organized by gender. The thumb, called the mother finger in Quechua, was the oldest ancestral digit while the last finger represented the youngest. Reproduction provided the metaphors for Quechua numbers. Women may have had their own number symbols, which probably were sexual in nature. The number one in Quechua, for example, also may have meant an erect penis or a man with only one testicle.

Just as *ayllus* had parallel lines of descent, they also divided labor and even religious ceremonies by gender. After infancy, young boys became hunters and herders while girls helped take care of their households, herded, and learned to weave and make dyes. As they neared the age of twenty, young men herded animals in the high country, joined adult males in warfare, plowed, and acted as messengers.

Young women raised llamas and matured into weavers of cloth. Once married, the *ayllu* considered both men and women full productive members of the community. Upon marriage, they received property from both sides of their families and resources from the *ayllu*. Each partner's kin were now linked together and expected to treat each other as brothers and sisters.

Men and women had their own religious organizations and even managed separate property to support their ceremonies. "Illapa" was a male deity who controlled rain and conquest, and male heads of households built shrines to him in the mountains high above their *ayllus*. Pachamama, his consort, was the Earth Mother and goddess of fertility. Her shrines were made of long stones placed in the middle of fields. Both men and women worshipped Pachamama, but only women purified themselves in her name before planting seeds. Women felt especially close to "Saramama," the Corn Mother and the daughter of Pachamama. To worship their deities, women had their own religious organizations, inherited sacred staffs, officiated as priests, and heard confessions from other women.

In Andean society, adult male identity was primarily associated with plowing and warfare. Women supervised households and wove cloth. Even in death the genders were carefully demarcated. Women went to their graves with spindles and rolls of cotton. Men had their hoes and instruments of war.

As the Inca state grew in the fifteenth and early sixteenth centuries by conquering and absorbing hundreds of ethnic groups, it modified but did not fundamentally change the kinship and gender structure of the *ayllus*. Inca conquerors could not create a new social order because the *ayllu* provided the context for Andean conceptions of order and hierarchy. Like the *ayllus*, the Inca dynasty was organized into parallel lines of male and female descent, as were Inca sacred narratives. The Incas claimed that they were the offspring of the Sun and the Moon. The emperor represented all men while his wife ruled over all women.

The Inca empire, which treated *ayllus* as inferior imperial kin, reorganized their lands into three parts. The Sun God's territory helped maintain the Inca religion, the emperor's property supported the state, and remaining arable lands belonged to the local *ayllu*. Lands were always strictly cultivated in this order of importance. Whenever possible, the Incas retained local ethnic communities and traditional *curacas* to buttress their expanding state. If *curacas* led more than 100 households, the Incas considered them minor nobility and provided them with attractive benefits. The rationale for this structure of inequality had been established by the original Incas, who were divine beings. In the first *ayllus*, they had created commoners and nobles within their empire.

The strongest, bravest young men became soldiers in the imperial army while peasants cultivated Inca lands and manufactured clothing and weapons for the imperial troops. The Incas chose beautiful *ayllu* women to be their spouses and forced others to become *acllas* [special imperial servants]. Living in monasteries, they cared for the imperial temples, produced beautiful cloth for gifts and religious ceremonies, and cooked large quantities of food for public ceremonies.

Ayllus also provided sacrificial victims for the Inca state. Besides sacrificing llamas, in Cuzco the Incas used men, women, and especially very young children to propitiate their gods on important ceremonial occasions—the beginning of a new reign, the illness of an emperor, or the appearance of dangerous natural calamities like droughts and earthquakes. Sacrificial children had no body blemishes and were treated with exceptional kindness before they died. Many were buried alive; others had their hearts torn out of their bodies after their chests had been cut open. Major temples also received yearly quotes of sacrificial girls from the empire. Before they were killed, they were anesthetized with *chica* [corn beer made by temple women] and consoled with the thought that they had been "called upon to serve the gods in a glorious place."

The Inca empire, like the *ayllus*, operated on the principle of imperial reciprocity and redistribution, however unbalanced and oppressive it appeared to conquered *ayllus*. Inca rule extracted labor, tribute, and people from conquered communities to strengthen the ruling elite in Cuzco. In exchange for their loyalty, service, *acllas*, and tribute, which were all considered gifts, the Incas retained the structure of the *ayllus* and might even give some communities grants of fertile land and special privileges. Workers on state lands were compensated by the Incas, and public granaries fed the empire's subjects during famines.

From the wealthy court of the Incas down to the poorest household of an *ayllu*, Andean society ranked the Inca empire, human society, the forces of nature, and even the heavens along parallel lines of gender. This social and cultural system separated men and women into complementary spheres with clearly demarcated duties, rights, and mutual obligations.[3]

Ona Hunting Tools

The boreal forest interior of cold Tierra del Fuego at the southern tip of South America supported the mobile Onas for thousands of years. There they lived in small bands of forty to 120 people in clearly defined hunting territories, moving about sixty times a year in search of food. The Onas depended on the guanaco for most of their diet. Their shelters were built of guanaco skins supported on poles; they wore caps and robes made of the light, warm wool of the guanaco; and they ate little else but guanaco meat and some fish.

The primary hunting weapon was the bow and arrow, the Ona male's most prized and dangerous possession. Arrows were made from the twisted trunk of a wild barberry, split into four pieces, and heated so that they would be straight. Then they were smoothed in a grooved stone and polished with dust and the skin of a fox. The arrow was notched on both ends, and a split feather was fastened below one notch with a guanaco tendon and white clay. A chiseled pointed stone was lashed in the other notch. To make their arrows, the Onas used six different materials scattered around their territory and seven different tools.

With their beechwood bows, the Onas were deadly hunters. They could kill other Onas invading their territory, capture wives, or bring down a guanaco at over 100 yards.[4]

The Toba First Woman

"The women were up in the sky. The men were down on earth, and they had no wives and did not know about women. Those people were the parrot, the hawk, the fox, the armadillo, and other animals.

They used to go out early to hunt and fish, leaving their food on a table. After the men had gone the women would descend on a chain, steal and eat the food, and climb up again. When this had been going on for many days, the men decided to leave someone to watch over their provisions.

First, they chose the parrot. When the women came down the next time the parrot wanted to call out, but the women bent his beak and beat him up.

The next day the hawk stayed behind to keep watch over the food. The parrot had told him what had happened, so, armed with a machete, the hawk hid. When the women descended he flew over and cut their chain, and they fell down and went to the ground, deep in the earth.

Since the armadillo was good at digging he started to dig, pulling out the women. As he got them to the surface the others seized them, and no one was left for him. Finally he grabbed the last woman, and as he did she escaped from his claws and he gouged out one of her eyes. The armadillo then caught her, wondering whether they should let her go because she had only one eye, although in other respects they could do with her as with the others.

But these women had toothed vaginas, and there was no way to have intercourse with them. The fox, lecherous as always, began to have sex with one woman, but the teeth in her vagina caught his penis and cut it off. The fox found a bone and put it there, thus getting a new penis. That's why the fox has a hard penis, because he used a bone to replace the penis that the teeth in the woman's vagina had cut off.

Then they seized the leader of the women. The fox made her sit down and opened her legs, and they could see her teeth. They hit her there and broke the teeth, which fell out. As her teeth fell, so did the teeth in the other women's vaginas, all by themselves. And thus it happened; each man got a wife."

Note: Johannes Wilbert and Kevin Simoneau, eds. *Folk Literature of the Toba Indians* (Los Angeles: University of California Press, 1982), vol. 1, pp. 141–142.

Hawks and Ancestors

The Mapuches of central Chile have always believed that their ancestors become influential spirits that have a very active relationship with the world of the living. When Mapuches die, they may be transformed into hawks of the sun, butterflies, and blueflies, or reborn as dangerous night creatures who haunt the living. Mapuche ancestors must be treated with great care and respect because the dead visit them at night in their dreams and during the day as nonhuman sentient beings. By performing the appropriate rites, ancestors can be propitiated. This is crucial for their sense of harmony and balance, for in the Mapuche universe the spirits of the dead constantly watch over human affairs.[5]

Chan Chan

Along the coastal desert of northern Peru six centuries ago stood Chan Chan, the largest city of its time in South America. As the capital of the state of Chimor, this metropolis of 25,000–30,000 inhabitants contained spectacular structures and objects of great beauty. Some of its earthen walls were twenty-five feet high and almost 2,000 feet long. In the middle of this nine-square-mile city was a gigantic adobe pyramid dedicated to the sun measuring 1,200 feet by 450 feet. An intricate irrigation system fed water into the city from the mountains fifty miles away, and the most productive fields surrounding Chan Chan were owned and operated by the state with tribute labor.

Chan Chan's royal rulers were considered semi-divine figures and lived in elegant palaces attended by many servants. Human sacrifices helped maintain the social and political order. The city also produced incredibly ornate pottery, textiles, silver, and gold for its elite, which was part of a rich, continuous cultural tradition of Moche art spanning over 1,000 years.

Perhaps Chan Chan's most unusual social custom was the royal system of split inheritance, which the Incas copied. Within the city were nine large royal compounds surrounded by adobe walls more than twenty feet high. Each of these compounds, with its plazas, courts, and storerooms, was the seat of a monarch. After he died, the compound became a mausoleum maintained by his noble relatives with the proceeds from the land and labor of his fields. As a result, each new monarch had to extend the boundaries of the Chimor empire because the state's best lands were controlled by the kinship lineages of dead monarchs.

Despite its wealth and power, however, Chan Chan could not maintain its independence beyond two centuries. The Incas eventually conquered the city, assassinated its rulers, replaced them with pliant leaders, and removed its wealth and most skilled craftspeople to their imperial capital of Cuzco. As the state of Chimor collapsed, Chan Chan quickly became a ghost town, a metropolis of crumbling buildings, looted burial sites, and blasted royal dreams.[6]

Moundbuilders of the Amazon

Over 1,500 years ago, large moundbuilding societies developed along the alluvial floodplains of Amazonia in places like the Lllanos de Mojos of Bolivia, the Middle Orinoco, the coastal plains of the Guianas, and at the mouth of the Amazon River. The largest and most influential of these cultures was Marajoara, which existed for almost a millennium on the gigantic island of Marajo astride the entrance to the Amazon. Marajoara was a seasonal floodplain over 1,000 square miles in size with fertile soils, plentiful savannahs, and forests. Because of heavy seasonal rains, its inhabitants constructed hundreds of massive mounds to maintain a population of more than 100,000 people.

The inhabitants of Marajoara lived in large communal dwellings that were spatially separated into extended family households. The communal dwellings surrounded an open space. Society traced descent through its women, and when men married, they moved into their wives' houses. Women fished, tended their manioc and maize plots, cared for their households and children, and acted as spiritual leaders. Because they produced their own food and crafts, senior women who ran households were powerful people. In their elaborately decorated pottery, they were portrayed with great religious powers.

Men, at least among the elite, were tall, powerful, and spent a great deal of time wrestling each other and fighting their neighbors. Marajoarca males lived in separate houses, made pottery for feasts and burials, and had their own special ceremonies. They apparently lived much like other Amazonians, but the scale of their society was unequaled in the tropical lowlands of South America.[7]

Hallucinogens and the Jivaro Soul

In the Ecuadoran tropical rainforest live the Jivaros, who believe that hallucinogenic drugs provided access to the invisible realm of the spirits. Until the past few decades, the Jiveros used mind-altering drugs to initiate young men into the violent life of a warrior.

In Jivaro society, hallucinogens were used by shamans, adults, and children. Soon after birth, babies received their first hallucinogenic drug to begin seeing the spiritual world. About the age of six, a boy might seek new souls with his father's assistance. Unless a boy received at least one before puberty, he might die. The first soul provided a male with power in fighting. The second one ensured that he could not be killed by his enemies.

To find an *arutam* soul, a boy and his father journeyed to a nearby sacred waterfall where souls and spirits lived in the breezes. On their pilgrimage, they sang a song "in order to have a very long life."

At the waterfall, they bathed naked and walked through the cascades with a magical balsa wood staff chanting *"tau, tau, tau, tau."* They slept by the sacred waterfall and fasted, drank tobacco water, and waited for the new soul to appear. Usually the boy encouraged its arrival by drinking a hallucinogenic juice.

After passing through a delirious state, the boy fell asleep. At midnight, he awakened to discover that the world has completely changed. The stars had disappeared, the earth violently trembled, and he was threatened by heavy winds, lightening, and falling trees. The boy grasped a tree trunk. Soon an apparition resembling an animal, snake, or human came toward him. He ran forward and touched it with a stick or his hand, and then it disappeared.

When the boy returned home, he told no one about the new soul but slept that night on the bank of the nearest river. The *arutam* in the form of an old man appeared and said to him: "I am your ancestor. Just as I have lived a long time, so will you. Just as I have killed many times, so will you." Immediately the new soul entered the body of the boy. He now had enhanced physical and mental powers and could not be killed by sorcerers or enemies.

Within a few months, he joined his father in a murderous attack that satisfied his desire to kill and enabled him to acquire more power by replacing his new soul with another one—that of his enemy. Becoming a brave warrior meant carrying out his sense of justice through constant warfare, blood feuds, and vengeance.

When a man died, his soul left him and drifted as a breeze at waterfalls until relatives found it. His soul also visited his male relatives in dreams, calling for revenge.[8]

Mesoamerica and the Caribbean

Monserrat

In the Lesser Antilles south of St. Kitts and Nevis lies the small volcanic island of Monserrat. When it was settled by Taínos migrating from South America's Orinoco River basin about 2,300 years ago, Monserrat had a diversified ecology of tropical rain forests, mangrove swamps, grasslands, coastal woodlands, and active volcanoes. The Taínos established two major villages along alluvial fans on the east and west coasts and grew fruits and vegetables they had carried from the mainland—maize, peanuts, sweet potatoes, squash, pineapples, papaya, beans, peppers, avocados, medicinal plants, tobacco, and especially manioc.

In Monserrat and the smaller islands of the Caribbean, the Taínos used weirs, hooks, and nets to catch fish, their major source of protein. They also captured sea turtles, turtle eggs, shellfish, and crabs, and hunted parrots and birds. The Taínos raised a kind of dog and a rodent-like animal for consumption, too. Because there were few large animals available, hunting was never an important activity.

Taíno food came primarily from their *conucos* [farms], which were tilled collectively by *naborías* under the control of *caciques*. Male *naborías* hunted, fished, gathered wild fruits from the forest, and cleared garden plots while female *naborías* harvested and prepared food. These people were not slaves but could be traded or given as gifts to other *caciques*. Most of their work involved cultivating manioc.

Using intricate irrigation systems to channel rain water, which began falling toward the end of March, the Taínos collectively grew manioc in large garden plots throughout the year. First, they destroyed all the vegetation in their plots by cutting and burning it. Then they sowed manioc seeds in mounds of dirt about four feet across and three feet apart. By placing manioc in mounds, it established a strong root system as long as three feet without exhausting the soil. The Taínos also grew beans, maize, and squash, which fertilized the mounds and kept the heavy rains from washing away their crops.

Taíno agriculture was remarkably productive. If twenty men worked six hours a day for only one month, they could grow enough manioc to feed 300 people for two years. After twelve to eighteen months, the heavy manioc plants were harvested by cutting away the roots with stone and flint tools. *Naborías* then squeezed the poisonous hydrocyanic acid from the roots, grated the dried manioc into flour, and baked it into a bread.

The Taínos ate two different kinds of manioc, sweet and bitter. Sweet manioc, which was roasted or boiled, came from a fast-growing plant the Taínos selectively bred. Bitter manioc, because it was poisonous, had to be carefully drained before baking. In the interior of Monserrat, the Taínos grew so much starchy and nutritious manioc that it became the basis for trade and the growing power of the *caciques*, who controlled *naborías* and village exchange with other settlements and islands.

In Monserrat, the Taínos developed a unique religion centered on the worship of *cemíes*, small cone-shaped objects made of stone, shells, ceramics, and wood. The *cemíes* were spirit mediums that could communicate with powerful cosmic forces, especially ones involved in divination, healing, and fertility.

When a Taíno walked by a tree that was moved by the wind more than the others, he might ask the tree's identity. If the tree responded, "Call here a behique or priest and I will tell you who I am," a priest or shaman would perform the appropriate ceremonies and ask, "What are you doing here? What do you wish of me? Why have you asked to have me called? Tell me if you wish me to cut you down?" The tree would be felled and carved into a *cemíe* if it answered these questions. The *cemíes* were sacred links that made possible direct communication between the supernatural and human worlds.

According to the Taínos, twelve basic *cemíes* formed two opposite orders. The "Spirits of Fruitfulness," for example, maintained flora and fauna, provided water, and ensured fertility. Their opposites were responsible for the destructive forces of the cosmos—hurricanes, death, sexual promiscuity, and the dead spirits' eruption into the world of the living.

In their fertility rituals, *cemíes* served as altars for harvested manioc because they helped fertilize crops. They were often placed on a highly decorated seat next to the *cacique* "to signify that he who sits there is not alone, but that he sits there with his rival." The Taínos ate, drank, and danced around these *cemíes* in ceremonies lasting several days. Shamans would use *cemíes* to heal people suffering from diseases such as syphilis, and in divination ceremonies their intricately carved nasal narcotic pipes resembled the *cemíes* they worshipped.

Taíno religious life was precariously balanced between complementary forces. For the Taínos, the cosmos was composed of opposites that could be stabilized, just as many of their *cemíes* had dual faces representing the human and the divine.[9]

Aztec Mother Earth

"Some say that the earth was created in this fashion: Two gods, Quetzalcoatl and Tezcatlipoca carried down from the heavens the goddess of the earth Tlalecuhtli, who was filled up at all joints by eyes and mouths with which she bit like a wild beast. Before they came down, there was already water, which they do not know who created and upon which this goddess made her way down. Which upon seeing, the gods said to one another: 'There is a need to make the earth'; and saying this they changed themselves into two large snakes, of which one seized the goddess from the right hand to the left foot, the other from the left hand to the right foot, and they pulled so much that they broke her in half, and from the half towards the shoulders they made the earth and carried off the other half to heaven, and by this the other gods were greatly angered.

After this deed, in order to recompense the goddess of the earth for the damage that the two gods had done to her, all the gods came down to console her, and ordered that from her would come all the fruit necessary for the life of men; and in order to do this, they made from her hair trees and flowers and grasses, from her skin the very fine grass and small flowers, from her eyes wells and fountains and small caverns, from her mouth rivers and great caverns, from her nose mountain valleys, and from her shoulders mountains. And this goddess sometimes wept at night, desiring to eat men's hearts, and would not be quiet until they were offered to her, nor would she bear fruit unless she was watered with the blood of men."

Note: Robert H. Markman and Peter T. Markman. *The Flayed God: The Mythology of Mesoamerica* (San Francisco: HarperCollins, 1992), p. 213.

Knowledge and Power in Panama

One thousand years ago, Panama was a fertile agricultural land of open savannah along great rivers. Panamanian society was divided into numerous small territories controlled by high chiefs, who ruled over vassals, commoners, and prisoners of war. In order to become powerful, chiefs had to demonstrate wisdom, strength, and gain access to long-distance travel and exchange networks.

In the Panamanian lowlands, chiefs exchanged fish, game, salt, cotton, and war captives for highland Colombian ceramics and intricately fabricated gold items, which symbolized leadership and sacred power. By accumulating beautifully crafted exotic objects that were produced far away, they proved their ability to tap into cosmic powers associated with distant places.

Chiefs demonstrated their importance by ritually contacting distant supernatural powers and gaining esoteric knowledge that set them apart from commoners. They could reach supernatural forces through a prophet, who could predict the future and control the weather, and a shaman, who could use his special herbs and powers to cure the sick and communicate with the supernatural realm.

But chiefs were not content to rely on others for power. They also thirsted after esoteric knowledge that would give them a profound wisdom known only to the few. High chiefs eagerly traveled to distant places, studied under renowned men of knowledge among the Chibchas in Columbia, and even learned special languages that closely allied them with cosmic sources of energy. This arduous training enabled them to recount sacred narratives, history, and sacred lore before their subjects and rivals.

By using contact with distant peoples and places to enhance their supernatural authority, chiefs convinced themselves and others that they were fit rulers. In ancient Panama, rulers acquired power and princely legitimacy by establishing long-distance trade and spiritual relations that elevated them above mundane, everyday concerns.[10]

Royal Blood

In classical Mayan society, royal families were priestly leaders. Claiming descent from the gods, they embodied the sacred within the human community and functioned as the literal centers of heaven and earth. Their lineages, clothing, ritual actions, specialized knowledge of astronomy, and willingness to sacrifice their blood helped align the earthly world with the supernatural realm. By praising and imitating the gods, Mayan rulers ensured the stability of the cosmos. One of their most important rituals was bloodletting, which nourished the gods with the divine forces they had implanted in the human body.

Bloodletting occurred in Mayan society whenever important events or ritual ceremonies occurred. At coronations, childbirth, military victories, changes in the sacred calendar, and building dedications, Mayan nobles and commoners freely gave their blood to honor the gods and nurture the universe. Through bloodletting, the Mayas spoke to their gods and strengthened their powers.

In a magnificently carved lintel that once graced the northern Guatemalan center of Yaxchilan, the elderly king Shield-Jaguar and his ritual partner Lady Xoc can be seen shedding blood in a ceremony that took place on

October 28, 709 CE. Shield-Jaguar, "the captor of *Ah Ahaual*" and "a blood lord of Yaxchilan," is ornately dressed with a shrunken head on his headdress symbolizing the importance of sacrifice in praising the gods. Around his neck he wears a rope collar signifying his participation in this bloodletting rite.

Lady Xoc, his middle-aged maternal first cousin once removed and one of his wives, is also beautifully attired and draws a thorny vine or rope through her tongue. At her feet is a woven basket with splattered paper, and her cheeks are smeared with scrolls symbolizing the blood she sheds to nurture the gods.

This royal sacrificial act occurred because Jupiter and Saturn were closely aligned in the sky near the Gemini constellation soon after Shield-Jaguar's son, Bird-Jaguar, had been born. By commemorating his heir's birth on such a propitious occasion, Shield-Jaguar was immortalizing in ritual and sculpture his newborn son as the rightful heir to the throne. Ten years after this bloodletting, Bird-Jaguar became king.

By piercing their tongues and other body parts, Mayan nobility helped regenerate time and the forces that made life possible. Since the gods also shed their own blood, royal bloodletting was the ultimate form of identification with the divine.

Yaxchilan, his ritual partner Lady Xoc, and their Mayan subjects were fascinated by the passage of time and the movements of the heavens because they believed that time and space were sacred and intertwined. In time, everything had its origins, and in space the forces of the divine periodically appeared and disappeared. The Mayas developed an extremely complex calendrical system in sculptures and books of day counts from previous Mesoamerican calendars that carefully charted the passage of time, natural phenomena, the rites needed to maintain them, and the fate of every individual. Their calendar was a dialogue between the human and heavenly worlds. By observing the stars and planets carefully, they tried to understand how the earthy order mirrored celestial patterns.

The first three basic units of the Mayan calendar were the *kin* [day], bundles of twenty days, and eighteen bundles of twenty days. The Mayan calendar was divided into eighteen months of exactly twenty days apiece corresponding to the number of human fingers and toes with an unlucky five days at the end of the year. Along with this calendar, they used a sacred almanac of 260 days that combined the numbers one through thirteen with the signs of twenty god names. In their "Calendar Round," which occurred every fifty-two years, all 18,980 dates included every possible combination of the 365–day calendar with the 260–day almanac.

The conclusion of a Calendar Round was a frightening event of cosmic significance. Would the sun rise again? Would a catastrophe destroy this age and another one begin? The Mayas believed time was an endless repetition of Calendar Rounds. Each moment of time on earth was an incredibly complex combination of celestial and underworld influences operating together.

The Mayas were haunted with time because it was an attribute of the gods that controlled their universe. *Kin*—signifying sun/day/time—was represented by a picture of the Sun God, and it contained endless cycles or circles of time, propitious and unlucky days, and the actions of divine beings. Time was not just divided into days, years, and cycles. The Mayas also arranged it into quadrants of 819 days, which were ruled by four gods—white Kawil of the North, yellow Kawil of the South, red Kawil of the East, and black Kawil of the West. The 819–day cycle represented the sum of seven times nine times thirteen, all sacred numbers. The Mayan notion of time involved duration, color, and direction, all acting together to sustain the universe.

In the beginning, "One-Maize-Revealed" or First Father, entered the sky and made a house with the eight directions. Next he established the World Tree, which was the literal center of the cosmos, and then First Father set the sky into motion. Afterward, time began on 1 Imix, which corresponds to August 13, 1359 BCE. By studying the heavens, the Mayan priests of sun and time could use their knowledge of mathematics and rites to counteract unfavorable days and destinies.

Each day, hundreds of gods effected events. Consequently, Yaxchilan and other Mayan kings made political decisions and acted based on the propitiousness of the time. They aligned their royal activities with godly activities to give them legitimacy and divine purpose. Time governed human affairs, but understanding it could lead to success and better fortune.

Mayan calendrical calculations were so important that each day was actually considered a pair of gods based on day's name and number. The cyclical repetition of time in the calendar revealed to the Mayas how their gods created and set the universe in motion. The present was but an emanation of their sacred origins, for the orderly and profoundly revealing mathematical movement of time was a form of cosmic history that determined Mayan earthly destinies.[11]

The Mayan Popul Vuh

"This is the account of how all was in suspense, all calm, in silence; all motionless, still, and the expanse of the sky was empty.

This is the first account, the first narrative. There was neither man, nor animal, birds, fishes, crabs, trees, stones, caves, ravines, grasses, nor forests; there was only the sky.

The surface of the earth had not appeared. There was only the calm sea and the great expanse of the sky.

There was nothing brought together, nothing which could make a noise, nor anything which might move, or tremble, or could make noise in the sky.

There was nothing standing; only the calm water, the placid sea, alone and tranquil. Nothing existed.

There was only immobility and silence in the darkness, in the night. Only the Creator, the Maker, Tepu, Gucumatz, the Forefathers, were in the water surrounded with light. They were hidden under green and blue feathers, and were therefore called Gucumatz. By nature they were great sages and great thinkers. In this manner, the sky existed and also the Heart of Heaven, which is the name of God and thus He is called.

Then came the word. Tepeu and Gucumatz came together in the darkness, in the night, and Tepeu and Gucumatz talked together. They talked then, discussing and deliberating; they agreed, they united their words and their thoughts.

Then while they meditated, it became clear to them that when dawn would break, man must appear. Then they planned the creation, and the growth of the trees and the thickets and the birth of life and the creation of man. Thus it was arranged in the darkness and in the night by the Heart of Heaven who is called Huracán.

The first is called Caculhá Huracán. The second is Chipi-Calculhá. The third is Raxa-Calculhá. And these three are the Heart of Heaven.

Then Tepeu and Gucumatz came together; then they conferred about life and light, what they would do so there would be light and dawn, who it would be who would provide food and sustenance.

Thus let it be done! Let the emptiness be filled! Let the water recede and make a void, let the earth appear and become solid; let it be done. Thus they spoke. Let there be light, let there be dawn in the sky and on the earth! There shall be neither glory nor grandeur in our creation and formation until the human being is made, man is formed. So they spoke.

Then the earth was created by them. So it was, in truth, that they created the earth. Earth! They said, and instantly it was made.

Like the mist, like a cloud, and like a cloud of dust was the creation, when the mountains appeared from the water; and instantly the mountains grew.

Only be a miracle, only by magic art were the mountains and valleys formed; and instantly the groves of cypresses and pines put forth shoots together on the surface of the earth.

And thus Gucumatz was filled with joy and exclaimed: "Your coming has been fruitful, Heart of Heaven; and you, Huracán, and you, Chipi-Caculhá, Raxa-Caculhá!"

"Our work, our creation shall be finished," they answered.

First the earth was formed, the mountains and the valleys; the currents of water were divided, the rivulets were running freely between the hills, and the water was separated when the high mountains appeared.

Thus was the earth created, when it was formed by the Heart of Heaven, the Heart of Earth, as they are called who first made it fruitful, when the sky was in suspense, and the earth was submerged in the water.

So it was that they made perfect the work, when they did it after thinking and meditating on it."

Note: Popol Vuh, the Sacred Book on the Ancient Quiché Maya, trans. Delia Goetz and Sylvanus G. Morley (Norman: University of Oklahoma Press, 1965), pp. 81–84.

Cuna Trees

Throughout the native world, trees were usually considered sacred beings. They provided humans with shelter, medicine, food, and transportation, and symbolized beauty, generosity, fertility, strength, and abundance.

Among the Cunas, who live on the San Blas archipelago off the east coast of Panama, the symbol of life has always been a jaguar with an umbilical cord made of the Tree of Life. Since the Cunas believe they are descended from trees, they have worshipped them and sought their wisdom and guidance. Trees were their friends, advisors, and honored members of the community. Along with plants and animals, trees have souls and used to talk to each other and exchange scared chants. In previous lives, their chiefs were the most powerful trees in the Panamanian jungle.

Their prophets consulted trees, and if the Cunas wanted to chop one down, they had to get permission from the community assembly. After receiving authorization, Cunas also had to obtain permission from the tree before cutting it.[12]

North America

The Seasonal and Spiritual Ecology of New England

About 17,000 years ago, the glaciers of the last ice age retreated from New England, leaving a tundra region that eventually developed into three basic forest regions: oaks and chestnuts in the south; hemlocks, white pines, and hardwoods in the center and northeast; and spruce and hardwoods in the far north. As the climate became warmer and the land more fertile, large mammals such as the mastodon and the caribou entered the region along with the first humans. Around 6,000 years ago, southern New Englanders began supplementing their protein-rich diets with domesticated plants such as squash, beans, and later maize.

The first New Englanders were Algonquian speakers who had migrated from the Great Lakes and northern Plains. In the North were the Malecite, Passamaquoddie, and Abenaki peoples. Southern New England contained the Massachusets, Pocumtuck-Nipmucks, Narragansetts, Pequot-Mohegans, Wappingers, and the Nausets. Languages and dialects varied widely, closely conforming to the river drainage systems that helped determine settlement patterns.

New Englanders created a stable and abundant regional culture by harmonizing their social and natural worlds. Societies were ruled by chiefs, and their villages, which rarely exceeded several hundred people, contained extended bands of kin. Male and female leaders, called "sagamores" in the North and "sachems" in the South, gained their positions through marriage or inheritance but maintained them by popular consent. Their authority was primarily ceremonial and advisory, but Naragansett sachems had great power and even punished miscreants.

Men were responsible for hunting animals and birds, which accounted for only about 10 percent of the southern New England diet. The remainder came from agriculture and gathering activities controlled by women. Men broke up the fields and sometimes weeded and hoed, but women were responsible for planting shifting gardens near their villages with hills of corn, beans, and squash. Fertilizer came from potassium and phosphoric acid, the result of burning the forest and its undergrowth in the early spring. Slash-and-burn agriculture also encouraged the growth of berry bushes, which attracted animals and birds.

Corn was the principal food in southern New England and could be grown further north when weather conditions were favorable. After the September harvest, maize was cooked with beans, fish, nuts, and Jerusalem artichokes. An adult woman typically harvested between twenty-four and sixty bushels of shelled corn in one- and two-acre plots. In the summer, women gathered nuts, berries, animal and birds' eggs, and wild fruits. During the fall, women and younger children also collected acorns, walnuts, and chestnuts, which they roasted or ground into meal.

Because the climate was harsh, the northern New England diet was dependent on hunting and gathering rather than farming. During winter, the most difficult and dangerous season of the year, men in small family bands hunted animals while women prepared meat and maintained shifting campsites. When spring arrived, villagers came together again. By March, men were hunting game and fishing. Along the shores women and children gathered crabs, clams, mussels, clams, and scallops. Bird eggs and Canadian geese supplemented their diets. In the summer, hunters killed coastal mammals such as porpoises and seals, and villagers feasted on the ample wild food women found.

In the darkest, coldest months of winter, New Englanders survived by sharing whatever meager food they could find. And in their many seasonal festivals, villagers gained power and prestige by giving away wampum, food, and possessions to their needy neighbors. In a seasonal migratory society where goods were easy to acquire but difficult to transport, nature and culture combined to promote a rough material equality.

Despite the harshness of the climate, the woods were a bountiful provider. In a typical ten square-mile forest, there were about 750,000 trees larger than three inches in diameter, almost 300,000 shrubs, more than 125 billion plants, and countless wild animals. New Englanders used the forests for fuel, canoes, weapons, building materials and furniture, and hunting. They also planted their crops on cleared forest land.

In southeast New England, the average adult was well-nourished by the standards of Renaissance Europe and many countries today in Africa, Latin America, and Asia. Although the food intake was modest compared to today's affluent American middle class, New Englanders consumed approximately 2,500 calories a day. A balanced diet of meat, fish, vegetables, fruits, and seeds provided them with plenty of protein and carbohydrates, oil, and vitamins and minerals from undepleted soil. The diversity of their diet was the best hedge against starvation.

In comparison to Renaissance Europeans, the average New Englander was taller, suffered from fewer infectious diseases, and had a longer life span. The infant mortality rate in New England was lower than in Europe, where even in prosperous Geneva, Switzerland, fewer than half of all children survived to the age of ten.

Local religions reflected the different ecologies of the region. In the North, New Englanders believed they were descended from the animals that sustained them. The Eastern Abenakis, for example, thought that "Grandmother Woodchuck" had raised their immediate ancestor. To kill the animals that were the mainstay of their diet, they followed elaborate hunting rituals to appease the "Keepers of the Game" who controlled the animals.

In the South, sacred narratives and rituals honored the "Corn Mother," who sacrificed herself so that New Englanders could sustain themselves with maize. During the early spring and late summer, sachems and shamans hosted long ceremonies to celebrate Corn Mother's bounty. In their longhouses, indigenous peoples danced, feasted, and exchanged gifts as their corn ripened. The Keepers of the Game and the Corn Mothers, who helped maintain the orderliness of the cosmos and nourish life, protected New Englanders and ensured their survival every season.[13]

Cherokee Genesis

"The earth is a great island floating in a sea of water, and suspended at each of the four cardinal points by a cord hanging down from the sky vault, which is of solid rock. When the world grows old and worn out, the people will die and the cords will break and let the earth sink down into the ocean, and all will be water again. The Indians are afraid of this.

When all was water, the animals were above in Galun'lati, beyond the arch, but it was very much crowded, and they were wanting more room. They wondered what was below the water, and at last Dayuni'si, "Beaver's Grandchild," the little Water-beetle, offered to go and see if it could learn. It darted in every direction over the surface of the water, but could find no firm place to rest. Then it dived to the bottom and came up with soft mud, which began to grow and spread on every side until it became an island which we call the earth. It was afterwards fastened to the sky with four cords, but no one remembers who did this.

There is another world under this, and it is like ours in everything—animals, plants, and people—save that the seasons are different. The streams that come down from the mountains are the trails by which we reach this underworld, and the springs at their heads are the doorways by which we enter it, but to do this one must fast and go to water and have one of the underground people for a guide. We know that the seasons in the underworld are different from ours, because the water in the springs is always warmer in winter and cooler in summer than the outer air.

When the animals and plants were first made—we do not know by whom—they were told to watch and keep awake for seven nights, just as young men now fast and keep awake when they pray to their medicine. Men came after the animals and plants. At first there were only a brother and sister until he struck her with a fish and told her to multiply, and so it was. In seven days a child was born to her, and thereafter every seven days another, and they increased very fast until there was a danger that the world could not keep them. Then it was made that a woman should have only one child a year, and it has been so ever since."

Source: James Mooney, *Myths of the Cherokees and Sacred Formulas of the Cherokees* (Nashville: Charles and Randy Elder, 1982), pp. 239–240.

The Dead

Along the far northwest coast of Newfoundland, for almost 1,000 years indigenous peoples buried their dead in the soft, fine sands along the shore. In one location, there are more than 100 graves and a great variety of decorative and religious objects. The dead were buried in the same area without regard to gender, age, or status. The number of males and females were about equal, and almost half were adults. Twelve burials were newborns, fifteen were two years old, and another fifteen were between the ages of six and eighteen years old. The dead included only seven individuals over the age of fifty.

Infants and young children usually were interred in an extended position, and their burial sites often had little or no ornaments and religious objects. Older children and adults, in contrast, were better dressed, better ornamented, and buried in a fetal position. At one grave site, a young woman was buried on her left side with a small child in her arms. Around them were decorative white quartz pebbles and a barbed hunting point made of caribou antler. At another site, an adult man and woman were buried with two large dogs. One of their skulls had been crushed by a blunt object. Nearby, a young woman was buried in a hooded garment with small shell beads of marine snails draped around the neckline of her clothing. And a young man went to his grave accompanied by a barbed harpoon head near his skull, two harpoon foreshafts across his chest, and the effigy of a killer whale near his lower jaw.

Some people were even buried after their bodies had badly decomposed. They probably had died over the winter and could not be placed in the ground until the late spring thaw.

People were interred with both utilitarian and religious objects belonging to a single cultural tradition even though the grave sites spanned a millennium. Practical objects included woodworking tools and hunting objects, such as daggers made from walrus ivory, caribou antlers, and slate. Some of them were broken before they were placed in graves.

Many cemetery objects had nothing to do with hunting or preparing animal skins. They included decorative articles such as shell beads, clothing, skin pouches, fish teeth, and pendants depicting animals and humans made from cooper, soapstone, and slate. Some men and women wore amulets that probably represented guardian or animal spirits, such as the effigy of a swimming killer whale. Others were interred with special articles linked to the sacred. Seal teeth probably were associated with success in maritime hunting, the leg bone of an aquatic diving bird could lead to good fortune in fishing, and dangerous enemies might be defeated with the increased strength that came from possessing a bear claw. The burial ground faced east, toward the rising sun, and red ocher was used at almost each grave site.[14]

The Chumashs and the Sun

The Chumashs of the central Californian coast were avid astronomers who believed that the universe was divided into three flat, circular worlds. A giant eagle supported the "Upper World" where the celestial beings lived. The center of the "Middle World" was a sacred place where the earth trembled and spirits lived. And in the "Lower World," which shamans could visit, lived menacing supernatural forces.

Five hundred years ago, each densely populated Chumash village had its own 'antap, a group that performed ceremonies, regulated the solar calendar, and maintained balance in the universe. Within this group, the 'alchuklash [astronomers] had the awesome responsibility to influence the Upper World. These shamans possessed strong spiritual powers and named Chumash babies according to the calendar and the position of the stars.

The Sun, "radiance of the child born on the winter solstice," was the most powerful deity of the Upper World. Daily he traveled across the Middle World with his torch to light and warm the Chumashs. He also snatched people from the earth, partially cooked them, and shared the bloody feast with his daughters, who lived in a house of quartz crystal.

Every night the Sun and the "Sky Coyote," a trickster God, played a gambling game with cosmic consequences. With the Moon as scorekeeper, on the night before the winter solstice, both sides calculated who had won the most games that year. If the Sun triumphed, the weather would be dry and the crops poor. If Sky Coyote won, there would be ample rain and plentiful food. The 'alchuklash had to predict the game's outcome and ensure that the next year would be a fertile one.

The most important 'alchuklash ceremony occurred around the winter solstice, when the Sun had to be driven northward. The three days of rites began with villagers settling any debts to purge themselves of impurities. On the afternoon of the second day, the "Image of the Sun" and the twelve "Rays of the Sun"—the chief 'alchuklash and his assistants—erected a wooden sunstick in the main plaza. Attached to the sunstick was a sandstone disk with markings representing the sun's yearly passage across the Middle World.

While the Image of the Sun stood next to the sunstick, his twelve attendants gathered around him and tossed a feather into the air. The Image of the Sun hit the disk twice and said: "It is raining. You must go in the house!" The afternoon ceremony ended with a speech about the Sun's power and a dance by the Rays of the Sun.

That evening, villagers danced clockwise around sunpoles to imitate the sun's direction. Between midnight and sunrise, they danced in the opposite direction and participated in a song-filled sexual orgy. The next night, everyone performed the "Dance of Widows" to console any females who had been widowed or orphaned that year. After midnight, they cried over departed husbands and fathers.

The ceremony ended on the morning of the third day when the sunstick was placed in a box until the next solstice. Outside the village, the *'alchuklash* inserted four feathered sunpoles in the ground representing the four cardinal directions and one feathered sunpole for the northward movement of the sun. When the last pole was planted, he intoned, "This is the pole symbolizing the center of the earth, this is our kingdom." The Chumashs could now face the future with hope. The powerful Sun was traveling northward, and perhaps this year the crops might be good.[15]

"Thinking Woman" and Her Descendants

At the creation, according to the Keres of Laguna Pueblo in New Mexico, Thinking Woman "finished everything, thoughts, and the names of all things. She finished also all the languages. And then our mothers, Uretsete and Naotsete said they would make names and they would make thoughts. Thus they said. Thus they did." Thinking Woman brought the Keres their religion, rituals, corn, memory, and gave her people the power and confidence to sustain themselves.

All over North America, Thinking Woman's descendants exercised power and authority in many native societies. Women gathered, planted, harvested, cooked; fished, built and maintained homes; made mats, baskets, and pottery; and traded within their own communities and with other peoples. They also distributed food, healed the sick, participated in communal ceremonies, acted as shamans, regulated domestic affairs, made political decisions, served as clan leaders and chiefs, and nurtured their children. In some communities, native peoples worshipped female deities and spirits such as the Shawnees' *Kokomthena* [Our Grandmother], who created the world, or White Calf Buffalo Woman, who brought the sacred pipe to the Lakota Sioux.

In the Southwest, woman functioned as white chiefs to promote peace and balance in village internal affairs. In the Southeast, the Cherokees had a Women's Council led by the Beloved Woman of the Nation. In the Upper

Midwest, the Crows, who produced great warriors, also had women of great power. They controlled the disposal of land, food, and crafts, and influenced political decisions. In the Northeast, Iroquois women chose clan sachems, took away titles from erring War Chiefs, and decided whether to adopt or torture prisoners. Along with the Iroquois, many other North American societies traced descent through females, and their matrilineal clans regulated village life.

Among the coastal Algonquians from the Wampanoags and Massachusets of New England to the Powhatans of the lower Chesapeake Bay, women played critically important roles. They could become chiefs or inherit the position on the death of their husband or their sister's husband. Women functioned as shamans, powerful visionary herbalists who could communicate with the dead, and love doctors who used special herbs and rites to choose spouses or wreck marriages. Elderly women, who were thought to have great wisdom and spiritual power, might prepare charms, potions, and produce rain.

Coastal Algonquian women also hunted with their husbands for deer, fished together, traded with neighboring villages, and controlled the corn harvest. So great was their power and independence that when they died, their husbands did not inherit their property.

In warrior societies like the Iroquois, women became powerful partly because males were often absent hunting and fighting and produced only small amounts of food. Access to strategic resources like corn meant that women needed to be consulted and respected by males.

Throughout North America, many women were ritually, politically, and socially powerful. As the Abenakis said, First Woman "was born of the leaf of the beautiful plant and . . . her power should be felt over the whole world."[16]

➤ 2 ◄

Toward a New World Order

During the Middle Ages, Europeans dramatically enlarged the boundaries of the Christian world through travel, trade, exploration, and conquest. But Europe's remarkable powers of expansion developed very slowly after the fall of Rome. By about 1,000 CE, the social fabric of Europe was transformed by knights who established landed estates based on their military power and control over formerly free laborers. Peasants, who lived in an uncertain world of famine, disease, and violence, had little choice but to support the clerics who prayed for them and the warriors who pledged to protected them. Insecurity and fear ruled their lives, and their existence was marginal at best.

Over the next four centuries, however, feudalism was gradually transformed by the revival of agriculture, population growth, the establishment of independent cities such as Genoa and Venice, and the development of industry and international commerce. The state became more powerful as wealth and legal supremacy slowly replaced personal allegiance as the foundation of royal government. Despite the terrible disasters of the fourteenth century —famines, the onset of a wetter, colder climate, and the devastating plague called the "Black Death"—the walled cities and open countryside of Europe developed a dynamic economy and a thirst for change unprecedented in human history. Capitalism appeared with long distance trade, and travel and conquest became intertwined. By the fourteenth century, Europe had dramatically enlarged its geographical and intellectual boundaries.

The precariousness of life was one major stimulus for European expansion. Throughout the Middle Ages, rampant epidemic diseases—plague, typhus, measles, diphtheria, and smallpox—decimated Europe's cities, especially during the summer. Without continuous youthful migrations from rural areas, every major European city would have declined in population. During the winter, famine stalked both the cities and the countryside, and many poor people died of malnourishment. The very young fared no better. Probably half of all children who survived childbirth died before the age of ten.

With an economy based on the extraction of increased amounts of energy from animals, fossil fuels, timber, and plants, and a society based on radically unequal access to the necessities of life, Europeans lived on the edge of ecological disaster. Disease, famines, poor harvests, high infant mortality, and frequent wars constantly reminded Christians that their continent could not easily support its contentious population.

Military expenditures and foreign wars also fueled European expansion and conflict. Throughout the Middle Ages, more than 70 percent of annual government budgets were devoted to warfare. State bureaucracies were constantly enlarging to maintain their military prowess, subdue rebellions, attack their neighbors, and expand their boundaries, usually at the expense of the peasantry.

Medieval governments also fought wars to protect and expand their commercial enterprises from the violent depredations of rival powers. Both Venice and England, for example, began their illustrious maritime histories with state-sponsored piracy. Venice also warred unceasingly to control the Adriatic sea, to establish secure trading routes to the Levant, and to dominate overland trading routes in northern Italy. In the Middle Ages, warfare and commerce were complimentary rather than opposing activities.

The expansion of Christendom, however, was never just a predatory or economic affair. From the perspective of princes, prelates, and canon lawyers, internationalism always had a higher purpose. According to the laws of European nations and the decrees of the Roman Catholic Church, Christians had a sacred mission to convert infidel and heathen peoples. Since Christianity was superior to all other religions, Europeans believed that outsiders could be redeemed from their ignorance and barbarism only through the saving grace of the Church.

Since late antiquity, Christians had taken seriously Jesus's call in the bible to "go ye therefore, and teach all nations, baptizing them in the name of the Father, and of the Son, and of the Holy Ghost: Teaching them to observe all things whatsoever I have commanded you" (Matthew 28: 19–20). Christianity proclaimed itself a religion for all humanity, and Christian nations were admonished by the papacy to proselytize unceasingly. By the First Crusade to conquer the Holy Land in 1096, militarism and territorial expansion had become deeply interwoven with Christian spirituality. Knowledge of the one true God justified imperial expansion and gave Europe a dynamic orientation around the globe.

Europe's history has always been the chronicle of a divided culture in perpetual conflict over its identity. This Christian identity, though, was forged by contact with peoples and societies far different than itself. Europe created its distinct character and place in the world partly by identifying certain peoples as outsiders and inferiors because they were not Christians—Jews, Muslims, and people labeled barbarians. Jews and Moslems, in fact, provided Christians with their model for the understanding and treatment of outsiders.

Fear of outsiders was hardly a unique perspective in the medieval world. But to a degree unmatched by other contemporary civilizations, Christians not only feared peoples different from themselves, but felt compelled to change them as part of their religious mission. By the mid-fifteenth century, a consensus had emerged among popes and political rulers about territorial expansion. Because the rest of the world was not as fully human as Europe, infidels and heathens had no real sovereignty over their domains or possessions. Their unnatural ways of life were shameful in the eyes of the Creator. As conscripts in Satan's army, they had to be conquered to redeem humanity and God's name.[1]

Society and Culture

Feudalism and Serfdom

Between the Rhine and the Loire Rivers, feudalism appeared on the ruins of the Carolingian empire in the eleventh century. It was a fragmented, decentralized system of government where local administrative, legal, and military authority was in the hands of vassals who owed allegiance to great lords and kings. Feudal lands were dominated by fortified castles and worked primarily by serfs, who farmed the soil but were not its owners. In return for land and protection, the nobility extracted compulsory labor services, rents, and dues on their manorial estates and tenant farms.

In the thirteenth century, a royal lawyer named Philippe de Beaumanoir wrote a brilliant treatise on the law of Clermont-en-Beauvaisis, a county forty miles northwest of Paris, and gave four reasons why serfdom had appeared there. First, "it became so difficult to sow the fields in olden times because of the armies in the field and the battles against the crown, that those who were unable to obtain justice became and remained serfs, both themselves and their heirs." Second, "in past times many gave themselves, their heirs, and their property to the saints out of great devotion." Third, people sold themselves to pay off their debts. And last, "sometimes they became so by outright gift of themselves, so as to be protected from other lords or from some enmity afoot against them."[2]

The Abandoned

Throughout the Middle Ages, about one-quarter of all children from Scandinavia to the Balkans were abandoned by their parents. They were abandoned at church doorsteps, along busy roads, in trees, formally given to the Roman Catholic Church and foundling houses, or sold as servants and laborers. The principal reason for abandonment was poverty. Even in the best of times, children were abandoned so their families could survive plagues, wars, famines, and terrible economic conditions. The wealthy, who were concerned about questions of inheritance and property, also abandoned their children frequently.

Although clerics and royal officials recognized that abandonment was common, they neither disapproved of the practice nor prosecuted those who admitted relinquishing their children. Into the nineteenth century, abandonment was probably Europe's principal means of family limitation.

Note: John Boswell, *The Kindness of Strangers: The Abandonment of Children in Western Europe from Late Antiquity to the Renaissance* (New York: Pantheon, 1988), pp. 3–22, 296–427.

Capitalism and the City

The medieval European city was unique in the world. Especially in Italy, Flanders, and Germany, cities declared themselves free and carried out all the political functions associated with sovereignty. They fought wars, coined money, sent ambassadors to foreign countries, defined citizenship, and made their own laws. These cities, which modestly began as associations of merchants and craftsmen, owed their independence and power to commerce. They produced hundreds of specialized goods from London's woolens to Brescia's military arms, and in the process their entrepreneurial spirit and global trade led to a new kind of economic system—capitalism.

No medieval city illustrated the restless, ambitious spirit of merchant capitalism better than Genoa. Like its rival Venice, Genoa rose to prosperity through piracy and trade with Muslims and Europeans in the western Mediterranean. When the Crusaders entered Jerusalem, Genoa was making hefty profits in Byzantium and the Levant through its control of far-flung trading routes. Genoa was not interested in developing a colonial empire. Instead, Genoese merchant families sailed the Mediterranean and later the western Atlantic to establish themselves wherever profits could be made. Although they had small colonies in the eastern Mediterranean, Genoans were usually content to submit to foreign rule and marry into the local aristocracy while remaining loyal to their distant home.

At first the East's spices attracted them, but by the fourteenth century they were involved with sugar estates in Sicily, grain in Cyprus, Danube and Black Sea timber and slaves, mastic from Chios, and alum from Phocaea. As Portugal and Spain developed island empires in the western Mediterranean and Atlantic, Genoese trading families built business enterprises in Seville and Lisbon that were the envy of Europe.

By the fifteenth century, they had become especially active in the Portuguese Algarve, Madiera, the Azores, and the Canaries. Genoese merchants and bankers lent money to royal courts, contracted for naval stores, handled trade between Italy, England, and Flanders, and raised the capital needed to finance the risky commerce of the Atlantic. They also marketed and distributed sugar throughout Europe and helped finance the African slave trade. Unlike the Venetians, the Genoese rarely fought wars to establish colonies. They only wanted to protect their ability to trade. Throughout the late Middle Ages, Genoa played a critical role in shipping Mediterranean and Atlantic luxury goods throughout Europe.

The career of the thirteenth-century Genoese merchant Benedetto Zaccaria typified the restless mercantile spirit of urban capitalism. Zaccaria earned money and fame as a skilled naval commander for his own city and the kings of Castile, Portugal, France, and the Byzantine Empire. During his busy life, Zaccaria also was a pirate, diplomat, crusader in the Holy Land, governor of a Spanish seaport, and a clothing merchant.

On one of his innumerable business trips, Zaccaria noticed near the Anatolian seaport of Phocaea a large deposit of alum, a double sulfate widely used by pharmacists, tanners, and dyers. In 1274, the Byzantines granted him land in the Phocaea area as a reward for his naval exploits. He built a large refinery and fortress outside the seaport, weakened competitors through his political connections and commercial guile, and processed the alum with the help of Italian technicians and Greek laborers. Afterward, he shipped it as far as England for use in the cloth industry.

Zaccaria may have gained more wealth in repulsing pirates attacking his alum fleets than in mining. As one commentator noted with admiration, Zaccaria's soldiers "seized many vessels of Latin corsairs, killed or blinded the pirates," and then "loaded their own ships with booty and returned home very wealthy." When not fighting pirates, Zaccaria traded in Egypt,

North Africa, Corsica, Sardinia, Spain, France, and along the Black Sea and the Crimea.

When Zaccaria died, his refinery housed 3,000 workers, the largest single alum mining operation in Asia Minor. By 1330, the Zaccaria family's commercial empire extended from London to Byzantium.[3]

Pushing Back the Frontier in Rijnland

Despite wars, famines, epidemics, political instability, and constant invasions, during the Middle Ages almost two-thirds of the land currently occupied by Europeans was turned into settlements. Expansion occurred in two directions: externally and internally. On the external frontier, military conquest and colonization led to the migration of Christians into the British Isles, northern Europe, southern Italy, the Iberian peninsula, eastern Germany, Bohemia, and into the Baltic region. On the internal frontier, from Sicily to the Baltic Sea, formerly uninhabited lands were turned into farms, villages, and cities. Land reclamation led to greater agricultural production and a huge growth in population. Between 650 and the onset of the Black Death around 1350, the population of Europe increased sixfold.

This process happened almost everywhere, even in western Holland's inhospitable Rijnland. There, on a narrow twenty-five square kilometer strip of barren land north of The Hague along the Oude Rijn (Rhine) River and the North Sea, land reclamation led to a burst of agricultural productivity and population growth that helped make Holland one of Europe's most prosperous and urbanized countries. Until the tenth century, this area of soggy peat bogs was sparsely inhabited. Frisians from the North settled in small numbers along the sandy ridges of the coast and the riverbanks where they grew cereals, raised cattle, and used local waterways to trade with the interior.

The Rijnland gradually changed its soggy appearance, however, after the tenth century. No longer did the giant peat bogs surrounding the Oude Rijn act as a barrier to human settlement. Into the fourteenth century, energetic residents built drainage ditches, dikes, canals, dams, and sluices to lower the water table and dry out the bogs. Over a century, most of the Rijnland's peat bogs lost 90 percent of their water and subsided one meter.

Once the peat had dried out, it resembled sod and could be used for farming and raising livestock. Frisians also built *terps*, large mounds of earth almost thirty feet high, to protect themselves from the savage sea that always threatened their reclamation projects. In four centuries, over forty agricultural towns appeared on land where once only cattle had grazed and hunters killed waterfowl.

As the peat bog wilderness was reclaimed and colonized, Rijnlanders moved away from the maritime world of the Frisians and became part of the farming culture to the east and south of them. Many stopped considering themselves Frisians and started calling themselves Hollanders (people who came from the peat bogs along the Oude Rijn), using a dialect of proto-Dutch that became popular in commercial transactions and urban documents around the twelfth century. Farms and agricultural towns sprouted everywhere across western Holland, and supplying peat fuel for nearby Rotterdam, Delft, Leiden, Gouda, and Schiedam became a major enterprise in the countryside.

Holland became one of Europe's most urban and commercial societies in the Middle Ages because of dramatic changes in the countryside. By radically modifying the natural landscape, the remote and seemingly barren Frisian land along the North Sea had developed into a thriving commercial society by the fourteenth century.[4]

Rose the Retailer

In William Langland's late fourteenth-century English poem, *Piers Plowman*, the wife of Covetousness is a wily woman named "Rose the Retailer." According to Langland, she was highly skilled at fleecing her customers. She bought soft wool from the widow so it could be stretched, and cheated her in the transaction by measuring the wool with a pound and a quarter instead of a one-pound weight. Rose also divided her almshouse ale into thicker, more expensive pudding-ale and thinner, less expensive penny-ale, but illegally mixed the two and then sold barleymalt at the price of pudding-ale, making four pennies a gallon profit.

Throughout England and continental Europe, women like the fictitious Rose were an important part of household production, the foundation of the medieval economy. In the countryside, women kept gardens and animals, provided food and clothing for their families, and supervised domestic help while they raised their children. In England, urban women often functioned as traders. Rose wove more wool and brewed more ale than her family needed and sold the surplus to earn cash, purchase consumer goods, and to pay rent and taxes.

Under English common law women could make contracts and wills, sell property, and sue others. Women had the right to one-third of their husbands' estates, widows could serve as guardians of their own children, and a married woman could even act as her husband's attorney.

Rose the Retailer lived in a society that was already oriented around the marketplace and the profit motive. Its merchants, bankers, money changers, and retailers lived in an acquisitive and calculating environment. Especially in towns and cities, land and labor were treated as commodities, and over half the adult male population worked as servants and laborers. Although England was overwhelmingly agrarian, it was a society based on contractual relationships and the mobility of labor.

Four centuries before Adam Smith, the division of labor and occupational specialization were common in England. Rose's entrepreneurial spirit and commercial orientation were typical of her country in the Middle Ages.[5]

The Conquest of Europe

Holy War in the Baltic

In 1196, Emperor Frederick II, the Holy Roman Emperor, established the military brotherhood of the Hospital of St. Mary of the Teutons in Jerusalem, which was dedicated to performing good works for Christian pilgrims and defeating the infidel. After the Crusades ended, the Teutonic Knights left the Holy Land and relocated to eastern Europe where there were more peoples to attack in the name of Christianity. First they helped the king of Hungary defeat the Cumans, and then the Knights started undertaking crusades in Prussia and the Baltic region, the last non-Christian lands of Europe.

Beginning in 1147, the papacy authorized Christians to undertake holy wars against northern heathen peoples. In fact, crusaders to the Baltic region were explicitly compared to those brave Christians who tried to retake the Holy Land from the infidels. The famous preacher of crusades and future St. Bernard of Clairveux was even blunter. He urged crusaders to attack the pagans of the North "until such a time as, by God's help, they shall be either converted or deleted."

The Baltic region was fertile ground for Christian conquest and missions. Many of the Baltic peoples worshipped a male sky god, a female sun god, a thunder god, a moon god, a guardian of wizards and sages, a goddess of fate, and an earth mother. Estonians believed that spirits ruled the forests. They prayed to the linden tree, the ash, and the oak in sacred groves. In Lithuania, the inhabitants venerated large oak trees where their deities lived. The chief Lithuanian forest priest commanded seventeen religious orders who helped honor the abode of the gods and place offerings at their roots.

The Teutonic Knights believed that a Baltic holy war was justified because the region was occupied by "enemies of the cross of Christ and of the Christian name, that is, by the Prussians, the Lithuanians, and by other infidels." Because these barbaric peoples were "worshippers of idols" who refused to subject themselves to their Creator, war was both necessary and just. The Baltic peoples were "Northern Saracens," and "who fight us, fights Jesus Christ." Germans called the Baltic region *Unland* and its peoples

44

undeutsche, implying that the indigenous inhabitants became humanized only after their arrival.

Throughout the German military conquests, intrepid clergy traveled throughout the Baltic region to spread the gospel. In the early thirteenth century, German settlers under the leadership of Bishop Albert of Buxhovden, who had convinced Pope Innocent III to announce a crusade against the "pagan Balts," founded Riga with 500 Saxon troops. Immediately he started Christianizing the Livonian countryside by attacking local confederacies. His soldiers, called the Knighthood of Christ in Livonia, or the Swordbrothers, carved out large ecclesiastical lands for themselves as they overcame the native peoples who had lived there for thousands of years.

After the Swordbrothers had been defeated by a combination of the Lithuanians and internal feuds, they were incorporated into the Teutonic Knights. The Knights were powerful and disciplined fighters. Stone castles, metal armor, deadly crossbows, and big ships that could carry 500 soldiers gave them powerful advantages over their scattered enemies, who feared each other as much as they hated the Germans. Any German who promised to help "wage the Lord's battle most forcefully" was granted a fief of roughly 300 acres, and Catholic bishops often administered lands conquered by soldiers and settlers.

By the middle of the thirteenth century, the Teutonic Knights' systematic campaign of atrocities, devastation, and extermination had led to the conquest of Prussia, Livonia, and Estonia. Eventually, however, they ran afoul of the church that had first sanctioned their crusade. Even after the Lithuanians had converted to Christianity, the Knights continued taking their lands. Critics complained that old-fashioned greed and political power had become more important to the Knights than missionary activities. They also pointed out that conquest and conversion were not always synonymous in the Baltic region. In 1432, a monk from Prague visiting the interior of Lithuania met worshippers of fire, sacred trees, snakes, and the sun.

In 1557, the last leader of the Livonian Knights became a duke after he renounced his religious and military vows. The Baltic had been partitioned by Poland, Sweden, Denmark, and Moscow, but the Teutonic Knights had triumphed in spirit, if not in politics. By the sixteenth century, Prussia and the are region were Christian lands. The Baltic religions had been vanquished, and now the entire area was a Roman Catholic sea.[6]

Satan and the Jews

During the early Middle Ages, Jews were granted communal autonomy in Christendom. Jewish life, however, was always precarious because it depended on the goodwill of Christian princes and clergy, who could withdraw their toleration at any moment. Beginning in the eleventh century, their status began dramatically declining all over western Europe, and by the fifteenth century Jews had disappeared from Spain, France, England, Belgium, Holland, and many parts of Germany.

In 1201, Innocent III issued a papal bull defending the validity of coerced baptisms. Since Jews resisting forced baptism were usually killed, anyone who converted under force had consented to receive the "stamp of Christianity." Four years later, another bull of Innocent III declared that although Jews killed Jesus, they were not to be murdered. Instead, because the Jews were comparable to the bible's Cain, they "must remain vagabonds upon the earth, until their faces be covered with shame and they seek the name of Jesus Christ the Lord." The pope declared Jews pariahs who could only be redeemed by denying their faith.

Finally, at the Fourth Lateran Council in 1215, the Roman Catholic Church made two more important decisions about the treatment of Jews. Saracens, lepers, prostitutes, and Jews were ordered to wear special clothing to distinguish themselves from the faithful because they worked for the devil and constituted a dire threat to Christian society. The Church also declared that confessions, which had been public and communal affairs, were now a compulsory and private matter between the faithful and their priests. Because Jews were so wicked and untrustworthy, only through private confession could converts be monitored to ensure that their devotion was sincere and correct.

During the same century, Jews lost their corporate freedoms and were condemned to perpetual servitude as royal serfs, for the "Jew can have nothing of his own, for whatever he acquires he acquires not for himself but for the king." Similarly, in German law all Jews were classified as *servi camerae* [serfs of the royal chamber]. Throughout Christendom, Jewish property was legally owned by the monarch and could be seized at any time.

Many Christians believed that Jews were dangerous subversives who killed Christ, denied the truths of Christianity, and acted in despicable ways. Jewish history and behavior, Christians argued, proved that they were actually the minions of Satan. Christians thought that by betraying God and abandoning their true savior, Jews condemned themselves as outsiders and heretics. Christians also believed that Jews prayed for the death of Christians; that their religion taught them to swindle anyone not of their faith; that they used Christian blood on their holy days of Purim and Passover, and at weddings and circumcisions; and even that some of them had horns and tails like the devil.

Jews spoke a secret language—Yiddish—and their holy books were magical. They were sorcerers, poisoners, and particularly enjoyed desecrating the host and destroying Christian images. Not surprisingly, the Antichrist was Jewish, for whoever did not believe in Jesus was of the devil. Many Christians considered Judaism little more than a despicable conspiracy against Christian society.

Medieval prejudice against Jews had its theological roots in the New Testament, which vividly described them as a satanic people who rejected the forgiveness and redemption Jesus offered them. This damning characterization developed out of bitter disputes during the first century between Jewish sectarians, Jewish supporters of Jesus, and gentile converts to Christianity. In John 8: 42–47, Jesus condemned the Jews, saying that "if God were your Father, ye would love me: for I proceeded forth and came from God. . . . Why do ye not understand my speech? even because ye cannot hear my word. Ye are of your father the devil, and the lusts of your father ye will do. . . . He that is of God heareth God's words: ye therefore hear *them* not, because ye are not of God." For their blasphemy, Jewish worship was called "the synagogue of Satan" (Revelation 2:9), and the Jews became, in Paul's chilling words, the "servants of Satan."

Although they were considered heretics by most Christians, Jews were allowed to exist because their souls were unredeemed. Jews were an object lesson, a terrifying example of how pitiful a people could become when they refused to renounce their superstitions and falsehoods for the one true faith. As St. Augustine had argued, the inability of Jews to understand the true meaning of their own prophecies testified to the truths of Christianity.

Jews were also a missionary challenge, a people whose conversion would herald the Second Coming of Christ. When Christ returned, one of two things would happen to the Jews: They would either finally acknowledge the religious errors of their ways or be condemned to perpetual damnation. As a result of this dual Christian attitude, Jews were both butchered and converted almost everywhere in Europe.

When a German Dominican monk named Felix Faber went to the Holy Land by galley in the late fifteenth century, he was shocked in the baths of Gaza where he mingled with Jews and Muslims. Their odor, he claimed, was markedly different from that of Christians. Faber discovered what many medieval Christians already had claimed—Jews emitted a horrible smell because of their crimes against Christians. "Stench and unbelief," according to a thirteenth century Austrian poet, characterized this foul people. Jews were so different from Christians that they belonged to virtually another species.

This is why Jews were the greatest aliens in medieval Europe and why the polemics used against them were applied to people labelled heretics or barbarians. By legal definition, Jews were *extra ecclesiam* or not of the Church, and so Christians naturally extended their analysis of Jews to others outside the faith. Because the powers of the Roman Catholic Church were frequently used to define what Jews could and could not do, popes and canon lawyers argued that these same powers could be applied to nonbelievers beyond Europe's borders.

Christians claimed there were close resemblances between Jews and barbarians because of their "way of life, ceremonies, and superstitions, omens and hypocrisies." Jews resembled barbarians because they worshipped the devil, sacrificed children, practiced cannibalism, and were the enemies of Christ. For many Europeans, the Jewish religion was really a thinly disguised satanic sect. As the great Renaissance humanist Erasmus of Rotterdam said, "if it is the part of a good Christian to detest the Jews, then we are all good Christians."[7]

Europe Abroad

Viking Exploration and Conquest

In antiquity and the early Middle Ages, travel was often considered a form of suffering or penance, and long journeys were usually dangerous, extremely uncomfortable, and completely unpredictable. The Vikings were the first medieval Europeans to undertake successful long-distance military expeditions in search of fame, power, wealth, slaves, and pleasure.

They equated territorial mobility with enhanced social status, projected their power over three continents, and expanded Europe's frontiers. In just two centuries, Viking warriors initiated the travel patterns other Europeans would use for 1,000 years to build empires. Beginning in the ninth century, Vikings from the kingdoms of Denmark and Norway invaded and settled England, Scotland, and Ireland. Men from *Rus*, as the Finns called Sweden, established military posts in Novgorod and Kiev, and traded with Jewish Khazars, Moslems, and Eastern Orthodox Byzantines. Traces of their runic alphabet can be found from the North Cape to Athens, and from Greenland to the Black Sea. During the early Middle Ages, the Vikings had no competitors. They were the most dynamic and disruptive peoples of Europe. "From the fury of the Norsemen, O Lord, deliver us" was a prayer heard throughout the land.

The Vikings left their cold, snowy lands for many reasons. They wanted pasture for their stock and fertile soil for farming, customers for their furs, slaves, timber, and fish, and lands to plunder. In Viking society, almost any free man could become a respected leader through piracy and great deeds of courage. With sleek wooden sailing ships and superb navigational skills, they could travel great distances without a compass and chart. "No landing place, no stronghold, no fort, no castle might be found," said the Irish, "but it was submerged by waves of vikings and pirates."

In the ninth and tenth centuries, Norwegians searching for land and pasture settled in Iceland. In 982, Eirik the Red, who had been banished from Norway, explored Greenland. A decade later, 3,000 Icelanders established communities in Greenland and were exporting furs, hides, and ivory to Norway in exchange for corn, iron, cloth, and timber. According to the *Greenlanders' Saga*, the European discovery of America was made around the year 1,000 CE by Leif Eiriksson, the eldest son of Eirik the Red. The Vikings explored the coasts of Baffin Island, Labrador, and northern Newfoundland, where they established a settlement at L'Anse aux Meadows.

There the Vikings initiated the first European contact with indigenous peoples in the Western Hemisphere. They met Skraelings, or "wretches," and described them as "small ugly men with coarse hair; they had big eyes and broad cheekbones." On an expedition to Vineland, early one morning the Vikings saw nine skin-boats. "Then the strangers rowed towards them, stared at them with astonishment, and came ashore."

The Vikings treated the Skraelings as they would any other outsiders. When the opportunity arose, they killed the adults and enslaved their children. On other occasions, they traded bolts of red cloth for furs. The Vikings intended to establish permanent colonies in Vineland, but hostilities between themselves and the menacing Skraelings doomed the venture. They continued visiting the North American coast in search of timber and furs, but after 1300 the climate grew colder and travel became more difficult. The last European Greenlanders disappeared by 1,500, and all Viking contact with North America ceased.

The Vikings took Skraelings to Norway and perhaps Iceland. They learned Norse, became Christians, and were memorialized in one of the Icelandic sagas. Over the next three centuries, the Vikings brought other Skraeling slaves to northern Britain and Scandinavia.

By the middle of the thirteenth century, the heroic Viking Age had ended as the Vikings ceased being a threat to northern Europe. After they became residents in their conquered lands, intermarried, and converted to Christianity, the Vikings quickly became indistinguishable from the people they had once ravished. Outside Scandinavia, hardly anyone remembered Greenland, Iceland, or Vineland.

As a result, Viking travels were not integrated into medieval Christendom's geographical knowledge, and North America never became part of the medieval expansion of Europe. The Vikings had demonstrated to the rest of Christendom, however, that international predatory military expeditions were an attractive route to wealth and power.[8]

King Chilperic's Ambassadors Visit Constantinople

In the late sixth century, Chilperic, King of the Franks in Gaul, sent ambassadors to Emperor Tiberius II of the Byzantine Empire. Their trip to Constantinople—about 1,000 miles away—took three difficult years, and they "suffered serious hardship and considerable loss on their return journey." Near home, they could not land at Marseilles because Chiperic was fighting two other kings for possession of the city. When they were ready to disembark, a storm destroyed their ship and the local inhabitants stole most of their possessions that had washed ashore.

Note: Gregory of Tours, *The History of the Franks*, trans. Lewis Thorpe (New York: Penguin Books, 1974), pp. 327–328.

An Armed Pilgrimage

At the time of the Crusades, Jerusalem was the geographical and spiritual center of Christianity—the "navel of the world, the land fruitful above all others, like another paradise of delights"—because Jesus had lived, been crucified, and resurrected in this holy city. Medieval maps showed the oceans on the periphery and three continents (Europe, Africa, and Asia) shaped like the letter "T" with Jerusalem exactly at the center.

As the Roman world became Christian, the Holy Land was rebuilt to demonstrate the truths according to the bible, and the new Christian sites served to purify and make sacred a formerly Jewish and pagan land. The construction of the restored Jerusalem began in 324 CE when the newly converted Emperor Constantine declared Christianity the favored religion of the Roman Empire. Two years later, his mother the Empress Helena visited Palestine and found the twelve stations of the cross, the stable where Jesus was born, and the place where Jesus was crucified (Calvary), as well as Jesus's cross, nails, and lancet.

Based on her recommendations, Constantine destroyed temples, built churches, and removed the soil around any pagan shrine "inasmuch as it had been polluted by the defilements of demon-worship." Helen was honored as the first Christian pilgrim to Jerusalem, and her piety became a model for future visitors to the holy city.

For Christian pilgrims, Jerusalem's most important site was Christ's tomb, which had been miraculously found by a bishop in the rubble of the Roman Temple of Aphrodite. After the area was duly excavated, Constantine con-

50

structed a magnificent rotunda and basilica called "the Holy Sepulchre" that included a slab of marble where the tomb once allegedly existed.

By the fifth century, Jerusalem had become a Christian city with new churches and over 300 monasteries and hostels for pilgrims. For them, the apostolic city was a sacred space—a visible sign of the demise of Judaism and the triumph of Christianity. By remaking Jerusalem, they transformed the land of Israel into a Christian Holy Land.

In the early seventh century the city fell to the Moslems, who also had a strong religious interest in the city because of its association with events in the Quran, Islam's most holy book, and the life of Muhammad, the founder of Islam. Christians called the invaders Ishmaelites and lamented the loss of Jerusalem, but they continued living throughout Palestine and even built sumptuous new churches. With the Moslem conquest, Christians began dreaming of Jerusalem's deliverance. This sacred land, they thought, could not long remain under the control of infidels.

In 1093, Alexius Comnenus, the Emperor of the Byzantine Empire, asked Pope Urban II for military assistance against his powerful new enemy, the Seljuk Turks. The pope agreed, and two years later called on the French nobility to undertake a holy crusade against the Turks, who slaughtered Christians and "sacrilegiously defiled" the Holy Sepulchre. "Christian warriors," he said, "if you must have blood, bathe in the blood of the infidels. I speak to you with harshness because my ministry obliges me to do so. Soldiers of Hell, become soldiers of the living God!"

Over the various Crusades, the Papacy carefully articulated a powerful and influential argument for world domination: Christians had a moral and legal responsibility to convert all peoples to the one true faith. The Catholic Church, pontiffs and jurists argued, was Christ's universal Christian commonwealth, and the Pope functioned as God's vicar on earth. His responsibilities not only included Catholics, but also infidels who denied Christ and heathens who were ignorant of the Church's saving grace.

Because these deluded peoples did not share the Church's understanding of salvation, Christian nations had a sacred responsibility to bring them under their tutelage. And because these peoples lived outside the Church or threatened Christian lands, they could be rightfully converted or conquered by European princes.

The opening battles of the First Crusade, however, took place not in the Holy Land but in the Rhineland as knights traveled toward Jerusalem. In Cologne, Worms, Speyer, Maiz, Nuremberg, and Regensberg, Christians massacred thousands of Jews in the name of Christ. In the Jews' memorial books commemorating the victims, these places were called "cities of blood." As one crusader said, "we have set out to march a long way to fight the enemies of God in the East, and behold, before our very eyes are his worst foes, the Jews. They must be dealt with first." Although some nobles and prelates bravely defended the Jews, entire communities disappeared in an orgy of violence that left the terrified survivors stunned and demoralized.

As the pope was readying his forces in Flanders, a charismatic monk named Peter the Hermit appeared to lead a motley, unruly army of over 100,000 men, women, and children to Jerusalem. His followers believed that a letter written in heaven had commissioned him to liberate the Holy Sepulchre, and "everywhere with an amazing authority he restored peace and concord in place of strife." On their way to the Holy Land, Peter's army savagely attacked both Christian and Turkish communities, and many attained a "blessed martyrdom in the name of the Lord Jesus." By the time they were rescued from the Turks, only 3,000 of his followers remained. Peter, ever the optimist, survived the debacle to lead a peasant militia into Jerusalem.

On July 15, 1099, Peter's dream came true. After marching around Jerusalem barefoot with crosses and holy relics, the Crusaders fought their way through its fortified walls and methodically slaughtered all its inhabitants. Jews who had taken refuge in a synagogue were burned alive. In their moment of exaltation, the Crusaders believed that the Christian faith had broken "the strength of the Saracens and of the Devil," and now the Church's kingdom could extend "from sea to sea and over the whole world." Before the joyous Crusaders buried slain Muslims, they mutilated their corpses and shipped home thumbs and noses as trophies. Jerusalem had finally been cleansed of its Moslem and Jewish inhabitants.

The Christian conquest of the Holy Land, however, was never permanent. After the First Crusade, Christian princes quarreled over the spoils, and the Moslems soon returned to besiege them. By the end of the century, a new pope was calling for yet another crusade to recover Jerusalem.

When Acre fell to the Moslems in 1291, the Kingdom of Jerusalem disappeared and the Crusades finally ended. Despite their failure, however, the Crusades were a watershed in European history because they were the first of many armed pilgrimages abroad. Pilgrimages had begun as pious moralizing journeys to walk in the footsteps of Christ, but the Crusades turned pilgrims and missionaries into soldiers and builders of empire.

Until the papacy of Urban II, Church law emphatically stated that pilgrims could neither bear arms nor fight on their journeys to holy places. With the First Crusade, however, pilgrims became engaged in holy wars sanctioned by the Papacy as the Church artfully combined the venerable tradition of penitential pilgrimages with Europe's growing zeal for expansion and conquest.

After the Christian defeat in the Holy Land, over the next three centuries other crusades would be launched with the Church's blessing in the Iberian peninsula, eastern Europe, Russia, and the Baltic region. They were carried out partly by international military brotherhoods first established in Palestine—the knighthood of the Temple of Solomon of Jerusalem (Templars), the Hospital of St. John of Jerusalem (Hospitallers), and the Hospital of St. Mary of the Teutons in Jerusalem (Teutonic Knights). The Templars, Hospitallers, and Teutonic Knights were monastic orders supported by the papacy and royal patronage to protect Christian pilgrims in the Holy Land.

During the crusades, however, these military orders became heavily involved in defending the newly created Christian kingdoms in the Levant. Once Acre fell to the Moslems, they left the Holy Land and spread out across the borders of Christendom to attack idolaters and "convert the nations to take up the standard of salvation."

The Templars fought heretics in southern France and Moors in Aragon and the eastern Mediterranean. In England, they became diplomats, members of Parliament, and advisors to the king. Meanwhile, with the blessings of the papacy the Teutonic Knights launched campaigns against unbelievers in eastern Europe and the Baltic region. After the Templars declined in power, the Hospitallers became valued allies in Rhodes, Malta, and other outposts along the Christian-Muslim frontier. The Crusades were just the beginning of Christendom's aggressive attempts to vanquish heretics and unbelievers, wherever they might dwell.[9]

The Canary Islands Become European

About 2,000 years ago, Berbers from northwest Africa became the first human settlers on the seven Canary Islands—Palma, Gomera, Hierro, Tenerife, Gran Canaria, Lanzarote, and Fuerteventura. Although the Canarians had little contact with each other, periodically they were visited by sailors from the African mainland and Europe. In the fourteenth century, visitors became more frequent as European ships sailed around Morocco's west coast to trade metallic items for the skins of goats and seals and to harvest the orchil, a dyer's lichen heavily in demand.

Trade, however, was soon replaced by deadly Portuguese and Castilian wars of conquest. In 1341, Niccoloso da Recco raided the islands on behalf of Portugal. According to the Italian humanist Giovanni Boccaccio, the Recco expedition found islands "inhabited by naked men and women, who were like savages in their appearance and demeanor." Boccaccio described them in very flattering phrases. "They sang very sweetly," danced almost as well as Frenchman, and were "gay and merry, and much more civilized than many

Spaniards." Married women wore aprons like the men, but the "maidens went quite naked, without consciousness of shame."

Although Boccaccio sympathetically depicted a people uncorrupted by civilization, Portugal and Spain displayed no sentimentality toward the Canarians. Under Castilian contract, a French force led by Jean de Béthencourt of Normandy conquered three of the Canaries from 1402 to 1406. His expedition was financed by the same Genoese and Sevillan slave traders who had already brought misery to the islands.

The Infante Dom Henrique of Portugal, better known as Prince Henry the Navigator, contended with Castile for control of the Canaries. Although Henry's maritime interests included both commerce and piracy, religious motives also propelled him southward. In 1418, a papal bull encouraged Christians to follow Portugal in its crusade against the infidel. As Administrator of the Order of Christ, Henry hoped to weaken the Moslems as he diverted West African riches toward Portugal. A devout Roman Catholic who constantly wore a hair shirt, a coarse garment worn next to the skin as penance, Henry wanted to "extend the Holy Faith of Jesus Christ and bring it to all souls who wish to find salvation."

King Duarte of Portugal was guided by similar sentiments. In a letter to the pope, he said that the Canary Islanders were "not united by a common religion, nor are they bound by the chains of law, they are lacking normal social intercourse, living in the country like animals." On behalf of the Church, Duarte offered to conquer the Canaries "for the salvation of the souls of the pagans of the islands," which would lead "toward an increased devotion toward Your Holiness."

Duarte also claimed that the Canary Islanders refused to let Christian missionaries preach, a telling sign of their barbarism and ignorance. The Church agreed and authorized him to conquer the Canaries so that the Pope could "bring the sheep divinely committed to him into the one fold of the Lord, and may acquire for them the reward of eternal happiness, and may obtain pardon for their souls."

Portuguese military expeditions attacked the islands throughout the midfifteenth century, capturing Canarians for the nearby Madeira and Azores Islands where they labored with recently arrived African slaves on new sugar plantations. Madiera, Portugal's first plantation slave economy, would become a model for the development of Brazil. In 1479, however, a treaty recognized the Canaries as a Castilian possession.

The Canarians fought bravely against the Spanish, especially on the larger islands, but they could never defeat their adversaries. The Canarians were disunited, and the Spanish used their sea power to raid the islands for male slaves. Perhaps Spain's greatest military advantages were biological. In the later stages of the struggle, soldiers mounted on horseback forced the Canarians to surrender level parts of the islands along with their grain and flocks. In the cold, inhospitable mountains, the Canarians died from hunger and succumbed in massive numbers to European diseases.

For a thousand years, the Canarians had been isolated from Africa and Europe, and as a result, they had no immunity to measles, smallpox, typhus, dysentery, pneumonia, and other devastating maladies brought by the invaders. An avenging God, said one of the Spaniards, sent them the plague, "which in a few days destroyed three-quarters of the people."

In the fifteenth century, the conquest of the Canary Islands sparked a spirited debate about the nature of its inhabitants that continued into the conquest of the Western Hemisphere. Were the Canarians humans or Wild Men? How should they be treated? Were they capable of exercising sovereignty? Did they possess a religion and a culture? These questions actually had been raised for over 1,000 years.

According to the Roman writer Pliny the Elder, in western Africa lived a bizarre race of Dog-Men whom he called "the Canarii" because they looked like dogs. Later the Canary, or Canine Islands, were identified as the home of these Dog-Men. Building on Pliny, medieval Germans pictured the Canarians as people with pig and dog heads. The Irish were equally unflattering. In their legends of St. Brendan, a race of aggressive Dogheads came from islands off the western coast of Africa.

Early medieval mapmakers pictured naked men with only one foot or eyes in back of their heads. At the same time, the Canary Islands also conjured up more favorable images. The western coast of Africa was considered the Garden of the Hesperides, the Land of the Blessed Dead, and the Fortunate Isles from the Greeks down through the Middle Ages. This fabled land was guarded by a dog named "Orthros," the brother of Cerberus, a three-headed dog who guarded the entrance to Hades.

Once the Portuguese and Spanish actually began encountering real Canarians, they were both revolted and fascinated by them because of their nakedness and way of life. As Canarian slaves appeared in Lisbon and Seville, Iberians concluded that they resembled the Wild Men of European legend, living outside the boundaries of civilization. These grotesque, hairy, and naked creatures, half human and half animal, supposedly inhabited the forests and desolate places of the earth and survived on wild plants and animals. Incapable of political organization, a stable family life, or of understanding Christian morality, Wild Men had degenerated into beasts because they lacked the faculty of reason and lived under conditions of extreme hardship. Subhumans, their lives had not yet been touched by civilization.

The Canarians quickly became Christendom's first real Wild Men. "Idolaters without law," "thoroughly rustic and beast-like," and "constrained by no bonds of law" were the judgments made about them by their captors. These barbaric peoples, Christians said, were brutal, cruel, lusty, and cunning. Their social customs were bizarre, family life were unknown among them, and they had no access to the institutionalized grace of the Roman Catholic Church.

Popes, jurists, theologians, and philosophers provided the justification for military conquest when they judged Canarians to be barbarians. These pitiful people, they argued, lacked all the characteristics associated with civilization—writing, cities, formal laws, proper religion, proper clothing, and disciplined work habits. In a society obsessed by dress as a mark of rank and breeding, the Canarians appeared hardly human. They worshipped "only the sun and the moon," lacked "normal social intercourse," and lived "in the country like animals."

Their nakedness was not a sign of Adamic innocence, as Boccaccio suggested, but a revealing metaphor for a terrible cultural void. The only Europeans permitted to be naked were condemned criminals, who were deprived of their clothing before execution. If the Canarians were to be civilized, Christians must have sovereignty over them. With minor alterations, these arguments would be tirelessly repeated in the Western Hemisphere over the next three centuries.

These negative evaluations of the Canarians were produced in papal and court societies whose members were slowly creating new aristocratic norms of behavior. No longer were fear, rage, revenge, lust, joy, and sadness permitted uninhibited self-expression. In Europe's palaces, the rough manners of warriors were being slowly remolded with a wide range of new constraints—handkerchiefs, knives and later forks, nightgowns, elaborate table manners, and courtly etiquette—that created a widening gulf between aristocrats and peasants. The Canarians represented everything the aristocracy were trying to transcend, for these unfortunates were not properly distanced from animal life and their own bodies.

This was especially distressing from the Roman Catholic Church's perspective. Since late antiquity, the Church had prided itself on its commitment to sexual renunciation. By the Middle Ages, the Church, which was run by men who "have made themselves eunuchs for the kingdom of heaven's sake" (Matthew 19:12), taught that Adam's fall had brought upon the human body two great dishonors, death and sexual desire. Although the Church had long since made its peace with sexuality and marriage by making marriage a holy sacrament and procreation a religious duty, its ideal was still the untouched human body. With this theology, it was easy to condemn the Canary Islanders and later the indigenous peoples of the Western Hemisphere. Their nakedness and allegedly bizarre sexual customs branded them as barbaric and repulsive brutes, fit only for conquest.

Once the Canarians were defeated, Spain rapidly remade the islands into a Christian colony. Surviving males became slaves in the Madeiras, Azores, and the Iberian peninsula. Women were retained as mistresses and house servants. Native religious objects and sites vanished. Clerics built convents, hermitages, monasteries, and churches everywhere. Religious images miraculously washed up on the beaches or were discovered at the tops of trees. The Inquisition, which arrived in 1499, never persecuted Canarians for their pre-Christian beliefs, but priests tormented them if they could not remember vigils, feast and fast days, and the Paternoster in Latin.

Priests used church doctrines to inculcate a regimen of guilt, fear, loyalty, and religious devotion among surviving Canarians. In the confessional box, the Canarians' personal behavior and thoughts were constantly scrutinized by Spaniards. For them, evangelization did not just spread the true word of God. Through confession, the barbarism of the Canarians would be replaced by a new way of thinking that stressed constant self-examination, a consuming desire for repentance, and loyalty to Spain and the Roman Catholic Church.

As the Canarians died or became absorbed into the European population, they were replaced by a new work force—African slaves, large numbers of Portuguese, Italian, French, and Dutch settlers, and camels, mules, and cattle. By 1513, there were only 600 native Canarians left in the largest island of Tenerife, and by the end of the century they were no longer a distinct ethnic group.

The experience of Spain and Portugal in the Canaries was a decisive moment in European history because the conquest of these islands became the foundation for Christendom's understanding and treatment of native peoples in the Western Hemisphere. The struggle against the Canarians gave Europeans the religious justifications and legal arguments they would use to subjugate indigenous peoples throughout the world. In the Canaries, the Spanish and Portuguese also learned that a combination of deadly European diseases, constant military pressure, and state-sponsored terrorism could defeat indigenous peoples. These powerful lessons would transform both Europe and the Western Hemisphere.[10]

The Birth of the Caravela Redonda

In 1400, Europeans used two kinds of ships for trade and warfare. On the Mediterranean, galleys powered by oars won the famous battle of Lepanto in 1570 and only disappeared in the eighteenth century. Galleys were strong, stable, and reliable, but totally unsuited for ocean travel. In the Atlantic, square-rigged ships with one mast carried heavy cargoes on short trips along the coast; but bulky construction and the use of a square rig made them difficult to control unless the wind was nearly astern.

The Portuguese, who had close trade contacts with the Arabs along the African coast from the thirteenth century, successfully combined square-rig construction and Arab shipbuilding technology to create the *caravela redonda* (from the Arabic *karib*), or the square-rigged caravel. In the Indian Ocean and the Mediterranean, the Arabs used lateen-rigged sailing ships called "dhows" they had copied from Indian boats in the Sea of Oman. Made of coconut palm wood or teak from western India, their timbers were bound with ropes made of coconut fiber and caulked with whale and shark oil grease.

Lateen or triangular sails enabled the Arabs to navigate under almost any wind conditions on the open seas, but because of the weight of the palm wood spars, each mast could hold only one sail. As a result, the Arabs never built large sailing vessels. They also developed the sternpost rudder, which eventually replaced the centerline rudders used by Europeans.

Around 1430, the Portuguese developed a square-rigged caravel with three masts, two European sails, and one Arabic lateen sail. Square sails, which would carry European ships across the Atlantic from the Canary Islands to the Caribbean and around Africa to India, were rigged along the boat's width to capture astern winds. The lateen sail ran lengthwise to help turn and steer the boat. Eventually, the caravel developed into a large round ship with three square-rigged masts and a wide hull that displaced little water, permitting mobility and long voyages far from any coastlines. They could also hold more cannon and small caliber guns than galleys, and their squared rigging made them more maneuverable in military battles than traditional oceanic vessels.

Note: J.H. Parry, *The Age of Reconnaissance* (Cleveland, World Publishing, 1963); J.H. Parry, *The Discovery of the Sea* (Berkeley: University of California Press, 1981), pp. 12–23, 139–144; Fernand Braudel, *The Structures of Everyday Life: The Limits of the Possible*, trans. Siân Reynolds (New York: Harper and Row, 1981), pp. 509–525; Roger C. Smith, *Vanguard of Empire: Ships of Exploration in the Age of Columbus* (New York: Oxford University Press, 1993), pp. 30–49.

Christopher Columbus: The Last Medieval Explorer

In May 1486, a merchant and navigator of Genoese descent named Christopher Columbus received a royal audience with King Ferdinand of Aragon and Queen Isabella of Castile. "He told them his dream," according to one of Columbus's friends, but they were very skeptical. After Columbus showed them a map, he "aroused their desire to hear more about those lands."

The lands Columbus portrayed were the fabled Orient of Marco Polo, described in the beautiful Catalan Atlas of 1381 as 7,548 islands in the Indian Ocean "containing marvelous riches . . . as well as gold and silver, spices and precious stones." After seven frustrating years of petitioning and pleading, Queen Isabella decided to support his venture, gave Columbus the title "Admiral of the Ocean Sea," and promised him a generous 10 percent of the profits from the lands he claimed for Spain.

His plan was bold and visionary—to reach the East by sailing West—and the Iberian peninsula was the ideal place to support it. First, he petitioned the adventurous, seafaring nation of Portugal for assistance. In 1415, the Portuguese boldly crossed the Straits of Gibraltar and captured the Moorish fortress of Ceuta and later Tangier. During the same century, they settled the Azores, Madeira, the Cape Verde Islands, and Sao Tomè; attacked the Canaries; established profitable trading and slave trading posts along the West African coast; and rounded the Cape of Good Hope in 1488. By the end of the fifteenth century, Portugal had displaced Venice as Europe's major importer of spices, and sugar became the chief product of her Atlantic possessions.

After Portugal rejected Columbus, he began promoting his venture at the Spanish court. Since the early eighth century, the first and longest Spanish civil war had been the *Reconquista*—the reconquest of the kingdom from the Arab-Berbers who became known as Moors. They had overrun most of the peninsula in the eighth century and established the powerful kingdom of Al-Andalus. But they never destroyed the Visigoth kingdom of Asturias-Leon in the northern part of the peninsula, and from there defenders of Christian Spain began their long, intermittent struggle that would last seven centuries. In 1002, the great caliphate of Cordoba broke into twenty small kingdoms. About 200 years later, the Moors were driven from Cordoba and Seville, and by the middle of the thirteenth century they were confined to the southern kingdom of Granada.

As the Spanish slowly reclaimed formerly Moslem territory, they also became a powerful maritime power in the western Mediterranean and Atlantic. In the thirteenth century, the House of Barcelona captured the Balearic Islands (Majorca, Minorca, Ibiza, and Formentera) from the Moors and resettled them with Catalans, who established textile industries and dynamic trading centers between Europe and North Africa. The conquest of the Balearics and the southern Iberian peninsula put Spain closer to North Africa, the fabled source of gold and slaves.

By 1286, the islands of Jarbah and Qarqannah were Europe's first colonial African possessions, producing wine, dates, and wool for Aragon. Gold, however, attracted the Spanish much more than agriculture. "Moorish ducats" were traded north along the Niger and Volta Rivers by the empire of Mali, and the Catalan Atlas described Mali's ruler as "the richest and noblest king in all the land."

By the late fourteenth century, Sicily had became an Aragonese fiefdom and a major source of wheat. As the Castilians expelled the large Moorish population, the coastal communities of Andalusia became their springboard into the Atlantic. By the middle of the thirteenth century, the Straits of Gibraltar, once under Moslem domination, were now controlled by Castilian ships built in Seville.

Through their territorial and maritime conquests, Aragon and Castile became the largest and most powerful Spanish kingdoms. After Ferdinand and Isabella married in 1469, they took bold steps to build a powerful, united Spain. The Crown established a centralized Inquisition, or judicial tribunal to suppress heresy, in 1478 to appease the strong sentiment throughout Spain against New Christians, whose parents and grandparents had converted from Judaism to Christianity. Ferdinand and Isabella also conquered Granada and later forcibly baptized its Moors, expelled Jews from Castile who would not convert to Catholicism, and helped finance the expeditions of Columbus.

Columbus's first voyage was the most momentous of the four journeys that he took between 1492 and 1504. Early in the morning on October 12, 1492, thirty-two days after leaving the Canaries, one of the Bahamas was sighted. At dawn, Columbus and his crew came ashore and claimed possession in the name of Spain. "I believed it to be no island but the continental province of Cathay visited by Marco Polo," Columbus later wrote.

During the next two weeks, Columbus explored the Caribbean and planted crosses on every island he visited. Although he found little gold, few precious spices, and no representatives of the Chinese emperor, Columbus was convinced that these islands were "set down in the maps at the end of the Orient." On subsequent voyages, Columbus explored the Caribbean and South America and established Christendom's first colony in the Americas.

Columbus's four voyages changed the globe in ways neither he nor his sponsors ever could have imagined. He literally opened up another part of the globe for Europe by navigating and describing the central Atlantic and the Caribbean for the first time. And the lands and peoples he encountered became the source of unimaginable wealth, huge empires, and dizzying new ideas. Columbus's impact on world history has been matched by few men or women. By linking Europe and the Americas, he began Europe's great age of discovery.

What motivated Columbus to spend so many years imploring monarchs for support and undertaking perilous voyages? Social ambition was probably an important factor. His family were modest Genoese clothiers, and like many of the conquistadores who followed, Columbus hoped his expeditions would bring him wealth and power.

Before reaching the Iberian peninsula, Columbus had worked in a Genoese merchant house; voyaged throughout the Mediterranean; and visited Ireland, Iceland, West Africa, and Madiera. Columbus was also a veteran slave trader, for after capturing some indigenous Caribbean peoples for transport back to Spain, he wrote that "already it has many times been my business to bring men from Guinea." Although he had "sprung from plebeian parentage," Columbus believed he could acquire fame, riches, and titles by sailing westward to the Orient.

But Columbus's material dreams were no less important to him than his religious vision. From the beginning of his Enterprise of the Indies, he fervently believed that his voyages would lead to the conversion of Asia, the liberation of the Holy Land, and the advent of the millennium. Columbus certainly was an intrepid navigator, but he was also a latter-day Crusader and a man intoxicated by biblical prophecies.

Columbus told Ferdinand and Isabella that when he was a young man, the Holy Spirit appeared in a vision and told him that "God . . . will cause your name to be wonderfully proclaimed throughout the world . . . and give you the keys of the gates to the ocean which are closed with strong chains." He had been divinely chosen to spread Christianity throughout the world and recover the Holy Land. "In this voyage to the Indies Our Lord wished to perform a very evident miracle in order to console me and the others in the matter of this other voyage to the Holy Sepulchre."

The first steps toward making the Gospel universal had already been taken by Ferdinand and Isabella, "who love and promote the holy Christian faith, and are enemies of the doctrine of Mahomet, and of all idolatry and heresy." Now that the Moors had been conquered and the Jews forced to embrace the Church or leave Castile, Columbus was poised to extend the boundaries of Christendom by visiting the court of the Chinese emperor.

This Asian monarch, Columbus claimed, had "sent to Rome soliciting instructors who might teach him our holy faith," but the pope "had never granted his request, whereby great numbers of people were lost, believing in idolatry and doctrines of perdition." Columbus felt confident that by sailing west he would be able to reach the East in a brief voyage and learn "the proper method of converting them to our holy faith."

Although Columbus failed to reach the Mongol court, his sense of prophetic mission increased after his first voyage. After 1492, he began signing his name Christoferens or "bearer of Christ," and used Latin initials above his name that stood for "Servant I am of the Most High Savior, Christ Son of Mary." According to Ferdinand, Columbus's son and first biographer, his father's name really meant *dove* "because he carried the grace of the Holy Ghost to that New World which he discovered, showing those people who knew Him not Who was God's beloved son, as the Holy Ghost did in the figure of a dove when St. John baptized Christ." Similar to the dove that Noah sent from the ark to search for land, Columbus "bore the olive branch of baptism, to signify that those people who had been shut up in the ark of darkness and confusion were to enjoy peace and union with the Church."

Columbus's sense of himself as a prophetic figure became most explicit on his third voyage of discovery. As he explored the coast of South America, he claimed that the mouth of the Orinoco River was literally one of the Garden of Eden's four rivers because of the immense amount of fresh water it emptied into the sea. "I believe that the earthly Paradise lies here, which no one can enter except by God's leave." In his impassioned speeches and writings, Columbus was convinced that he had discovered the site of Paradise predicted by "those holy and wise theologians."

While Columbus explored the Caribbean, he also worked on a *Book of Prophecies* that would explain his vision of history and the providential role he was destined to play. This manuscript of eighty-four numbered leaves bound in vellum with writing on both sides was never completed, but the surviving materials in Castilian, Latin, and Italian—biblical quotations, selections from ancient and medieval authors, Columbus's commentaries and his preface—clearly revealed the Admiral's religious motives and goals.

In this extraordinary document, Columbus quoted heavily from the Book of Isaiah to demonstrate that a stage of prophecy had been fulfilled by his voyages of discovery. Now Spain stood poised to recover "God's Holy City and Mount Zion" and evangelize the "islands of the Indies and of all other peoples and nations." Columbus believed that the world would end in a little over a century, and thus all idolaters in the new lands he had discovered must be converted quickly. Based on his careful study of medieval maps, ancient and medieval books, and the Bible, Columbus was certain that he was living at a great moment when the history of the world was about to alter dramatically.

But Columbus was not content just to convert the Orient to Christianity. He also wanted to use the legendary wealth of the Indies to drive the infidels out of Jerusalem. Just as the biblical David and Solomon had mined precious stones to build the First Temple, so Columbus would give the Spanish monarchs the gold they needed to storm the Holy Land. He identified what is today Panama as the original site of the Temple's jewels and expected to find the lost mines of Solomon somewhere in the Far East near the equator. The conquest of the Indies would lead to "certain victory in the enterprise of Jerusalem," liberating the city that had given birth to Christianity.

"God," he wrote, "made me the messenger of the new heaven and new earth." Columbus believed himself a fifteenth-century John the Baptist who would bring Christianity to the Orient and provide his Catholic monarchs with the wealth to fulfill their prophetic roles in Jerusalem.

In the earliest map of the Americas, published in 1503 by a cartographer on Columbus's second voyage, far to the west of Europe lies an indistinct coastline. There stands Columbus—Christoferens—carrying the Christ child on his shoulders to the interior of the continent. With Columbus, the Western Hemisphere would serve as a stage for transcendence and renewal, and perhaps Europe could now realize its age-old dream of a universal Christian empire.[11]

➤ 3 ◄

Suffering a Great Misery

––––––––
–––––

At first, reports about the European discovery of America appeared almost too fabulous to believe. The Genevan Jean de Léry, who briefly lived among the Tupinambás of Brazil as a Huguenot pastor in 1557, made an eloquent and remarkable confession in his provocative book, *History of a Voyage to the Land of Brazil, Otherwise Called America* (1578). Since "I have been in this land of America, where everything to be seen—the way of life of its inhabitants, the form of the animals, what the earth produces—is so unlike what we have in Europe, Asia, and Africa that it may very well be called a 'New World' with respect to us."[1]

These kinds of confessions became common in early descriptions of the Americas. Because the European discovery of indigenous societies challenged so many centuries of venerated texts and traditional assumptions, the Western Hemisphere was difficult to comprehend and describe. Ancient texts and ideas were both useful tools and frustrating obstacles for explorers in the Americas. Beginning with Columbus, as Europeans tried to understand the Americas, they challenged and eventually displaced their traditional conceptions of the earth. The discovery and colonization of the Americas became the new model for understanding nature and human society.

Early descriptions of native peoples were ambiguous. On the one hand, explorers from Spain, Portugal, France, and Britain praised many aspects of indigenous cultures. Native peoples had powerful and graceful physiques. They were dignified, courteous, hospitable, temperate, and free from envy, cheerfully sharing what they had with their neighbors. They practiced marriage and loved their children.

Their leaders seemed grave and wise, and people understood their rights and duties. They recognized rank in their societies, built towns and cities, and practiced agriculture. Although their technology was primitive, explorers were impressed with their large cities, canoes, and ability to grow corn. They were idolaters, but acknowledged the existence of a supreme being.

The inhabitants of the Americas were clearly inferior to Europeans, but they also were recognizably human. As one Frenchman said, "our savages though they be naked, are not void of those virtues that are found in men of civility."

On the other hand, Christians quickly came to two damning conclusions about the peoples of the Americas that led to wars of conquest.

First, Christians thought that the inhabitants of the Western Hemisphere lived closer to nature than to human culture. Although some admired the natives' seeming innocence, explorers often concluded that they were Wild Men—semi-humans governed by the most basic instincts and desires in a world that was violent and disorderly because it lacked the rule of human law. Because nature was so unpredictable and associated with animality, it could only produce humans who resembled beasts. In the sixteenth century, the word savage no longer referred just to wild woodlands, but now included people who lived and acted like barbarians. The Americas were engulfed in savagery. Building materials and techniques were primitive. Many societies lacked an alphabet and written records, private property, monetary systems, agricultural surpluses, or governments. Their religions were diabolical, childish, and full of superstition. They wore no clothes and engaged in indiscriminate sexual relations. Some practiced cannibalism. Native peoples were so brutish they did not even observe the incest taboo.

Second, when Europeans voyaged to the Americas, they equated traveling great distances from Europe with moving backward in time. Consequently, the peoples they encountered were considered human atavisms, throwbacks to a cruder age that resembled the original condition of humanity before the advent of civilization. By definition, indigenous peoples existed outside of history because they had not yet transcended their barbarism. The Americas were something quite strange and inexplicable—an antiquity not of Greece or Rome, but of barbarism. As the English philosopher John Locke wrote, "In the beginning all the World was *America*."

These primitives, Christians argued, shared neither a common past nor a common present with themselves. Therefore, indigenous peoples had no common future with Europeans, except as their wards. The fate of native peoples was sealed when they were declared inferior and barbaric. Like the inhabitants of the Canary Islands, the peoples of the Americas could be conquered and brutalized with few moral qualms.

The term "New World" had at least three meanings to Renaissance explorers. First, it literally meant the discovery of a part of the world previously unknown to Europeans. Second, it referred to a place where Europeans could establish new cities, new colonies, and new empires. Not surprisingly, the word "new" was affixed to many colonial possessions throughout the world (e.g., New Spain, New Mexico, New Granada, New Galicia, and New England). By effacing local names and renaming towns and regions in their own vernacular languages, Europeans signified that these newly claimed lands would experience a new birth as they were brought into the orbit of Europe. And third, by calling the Western Hemisphere a "New World," Europeans were saying that it was inhabited but empty because no civilized beings lived there. Thus, it was available for settlement. The term "New World" was a European projection and an adjunct to conquest, just like the word "Indian."

The indigenous peoples of the New World also had problems of comprehension when they first encountered Europeans. Because these unusual strangers had arrived from great distances beyond the horizon and seemingly to them from out of the sky, native peoples thought that they must be great chiefs, shamans, reincarnated ancestors, spirits disguised in human form, or humans with unusual powers.

The indigenous peoples thought that the Europeans looked, dressed, and behaved oddly; smelled differently; and possessed exceptional technical skills. They believed that the Europeans' horses, guns, ships, beards, skin and hair color, books, clothing, and navigational instruments indicated they must have a special relationship to the spirit world. Because Europeans appeared very powerful and because their novel material goods were mystifying and sometimes very frightening, native peoples immediately wanted to befriend Europeans and obtain their goods.

At first, the peculiar appearance and seemingly great powers of Europeans inspired awe among indigenous peoples. The Mohawk word for the Dutch was *Kristoni* [I am a metal maker], and the Yuroks of California called white settlers *wo'gey*, the same name as their cultural heroes. Similarly, the Aguarunas of northern Peru named Europeans *wiakuch*, a word closely related to *Wiracocha*, the major Inca god.

Indigenous peoples thought they could share the powers of their visitors by welcoming them and possessing their goods. Long-distance exchange, after all, had always been associated with spiritual power and prestige in native cultures. New World peoples at first happily traded their gold, pearls, and furs for glass beads, metal, clothing, and other items of seemingly little value because they attached great power and spiritual significance to everything European.

European glass beads and copper, for example, were associated with native crystal, shells, and other minerals that had supernatural properties. European technology—especially large ships and booming guns and cannon—particularly impressed indigenous peoples, for they seemed visible signs of god-like faculties. The Oglala Sioux still refer in their own language to guns as sacred objects.

Indigenous peoples quickly learned, however, that Europeans were not from another world but mortal beings who had great wealth, unusual skills, and desirable products. As a result, they began appraising European intentions and behavior according to their own standards.

The great encounter between Europeans and native peoples began badly with Columbus in 1492 and hardly changed over the centuries. Despite cultural and political differences, the people of Spain, Portugal, France, and Britain behaved in similar ways toward the people of the New World because they believed that the creation was most orderly in Europe and increasingly incomprehensible and grotesque on the periphery. According to the Europeans, the inhabitants of the New World lived and worshipped in ways that denied God's truths; thus, they could not legitimately exercise sovereignty over themselves and their possessions. Consequently, indigenous peoples had to be subdued and converted to Christianity.

This attitude was puzzling to New World peoples, who at first welcomed Europeans and treated them warmly and generously. Europeans did not conform to the standards of the peoples they encountered, and their greed for gold and silver, discourtesy, and sexual avarice deeply offended them. With the arrival of Columbus and other European explorers, indigenous peoples began to "suffer a great mystery," in the words of an advisor to the Aztec leader Moctezuma. They could not understand why Europeans consistently behaved in ways that were so disruptive, brutal, and contemptuous toward those who wanted to befriend them. The Europeans' predatory and crusading mentality simply made no sense to them.[2]

Mesoamerica and the Caribbean

Columbus Tries to Reach Cathay

In August 1492, Columbus left Spain, stopped at the Canary Islands, and "shaped his course to the West." Columbus noted in his log book that he needed better sailing conditions "because nothing like this had occurred since the time of the Jews when the Egyptians came out against Moses who was leading them out of captivity."

On October 11, 1492, land was sighted. The next day, Columbus raised the royal standard and came ashore to claim the island "for his sovereigns and masters the King and Queen." While he was making the required declarations, the Taínos watched their strange visitors closely. So did Columbus. According to him, "they were very well built with fine bodies and handsome faces. . . . They are the color of the Canary Islanders (neither black nor white)." They did carry arms and when Columbus showed them swords, they "cut themselves out of ignorance. They have no iron. Their spears are made of cane."

Because Columbus thought he had landed east of the Indus River near the Asian coast, he called these people "Indians," and immediately concluded from their appearance and behavior that they would make good servants and "would easily be made Christians, for they appeared to me to have no religion. God willing, when I made my departure I will bring half a dozen of them back to their majesties, so that they can learn to speak."

From his first day in the Bahamas, Columbus claimed all the islands he visited for his sovereigns, believing that "having annexed one, it might be said that we had annexed all." By the time Columbus triumphantly returned to Spain, he laconically noted in his diary that "I found many islands with large populations and took possession of them all for their Highnesses" by proclamation and by unfurling the royal standard.

Throughout his four voyages, Columbus acted as if his Catholic monarchs were "just as much political lords of this land as of Jerez or Toledo." After 1493, part of this claim was based on the incredibly generous papal donation of Rodrigo Borgia of Valencia, who as the corrupt and worldly Pope Alexander VI granted the Spanish Crown "full, free, ample, and absolute authority and jurisdiction" over non-Christian lands it discovered. Underlying this donation was a basic principle that any Christian power could apply to the Western hemisphere.

For centuries, Christendom had acted firmly on the belief that the world outside Europe was chaotic, disorderly, uncivilized, and populated with barbarians, infidels, and heathens. These benighted peoples did not exercise true sovereignty over their domains because they lacked reason or knowingly worshipped false gods. By taking possession of land in the name of Jesus Christ, Columbus and other explorers ritually consecrated the land and began enclosing it within the Christian cosmos.

The crosses they erected symbolized a new religious birth and sovereignty over the people who lived there. As King Ferdinand said in 1511, all Indians were supposed to become part of "our holy Catholic faith, for this is the principal foundation upon which we base our conquest of these regions."

As Columbus claimed the Caribbean for Castile, he frantically searched for the gold and jewels that had lured the Portuguese and Spanish to North Africa and the Canary Islands. Columbus's mania for precious metals surfaced on the second day of his landing and never abated, for gold or rumors of gold invariably determined his sailing course and dealings with Indians.

Like the Christians, who followed him, Columbus was seeking salvation in gold. "Our Lord in His goodness guide me," he prayed on his first voyage, "that I may find this gold." By his fourth voyage in 1502, Columbus had become almost crazed by his search for wealth. "Gold is most excellent," he wrote. "Gold constitutes treasure, and he who possesses it may do what he will in the world, and may so attain as to bring souls to paradise." Gold and salvation, which were always closely linked in Columbus's mind, always seemed to beckon just beyond the next horizon.

Although Columbus found few precious metals or spices over the next three months, he returned home undaunted, coyly telling Ferdinand and Isabella that he would "give them as much gold as they require, if they will render me some very slight assistance." Furthermore, he boldly predicted that "all Christendom will receive encouragement and profit" by the "conversion of so many peoples to our holy faith."

The Crown's fervent belief that "temporal benefits" and "holy faith" were closely intertwined had deep medieval roots in Iberian culture. Both the *Reconquista* of Spain and the annexation of the Canaries were jointly financed by the Crown and private interests. In Spain, monarchs had given knights contracts to fight the Moors—which recognized the Crown's sovereignty over conquered Moorish lands—but also awarded successful military leaders land, property, slaves, official government posts, and titles of nobility.

Columbus's private contract with the Crown resembled the contracts used so effectively against the Moors and Canarians. He and his descendants would become the viceroys of all the places he discovered and receive a handsome profit for their efforts, but the Crown owned the lands Columbus might find.

When Columbus met the Taínos rather than the Great Khan, their appearance and culture immediately reminded him of the Canary Islanders, who were being conquered by the Spanish as he set sail for the Orient. Columbus claimed to admire the Taínos and described them to his sovereigns in very flattering terms. "They are so affectionate and have so little greed and are in all ways amenable that I assure your Highnesses that there is in my opinion no better people and no better land in the world. They love their neighbors like themselves and their way of speaking is the sweetest in the world, always gentle and smiling."

These same Taínos, Columbus claimed, would make good servants and willingly give the Spanish all they possessed. He even suggested that "should your Highness command it, all the inhabitants could be taken away to Castile or held as slaves on the island, for with fifty men we could subjugate them all and make them do whatever we wish."

Columbus's maiden exploration of the Caribbean in 1492—with its emphasis on territorial possession, the frenzied search for precious metals, and the belief that the Taínos were an inferior human species ripe for conquest and slavery—typified not just the Spanish approach to the New World, but all of Christendom's approach to the New World over the next centuries. The heir to centuries of military and commercial expansion in the Mediterranean and the western Atlantic, Columbus embodied a culture of domination that said, "There is nothing inside you or inside your societies of value. To become truly human, you must surrender your freedom and acquire what only we possess."[3]

Michele da Cuneo

During Columbus's second voyage in 1493, the sailor Michele da Cuneo was very excited by the native women he met. Although they lived "like veritable animals" and even "copulated openly whenever they feel like doing so," the boyhood friend of Columbus was still strongly attracted to them.

According to da Cuneo, on a military expedition to a local village "while I was in the boat, I captured a very beautiful Carib woman, whom the said Lord Admiral gave to me. When I had taken her to my cabin she was naked—as was their custom." Cuneo tried to rape her, but she resisted and "treated me with her nails that I wished I had never begun." Then he took a rope and as he whipped her, "she let forth such incredible screams that you would not have believed your ears. Eventually we came to such terms, I assure you, that you would have thought she had been brought up in a school of whores."

Note: Antonello Gerbi, *Nature in the New World: From Christopher Columbus to Gonzalo Fernandez de Oviedo*, trans. Jeremy Moyle (Pittsburgh: University of Pittsburgh Press, 1985), p. 34; Christopher Columbus, *The Four Voyages*, trans. J.M. Cohen (New York: Penguin, 1969), pp. 138—139.

Quetzalcoatl Returns to Mexico

As strange and terrible omens appeared throughout Mexico, the Aztec emperor Moctezuma summoned magicians to his palace. As they "knelt before him, with one knee on the floor, and did him the greatest reverence," Moctezuma asked them about the "omens in the sky and on the earth." But they could not help the emperor, and in anger Moctezuma had them locked up in prison until they made their predictions.

They told the head steward that the "the future has already been determined and decreed in heaven, and Moctezuma will behold and suffer a great mystery." When the steward gave Moctezuma this message, he questioned them again.

"Ask them if it will come from the sky or the earth, and from what direction or place it will come, and when this will happen." But when the steward returned to his prison, he discovered that the magicians had become invisible and flown away. Moctezuma was infuriated at their escape, and ordered his village chiefs to kill the magicians' families by hanging their wives and killing their children.

Several days later, a *macehual* [common man] came to the palace with this message for Moctezuma. He had seen a "mountain range or small mountain floating in the midst of the water, and moving here or there without touching the shore. My lord, we have never seen the like of this, although we guard the coast and are always on watch." Moctezuma thanked him for the information and placed the man in prison.

He sent a priest and ambassador to investigate the "strange things that have appeared on the great sea." After they arrived in Cuetlaxtlan, they "came back in great haste to report that it was true: They had seen two towers or small mountains floating on the waves of the sea." The priest, hiding himself in a tree, "saw what was floating there, beyond the edge of the water," and observed strangers nearby fishing in a small boat. They all had long beards, and their hair only came to their ears.

Moctezuma was very downcast when he heard this report. He told the emissaries to bring him the imprisoned *macehual*, but he too had vanished from his cell. This astonished and terrified Moctezuma, who then called for two silversmiths and two jewelers. He told the craftsmen to make a gold chain with emeralds, gold bracelets, beautiful earrings, and two great fans with feathers and gold.

He also warned them that if they revealed his purpose, "it will mean the ruin of your houses to their foundations, and the loss of your goods, and death to yourselves, your wives, your children and your kin, for all shall die." After they completed their tasks, Moctezuma gave them cloth and food.

Later, the towers again appeared along the shoreline. When Moctezuma heard about them, he thought that Quetzalcoatl, the Aztec god who had founded Mexican culture, had returned, "as he had said he would when he set out eastward long ago, to resume the rulership from which he had been driven." Moctezuma chose five emissaries to bring them the beautiful gifts his craftsmen had created.

When they paddled out to the towers, the strangers asked them: "Who are you? Where do you come from?" The Mexicans brought baskets of gifts, and one by one they honored the vessel's leader "by touching the ground before him with their lips."

71

They said to him: "May it please the god to hear. His deputy governor, Moctezuma, who rules Mexico for him, prays to him and says, 'The god has traveled far; he is tired.'" Then they dressed the strangers' leader with incredibly beautiful gifts that the priest-king Quetzacoatl should wear, including a turquoise mosaic mask, decorated vest, armbands of gold, shells, and quetzal feathers, and a mirror.

He was not impressed with the finery, however. "And this is all," he said through his interpreter. "Is this your gift of welcome?" The emissaries were bound in irons, and then the strangers produced a loud explosion with a device that smoked. The Mexicans fainted until the strangers revived them with strong drink and food. After they felt better, the leader told them he had heard that the Mexicans were very brave conquerors. One warrior could defeat even twenty of his foes. But the leader was not convinced and wanted to see them fight. "We are going to fight each other in pairs, and in this way we will learn the truth. We will see who falls to the ground!"

The emissaries politely replied that their lord deputy Moctezuma had not sent them to fight with the strangers. If they did, Moctezuma would be angered and surely execute them. But the leader still insisted that they fight the next day. The Mexicans paddled away from the towers very rapidly, "so fierce was the anxiety burning in their souls. We must report to our king, Moctezuma," they said. "We will tell him what we have seen, and it is a terrifying thing. Nothing like it has ever been seen before!"

After the emissaries left the palace, Moctezuma could neither eat nor sleep. "He was lost in despair, in the deepest gloom and sorrow. Nothing could comfort him, nothing could calm him, nothing could give him any pleasure." He wondered what would happen to himself and his people and felt his heart aching.

When his emissaries returned, Moctezuma decided to hear their report in the Coacalli building where visiting dignitaries met the emperor. But first he commanded that two captives covered with chalk be brought to the Coacolli. First their breasts were torn open, then their hearts were torn out, and finally the messengers were sprinkled with their warm blood. Moctezuma had ordered the sacrifices because his emissaries had "gone into great danger; they had looked into the very faces of the gods; they had even spoken to them."

Afterwards, they told the emperor what they had seen and even produced samples of their food. Moctezuma was "astonished and terrified by their report, and the description of the strangers' food astonished him above all else." He almost fainted when they described the device that exploded. "A thing like a ball of stone," he heard, "comes out of its entrails: It comes out shooting sparks and raining fire. The smoke that comes out with it has a pestilent odor, like that of rotten mud."

Moctezuma also learned other amazing things. The strangers dressed in iron and their bows, shields, and swords were also made of iron. The strangers' bodies were always completely covered except for their faces. Their skin was white as if it had been made of lime. They wore long beards colored yellow and black, and "there were some black-skinned ones with kinky hair." Their food was like human food but tasted like a cornstalk.

"The animals they rode—they looked like deer—were as high as roof tops." Their dogs seemed enormous. They had flat ears and long, dangling tongues. Their eyes were a burning yellow, and they seemed to flash fire and shoot off sparks.

After Moctezuma heard this report, he became terrified. "It was as if his heart had fainted, as if it had shriveled. It was as if he were conquered by despair."[4]

Cortés Meets Montezuma's Emissaries

After Castilian expeditions from Cuba had explored the Mexican coast looking for slaves, Hernán Cortés left Havana with eleven ships in February, 1519, for Cozumel, an island off the coast of Mexico. There he found a survivor from a previous expedition, Geronimo de Aguilar.

When Spaniards washed up on the Mexican coast after a shipwreck in 1511, a local *cacique* sacrificed five of them and let the others live so they could be fattened for future offerings. They escaped to another *cacique* and willingly became his slaves. "All died of grief," and only Aguilar and another Spaniard survived.

When Hernán Cortés heard the word "Castilan" from the Indians on Cozumel, he thought there might be Spanish captives nearby. After local *caciques* reported that there were Indian traders who had spoken to Spaniards only two days before, Cortés gave them beads and a letter announcing that their deliverers had arrived. The Indians took this message wrapped in their hair and delivered it to Aguilar. After reading it, he gave his master the beads and was released to rejoin his countrymen. A naked Aguilar accompanied by other Indians crossed the twelve-mile channel to Cozumel in a canoe. When he met Cortés's men, who thought Aguilar was an Indian, he asked in awkward Castilian whether they were Christians. When they replied, "he wept for joy and falling on his knees gave thanks to god." Aguilar became one of the expedition's most important translators and supplied Cortés with critical information about the challenges his expedition would face on the mainland.

Cortés had been born in the stony and isolated Spanish province of Extremadura, where leprosy, poverty, and emigration were common. For almost eight centuries, Extremadura had sent its sons to the holy wars against the Moors. Later, others distinguished themselves among New World conquistadors. Many of Spain's greatest New World adventurers—Francisco Pizarro, Hernando de Soto, Pedro de Alvarado (called "the Sword of Extremadura" by Spaniards and "he who goes along getting hot" by the Aztecs), Nicolás de Ovando, and Vasco Nuñez de Balboa—hailed from the inhospitable land along Portugal's border that bred valiant warriors.

Cortés was no exception. The son of wealthy parents, Cortés attended the university at Salamanca for two years where he studied Latin grammar in preparation for a legal career. Afterwards, he served as a notary in Seville and then spent fifteen years in Hispaniola and Cuba as a notary, government official, and landowner with Indians attached to his estate. But Cortés did not see himself as simply a conqueror.

In good Renaissance fashion, he criticized the Catholic Church for its worldliness and corruption and hoped that in Mexico would appear a "new church, where god will be served and honored more than in any other region of the earth." Cortés believed that God had chosen him to bring millions of primitive heathen to Christ. Like Columbus, he dreamed of a universal Christian empire reaching from Spain across the New World to Cathay and thought his work in Mexico would hasten the advent of the millennium.

A man of strong faith, Cortés attended mass daily and always carried a picture of the Virgin Mary. He also had two banners. One had a statement in Latin emblazoned "The judgment of the Lord overtook them; His might lent strength to my arm." The other had a picture of the Virgin Mary on one side and Castile and León's coat of arms on the other.

When Cortés reached Mexico with his army in March, the gold and silver he saw led him to conclude that "it is entirely possible that this country has everything which existed in that land from which Solomon is said to have brought the gold for the Temple." Along with precious stones, Cortés received an equally valuable gift from the defeated village of Tabasco, a young female slave who was "good-looking, intelligent, and self-assured" whom he renamed Dona Mariña.

According to one soldier, Dona Mariña "was the great beginning of our conquests, and thus, praise be to God, all things prospered with us." She became Cortés's mistress and the mother of his child and ably served him as an interpreter. In conversations with the Aztecs, she translated their Nahuatl into Yucatec Mayan, and then Aguilar translated her words into Castilian. Once Dona Mariña converted to Catholicism, she also helped Cortés preach against the Mexican religions he encountered.

On Holy Thursday, as the fleet arrived off the mainland, large canoes full of Mexicans came to the ship and asked who was the master. Dona Mariña pointed Cortés out, and the Indians paid him great respect. "They said that their lord, a servant of the great Montezuma,* had sent them to find out what kind of men we were and what we were seeking, also to say that if we required anything for ourselves and our ships, we were to tell them and they would supply it."

Through his interpreters, Cortés thanked them and said that he had come to visit and trade with them. Over the next two days, Cortés moved 300 soldiers ashore and built a fort with the assistance of the Indians, who also supplied the Spanish with plums, fowl, maize cakes, and gold jewels. On Easter Sunday, two emissaries of Montezuma arrived with more presents, humbly bowing three times before Cortés and his soldiers.

Cortés celebrated a mass before them and then explained that he and his men were "Christians, and vassals of the Emperor Don Carlos, the greatest lord on earth, who had many great princes as his vassals and servants, and that it was at his orders we had come to their country, since for many years he had heard rumours of it and the great prince who ruled it." He wanted to have a meeting with Montezuma.

One of the emissaries was shocked at Cortés's effrontery and suggested that the visitors accept their presents and explain what they wanted to tell Montezuma. He gave them a chest full of golden objects, ten bales of white cloth made of cotton and beautiful feathers, and many delicious foods. In return, Cortés presented him with twisted glass, a few beads, and a carved, inlaid armchair.

Cortés asked again "that a day and place might be fixed for his meeting with Montezuma." Tendile, one of emissaries, promised to deliver the gifts and return with a reply. As the Aztecs talked with Cortés, skilled painters made large portraits of him and his ships, sails, greyhounds, and army for Montezuma to see.

Afterwards, Cortés decided to impress Montezuma's emissaries by ordering his men to gallop by them on horseback as cannon were fired into the nearby forest. Not surprisingly, the Aztec entourage was thoroughly frightened both by the horses and the great din of the cannon. Tendile then asked to see the rusty, half-gilt helmet of a Castilian soldier and told Cortés that "it was like one they had possessed which had been left them by their ancestors" and worn by their god Hitzilopochtli. Cortés gave him the helmet and asked whether the gold of the Aztecs "was the same as the gold we find in our rivers," for he would like to send the helmet back to his emperor filled with gold.

---

*The Spanish called the Aztec emperor "Montezuma," but in Aztec accounts his name is often "Moctezuma."

Tendile returned with more than 100 porters bearing great gifts for Cortés. They kissed the earth and perfumed the visitors with incense from earthenware braziers. Cortés was given a large golden disk shaped like the sun worth more than 10,000 pesos, a heavy silver disk, and his soldier's helmet full of gold worth 3,000 pesos. He also received golden objects in the shape of birds and beasts, beautiful green feathers, and thirty bales of decorated cotton cloth.

Cortés graciously accepted these gifts and told Tendile that he thought Montezuma "would much like to see our great Emperor, who was such a mighty prince that his fame had reached him even from the distant lands whence we came." Again, Tendile politely but firmly turned down his request to meet Montezuma.[5]

North America

Newfoundland Slaves

On May 12, 1500, King Manoel V of Portugal gave his son Gaspar Corte Real a charter "to discover and find any island or islands, or mainland" in the New World. One year later, Corte Real reached "Newfoundland" and told his father that he had discovered a "land that was very cool and with big trees." The inhabitants seemed "very barbarous and wild," reminding him of the Brazilians his countrymen had recently met. According to Corte Real, "Newfoundlanders" were white but turned brown with age from the cold climate. They lived in rocky caves and thatched huts, had no religion, and were very jealous of their wives, like the Lapps of Scandinavia.

While exploring the coast, he kidnapped fifty-seven Beothuks for his father to inspect. According to an Italian visitor at the Portuguese royal court who had "seen, touched, and examined these people . . . their manners and gestures are most gentle; they laugh considerably and manifest the greatest pleasure." The women had small breasts, beautiful bodies, and pleasant faces. "In fine, except for the terribly harsh look of the men, they appear to me to be in all else of the same form and image as ourselves."

The king was excited by his son's discovery. He thought that because this new land was near Portugal, he could conquer it without much difficulty and gather "a very large quantity of timber for making masts and ships' yards, and plenty of men-slaves, fit for every kind of labour."

The king's prediction proved accurate. Portuguese ships began visiting the Grand Banks of Newfoundland for fish, and Newfoundlanders were regularly sold in the slave markets of Seville and Valencia.[6]

Coronado and the Zuñis

After a Mexican friar returned from a disastrous expedition to Arizona with fanciful tales of seven terraced cities and ample gold, Francisco Vázquez de Coronado, the young governor of Nueva Galicia in northern Mexico, was appointed to explore this area. In the spring of 1540, a military expedition of over 300 Spanish soldiers and native peoples accompanied Coronado northward along Indian trails into the lands of the Pueblo Indians.

In early July, they met a ceremonial party of Zuñis at a sacred lake near their village of Hawikuh. Every two years, nine days after the summer solstice, Zuñi pilgrims visited the sacred lake to pray and kindle a sacred fire that would be brought back to the Zuñi pueblo. When the Spanish used their sacred kachina dolls that symbolized ancestral spirits for firewood that night, the enraged Zuñis attacked them.

After wounding Coronado, the Zuñis returned to their village to finish their sacred ceremony with joyous dances and songs. Coronado arrived at the Zuñi pueblo ten days later, but he found only a few old men. The rest of the villagers had fled into the mountains to avoid the strangers who had desecrated their sacred site. Into the twentieth century, the Zuñis forbade Spaniards to observe their ceremonies.

Note: Elizabeth A.H. John, *Storms Brewed in Other Men's Worlds: The Confrontation of Indians, Spanish, and French in the Southwest, 1540–1795* (Lincoln: University of Nebraska Press, 1975), pp. 12–16; J. Wesley Huff, "A Coronado Episode," *New Mexico Historical Review* XXVI, no. 2 (1951): 119–127.

Cartier in Canada

When King Francis I visited the beautiful island monastery of Mont-Saint-Michel in 1532, the bishop introduced him to Jacques Cartier, master mariner of the nearby port city of Saint-Malo. According to the bishop, Cartier, who had already visited Brazil and Newfoundland, could "discover new lands in the New World" and find a passage to Asia through the Gulf of the St. Lawrence River. Francis I was very intrigued by Cartier's account because he desperately needed money to finance his European wars. Perhaps somewhere between Florida and the frozen northern icy wastes a navigable passage could be found to the riches of Cathay.

The king had Cartier undertake three voyages into the interior of North

America from 1534 through 1543. Cartier planted the first European colony in the St. Lawrence River Valley and established the foundations for France's great fur empire in Canada. Although Cartier had no information about the Canadian interior, European fisherman and fur traders already had been visiting Maritime Canada and knew about the entrance to the St. Lawrence River. From their travels, Cartier understood that Canada's native peoples were very eager to trade their plentiful furs for cheap metal and glass beads.

In July 1534, Cartier's expedition encountered Micmacs in the Bay of Chaleur. As his men explored, "we saw boates full of wild men that were crossing the river." The next day, "we sawe a man running after our boates" signaling that they should return to the spot Cartier had visited the previous day. But when they rowed toward him, he fled in terror. The French left the frightened man a knife and a "woolen girdle on a little staffe."

Several days later, about forty or fifty boates of "wilde men" appeared, beckoned them to come ashore, and displayed animal skins stretched on wood. Cartier, however, was too worried about his defenseless position to land on the beach. Seven Micmac canoes followed him, "dancing, and making many signs of joy and mirth, as it were desiring our friendship." But when they surrounded Cartier's boat and ignored pleas to leave, the French fired "two pieces among them, which did so terrifie them, that they put themselves to flight . . . making a great noise." Again they came near Cartier's boat, and "wee strucke at them with two lances, which thing was so great a terrour unto them, that with great haste they beganne to flee, and would no more follow us."

The next day, Cartier met nine more boats signaling that they "came to trafique with us" by exhibiting valuable furs. Two Frenchmen went ashore with knives, iron objects, and a red hat for their leader. The Micmacs danced, dripped sea water on the Frenchmen's heads, and traded so many furs that they were completely naked.

A few days later, the same transaction was repeated at another location with more than 300 Micmac men, women, and children. Some of the women stood up to their knees in the water singing and dancing; others rubbed the French sailors' arms and lifted "them up toward heaven, shewing many signs of gladnesse." Again the Micmacs gave away all their goods "til they had nothing but their naked bodies."

Cartier had a mixed opinion of the Micmacs. He considered these "wild men" so simple and friendly that "this people might very easily be converted to our Religion." But they also seemed "great theeves, for they will filch and steale whatsoever they can lay hold of. All is fish that commeth to net," he tartly concluded.[7]

The Desecration of Crosses

The Ojibwas of the western Great Lakes region were horrified by the first Europeans they met, for these strange beings built crosses everywhere. The Ojibwas thought that these crosses were acts of desecration because they constructed wooden memorials only at funeral ceremonies to remember the dead. Consequently, they concluded that Europeans were mocking their ceremonies and ancestors by planting wooden objects outside Ojibwa burial grounds.

Note: Basil Johnston, *The Manitous: The Spiritual World of the Ojibways* (New York: HarperCollins, 1995), p. 1.

Elizabethans Abroad

While Spain and Portugal were establishing their great maritime empires, England slowly became involved in the New World. John Cabot and his son Sebastian, Venetians in the service of English kings, explored Newfoundland, Labrador, Nova Scotia, and Hudson Bay in 1497 but planted no colonies. Meanwhile, ships from Bristol and England's West Country fished off the rich Grand Banks of Newfoundland and bartered Canadian furs for European goods.

England's interest in New World colonization grew slowly, partly because she was allied with Spain until the late sixteenth century. Into the reign of Henry VIII, France had been England's protagonist and Spain her ally. England supported Spain's bountiful claims in the New World, and the Roman Catholic Queen Mary even married Philip II of Spain.

But after Queen Elizabeth began her long reign in 1558, the Protestant English gradually concluded that Spain's aggressive Roman Catholicism constituted a dangerous threat to English political liberty, the newly established Church of England, and to its international commerce. By the 1580s, Elizabeth, who had been excommunicated by the pope, felt strong enough to challenge Spain, which had become associated in the English popular mind with bigotry and unspeakable cruelty toward Indians.

While England was becoming a commercial power, it developed considerable military and colonial skills fighting the Irish. As they battled the Irish beyond the Pale of Dublin to Munster and Ulster, the English reduced "that savage Irish nation to better government and civility" in ways that served as a prototype for American colonization. Ireland was England's Granada and

Canary Islands, and colonization efforts in Ulster led directly to the Roanoke and Jamestown ventures.

Irish land was taken from local chieftains, who were considered wild and completely untrustworthy, divided into administrative units, and given to English proprietors who in turn sold their property to loyal English and Protestant Lowland Scottish settlers. Although this idea of establishing plantations took hold slowly, after the bloody Munster rebellion of 1580–81, it became part of Elizabeth's official policy in Ireland. Through private colonization and the extension of Crown government, Ireland gradually came under English control. The Crown's contracts with private colonizers were modeled after the ones granted military adventurers in the Iberian peninsula, the Canary Islands, and the New World.

According to the English, they had a solemn moral responsibility to reclaim Ireland "from desolation and a desert (in many parts) to population and plantation; and from savage and barbarous customs to humanity and civility." Sir Francis Bacon thought that the planting of English colonies in Ireland would lead to a time "when people of barbarous manners are brought to give over and discontinue their customs of revenge and blood and of dissolute life and of theft and rapine."

The Irish had no government, no cities, and led a nomadic, licentious existence. Warfare and revenge dominated their coarse lives. Although they were nominally Roman Catholic, their religion contained many vestiges of paganism. In the words of the English poet Edmund Spencer, Irish life was characterized by "salvage brutishnes and fylthynes." They were barely human.

Because Ireland and America were settled at the same time, they became closely intertwined in the English imperial imagination. One writer, for example, stated that Newfoundland "lieth near the course and half the way between Ireland and Virginia." Another described Ireland as that "famous Island in the Virginian Sea," and a third believed that English culture would humanize "the Irish, the Virgineans, and all other barbarous nations." And in the dedication to one of his poems, Spencer called Elizabeth I "Queene of England, Fraunce, and Ireland and of Virginia." Three of the most enthusiastic supporters of Elizabethan military expansion into Ireland—Humphrey Gilbert, Walter Ralegh, and Richard Grenville—helped finance and direct England's first American colonization efforts.

Out of England's burgeoning commerce, rising nationalism, and colonial successes in Ireland came a major challenge to Spain. When the Spanish ambassador to England complained to the Crown about Francis Drake's bold international piracy, he was told that the "queen does not acknowledge that her subjects and those of other nations may be excluded from the Indies on the claim that these have been donated to the king of Spain by the pope. . . . Prescription without possession is not valid."

The rise of Protestantism, Elizabeth believed, had broken the Roman Catholic Church's religious monopoly in the Western Hemisphere. Now there could be only one criterion—the successful planting of colonies—to determine European sovereignty abroad. Although the English considered themselves superior to the supposedly fanatic Spanish, they had the same attitudes toward the indigenous inhabitants of the New World. Because sovereignty was an attribute only of Christian nations, native peoples really did not possess their lands.

In 1578, Gilbert, representing West Country merchant adventurers, received a Crown patent to establish a colony in North America on lands not possessed by any Christian monarch. He failed, but his half-brother Ralegh carried on his efforts with greater zeal and determination. That same year, two ships departed England for America under Ralegh's instructions to find a site for a colony north of Spanish Florida.

After stopping in the Canaries and the West Indies, the military expedition sailed up the eastern coast of North America in June, "which we supposed to be a continent and firm land." Immediately, the English took possession of the area in the name of the Queen. On the third day, as they were admiring the bounty of the Carolina coast, three Indians appeared. One came aboard and received a shirt, hat, and his first taste of English meat and wine. After the man left, he fished for thirty minutes and left half his catch for the English.

The next day, about fifty "handsome and goodly men" accompanied their leaders to meet the explorers. A few days later, the English and Indians traded European goods for deerskins and other items. The Indians were so friendly that they even showed the English their fort at a place they called Roanoke.

During their stay, the Indians treated them with "all love and kindness, and with as much bounty (after their manner) as they could possibly devise." After the ships returned to England in September, the captains wrote a detailed report to Ralegh which "certified you of the country taken in possession by us, to her majesty's use, and so to yours by her Majesty's grant."

But land was not all they had claimed for England. In the last sentence of their report, the captains noted that "we brought home also two of the savages being lusty men, whose names were Wanchese and Manteo."[8]

Heavy Sticks and Little Kettles

According to Waioskasit of the Menominis, who lived along the western Great Lakes, one day they saw "on the shores of the sea . . . some large vessels, which were near to them and wonderful to behold." Suddenly they were startled by an explosion that sounded like thunder. Men with light-colored skin left the vessels and came ashore. They had hair on their faces and carried long, heavy sticks decorated with shining metal. As they approached, the Menominis thought their leader was a great manido, or spirit.

The chief rubbed some tobacco into the leader's forehead, and then the manido and his companions sat on the ground and smoked tobacco with the Menominis. The visitors drank a strange liquid and offered it to their guests. The Menominis, however, were afraid to drink the pungent liquid because they feared it would kill them. Instead, they selected four old men to determine its affects.

The men "began to talk and grow amused" after they consumed part of it. When they arose and staggered about, the Menominis feared they were dying. After the men collapsed, the Menominis thought about attacking their guests for trying to kill them. But before any violence occurred, the men regained consciousness, rubbed their eyes, and said that the liquid made them feel very happy.

The manido offered them food and presented one of their hosts with a rifle "after firing it to show how far away anything could be killed." The manido also gave them large, heavy kettles and demonstrated how to boil water with them. The Menominis, however, found the kettles too big and asked for cups the size of their clenched fists, "for they believed they would grow to be large ones." The Menominis received several small ones as gifts, but the cups never grew to be kettles.[9]

South America

In the Land of the Parrots

In 1489, Bartholomeu Dias presented an electrifying report to King Joao II of Portugal. In May of the preceding year, his flagship had rounded the Cape of Torments (later renamed the Cape of Good Hope) and entered the Indian Ocean before his terrified crew demanded they return home. The easiest road to the fabled Orient, the king concluded, was around Africa and not west beyond the Azores. In 1497, Vasco de Gama's four ships reached the southern Indian port of Calicut and returned with cloves, ginger, cinnamon, pepper, and other exotic spices.

Three years later, the king and his nobles financed a huge trading and military expedition to India consisting of thirteen ships and over 1,000 men. Commanded by Pedro Álvares Cabral, the fleet left Lisbon for the Cape of Good Hope but was blown off course by strong eastward winds. Six weeks later, Cabral's fleet landed in Brazil and spent nine days exploring the coast. With Cabral was a government official named Pero Vaz de Caminha, who wrote a detailed and lively letter to his monarch about the people they met.

According to Caminha, after they cast anchor opposite a river mouth, "we caught sight of men walking on the beaches." Cabral sent someone ashore to examine the river, and as he approached about twenty Indians awaited him. "They were dark and naked and had no covering for their private parts, and they carried bows and arrows in their hands." One Portuguese sailor "threw them a red cap, and a linen bonnet he had on his head, and a black hat. And one of them threw him a hat of large feathers with a small crown of red and gray feathers, like a parrot's. Another gave him a large bough covered with little white beads which looked like seed-pearls."

Cabral's fleet sailed along the coast and met two warriors in a canoe. The men were taken to the admiral's flagship and were "received with great rejoicings and festivities." Cabral appeared before them regally seated on a chair with a carpet at his feet. Although he was beautifully dressed and wore a very large gold collar to impress his visitors, the two men "made no gesture of courtesy or sign of a wish to speak to the admiral or any one else." Their indifference to rank shocked the Portuguese. "They go naked," Caminha reported, "with no sort of covering. They attach no more importance to covering up their private parts or leaving them uncovered than they do to showing their faces."

The visitors were shown a ram, but they seemed unimpressed. When the Portuguese gave them bread, boiled fish, sweetmeats, cakes, and dried figs to eat, "they spat it out at once" and had similar reactions to wine and water from a pitcher. After looking at other objects, the Indians "lay on their backs on the carpet to sleep. They did not try to cover up their private parts in any way; these were uncircumcised and had their hairs well shaved and arranged." Cabral ordered two of his cushions to be placed under their heads and had a cloak spread over them. "They consented to this, pulled it over themselves, and slept."

The next day, the Portuguese met more Indians. "Three or four girls went among them," Caminha wrote, "good and young and tender, with very long black hair hanging down their backs. And their privy parts were so high and tightly closed and so free from pubic hair that, even when we examined them very closely, they did not become embarrassed." Two of the women especially attracted Caminha's attention. One had her knees and calves painted with a black dye, and "her privy parts so naked and exposed with such innocence that there was no shame there." Another was "all dyed from head to foot in that paint; and indeed she was so well built and so well curved, and her privy part (what a one she had!) was so gracious that many women of our country, on seeing such charms, would be ashamed that theirs were not like hers."

The Portuguese were alternately titillated and exasperated by the Indians' unwillingness to wear clothes. After Cabral's visitors awoke, they were dressed in shirts, hats, and rosaries, but discarded their gifts quickly. And during a mass, sailors were bothered by the nudity of one Brazilian visitor. They gave her a cloth covering, "but as she sat down she did not think to spread it much to cover herself." Caminha could only conclude that the "innocence of Adam himself was not greater than these people's, as concerns the shame of the body."

The natives' hospitality and nakedness beguiled the Portuguese, conjuring up images of a people living in paradise. Diogo Dias, "a merry fellow," joined an Indian dance with a bagpipe player. Caminha concluded "if we could understand their speech and they ours, they would immediately become Christians, seeing that, by all appearances, they do not understand about any faith. . . . Any stamp we wish may be easily printed on them, for the Lord has given them good bodies and good faces, like good men."

Before the expedition departed for India, Cabral decided to establish trading relations with his hosts. In exchange for European items, Indians helped his men load hardwood logs that produced a red dye called *brasile* onto a supply ship, which immediately returned to Portugal with Caminha's letter. For the next three decades, European ships visited the "Land of Parrots" to barter metal knives and axes in exchange for Indian labor.

Cabral also left two convicts to intermarry among the natives. Sentenced to death, their lives were spared so they could begin spreading Portuguese culture in the New World. For the next half-century, Brazil became the final destination for many of Portugal's worst criminals. When the fleet was about to depart, they "began to weep, but the men of the land comforted them and showed that they pitied them." The convicts were joined by two cabin boys who had deserted their ships.

Before leaving, Cabral kidnapped four or five Indians for servants. Caminha thought that they should be "very handsomely treated, not only in the way of food, but also to a bed with mattress and sheets, the better to tame them."[10]

In the Land of the Clodhoppers

In 1519, Ferdinand Magellan, a Portuguese seaman sailing for Spain, landed on the South American coast during his epochal circumnavigation of the world. He named the land Patagonia, or Land of the Clodhoppers, after the people he met. The men reminded the Venetian Antonio Pigafetta of huge naked beasts "who sail upon the infernal marshes."

One man "had a large head and great ears like unto a mule, with the body of a camel and tail of a horse." The women, he wrote, were smaller than the men "but in return they are much grosser. Their drooping breasts are more than a foot long. . . . They were not beautiful to our eyes; nevertheless, their husbands were extremely jealous of us."

According to Pigafetta, one naked women sneaked aboard his ship to steal some items. In the captain's cabin, she found a nail, "grabbed it immediately, stuck it deftly into her vagina, then jumped overboard and got away."

Note: Ronald Sanders, *Lost Tribes and Promised Lands: The Origins of American Racism* (Boston: Little, Brown, 1978), p. 108; Antonio Pigafetta, *Premier Voyage autour du monde par Le Chevalier Antonio Pigafetta, 1525* (Paris: H.J. Jasen, 1801), pp. 30–31, 33, 36.

The First European Picture of New World Peoples

Probably the first European picture of the indigenous peoples of the Western Hemisphere appeared in a 1505 German edition of Amerigo Vespucci's *Mundus Novus*. It was based either on an account of the Cabral expedition from the King of Portugal to the Renaissance Florentine humanist, Pietro di Medici, or on a letter from Vespucci to him. The German translation stated that the description of Brazil's Indians was made from a Latin version of the letter.

In the engraving, there are eight Brazilian and three children, all dressed in feathers. The women's breasts are completely exposed. Two Portuguese ships hover offshore while a horrifying scene unfolds. In the foreground, two warriors are initiating sexual relations with each other. In the background, two women are kissing and fondling while another eats a human arm. Between the men and the women hangs the severed torso of a man roasting over a fire. Meanwhile, one women calmly nurses her child while cannibalism and homosexual relations take place around her.

According to the caption underneath the picture, they were naked, handsome, brown, and "well shaped in body." Everything is held in common, and the "men have as wives those who please them, be they mothers, sisters, or friends, therein make they no distinction." They fought and ate each other, "even those who are slain, and hang the flesh of them in the smoke. They become a hundred and fifty years old. And have no government."[11]

The Impostors of Wiraqocha

When Huayna-Capac, the last great emperor of the Incas, heard about the strange men who had just appeared in his empire, he became very disturbed because "it brought to his memory the ancient prediction according to which strangers never before seen would one day land in Peru and despoil their Empire and their faith." Three years before the strangers appeared, a bad omen had sown consternation throughout the land. During the celebration of the annual feast of the Sun, a royal eagle fell wounded at the emperor's feet, dying several days later.

Then violent earthquakes shattered huge rocks and collapsed whole mountains. The sea became furious, comets streaked across the heavens, and one night three bright rings appeared around the moon. Huayna-Capac asked his seers for advice, and they replied "with ominous forecasts, and the Empire lived in a state of fear, awaiting the direst misfortunes."

One day, Huayna-Capac fell ill after bathing in a lake near Quito. As his condition worsened, a green comet lit up the sky and lightening struck his palace. After saying farewell to his family, he died of smallpox sometime around 1525.

According to one native account, at dinner a messenger arrived wearing a black cape. After kissing the emperor reverently, he gave him a box and a key. When the emperor "opened the little box from which flew butterflies or fluttered little pieces of paper, which disappeared." Within two days, a general and many captains died of smallpox, their faces covered with scabs. "When the Inca saw all this, he ordered a stone building erected in which to hide himself away. And thus hidden, encased in stone, he too died." Eight days later, they embalmed his body and took it to Cuzco.

Many of his subjects also succumbed to this frightening illness, and the survivors became weakened and frightened. His son Huascar was made the new Inca ruler while Atahualpa, another son, led the imperial army. After several years of peace, the two brothers started fighting each other, and Atahualpa's armies crushed Huascar's militia. As the war was ending, strangers appeared again in Peru.

According to eyewitnesses, "they said they had seen beings quite different from us landing in their country, different as much by their conduct as by their clothing," who resembled the Wiraqochas. "This they named them, first because they were very different from us, in face and costume, second because they saw them riding on the backs of huge animals [horses] with silver feet."

These strange beings silently conversed with one another "by means of pieces of white cloth, just as easily as one man speaks to another by word of mouth." Some had black beards while other were reddish in appearance. Shrouded like corpses, their faces were covered with wool. Only their eyes could be seen. On their heads, they wore colored pots and ornamental plumes, and they "carried their penises, very long, hanging behind."

The strangers ate from silver plates and used *Illapas* [thunderbolts] from heaven. The Incas were frightened by these newcomers, for they did not sleep at night, their horses ate silver and gold, and their weapons were made of metal. Worse, they spent much of their time raping women and plundering the local inhabitants.

As the strangers marched along Inca roads through Peru, Huascar and Atahualpa tried to enlist their support. An emissary of Huascar asked for help "from the sons of his god Viracocha." Two days later, Atahualpa's brother Atauchi arrived at the head of a large diplomatic mission. He told them that the "Inca has sent me to welcome the sons of our god Viracocha and to offer them some of the fruits of the earth in order that they might know that we are happy to serve them with all our strength and in every way we can."

After his welcoming speech, the strangers were given lambs, llamas, deer, corn, fruit, parrots, monkeys, woolen goods, emeralds, and gold and silver bowls. The leader of the strangers sent Atahualpa a shirt and two glass goblets. After several days rest, the strangers continued in the direction of Atahualpa's encampment. They were welcomed as "descendants of the Sun," and told the inhabitants that if they wanted to make friends with them, they should feed their animals unlimited amounts of gold and silver bars.

Opinion soon turned, however, on the divinity of the strangers. Atahualpa heard that the bearded intruders' *Illapas* could fire only twice and that their huge animals had to rest at night. Worse, the strangers behaved more like "lordless people who ransack and loot" than like gods. One of Atahualpa's informants told him that "they think it fine to take for themselves young women and golden and silver glasses and fine clothing . . . and wherever they go they do not leave anything they have not looted." Although they at first appeared to be gods, they were really "itinerant, disorderly thieves." This man concluded that he would not call them Wiracochas but instead "demons."

These strangers were clearly rapacious mortals, not gods. Now that the civil war was ending, Atahualpa decided to lay a trap for them at his encampment.[12]

➤ 4 ◄

Rage Without Reason

———————

When Columbus left for the Orient in 1492, Christendom was in the throes of transformation, and during the next century western European countries established the world's first global capitalist economies. First Spain and Portugal and later Britain, France, and the Netherlands created huge maritime empires stretching from the cereal estates of eastern Europe to the ports of Southeast Asia and the silver mines of Peru. A new age had begun.

With Spain as the leader, Christendom created its New World colonies to extract an economic surplus through radically unequal exchange relations. European governments wanted to manage what indigenous peoples produced, how they produced it, what they received in exchange, and how they consumed it. Their goal was to strip New World societies of their sovereignty and wealth and turn them into dependencies ruled from the Old World.

Dependency brought a radically new ethic to the New World—the belief that acquisition and consumption were the chief means to achieve happiness; that the possession of property, people, and wealth was the predominant measure of success; and that individuals had the natural right to the unlimited appropriation of nature. When John Locke and other European philosophers defended property—in people and goods—as an inalienable right, they had Christendom's New World empires in mind.

Dependency, however, was never merely an economic process. With Granada, the Canary Islands, and Ireland as recent models, Christians waged a holy war against indigenous societies. To redeem the New World from its benighted condition, Christendom focused on changing two facets of indigenous life that differed most from its own, native spirituality and the place of native peoples in the cosmos.

Colonial powers tried to destroy the New World's spiritual inheritance by denying any value to indigenous religious beliefs and practices. Most Christians, whether they were highly educated priests, opportunistic settlers, or hardened soldiers, saw the New World as a Satanic inversion of Christianity and a savage land. Everywhere Europeans looked, Indians were under the control of the devil. Consequently, native spirituality had to be destroyed and the native spiritual environment made banal.

The technique was very straightforward. Everything—people, trees, gold, silver, land, labor, food, and even hammocks and feathers—would be turned into commodities defined by their usefulness to Christendom, and a once bountiful nature would be turned into inert, private property that excluded entire peoples. Beginning with Columbus on the island of Hispaniola in 1493, Christendom put up a gigantic "For Seizure and Sale" sign that covered the New World. Economic dependency, based on the relentless desacralization of the indigenous environment, would be the chief means to transform the native world and its inhabitants.

The conquerors also introduced new conceptions of land use and ways of representing geography into the New World. With European colonization, indigenous communities lost their power to name places, represent themselves in official maps and pictures, and use land as they saw fit. With the conquest, native lands lost their sacred and communal character and simply became pieces of real estate to be bought and sold.

In addition, Christendom tried to alter indigenous societies' traditional understanding of their place in the cosmos. Until the arrival of Europeans, all New World societies believed they existed at the center of the universe. By living according to their sacred traditions, they existed in harmony and helped sustain the world. With the conquest, however, indigenous communities were displaced from the center of the universe to its periphery. According to Europeans, it was impossible for native peoples to live moral lives and achieve salvation in their savage condition. Only by becoming obedient subjects of their Christian masters and jettisoning their most important traditions could they hope to overcome their crude inheritance.

Europeans also tried to obliterate the memories of native peoples by destroying their records and vilifying their traditions. They developed historical interpretations of the New World that described its peoples as vanquished and passive bit actors in a cosmic drama produced and directed by Christians with themselves as the lead performers. While Renaissance philosophers in Europe were heralding the newfound dignity and powers of humanity, Renaissance explorers and colonizers were systematically carrying out an anti-humanistic campaign in the New World.

Under European domination, millions of Indians were forced to obey abstract tribute and work schedules that bore no relationship to their sacred narratives, daily rituals, community traditions, or to the cyclical changes of nature. As Indians were relegated to the bottom of the social pyramid along with African slaves, they had to undertake massive sacrifices of their time for the benefit of Europeans and for eventual entry into the kingdom of heaven.

The exploration, conquest, and settlement of the New World was the greatest attempt at social engineering before the Nazi and Communist political revolutions of the twentieth century. Beginning with Columbus, the conquest was an incredibly audacious attempt by Christendom to change one part of the world based on a religious and political philosophy that grandly claimed to encompass the laws of historical development. Europe took its beliefs and customs, boldly universalized them, and then used them to measure the Western Hemisphere. Not surprisingly, all native societies were found seriously deficient.

The invasion of the New World was primarily a military and biological operation. In the tradition of the crusades and the conquest the Baltic region, the Canary Islands, and Ireland, indigenous peoples usually met Europeans through aggressive military and colonization expeditions. From North Carolina to Peru, the English, Spanish, and Portuguese usually behaved callously and brutally toward Indians because their goal was to conquer, exploit, convert, and degrade peoples they considered savage and inferior. Like their crusading ancestors, New World military and colonizing expeditions engaged in calculated campaigns of religious and state-sanctioned terrorism against men, women, and children.

Their invasion was also a biological triumph, for European germs changed the New World as much as settlers. Smallpox, measles, and other diseases were powerful elements of political and social transformation. As predatory and opportunistic as Christians, they quickly altered traditional ways of life by killing off most of the native population. Within a century of contact, about 90 percent of indigenous peoples died of European diseases.

In an incredibly brief period of time, some indigenous peoples became extinct, diminished greatly in number, or were displaced to less productive areas than they once had inhabited. Others were forced to establish new social patterns in the wake of slavery, various forms of forced labor, and the introduction of an international market economy. And perhaps most importantly, Christianity challenged their most sacred and honored beliefs.

Native peoples had been involved in armed conflicts for thousands of years, but they had never before met any people as fierce, organized, and single-minded as Christians. They quickly learned that what made them so dangerous was their dedication to completely remaking the New World. As the Mayas of the Yucatan described this invasion:

They came with a fury
with a rage without reason
with a thirst for blood,
for heads, for jewels.
Came into our lands
to conquer for no quarrel
to seize for the sake of seizing
to claim for an absent king
our lands, our corn, our people.

This process began with Columbus's colony in Hispaniola and swiftly spread to Mexico, Peru, and the rest of the hemisphere.

The West's greatest strength in the long run, however, was neither its military nor economic capacity but its cultural adaptability. Since the early Middle Ages, Christendom had learned to absorb, assimilate, and transform cultures and alien influences without losing its own identity or core beliefs. In the sixteenth century, Spain and Portugal demonstrated this remarkable capacity for adaptation by rapidly altering New World peoples and environments to establish their empires.[1]

Mesoamerica and the Caribbean

Europe's First Colony in the New World

When Columbus reached the Caribbean island of Hispaniola on his second expedition in 1493, he commanded a fleet of seventeen ships and the materials for Christendom's first colony in the New World—over 1,000 settlers, horses and other animals, and seeds and cuttings for fruit trees, sugarcane, and wheat. First, he stopped at La Navidad where his ship had sunk the year before. He had negotiated with a local chief to let his men establish their own settlement within the village of Guacanagari. Just one year later, there were no survivors. All thirty-nine had died from Taíno attacks after they began plundering the area for gold, kidnapping women, and burning Taíno *cemíes*.

After burying the dead and fruitlessly searching for gold that may have been hidden, Columbus established Isabella near the site of Navidad on the north shore of Hispaniola. His twin goals were to reach the Orient, which he believed was nearby, and to find precious metals. As Columbus explored Cuba and Jamaica, Isabella's settlers immediately began scouring the island for gold and slaves.

Columbus was attracted to Hispaniola partly because he identified the island with the isles of Tarnish and Ophir and with the Queen of Sheba. His shipmate Michele da Cuneo heard Columbus say that he had found biblical lands of gold and jewels. "Gentlemen," said Columbus to his crew, "I wish to bring us to a place whence departed the three Magi who came to adore Christ, the which place is called Saba."

Isabella's new settlers also wanted to become instantly wealthy, for many of them were convicted murderers who had been paroled directly from Spain's worst prisons to his ships. According to one account, they were "for the most part undisciplined, unscrupulous vagabonds, who only employed their ingenuity in gratifying their appetites." They carried off women in front of their families. "Given over to violence and thieving, they had profoundly vexed the natives."

When local Indian *caciques* begged Columbus to restrain his rapacious settlers, he decided that "to establish authority over the island, it was necessary to conquer the islanders and to break their power." Columbus built forts near Isabella and launched military expeditions into the interior. After an orgy of killing, raping, and looting had apparently subdued the Indians, Columbus initiated an onerous tribute system. For eight months each year, all islanders between the ages of fourteen and seventy had to provide the colony with gold, precious stones, food, and clothing. If the settlers were not satisfied, they plundered towns and returned with booty for their Admiral.

Meanwhile, Columbus's brother Bartholomew claimed that he had found gold "sixty leagues from Isabella in the direction of Cipangu," the name of Marco Polo's Japan. Since the quarry seemed very old, Columbus concluded that "he had rediscovered in those mines the ancient treasures which, it is stated in the Old Testament, King Solomon of Jerusalem had found in the Persian Gulf." A relieved Columbus left for Spain with the good news and gave command of the rebellious colony to his brother.

When Columbus returned to Isabella with three ships in 1498, conditions had seriously deteriorated. The Taínos had turned against their new masters, and a group of colonists openly defied his brother's authority. While Columbus was absent, "they would wander from town to town and village to village, eating at will, taking the Indians they pleased as servants and as many women as they liked, and making the men carry them on their shoulders or in hammocks."

Columbus responded by issuing pardons and generous land grants to his settlers, which included control over local *caciques*. The results were predictable. The Spanish forced more Indians to feed them, took more women, and worked still more Taínos to death digging for gold. The frightened Indians "trembled before them as if they were demons."

In addition to oppressing the indigenous peoples of the Caribbean, Columbus tried to enslave them. He strongly recommended to his sovereigns that the Indians of the Lesser Antilles, whom he considered "cannibals, a people very savage," be captured and sold as slaves. Bondage, Columbus argued, would civilize them. Besides, profits from their sale could be used to purchase cattle and other goods for Spanish colonies.

On February 17, 1495, Columbus and his men loaded their caravels with 550 captured Indian men and women. About 300 of them survived the voyage to the slave markets of Spain. By the end of his fourth voyage to the New World, Columbus had captured at least 3,000 Caribbean Indians for slavery in Europe and the Madiera, Canary, and Cape Verde islands.

In 1499, Columbus was replaced as the Viceroy of Isabella. The Crown graciously allowed him to keep his title and tribute, and he died a wealthy man. In 1502, Nicolás de Ovando—monk and Lord Commander of a military order in the wars against the Moors of Granada—became the new governor of Hispaniola. Ovando arrived with thirty ships and over 2,000 colonists. With even greater severity than Columbus, he subdued the rebellious colonists and waged war against the Taínos, forcing them to supply the colony with tribute and labor.

The Taínos gave Europe immensely valuable gifts—cassava, corn, sweet potatoes, peanuts, squash, guava, pineapples, tobacco, rubber, canoes, and the hammock. Hispaniola also supplied the Spanish with three to six tons of gold each year, which helped finance the Spanish conquest of the Caribbean. In exchange, the Spanish pulverized and destroyed the Taínos.

In 1504, Ovando was replaced by Diego Colón, one of Columbus's sons. With even greater brutality than his predecessors, he worked the Taínos to death mining gold. They died so rapidly that Indian slaves had to be imported from other Caribbean islands and Florida.

According to one account, the Indians were so "intolerably oppressed and overworked" that "many went into the woods and having killed their children, hanged themselves, saying it was far better to die than to live so miserably serving such ferocious tyrants and villainous thieves. . . . Some threw themselves from high cliffs down precipices; others jumped into the sea and rivers; others starved themselves to death."

When Columbus established Isabella, there were at least 300,000 and perhaps up to 1 million Taínos living on the island of Hispaniola. In 1548, only about 500 survived. As gold and the native population disappeared, African slaves replaced the Indians as the colony's chief source of labor on sugar plantations. Hispaniola produced the New World's first mulattos, or Afro-Indians, as Taíno slaves melded racially and culturally with the survivors of African slave ships.

On his first voyage, Columbus had dreamed of operating a trading post like the ones the Portuguese were establishing along the Gold Coast of Africa and hoped to grow wealthy by exchanging European manufactured items for slaves and gold. But the disastrous experience at La Navidad convinced him that the Taínos were uninterested in mining gold or converting to Christianity and would fight fiercely to keep their freedom. As a result, Isabella became a predatory colony based on plunder and enslavement. Recent wars and colonization efforts in Granada and the Canary Islands had given Columbus and his successors the blueprint for their New World settlement. In turn, Spain's treatment of the Taínos provided a model for future European colonies.[2]

The Last Judgment

While Columbus was terrorizing the Taínos on the island of Hispaniola, an elderly *cacique* visited the Admiral and presented him with a bowl of fruit. The *cacique* sat down next to Columbus and through an interpreter gave him some advice. The Taínos believed in an afterlife. Evil people went to a place that was bad and full of darkness while peace-loving people went to one that was good and full of happiness. Therefore, he concluded, "if you feel you must die and believe that every man answers for his deeds after death, you will not harm those who do not harm you."

Note: S. Lyman Tyler, *Two Worlds: The Indian Encounter with the European, 1492–1509* (Salt Lake City: University of Utah Press, 1988), p. 148.

We Have Seen Bloodshed and Pain

After Moctezuma heard reports about the Spaniards and their animals, he decided to send them a deputation of shamans, priests, and his noblest and bravest warriors. Moctezuma's envoys also took captives as sacrifices because the Spaniards "might wish to drink their blood." But when they were sacrificed before them, "they were filled with disgust and loathing. They spat on the ground, or wiped away their tears, or closed their eyes and shook their heads in abhorrence." They refused to eat any food that had been sprinkled with blood and acted "as if the blood had rotted." Moctezuma's shamans tried to harm them but failed. When they returned to the palace with their sad news, Moctezuma could do "nothing but resign himself and wait for them to come. He mastered his heart at last, and waited for whatever was to happen."

After his envoys failed to stop the Spaniards from disembarking, they began marching inland. When the Otomis met them in battle array and "greeted the strangers with their shields," all of them died. When the Spaniards met the Tlaxcalteca, they discovered that their enemy was the Cholulas, a people allied with the Aztecs. The Spaniards and the Tlaxcaltecas destroyed the Cholulas, and marched toward Tenochtitlan. "Their dogs came with them, running ahead of the column. They raised their muzzles high; they lifted their muzzles to the wind. They raced on before with saliva dripping from their jaws."

As the Spaniards approached Tenochtitlan, they met new Aztec envoys. After receiving gifts of gold necklaces and ensigns covered with gold and quetzal feathers, the Spaniards became frenzied. "They picked up the gold and fingered it like monkeys; they seemed to be transported like joy, as if their hearts were illumined and made new. . . . Their bodied swelled with greed, and their hunger was ravenous; they hungered like pigs for that gold." Moctezuma's shamans and priests again failed to dissuade the strangers from proceeding. When Moctezuma heard about their attempts, he bowed his head and was silent. "We will be judged and punished," he said.

In Moctezuma's capital there was apprehension and sorrow. "Everyone was in terror; everyone was astounded, afflicted." Fathers ran their hands through their sons' hair, and mothers wondered how they could live through the events that were about to happen.

In November of 1519, the Spaniards arrived in Xoloco. Moctezuma met them arrayed in his best finery. He showered them with gold necklaces and other gifts. After he identified himself, Moctezuma bowed low and said: "O our lord, you have tired yourself; you are weary. At last you have come to earth; you have come to govern your city of Mexico." Moctezuma finished his welcome by suggesting that they rest in his palace.

After their leader's female interpreter translated Moctezuma's address, Cortés said to her: "Tell Moctezuma that we are his friends. There is nothing to fear." At the conclusion of her translation, Cortés's retainers shook Moctezuma's hands and "patted his back to show their affection for him."

Once the Spaniards made themselves comfortable in Moctezuma's palace, they asked about the city's treasures and demanded gold by threatening him. At the treasure house of Teucalco, Moctezuma had gold and feathers brought to them. They stripped the feathers from their shields and ensigns and put all the gold "into a great mound and set fire to everything else, regardless of its value." Then they melted the gold into ingots. Next the Spaniards broke into Moctezuma's storehouse where he kept his personal treasure. "They searched everywhere and coveted everything; they were slaves to their own greed. . . . They seized these treasures as if they were their own, as if this plunder were merely a stroke of good luck." When they were fed, they acted as if they were wild beasts, "as if the hour were midnight on the blackest night of the hour." The Aztecs gave them food "with trembling hands, then turned and walked away."

After Cortés left the city of Mexico for the coast, the Aztecs begged Moctezuma, who was imprisoned in chains, to hold their celebration in honor of Huitzilopochtli, the patron god of the Aztecs. He consented, but when the feast began, Spaniards appeared in battle array and blocked the exits to the temple courtyard. "They first struck a drummer; they severed both his hands and cut off his head, which fell to the ground some distance away. Then they charged the crowd with their iron lances and hacked us with their iron swords. They slashed the backs of some, so that their entrails poured out."

As news of the massacre spread throughout the city, people wailed with grief and beat their palms against their mouths. Warriors appeared carrying spears and shields to do battle. Moctezuma told them to stop, but his enraged subjects no longer obeyed him. Finally the Spaniards killed Moctezuma and abandoned the city with their Indian allies, fleeing down the causeway over the water that led to Tlacopan.

But the Aztec celebration was brief, for in the month of Tepeilhuitl a great plague ravaged Tenochtitlan. "It began to spread during the thirteenth month and lasted for sixty days, striking everywhere in the city and killing a vast number of our people." Some could not walk while others died of hunger because no one would care for them.

After the plague left many Mexicans dead, blind, and disfigured, the Spaniards and their Indian allies returned. They surrounded the city, cutting off the water and food supplies. The fighting was very fierce. In the beginning, the warriors pursued the strangers and took fifteen prisoners. First they were plundered of their weapons and "while their comrades on the lake watched them being put to death." In another battle, the Aztecs captured a banner and fifty-three Spaniards, who were sacrificed along with their horses. But the siege caused great anguish. There was no fresh water available and many people starved to death after eating animal hides, bitter weeds, and dirt.

As the battle raged with great intensity, a fiery omen appeared in the night sky, circled the shores of the lake surrounding the city, and plunged into the water. "No one cried out when this omen came into view; the people knew what it meant, and they watched it in silence." The Aztec leaders decided to surrender. Once the siege ended, the victors robbed the starving inhabitants as they left their city and seized fugitives, "mostly our pretty women, the yellow-skinned ones."

Young warriors were branded with a hot iron on their cheeks or lips. Others were hanged from trees. The Aztecs were forced to give up their gold, jade, turquoise, quetzal feathers, and beautiful birds. As one poet lamented, "We have seen bloodshed and pain/ where once we saw beauty and valor." The Aztecs were consumed with grief. "Have you grown weary of your servants?" they plaintively asked. "Are you angry with your servants/ O Giver of Life?"[3]

"What Is It that Makes History? Well, Bodies."

We will never know exactly how many indigenous peoples inhabited the Western Hemisphere in 1492 because our demographic sources are incomplete, often inaccurate, and subject to varying interpretations. In the twentieth century, population estimates have ranged from a low of 8.4 million to a high of over 112 million people. When Columbus landed in the Bahamas, the New World may have contained around 50 million inhabitants with the heaviest population concentrations in Central Mexico, Middle America, and the Central Andes.

The New World covered 16 million square miles, one-fourth of the earth's total land surface, and it probably was as populous as all of Europe and Russia combined. In 1492, there were more speakers of Nahuatl, the principal language in the Valley of Mexico, than speakers of English. And Quechua, the official language of the Inca empire, was more widely spoken than Italian, French, or German.

The number of New World inhabitants, however, drastically declined in just a few centuries to less than 10 percent of their original numbers in 1492. Beginning with Columbus's arrival, indigenous peoples everywhere succumbed to the most lethal of all Old World conquerors—such acute viral infections as smallpox, measles, chicken pox, and influenza. Christians also brought the plague, scarlet fever, diphtheria, certain kinds of venereal diseases, typhus, cholera, typhoid fever, scarlet fever, mumps, diphtheria, influenza, and whopping cough to the shores of the New World. Africans contributed two deadly diseases born by insects, malaria and yellow fever. Together, these diseases and an accompanying decline in the native birth rate led to a precipitous population decline, especially in Central Mexico and Central Peru.

For thousands of years, indigenous peoples had lived in isolation from other continents, and consequently they had no exposure and immunity to many common diseases that periodically ravaged the rest of the world. Although Indians suffered from venereal syphilis, pinta, hepatitis, intestinal parasites, and yaws, deadly European and African diseases were quite foreign to them. As a result, the stage was set for a stunning biological disaster. By far the single most important cause of native population decline was the introduction of virulent diseases from abroad.

European diseases especially were virulent in the New World for three reasons. First, Europe's overcrowded and filthy urban centers provided deadly pathogens with an excellent environment in which to breed and survive. Second, Europe's long-distance trade routes with Asia and Africa acted as a viral highway for many different kinds of deadly international diseases, such as the plague that ravaged Europe in the fourteenth century. And third, Europeans raised large numbers of domesticated animals, such as sheep, cattle, goats, horses, and pigs, that were breeders and carriers of deadly diseases like swine flu. Consequently, when Europeans and their animals came to the Americas, they brought with them the most lethal pathogens in the entire world. As a result, death rates in the New World far surpassed the worst plague epidemics in Europe and Asia. In Mesoamerica, the Caribbean, and South America, the native population steadily declined for 200 years and only began increasing during the early eighteenth century. In North America, indigenous peoples reached their lowest point in the late nineteenth century.

For centuries, European diseases killed millions of Indians and crippled the survivors. European epidemics increased the nutritional requirements of indigenous peoples when they were least able to obtain food. Measles and chickenpox lowered vitamin A levels, vomiting and nausea from malaria led to severe malnutrition, and other diseases resulted in protein loss, iron deficiency anemia, and anorexia. Old World maladies raised infant and child mortality rates so high that in just a few generations many indigenous societies could not replace those who had died from previous epidemics. As native peoples were consumed by new and deadly parasites, chronic diseases, extreme hunger, and starvation stalked their communities.

This deadly process began immediately when Columbus landed in the Bahamas. Of the West Indians he kidnapped on his first voyage, only two survived to make the return trip. The same fate befell many of the 550 Taíno slaves whom Columbus took to Spain in 1495. When Ponce de León searched the Bahamas looking for slaves and the fountain of youth in 1513, he found only one old woman whom he derisively named *La Vieja*. In December of 1518, a smallpox epidemic reached Hispaniola and killed almost half the Taínos. After ravishing the Greater Antilles over the next year, in 1520 it arrived in Mexico with Cortés's army.

When Cortés entered the Aztec capital of Tenochtitlan, he and his soldiers were astonished by this opulent city of 250,000 people. Unlike the metropolises of Europe, Tenochtitlan's population was extremely healthy and lived in a remarkably clean environment. The Aztecs believed that a balanced diet and moderate behavior led to health, happiness, and the maintenance of the universe. Through irrigation, terraced farming, multi-cropping, *chinampas* (intensive cultivated farms along the southern edge of the lake surrounding

Tenochtitlan), and the development of superior strains of plants, the Aztecs grew plenty of corn, beans, squash, and amaranth. They supplemented their predominantly vegetarian fare with armadillos, gophers, weasels, rattlesnakes, mice, desert lizards, fish, frogs, and domesticated turkeys and dogs, consuming an average of about 2,600 calories a day, mostly from corn. This caloric intake is higher than the world average today.

Tenochtitlan's environment was far cleaner than any cities the Spanish had ever seen. The Aztecs used soap, breath sweeteners, deodorants, and dentifrices, and washed often. The Spanish, who seldom changed their clothes or cleaned themselves, were shocked that Moctezuma bathed twice a day. The city's streets were cleaned daily by state employees, fresh water was purchased from canoes plying the canals, and bodily wastes were collected from privies and pottery vessels for fertilizer and the treatment of cloth. Although the Aztecs suffered from rheumatism, dysentery, respiratory and gastrointestinal infections, and gout, in general they were well-nourished and healthy.

The Aztecs consumed more daily calories, had a more varied diet, and lived in a more sanitary environment than most Europeans until the nineteenth century. They suffered from far fewer infectious diseases than contemporary urban Europeans. Life expectancies in Tenochtitlan were also higher and infant mortality rates lower compared to European cities, where deaths usually exceeded births.

Five months after Cortés reached Mexico, however, smallpox ravaged Tenochtitlan. According to the Aztecs, the "pestilence lasted through sixty day signs before it diminished. . . . Many indeed perished from it. They could not walk; they could only lie at home in their beds, unable to move, to raise themselves, to stretch out on their sides, or lie face down, or upon their backs." Others died from malnutrition, and many survivors were disfigured or blinded. Probably half the population, including Moctezuma's successor Cuitlahuac, died in 1520 and 1521.

Throughout the rest of the century, Mexico was buffeted by recurring epidemics of smallpox, measles, typhus, and mumps. The population declined almost 90 percent in the Valley of Mexico during the first century of conquest. In contemporary Nahuatl documents, *micohua* [they died] became a commonly used phrase. As one native account lamented in 1582, disease overwhelmed the people of Mexico. "Many Indians hang themselves, others let themselves die of hunger, others poison themselves with herbs; there are mothers who kill the children to whom they have just given birth, saying that they are doing it to spare them the trials that they are undergoing."

In 1521, smallpox reached Guatemala and killed half of the population in the Yucatan Peninsula. Indians in Honduras declined from 800,000 on the eve of conquest to just about 48,000 in 1700. A similar process took place in Costa Rica. In just over a century, twelve native communities in Costa Rica's Central Valley lost more than 90 percent of their inhabitants.

Between 1524 and 1526, disease ravaged the densely populated Inca empire, where perhaps 9 million people lived in Peru. Smallpox killed the emperor Huayna Capac along with half of his subjects. By the end of the sixteenth century, Peru had experienced a demographic collapse. In many parts of the former Inca empire, four-fifths of the males died, and many communities were abandoned. In less than one century, Peru's indigenous population declined over 90 percent.

Although neither Christians nor native peoples understood the biological causes of this demographic disaster, both cultures understand that diseases could be caused by contagion. When the Black Death appeared in Europe around 1348, seaports such as Venice and Ragusa began quarantining ships, crews, and cargoes because they understood that the plague was spread by contact. As the Black Death ravaged Europe, Christians in the Canary Islands also learned that their contagious diseases were deadliest to people whom they had never previously encountered.

The same observations about contagion were made in the New World. As one Canadian Jesuit priest candidly admitted, "wherever we set foot, either death or disease followed us. . . . For it happened very often, and has been remarked more than a hundred times, that where we were most welcome, where we baptized most people, there it was in fact where they died the most."

Indigenous peoples made the same comments. By comparing a healthier past with a death-ridden present, Indians clearly understood that Europeans brought the strange epidemics that were destroying them. As the Mayas of the Yucatan lamented:

> Before the conquerors came
> there was no sin,
> no sickness, no aches,
> no fevers, no pox.
> The foreigners stood
> the world on its head,
> made day become night.

European diseases were especially devastating because they killed disproportionate numbers of males and females between the ages of fifteen and forty responsible for fighting, procuring food, and bearing children. As Indians succumbed to pathogens, there was also an increase in sterility, negligent child care, venereal diseases, infanticide, abortion, and infant mortality. Malnutrition and extreme stress followed in the wake of the European epidemics.

To a great extent, Christendom triumphed in the New World because virulent European diseases killed most indigenous peoples, drastically lowered the survivors' health and birth rates, and crippled their communities. At the same time, native societies frequently came under military attack. As their resources became more constricted, many died in large numbers from warfare and the destruction of their traditional resources and life ways. After 1492, the New World became a gigantic charnel house, a place for the bones and bodies of dead Indians.[4]

Nicaragua's Vanishing Population

When the Spanish moved southward into Nicaragua following the conquest of Mexico, they discovered that its Pacific coast was divided into large, populous chiefdoms. Immediately, military expeditions began plundering the new colony of its people. After Pedrarias Dávila became governor of Nicaragua in 1526, he quickly identified three potential sources of slaves—Indians captured by Spanish soldiers, nominally free Indians under the control of *caciques* dependent on the Spanish, and Spanish landowners willing to sell their tribute Indians into slavery—and organized a flourishing slave trade. At its height, over eleven ships a year regularly carried large cargoes of Indians branded with an identification mark from western Nicaragua to Peru and Panama.

Until 1548, when slavery was outlawed, perhaps up to 400,000 indigenous peoples left Nicaragua's Pacific coast in bondage. Most of them died before they could be sold, which further fueled the demand for slaves and led to the kidnapping of orphans, children, and free Indians. A similar number probably died as a result of warfare, disease, and starvation while others fled to safer areas. By 1574, there were just 13,000 Indians left in once populous western Nicaragua.

Note: David R. Radell, "The Indian Slave Trade and Population of Nicaragua During the Sixteenth Century," in *The Native Population of the Americas in 1492,* ed. William M. Denevan, (Madison: University of Wisconsin Press, 1996) pp. 67–76; Linda A. Newson, *Indian Survival in Colonial Nicaragua* (Norman: University of Oklahoma Press, 1987), pp. 84–109; Bartolomé Las Casas, *Devastation of the Indies: A Brief Account,* trans. Herman Briffault (Baltimore: Johns Hopkins University Press, 1992), pp. 56–57; William L. Sherman, *Forced Native Labor in Sixteenth-Century Central America* (Lincoln: University of Nebraska Press, 1979), pp. 30–67; Dan Stanislawski, *The Transformation of Nicaragua: 1519–1548* (Berkeley: University of California Press, 1983), pp. 9–13.

Friar Diego de Landa and the Mayas

In 1561, the Franciscan Order of Spain chose Friar Diego de Landa to be its first Provincial in the missionary province of Guatemala and the Yucatan. They had made an excellent choice, for Landa was energetic, brilliant, and determined to propagate Christianity. Since coming to the Yucatan at the age of twenty-five, he had learned to speak the local Mayan language and spent many hours observing Indian customs and earnestly discussing religion with Mayan elders. The Mayas trusted him so much that they showed Landa their sacred books and explained how they were read.

One year later, after a friar had found Mayan graven images and skulls near the Yucatan village of Mani, the Franciscans unleashed a reign of terror against any Indians suspected of what the Spanish considered heathenism. Strong measures were necessary, said an enraged Landa, because the Mayas were "idolaters and guilty." He predicted that "it would be impossible to finish with the province of Mani alone in twenty years, and meanwhile they would all become idolaters and go to hell." The Mayas, reported a horrified Landa, had even crucified some of their sacrificial victims.

Landa and his fellow priests understood that Catholicism and traditional Mayan beliefs were based on conflicting understandings of time, history, and ritual. After the Spanish had conquered the Yucatan, the Mayas formerly converted to Catholicism but viewed the Spaniards as rapacious outsiders who wanted to destroy their ancient beliefs and social customs. Their prophetic books of the *Chilam Balam*, written in Yucatec Mayan with Latin letters, stated that they did not "wish to join with the foreigners; they did not desire Christianity. They did not wish to pay tribute, did those whose emblems were the bird, the precious stone, the flat precious stone and the jaguar, those with the three magic emblems."

Their reasons for rejecting Spanish rule were very clear. "Then with the true God, the true Díos, came the beginning of our misery. It was the beginning of tribute, the beginning of church dues, the beginning of strife with purse-snatching, the beginning of strife by trampling on people, the beginning of robbery with violence, the beginning of debts enforced by false testimony, the beginning of individual strife, a beginning of vexation, a beginning of robbery with violence."

Since the foreigners "brought shameful things when they came," the Mayas resisted acculturation into the Spanish world. Few learned to speak Spanish. Many quietly continued adhering to their traditional beliefs. Others fled westward into the lowland tropical jungle where they established communities free of Spanish rule.

Into the forests
the Mayas will flee
take their beds and mats
forage like starving deer.

books of the *Chilam Balam*

Still others revolted against their oppressors. In 1546, Mayas east of the Yucatan tortured and murdered Spanish men, women, and children; destroyed all vegetation planted by the Spanish; and killed their horses, chickens, dogs, cattle, and pigs.

Perhaps the most creative religious adaptation of the Mayas to Christianity concerned the cross. In ancient Mayan society, the World Tree of the Center, shaped like a cross, was the literal center of the cosmos. Found in Mayan temples and communities, it was often clothed in fine jewels and worshipped. The Mayas made Christ's cross into their traditional World Tree of the Center and treated it as a living object possessing a soul that nurtured the universe. By feeding crosses with flowers, candles, copal, maize, and other foods, they helped maintain its power.

The Yucatec Mayas denied the legitimacy of Spanish rule, but as nominal Christians they also hoped that Jesus would arrive to end their suffering. "But when the law of the *katun* [twenty-year cycle] shall have run its course, then God will bring about a great deluge which will be the end of the world" and "those who are of the lineage shall come forth before their lord on bended knee so that their wisdom may be made known." At the end of Christian time, which the Mayas fit into their elaborate calendrical system, the Mayas would be redeemed. The Mayan prophetic tradition, now sustained with the Spanish alphabet, helped make sense of the Spanish invasion and justified an adversarial attitude toward the hated invaders.

In just three months, the Franciscans tortured over 4,500 Mayas. Almost 200 died as the result of brutal interrogations or suicide, and some were permanently crippled, their hands shaped "like hooks." According to one horrified eyewitness, when the Indians confessed, the friars "tied their wrists together with cord, and thus hoisted them from the ground, telling them that they must confess all the idols they had, and where they were." If the Indians said they had no more idols, the friars "ordered great stones attached to their feet" and flogged them "as they hung there, and had burning wax splashed on their bodies."

The *strappado* technique—hoisting victims onto a pulley and attaching weights to them—was the favorite method of the Spanish Inquisition to force confessions from converted Jews who had been accused of heresy. In the words of the books of the *Chilam Balam,* "with the coming of the cross . . . the trees become scaffolds bearing only the fruit of hanged men."

103

Those who confessed their sins had to undertake various penances, which might include five years of slavery, whippings, and the wearing of special clothing to distinguish them from their more devout brethren. The Franciscans even posthumously condemned over 100 Mayans for their alleged idolatry and cremated their burial remains.

Landa also decided to destroy the sacred books of the Mayas because "they contained nothing in which there was not to be seen superstition and lies of the devil." He confiscated twenty-seven Mayan sacred hieroglyphic books made with accordion-like bark paper and deerskin and burned them along with 5,000 native religious icons on July 12, 1562. Only three ancient texts survived Landa's devastating inferno. The Franciscans began eradicating the native written language by educating Mayan boys in Spanish and Latin ("The hieroglyphic sign will be lost, and lost also the teaching which lies behind it," predicted the books of the *Chilam Balam*). With a knowledge of Latin letters, the Mayas would be able to understand Christian documents and the questionnaires Franciscans developed to interrogate their new flock.

Eventually, Bishop Francisco de Toral stopped Landa's brutal Inquisition. After investigating the Franciscans' forced confessions, he concluded that the Mayans had fabricated stories of heresy to satisfy Landa and his fellow interrogators. According to Bishop Toral, the Mayas were neither worshipping their former gods nor sacrificing their children. They invented realistic stories of apostasy because their lives were in danger from Franciscan missionaries. Under Landa's suggestive questioning, some Mayas even confessed to ritual murders that eerily resembled accusations that had been hurled against Spain's New Christians, or Catholics whose ancestors had been Jewish.

In 1564, Landa was tried in Spain for his excesses, but a special committee absolved him of any misdeeds after he was condemned by the Council of the Indies. Two years later, he published an affectionate and insightful book on the Mayas, which only briefly mentioned the dramatic events of his rule as Provincial. He returned to the New World in 1572 as bishop of the Yucatan and resumed his crusade.

Sadly for him, however, the times had changed. When he began browbeating the Mayas again, they responded in good Spanish style by filing legal briefs against him. After failing to recoup his waning power by excommunicating the governor, a weary and contentious Landa died at the age of fifty-four.

Mayan distrust of the Spanish continued far beyond Landa's death. In 1618, when two friars tried to convert Can-Ek, the Mayan king of Itza, to Christianity, he told them that "the time had not yet arrived in which their ancient priests had prophesied to them they were to relinquish the worship of the Gods." The last independent Mayan kingdom in the Yucatan fell to the Spanish in 1697, over a century after the Franciscans' reign of terror began in the peninsula.[5]

Juan del Espinar, Guatemalan Encomendero

In 1524, the Spanish began attacking the Mayan peoples in the rugged Cuchumatán highlands of northwest Guatemala. As soon as the fighting began, a number of exceptional soldiers received highland *encomiendas* [grants of land] as rewards for their services. Juan del Espinar, a former tailor, became the richest land owner. He received Huehuetenango in 1525, and controlled it until his death in 1562. Five years after he was given Huehuetenango, Espinar supervised over 2,000 Mayas and received an annual tribute that included corn, cotton, cloth, beans, salt, chickens, chile peppers, and the use of personal servants. Tributary males worked in Espinar's mines, females harvested his crops and prepared food, and slaves augmented his huge *encomienda* labor force. Espinar earned 3,000 pesos each year from his agricultural operations and another 8,700 pesos from his mines.

Espinar had no illusions about the foundations of his wealth. Since the Indians, he said, were "evil, incorrigible, and unruly . . . it is no great sin to beat them, or to threaten to beat them. They must be punished constantly, a strong grip kept on them always." When Mayan nobles failed to pay tribute, he imprisoned them in his own house, bragging that "I put them in chains to scare them so that they would serve me." Through constant lawsuits against Mayas and Spaniards, the burning of Indian settlements, and outright thuggery, Espinar intimidated his *encomienda* Indians and anyone else who dared challenge him.

Note: W. George Lovell, *Conquest and Survival in Colonial Guatemala: A Historical Geography of the Cuchumatan Highlands, 1500–1821* (Montreal: McGill-Queen's University, 1992), pp. 97, 100, 105, 184–190; Wendy Kramer, W.J. George Lovell, and Christopher H. Lutz. "Fire in the Mountains: Juan de Espinar and the Indians of Huehuetenango, 1525–1560," in *Columbian Consequences: The Spanish Borderlands in Pan-American Perspective*, ed. David Hurst Thomas, (Washington, DC: Smithsonian Institution Press, 1991), vol. 3, pp. 263–282.

South America

Brazil from Barter to Coercion

When the Portuguese first arrived in Brazil in 1500, the Tupinambás, who lived on along the coast, helped them harvest brazilwood trees and traded manioc for European tools and trinkets. Although the Portuguese heavily depended on Tupinambá labor, food, and their knowledge of the forest, they considered the Tupinambás "fierce and savage people far removed from any courtesy or humanity."

In 1548, royal government was formally established in Brazil. Iberian monarchs believed that they were divinely charged with bringing justice to their realms and thus there were no elective positions or assemblies in Brazil. Officials governed by command and combined executive, legislative, and judicial functions, just as the Portuguese king did. At the apex of the colonial administrative structure were the governor-generals, who had supreme executive authority. Beneath them were hereditary captaincies who ruled as local feudal lords but were subject to the governor-generals, various officials, municipal councils, and a Supreme Court.

Although government officials, colonists, and Jesuits differed about the best ways to develop a dependable Indian labor force, they all agreed that Indians must be made into obedient Christians to save their souls and boost Brazil's economy. The Portuguese developed three systems of labor to meet this goal—Jesuit communal missions, wage labor, and plantation slavery—but all of them failed.

Brazil's Indians were confronted with new demands for their labor as the Portuguese Crown granted their lands to settlers. Colonization began with the rapid modification of the Tupinambá's environment, the tropical and subtropical primary forest ringing the Brazilian coast. When the Portuguese arrived, they began cutting down the largest and most valuable trees. The logging of brazilwood may have denuded one-half of the forest along the coast. With the introduction of metal tools, pigs, and cattle, settlers were able to cultivate larger plots of land than the Tupís. As towns grew, forests were turned into firewood and charcoal, especially around Rio de Janeiro. Forests also were burned to provide easier access to gold-bearing streams, and sugarcane plantations and sugar mills consumed huge amounts of wood for fuel.

As the coastal forests were drastically modified, the Jesuits created twelve villages in Bahía with about 40,000 Tupí-speaking Indians. Some arrived because their chiefs had converted to Christianity while others sought protection from slave raiders. Still others were attracted by the promise of food and shelter. As one Jesuit wrote in 1561, "they come in such humility that it is something for which to praise the Lord. . . . Whatever I teach them they accept." In the beginning, the Jesuits dreamed of rapidly converting thousands of Tupís to Christianity and to a European way of life.

Inside the missions, the Indians quickly discovered that the Jesuits wanted to destroy their traditional culture and turn them into local wage laborers, subsistence farmers, and ranchers. The Jesuits imposed a harsh, relentless discipline to wean them away from their customs and nakedness. Children were encouraged to inform on erring parents, and offenders received strict punishments. Any expression of Tupí mores or beliefs that clashed with Catholicism and Portuguese culture was systematically attacked. As one Jesuit wrote in disgust, "If they had a king it would be possible to convert them or if they worshipped something. But as they do not even know what it is to believe or to worship, they cannot understand the preaching of the Gospel." He was puzzled that God had given such good land to a people "who know so little." The Portuguese began calling Indians *gentio barbaro* [savage gentiles] or *gentio de cabello corredio* [straight-haired heathen].

Despite the Jesuits' energetic efforts, the mission system failed. One problem was that the Tupís were not as pliable as the Jesuits thought. Many of the Tupís concluded that the Jesuits were not their true friends and protectors, and they deeply resented attempts to emasculate their culture. When given the opportunity, they escaped to the interior or even became day laborers and plantation hands, working for only about one-fifth of the daily wage paid to settlers.

Another problem was disease. Early Portuguese visitors to Brazil were amazed at the number of Indians on the coast. "There are so many of them," one settler wrote in 1551, "and the land is so great that if they were not continuously at war and eating each other it could not contain them." Within several decades, however, northeastern Brazilian Indians were decimated by European epidemic diseases, especially measles and smallpox. The Tupís realized that these strange diseases only attacked them and claimed that they were being killed "with baptism." By 1590, there were only five missions in Bahía and Pernambuco and fewer than 6,000 Indians under direct Jesuit control. In the sixteenth century, probably 95 percent of the Tupís died from European diseases. Despite declining numbers, however, the Portuguese depended on loyal mission Indians to capture escaped African slaves and destroy fugitive slave communities.

In the first fifty years of Portuguese colonization, settlers had learned a harsh lesson. The Tupís would not become wards of the Portuguese voluntarily. As the Jesuits continued their missions, and colonists tried turning Tupís into poorly paid free workers, the Portuguese resorted to a third labor system—slavery. As one Tupinambá angrily said, "in the beginning the Portuguese did nothing but trade with us, without wishing to live here in any other way. At that time they freely slept with our daughters, which our women . . . considered a great honor." But then they began to "insist that the Indians help them build settlements, and fortifications to dominate the surrounding country." After that, they "wanted to take our children."

The Portuguese captured slaves by either ransoming war captives from tribes or undertaking raids against hostile Indians. Although Pope Paul III had decreed in 1537 that Indians "should not be deprived of their freedom," and Indian slavery was outlawed in 1570, the Portuguese found numerous reasons to wage what they called "just" or legitimate wars against Indians. Portuguese slavery began in 1511 with the harvesting of wood and greatly intensified as sugar plantations were established along the Atlantic coast.

By 1640, *bandeiras* [military companies] from Sãn Paulo had probably captured 60,000 Indians for sugar plantation slave labor in the Rio de Janeiro area. They came from raids on native villages and Jesuit missions. In Bahía, one observer estimated that slave raids netted 2,000–3,000 Indians every year. The sixty-six sugar plantations in Pernambuco used 4,000 Indian slaves in 1585, and around the same time Bahía's sugar plantations had 9,000 Indian slaves. Some of them were operated by the Jesuits. Indian slavery became so common that the Portuguese used the phrase *negros da terra* [blacks of the land] to describe indigenous peoples and *negros de Guiné* [blacks from Guinea] to describe Africans. By the end of the sixteenth century, there were three times as many enslaved Indians as Africans on sugar plantations. Surplus Indian slaves were even exported to Portugal's African possessions.

Brazil's large-scale sugar plantations were demanding places to work. Indians had to plant and harvest sugar almost all year, and during the nine-month harvest season, the sugar mills operated twenty-four hours a day. Plantation slaves suffered from exhausting and dangerous work, a poor diet, poor living conditions, and harsh discipline from masters who understood that labor comprised 80 percent of their operating costs. Not surprisingly, throughout Brazil both Indian and African plantation slaves had high mortality rates and short life spans in comparison to free laborers. Brazil's sugar plantations were never self-sustaining. Because of the excess of deaths, plantation owners constantly needed new slaves to make profits.

Indian slavery, however, failed to solve the need for cheap labor in Brazil. Epidemics ravaged many plantations, and the Portuguese discovered that Indians made poor slaves. Males considered agriculture women's work, and they loathed losing their independence. As one Bahían planter admitted, Indians disliked "working by obligation rather than out of desire, as they had in the state of freedom." As a result, in "captivity so many die that even at the lowest price they are expensive." African slaves, in comparison, could generate enough profits to cover their purchase price in just two years.

The Tupís also showed little respect for their masters' authority. Some deserted their plantations while others joined fugitive African slaves in a series of bloody insurrections in southern Bahía that lasted almost a century. Along the Brazilian frontier, escaped Indian and African slaves frequently became allies in constant guerrilla wars against Portuguese settlers.

By the early seventeenth century, plantation owners began replacing Indian with African slaves, and within a few decades they became the back-bone of the Brazilian economy. By the end of the century, between 10,000 and 15,000 African slaves were landing in Brazil every year. As a result, there was widespread racial mixing among Africans and indigenous Brazilians. Because many Indian slaves were women and most African slaves were male, slavery in colonial Brazil quickly took on a biracial character. A Bahían census of 1775 revealed that a majority of the population were either *mulatos* (African-Indian), *pardos* (African-Indian-European), or *mamalucos* (European-Indian).

Indigenous slavery, however, never completely disappeared in colonial Brazil. On the frontier, Indian slavery continued on cattle ranches and sugar plantations that could not afford African slaves. South of Sao Paulo, Paraná had more Indian than African slaves until the 1740s. Only in the nineteenth century did Indians disappear from Paraná's slave registers. In the seventeenth and eighteenth centuries, Indian slaves panned for gold and worked in the royal smelting houses that officially weighed and processed gold. And although the Portuguese monarch had prohibited Indians slavery yet again in 1758, into the nineteenth century miners and cattle ranchers in the interior were still capturing adults and children to sell, work, or "to prey upon Indian women, practicing with them the greatest debauches."

When the Portuguese first landed in Brazil, they hoped to create a prosperous colony by forcibly turning Indians into servile workers. After centuries of brutal coercion and devastating epidemics, however, Indians continued resisting Jesuits missionaries, sugar plantation owners, and the lure of the marketplace. African rather than Indian slave labor became the backbone of Brazilian society because too many native peoples perished from diseases, made poor slaves in comparison to Africans, or resisted becoming wards of the Portuguese.[6]

Tupinambás in France

In 1562, three kidnapped Tupinambás were presented to King Charles IX in Rouen. After he had talked to them through an interpreter, and they were shown the city, some Frenchmen wanted to know what they had found most amazing. The Tupinambás replied that "they thought it very strange that so many grown men, bearded, strong, and armed who were around the king . . . should submit to obey a child" and that "one of them was not chosen to command instead."

They were also shocked by the great disparities of wealth and poverty in France. After observing "men full and gorged with all sorts of good things" and "beggars at their doors, emaciated with hunger

109

and poverty," they wondered how they "could endure such an injustice" and why they "did not take the others by the throat, or set fire to their houses."

When the great Renaissance essayist Michel de Montaigne asked one of them through an interpreter "what profit he gained from his superior position," the Indian responded that he led his men to war. "Did all his authority expire with the war?" No, the man replied. "When he visited the villages dependent on him, they made paths for him through the underbrush by which he might pass quite comfortably."

Note: Jean de Léry, *History of a Voyage to the Land of Brazil, Otherwise Called America*, trans. and ed. by Janet Whatley (Berkeley: University of California Press, 1990), p. xxiv; Michel de Montaigne, *The Complete Essays of Montaigne*, trans. Donald Frame (Stanford: Stanford University Press, 1958), p. 159.

The Potosí Mita System

In 1532, seasoned Spanish troops under the leadership of Francisco Pizarro entered Peru, captured the Inca ruler Atahualpa, and after six years of bitter fighting, ended almost a century of Inca sovereignty. Immediately, the Crown began forcibly extracting goods and labor from Andean peoples.

The Crown argued that its New World empire was both just and necessary because Indians were natural slaves, incapable of rational and moral behavior. Sixteenth-century Spanish scholars used Aristotle, one of the pillars of late medieval philosophy, to label Indians natural slaves because they were not Christians and behaved more like savages than like humans. According to Aristotle, there were two kinds of slavery, civil and natural. Civil slavery involved debtors, criminals, and war captives. Natural slavery, said Aristotle and the great medieval theologian Thomas Aquinas, referred not to the institution of slavery, but to a kind of person. Natural slaves were unfortunates whose passions dominated their intellectual and reasoning faculties. They could only achieve virtue and happiness, the true ends of life, by serving their masters.

Many Spaniards argued that Indians behaved much like Aristotle's natural slaves. A Colombian bishop thought that Indians were "not men with rational souls but wild men of the woods, for which reason they could retain no Christian doctrine, nor virtue nor any kind of learning." Another claimed that both Africans and Indians were barbarians because "they are never moved by reason, but only by passion." Some officials in Mexico considered their Indian subjects "children with beards," "brutes," "extremely short on intelligence," and "barbarous people of vile inclinations." One friar thought that if Indians "are not obliged through fear and compelled by force like children, they will not obey." "If you don't hit an Indian," said yet another, "he can't make his limbs move."

Like the Canary Islanders, the inhabitants of the New World were not fully human. As one Spanish royal officer and court historian contemptuously wrote, "their marriages are not a sacrament but a sacrilege," and they were idolatrous, libidinous, and committed sodomy. Unfortunately, their chief desire was to "eat, drink, worship heathen idols, and commit bestial obscenities." Their skulls were so thick that the "Spaniards had to take care in fighting not to strike on the head lest their swords be blunted."

In the Andes and other Spanish possessions, conquest was followed by the imposition of the *encomienda* system, an Iberian institution developed in the wars against the Moors. To encourage privately financed bands of knights from northern Spain to fight Moslems in Andalucia, the Crown had granted victorious warriors titles of nobility, ownership over castles, towns, and lands with jurisdiction over their inhabitants, and exemption from personal taxes. Christian military orders also gave some of their members *encomiendas*—communities, land, and vassals owing them tribute and personal service—in newly conquered territory as long as they maintained an armed presence and promoted Catholic worship.

The Crown continued this policy by awarding *encomienda* grants to its most successful soldiers and officials. *Encomiendas* in the New World resembled their predecessors in Iberia and the Canary Islands, even in the language of the grants and the ceremonies of investiture.

Encomiendas, however, failed in the Andes. European diseases decimated over 90 percent of the conquered population and weakened the productive capacity of surviving *ayllus*. Famine, onerous taxes, and the loss of traditional native lands to Spanish settlers further reduced the economic viability of the *encomiendas*. Finally, once the conquerors claimed their *encomiendas*, they faced strong economic competition from other Spanish immigrants, especially in the cities, farms, and mines of the new empire.

According to Spanish law, all married Indian males between the ages of eighteen and fifty were tributaries and liable for periodic tribute payments. Tribute, collected twice a year by village leaders or *curacas*, was usually in the form of local goods later sold by Crown officials at public auctions. If *curacas* failed to meet their tribute quotas, they were threatened or arrested. Indians paid tribute to land owners or directly to the Crown. Some unfortunates had to pay both.

In addition, Indians were forced to maintain trails, roads, work in mines and factories, and carry heavy sacks of grain to market. As *repartimiento* labor [forced distribution of Indian laborers], Indians even served as auxiliaries for Spanish military forces. The Spanish government also created a *mita* [labor draft] to provide inexpensive labor for Peru's silver mines, the backbone of its wealth in the Andes.

The Inca empire had always mined precious metals and stones, which Andean peoples considered sacred objects that came from their Sun god. Gold and silver were "esteemed only for their beauty and brilliance, as being suitable for enhancing that of the royal palaces, Sun temples and convents for virgins." Mining was a minor enterprise because the Inca state did not have a monetized economy.

Like other kinds of labor tribute, mining intensified dramatically under Spanish rule. By the middle of the sixteenth century, the Spanish understood that the rich silver deposits in the Bolivian Andes were their greatest resource. Under the energetic and autocratic administration of Viceroy Francisco de Toledo, in 1573 the state began forcibly harnessing the labor of Andean peasants to create a cheap and dependable supply of miners to extract silver from the former Inca empire.

He decreed that 139 villages in sixteen provinces surrounding Potosí must supply a revolving yearly workforce of about 13,500 men, or one-seventh of their total male inhabitants, to work its mills and mines every seven years. Some of them would have to travel 600 miles over several months with their families and llamas to reach the mines. He understood that the *ayllus* would resist this drastic form of tribute, and so over 1 million Andean peoples were uprooted from their traditional lands and forcibly moved into new and ethnically mixed settlements.

This relocation process drastically changed the Peruvian social landscape. Large estate owners conveniently took over land once collectively controlled by *ayllus*. Many Indians sold their lands to pay tribute or to cover expensive events such as baptisms, funerals, and lawsuits. Others were driven out by marauding European livestock and the loss of control over precious water rights.

These *mitayos* [forced laborers] received about half the pay of free mining laborers and no bonuses, and they could not quit work if mining conditions were too harsh or their crops needed harvesting. Because wages were so low, *mitayos* had to hire themselves out during their rest days or rely on assistance from their families and communities.

By the early seventeenth century, *mitayos* toiled twelve-hour shifts, lived completely underground twenty-three weeks out of the year, wielded heavy iron bars, and carried sacks of silver ore weighing twenty-five kilograms on wood and rawhide ladders more than 300 meters to the surface with a candle to guide them. They were frequently beaten and whipped by the mine owners and forced to work incredibly long hours to fulfill their quotas of ore. Many died or were injured in mining accidents. Others were poisoned by underground toxic gases and the mercury used to remove silver. The mines and smelting furnaces were so lethal that no vegetation grew around Potosí for twenty miles. Not surprisingly, many adult males fled their communities to avoid *mita* labor and became part of Cuzco's growing native population or peons on rural estates.

Potosí, "the mistress of treasures and fortunes," grew from a small mining town of 14,000 people in 1545 to a large and wealthy city of 150,000 by 1600. Within several decades of its founding, mining output grew almost sevenfold and the volume of trade averaged about 60,000 silver pesos each day. In 1592, 42 percent of the Crown's total domestic budget came from the 202,000 kilograms of silver mined in Potosí.

Mine owners donated hundreds of thousands of pesos to build lavishly decorated churches near the hovels of *mitayos*, and religious orders profited from their involvement in the mining industry. One priest, who managed a silver refining mill, proudly told a relative in Spain that if he decided to stay, he would buy a very good farm with a vineyard to support himself when he retired. Too many Spaniards benefited from Toledo's oppressive regime for conditions to improve at Potosí.

As Toledo's new communities lost men to migration and death in Potosí, mine owners extorted and tortured village leaders to supply them with workers. When they could not produce enough able-bodied *mitayos*, villagers had to pay mine owners silver as compensation, putting a further strain on their besieged communities.

The *mita* system, as Toledo recognized, was an incredibly profitable form of labor because wages accounted for two-thirds of the mine owners' total operating costs. If Toledo had relied on a voluntary Indian workforce, the mining industry would have had to pay much higher wages and provide better working conditions to Indians with strong traditions of autonomy and local work alternatives.

Through forced Indian labor, Toledo and his successors helped make silver the Spanish empire's most valuable export. By the end of the eighteenth century, Potosí had produced almost 1 billion pesos worth of silver, or about half of all the silver mined in the New World. Although the mines gradually declined in importance, the *mita* system was not officially abolished until 1825.[7]

North America

Manteo and Wanchese in England and Virginia

When Arthur Barlowe returned from his military expedition to the coast of North America in 1584, two Indians named Manteo and Wanchese accompanied him. Ralegh, who kept them in his household several months, used the Indians to build up interest in his colonization scheme. Parliament noted that "some of the people borne in those parties" had been "brought home into this our Realme of England by whose means and direction and by suche of her majesties subjectes as were sent thyther by the said Walter Rawleigh."

The Indians were formally presented to the court in English clothing, learned basic English, and taught some Algonquian to Thomas Harriot, the prominent Elizabethan astronomer and mathematician. Manteo received more attention from Harriot than Wanchese because of his intellectual curiosity and ability to learn English rapidly. Early in 1585, Ralegh named his land Virginia in honor of Queen Elizabeth. She in turn knighted Ralegh and appointed him governor.

That same year, a military squadron of five ships under the command of Richard Grenville landed at Roanoke Island in North Carolina with about 100 colonists and established a naval base for English ships to plunder the Spanish treasure fleet. Harriot communicated with the Indians and used Manteo and Wanchese as interpreters. Manteo liked the English and skillfully acted as a bilingual mediator between the two cultures, but after Harriot's departure Wanchese became hostile towards them and went home to the Roanokes.

When Grenville returned to England, Ralph Lane, another Irish war veteran, took over as governor. Lane believed that Virginia's Indians were very similar to the Irish clans he had recently defeated and thus must be intimidated into submission. Although they inhabited a huge and fertile land, "being Savages . . . they know no use of the same." Barbarism must give way to civilization. Over time, the Indians would leave their uncultivated state and adapt themselves to English culture.

Now, however, Lane concluded that the Indians must be violently intimidated. When the local chief refused to provide Lane with more gifts of maize in the early spring of 1586, Lane killed him in an attempt to terrify the Indians into surrendering their dwindling food supply. As Lane guiltily acknowledged, the "wylde menn of myne owene naccione" oppressed the Indians, and he was not surprised that the "hande of God came upon them for the crueltie, and outrages committed by some of them against the native inhabitants of that Countrie." Lane never recognized that these colonists were simply modeling themselves on his contemptuous attitude and brutal behavior.

Harriot echoed Lane, admitting that the English had badly mistreated the Roanoke Indians by being "too fierce." When Francis Drake arrived in Roanoke after destroying the Spanish fleet in the West Indies, the beleaguered colonists eagerly abandoned their struggling colony and returned with him to England.

In 1587, the English reappeared in Roanoke with three ships and the first English families to settle the New World. John White, the leader of the colony, promptly rewarded Manteo for his loyalty by baptizing him into the Church of England and named him Lord of Roanoke and Dasemunkepeuc. That same year, Wanchese chose a different path. According to one colonist, in July "George Howe, one of our twelve assistants was slain by divers savages" after he strayed two miles away from his company. Wanchese may have been a member of this war party or helped plan the murder.

When the English visited Roanoke in 1590 after a three-year absence, they found neither colonists nor Indians. White thought the settlers might be at Croatan with Manteo, but his ship quickly departed to attack Spanish galleons. Manteo and Wanchese, Ralegh's bridges to Indian Virginia, never again met any English.

Although the Roanoke colony was a failure, it was a crucial step in developing an English empire across the Atlantic. As Spain became England's most dangerous enemy, the English developed a justification for their New World empire that combined the medieval Roman Catholic Church's traditional doctrines about the right to subdue barbarians with a fervent Reformation Protestantism and desire for "temporal profit and glory."

Flush from their military successes in Ireland and the defeat of a Spanish invasion fleet in 1588, England believed that the New World was part of its manifest destiny. They had learned at Roanoke, however, that they could succeed only by contending "against such stubborn savages as shall refuse obedience to her Majesty."[8]

➤ 5 ◄

Black Rainbows and Sinister Hailstorms

—————

When Spain, Portugal, Britain, and France established global empires in the New World, they used the venerable example of Rome as their model. These fledgling empires, however, only remotely resembled their ancient predecessor. New World colonies were far from Europe and established out of a need for gold, silver, and other valuable commodities. And unlike pagan Rome, they were based on the premise that worldwide empires could only be founded on Christianity—a universal faith that supposedly applied to all peoples and nations for all times. Renaissance humanists prided themselves on their supposed cosmopolitanism, but in reality their religious and cultural horizons extended no further than the Straits of Gibraltar.

The Spanish, Portuguese, British, and French empires had different approaches to controlling indigenous peoples and territories based on their varying cultures and the nature of the New World societies they encountered. The Spanish Crown saw itself as the rightful heir to Rome and the defender of the faith, and its new possessions had been legitimated by the Catholic Church even before Columbus reached America. Imperial rule was a means to a higher end, for the Spanish insisted that all peoples must become Catholic to be fully civilized and human.

Spain was obligated to wage "just wars" against heathen and infidel peoples so they could become part of the "congregation of the faithful." Because there could be no salvation outside the Church, indigenous peoples needed to "acknowledge the Church as the ruler and superior of the whole world, and the high priest called Pope, and in his name" the Spanish Crown. *Drecho de conquista*—force of arms to wage holy wars against infidels—provided the justification for Spain's providential empire.

Columbus and his successors discovered peoples radically different than their own but refused to consider their societies legitimate because they were barbaric and degenerate. There was really no need to explain the belief systems or social behavior of Indians except to say that they were pagans. As one Spanish scholar wrote, "for the Prince of darkness being the head of all Infidelitie, it is no new thing to find among the Infidells, cruelities, filthines, and follies fit for such a master."

The Spanish defined Indians by their absence: They were non-Christians. Native peoples had lived in "the great darkness of idolatry and faithlessness" because of "our ancient enemy Satan." Although Pope Paul III had declared in his papal bull of 1537 that Indians were "true men," they could not be the equals of Europeans because of their "heathen beliefs, deceits, and imperfections." From Columbus through the nineteenth century, Spain's evaluation of New World societies never altered. Indians were an inferior human species.

From this damning indictment of the New World, however, the Spanish drew an optimistic and bracing conclusion. Because native peoples were human, they could be converted to Catholicism. From Spain's perspective, this was the lasting significance of Columbus. He was the "first who opened the doors of this Ocean Sea, through which he entered and introduced to these so remote lands and realms, until then so unknown, our Savior Jesus Christ." Columbus should be honored for all the gold that is sent to Spain, but "he is still worthy of fame and glory for having brought the Catholic faith to these parts."

New World pagans, despite their devilish behavior, were not beyond salvation, for "what is certain is that all these people are our brothers, proceeding from Adam's stock even as we ourselves." Although native peoples were idolatrous and barbaric, this need not be their permanent condition. The inhabitants of New World were potential Christians and loyal Spanish subjects, given sufficient imperial force and a massive religious crusade.

As Pope Alexander's papal bull of 1493 made clear, if Indians were to be Christianized and civilized by the Spanish Crown, they must be denied their spurious freedom and put under the domination of their betters. King Ferdinand agreed when he established the *encomienda.* "Because of the excessive liberty the Indians have been permitted, they flee from Christians and do not work. Therefore they are to be compelled to work, so that the kingdom and the Spaniards may be enriched, and the Indians Christianized."

Ironically, the Spanish were the most parochial of all the European powers because they ardently believed in the religious unity of the human species. As crusading Christian humanists, they could only define humanity in relation to themselves. Assimilation was the logical outcome of humanism, and thus Spanish ethnocentrism always wore the mask of a benevolent universal empire based upon submission to Church and Crown.

The key to enrichment and Christianization was control over native communities. Spain needed Indians to work for them, to pay tribute to the Crown, and to fulfill their religious mission. Because the Spanish discovered large deposits of gold and silver and conquered the tributary empires of the Aztecs and Incas in the early sixteenth century, their New World venture was heavily dependent on mining precious metals and harnessing Indian labor.

By the end of the seventeenth century, Spain had established the largest, the most profitable, and seemingly most entrenched of all Europe's maritime empires. Although the Crown earned income from duties on maritime commerce, most revenue came from taxes directly levied in the New World, especially the *alcabala* [sales tax], the *quinto* [silver tax], and annual tribute payments from Indian male and female adults.

After 1519, Spain's New World empire was considered a direct possession of the Crown. As Christian monarchs, Spanish kings and queens governed in the community's interests and believed that authority needed to be concentrated for the beneficial governing of the realm. At the top of the administrative structure was the Council of the Indies, which next to the monarch was the ultimate authority in the New World. Beneath the Council was the viceroy, who ruled in place of the king, and the *Audiencia*, which governed by combining executive and judicial functions. Beneath them were governors, mayors, town councils, and treasury officials to collect taxes. There were no elective positions or assemblies in the Spanish colonies. Officials governed by command, just as did the monarch.

As native peoples struggled against their Spanish adversaries in the Americas throughout the seventeenth century, they developed a variety of strategies to deal with the invaders. In Paraguay, the Guaranís allied themselves with the Jesuits to avoid slavery, brutal encomienda labor, and the violence of everyday life under the Spanish. Throughout the Andes, Indians abandoned their villages for the anonymity of urban native barrios or established new *ayllus* in the high inaccessible sierras away from the Spanish.

Others, like the Araucanians of Chile, successfully fought the Spanish for three centuries rather than submit to imperial rule. In Peru, native shamans still exercised authority and villagers continued to worship stone *huacas*. They also melded Catholic saints with local gods to ensure their well-being. In the Guatemalan highlands, the Mayans resisted Spanish acculturation by turning inward to preserve the social and cultural social integrity of their communities. And all over the Americas, indigenous peoples tried to retain their languages, learned Spanish to write wills, property deeds, and bring lawsuits against the Spanish, and to record their own histories, traditions, and descriptions of Spanish rule. One of them—Felipe Guaman Poma de Ayala's *El primer nueva corónica y buen gobierno* [Letter to a King], completed in 1615—is one of the most excoriating indictments of any regime written before Aleksandr Solzhenitsyn's *The Gulag Archipelago* (1973).

The invasion of the New World initiated a profound religious, cultural, and social shock that has continued unabated for over 500 years. With Columbus's first military expedition, traditional indigenous communities started collapsing in the wake of epidemic diseases, debilitating armed conflicts, aggressive missionary activities, and the loss of sovereignty. Everywhere, native peoples saw "black rainbows" and "sinister hailstorms," in the memorable words of a Quechua elegy.

Some New World peoples broke under the Spanish onslaught and became thoroughly demoralized because their rituals and behavior no longer seemed to tap into the sacred sources of the universe. Others dwindled, joined larger Indian communities, or simply disappeared. Most of the survivors, however, creatively found ways to maintain their identities in an increasingly hostile and incomprehensible world.[1]

South America

A Jesuit Paradise in Paraguay

When the Jesuits first arrived in what is today Paraguay, they were shocked by their fellow countrymen. Once the Spanish realized that the Río de Plate region had no precious metals, tribute, or rich Indian states, they settled down with the local Guaranís and rapidly produced a huge mestizo population. In the early years of settlement, Spanish males had families of ten to twenty wives and mistresses. *Encomienda* grants were established in 1556, but they gradually disappeared as the Guaranís declined through disease and race mixture (*encomienda* Indians were called *tobaya*, or "in-law relative"). In no other part of South America were Indians so quickly integrated into colonial Spanish society.

Although the Jesuits exercised little influence over the Spanish, by the early seventeenth century they succeeded in establishing the world's largest experiment in cooperative living. About 200,000 Guaranís who had once occupied the territory between the Atlantic Ocean and the Paraguay River were forcibly resettled in thirty permanent communities. This arrangement left the Jesuits in control of the most fertile part of Paraguay for over a century.

The Jesuits, who were fine agronomists and shrewd businessmen, established permanent villages to convert the Guaranís to Christianity and a European way of life. Since "in their barbaric state the Indians possessed neither house nor field" and lived in large communal buildings and extended families, the priests tried to teach them the importance of private possessions and the nuclear family. Polygamy was forbidden, as was the keeping of concubines by chiefs and their families. Guaraní land was divided into family plots to grow manioc, wheat, fruits, vegetables, and cotton. On common land, they raised farm animals and especially the yerba plant, their chief export.

The Jesuits modeled their missionary villages on a Greco-Roman urban gridiron plan. Each town had a large central square dominated by a parish church and civic buildings. Guaraní houses stood behind the square, and beyond the walled perimeter of the town were farmlands, pasture, forests, and fresh water. Although the plaza, civic buildings, and individual dwellings were new to the Guaranís, Jesuit town planning was congenial to them because they had always lived in tightly packed settlements with stockades and moats to protect them against their enemies.

When the Jesuits first met the Guaranís, they were impressed with their messianic quest for *ywy mara-ey* [the Land-Without-Evil]. As their prophets promised, in the Land-Without-Evil there would no longer be any misfortune and the Guaranís would live among the gods. As one priest observed, "the shamans persuade the Indians not to work, not to go to the fields, promising them that the harvests will grow by themselves, that food instead of being scarce will fill their huts, and that spades will turn over the soil all alone, arrows will hunt for their owners, and will capture numerous enemies. They predict that the old will become young again."

Their search for the Land-Without-Evil became more desperate after the Spanish invasion of Paraguay. The world seemed to be disintegrating before their eyes as Guaraní society was rocked by warfare, disease, and Brazilian slave raids. Around 1630, Portuguese slave raiders kidnapped about 60,000 Guaranís from Jesuit missions. Many Guaraní villages disappeared, and the spiritual foundation of their culture crumbled because their shamans and leaders could not protect them against European violence and deadly epidemics. "The earth is old," they concluded, and the creation seemed exhausted. Chaos reigned, and for some their search for the Land-Without-Evil became a craving for surrender and death. With enticing promises of life after death, access to European goods and technology, and the ability to shield the Guaranís from harsh Spanish *encomienda* labor, the Jesuits succeeded their shamans and prophets as spiritual leaders.

Jesuit settlements, however, could not protect the Guaranís against European diseases and the cupidity of their Christian neighbors. Since encountering the Spanish, their population had declined almost 90 percent. At the same time, the powerful Jesuits became increasingly unpopular both in Paraguay and Spain. After the Crown banished them from the New World in 1767, the Guaranís fled for their lives when their settlements were destroyed by invading Portuguese and Spanish settlers. Many were killed or captured and auctioned off in Brazilian slave markets, and the Jesuits' magnificent library was burned as fuel.

Today, Paraguay is a mestizo nation with a palpable Indian heritage and Guaraní as its official second language. There are still some Guaranís who listen to shamans and dream of the Land-Without-Evil. They say it can be found by living according to traditional Guaraní principles that predate the appearance of Christians in Paraguay.[2]

The Origins of White People

The Cuiva Indians, who live in the forests and plains of eastern Columbia and western Venezuela, met Spanish explorers and Jesuit missionaries in the late seventeenth century. They have two stories about the origins of white people.

In one story, the first human beings were Indians. Later, say the old people, whites gradually emerged from the water. One man had ten cows while another emerged with five men mounted on horses. The Cuiva fled to the forest because they were afraid of white people. "The latter were still good then, as they had only just emerged."

In another story, Namoun and his son were visiting other people. When the son did not answer his father, Namoun shot him with his bow and arrow. Each time, however, the son came back to life again but said nothing to his father.

When they returned to their own shelter, Namoun placed his son in a hammock. The next day, the son ordered Namoun to build a fence and bring timber to build his house. After Namoun spent many days working, the son told him to do the cooking and then go and kill the Indians who were stealing his cattle. Namoun left and killed the robbers.

The next day, the son jumped on his horse and went to tend his cattle. "He had horses, cows, guns, cooking pots, machetes, mosquito nets, cloth hammocks, trousers, and other things." When he returned, the son scolded his father. "You never do anything. All you want to do is eat my nice, fat cows." The father neither replied nor looked at his son. Then the son killed his father with a gun.

The next day, Namoun came back to life and started laughing. "My son," he said, "you have become a white." That night, the son left with all his belongings. And that is how white people were created.

Note: Johannes Wilbert and Karin Simoneau, eds., *Folk Literature of the Cuiva Indians* (Los Angeles: UCLA Latin American Center Publications, 1991), pp. 73–74.

Sleeping with the Enemy

In 1615, an elderly member of a Peruvian noble family named Felipe Guaman Poma de Ayala (Hawk-Puma) completed one of the most extraordinary books ever written—a huge letter of over 1,000 pages and almost 400 drawings addressed to his sovereign King Philip III called *El primer nueva corónica y buen gobierno* [Letter to a King]. The first part of his book recounted the history of Peru from Adam and Eve through the reign of the Incas, while the second part described the Spanish conquest and the subsequent civil wars that followed the destruction of the Inca empire. Most of his book was a caustic description of contemporary Spanish and Indian life in the Viceroyalty of Peru. An unusual combination of biblical and dynastic histories, sermons, allegories, factual descriptions and fictional events, and captioned drawings, Guaman Poma's massive work in Spanish and Quechua can only be compared to the magic realism of contemporary Latin American authors or to the inventive stories of the Argentine writer Jorge Luis Borges. All of it, however, was written with a decidedly Andean perspective, even its maps.

In the book, there is a charming drawing of the author, his young son, his horse, and his two dogs walking from the central Andes to the Viceregal capital of Lima. Father and son are dressed in traditional Andean clothes and sandals, but the horse is Spanish, as is the caption under the drawing. Poma's bicultural drawings depicted well the ambivalence of his book. He was proud of his royal heritage and hated the Spanish, but Guaman Poma fully expected King Philip III to read *El primer nueva corónica y buen gobierno* and then name his son the native ruler of Spain's Andean empire.

Andean peoples, Guaman Poma argued, had always used their natural reason to live according to the Ten Commandants and Christian law until the Incas forced them to worship idols. Consequently, the Spanish had no right to oppress and degrade them by acting in unchristian ways. He was especially concerned about the social disorder the Spanish created through their rapacious sexual behavior. "Women had honor . . . during the epoch of the Incas in spite of the fact that they were idolatrous, but now the clergy and the parish priests are the ones who first violate them and lead them to sin."

Landowners and their hirelings were equally venal. "In the Indian villages, the encomenderos, their sons, brothers, and major-domos rape single women, married women—all women—whom they pervert, converting them into prostitutes. These men, as well as their servants, blacks, mestizos, and Indians wreck the lives of these women, destroying their possessions, land, and food."

This social system was disastrous, for now "women who are handed over to the priests and other Spaniards do not want to marry Indian men, nor do the men want to marry them." Young women were "converted into common prostitutes, and married women into bellicose prostitutes and adulteresses, who live outside their communities." In the Viceroyalty of Peru, Guaman Poma savagely concluded, men and women could survive only by becoming panderers and whores.

As Andean peoples lost their identity and became a mongrel race, divine punishment would strike the Spanish. "You say that you have to make restitution; I don't see that you give back either in life, or at the time of death," Guaman Poma lamented. "Even though you were to abandon yourselves in the desert and become religious hermits, as long as you do not make restitution and pay what you owe, you will be condemned to the inferno."

Guaman Poma understood that he lived in a topsy-turvy world where history, philosophy, and theology were being used to support a crushing colonial regime that sucked the life out of its suffering subjects. "Just imagine," he cried, "that our people were to arrive in Spain and start confiscating property, sleeping with women and girls, chastising the men, and treating everybody like pigs! What would the Spaniards do then?" Guaman Poma wrote that had I "set down all the misdeeds of priests and other Spaniards, I would have long since run out of paper."

In this surreal environment, he decided that his only recourse was to judge the Spanish by their own lofty rhetoric and religious ideals. "To write is to weep," he sadly concluded, realizing the futility of his remarks.[3]

The Mixing of Races in Latin America

Because so many more Iberian men than women migrated to the New World (in the early sixteenth century, there were eight male Spaniards for every Spanish woman in Peru), different races immediately began intermixing during the conquest. At first, the Spanish and Portuguese received women as gifts and tokens of friendship from indigenous peoples. At the same time, Europeans forcibly initiated sexual relations with Indians and Africans, who began appearing as slaves in Hispaniola during the first decade of the sixteenth century.

Although they considered Indians and Africans far inferior to themselves, widespread miscegenation occurred throughout Latin America from the beginning of European colonization. As one of the characters in a Gabriel García Márquez's novel *Strange Pilgrims* (1993) colorfully explained, Latin America was a "continent conceived by the scum of the earth without a moment of love; the children of abductions, rapes, violations, infamous dealings, deceptions, the union of enemies with enemies."

After the conquest, by law and custom a *Sociedad de Castas* [Society of Castes] developed throughout Spanish and Portuguese America. Iberians and Creoles (Spaniards born in the New World) had the highest social status followed by *mestizos* (mixed Spanish and Indian), and lastly African Americans and Indians. This caste society was supposedly based on *limpieza de sangre* [purity of blood], a fifteenth-century Spanish concept used to distinguish Catholics from Jews and New Christians (converted Jews) from Old Christians. This obsession with racial purity migrated with Iberians to the New World, where paradoxically it was grafted onto societies with many different ethnic groups and small numbers of Iberians and Creoles. By the seventeenth century, Latin America had developed an incredible racial mosaic of peoples who were impossible to classify with precision.

Note: Magnus Mörner, *Race Mixture in the History of Latin America* (Boston: Little, Brown, 1967), pp. 21–33, 53–58; Claudio Esteva Fabregat, *El mestizaje en Iberoamérica* (Madrid: Alhambra, 1988), pp. 127–186; W. George Lovell and Christopher H. Lutz, *Demography and Empire: A Guide to the Population History of Spanish Central America, 1500–1821* (Boulder, CO: Westview Press, 1995), p. xvi; James Lockhart, *Spanish Peru, 1532–1560* (Madison: University of Wisconsin Press, 1968), p. 152; Jane S. Gerber, *The Jews of Spain: A History of the Sephardic Experience* (New York: Free Press, 1992), pp. 127–129; J.H. Elliott, *Imperial Spain, 1469–1716* (New York: New American Library, 1963), pp. 214–221; Benzion Netanyahu, *The Origins of the Inquisition in Fifteenth-Century Spain* (New York: Random House, 1995), pp. 925–1069; Woodrow Borah, "The Mixing of Populations," in *First Images of America: The Impact of the New World on the Old*, ed. Fredi Chiappelli (Berkeley: University of California Press, 1976), vol. I, pp. 707–722.

Three Centuries of Araucanian Resistance

The Araucanians of Chile, who are Mapuches, first encountered Christians when a Spanish army appeared in 1536. Five years later, Governor Pedro de Valdivia founded the city of Santiago and established forts and villages throughout central Chile. Under Spanish rule, Araucanian life rapidly changed. From 1540 to 1620, many Indians died from brutal *encomienda* and mining labor. Even more Araucanians died from European diseases and warfare.

In 1553, an Indian servant from Santiago named Lautaro, who was once Valdivia's groom, led the first major revolt against Spanish rule. Araucanians killed Valdivia and then dismembered his body. So began more than three centuries of successful Araucanian resistance, which lasted until a formal peace with the Republic of Chile was signed in 1881.

Until the late eighteenth century, the Araucanians successfully confined the Spanish to Santiago and a few garrison towns in central Chile. They accomplished what the mighty Aztec and Inca empires failed to do—retain their independence and keep the Spanish at bay. Successful resistance was partly the result of Spanish weaknesses. Spaniards were far from their main supply lines in Peru and never outnumbered the Araucanians, even after smallpox epidemics ravaged them for years. In 1600, a census estimated that there were only 2,400 Spaniards in Chile and almost 500,000 indigenous peoples.

Spain's vaunted cavalry and soldiers could not function effectively in Chile's forests, and Spanish soldiers often were more interested in rape, theft, kidnapping, and acquiring Indian slaves than in fighting. Finally, Chile was not of strategic importance to Spain because the wealthier Andean provinces to the north provided far more silver and tribute to the Crown. As a result, Spain did not make the military defeat of the Araucanians as high a priority as the defeat of other indigenous peoples.

The greatest obstacle to imperial rule, however, was the Araucanians' ability to transform their culture in response to the Spanish threat. The Araucanians developed into a formidable military force. Although they relied primarily on traditional weapons—bows and arrows, lances, clubs, and slings—the Araucanians were often able to defeat Spanish troops. They attacked in carefully prepared ambushes and chose places where Spanish horses were ineffective or could be trapped in camouflaged pits lined with sharp wooden stakes. At first, the Araucanians were terrified of horses and retreated in panic whenever Spanish infantry approached. By the early seventeenth century, however, they had developed a highly mobile cavalry, raised the best horses in Chile, and refused to surrender them in exchange for peace.

The Araucanians also found ways to overcome their deep-seated localism. By using Spanish plunder to cement local alliances, the chiefs of central Chile created a formidable fighting force that even included mercenaries and Spanish deserters. By the seventeenth century, the area around Arauco coordinated the military resistance. To intimidate the Spanish, captives sometimes were crucified before being killed. Captured women were treated with the utmost contempt. Those with the highest status became the mistresses of chiefs, and when Spanish women were exchanged for Indian prisoners, they were returned filthy, naked below the waist, and pregnant.

Araucanian military and political power was based on the rigorous training of boys for a lifetime of combat. At the age of six, males were taught to become strong runners, swimmers, and fighters. By practicing on Spanish captives, they became specialists in the use of deadly weapons. Young Araucanians memorized verses celebrating the history of their people and recounting the cruelties committed by the Spanish. Their warrior creed was based on the power of their weapons. "This is my master: it does not order me to dig for gold, or carry food or firewood, nor to herd cattle, or to follow it about. And since this master sustains my liberty, it is with him that I wish to pass."

When the Spanish colonized Chile in the early sixteenth century, Jesuit priests wanted to bring the Araucanians "to the dominion of the king by peaceful methods, by good treatment and by teaching them the principles of Christianity." They complained to the Crown that the Araucanians resisted Christianity because of slavery and *encomienda* labor. Soldiers and civilians sneered at these arguments. The Moors in Spain had been enslaved for rebelling. Why should Araucanian men, women, and children be treated differently?

In 1599, the Archbishop of Lima ruled that the Indians of Chile were "without a king, without law, honor, or shame." Since they were even more "bellicose, and more dishonorable" than Peru's Indians, the Spanish had the right to wage just war against them. King Philip III agreed, and in 1608 he ordered that all young boys and girls captured in Chile's wars be enslaved and given to Christians "who would teach them the faith as was done with the Moors in the Kingdom of Granada." By the early seventeenth century, the Spanish and Araucanians were engaged in an unrelenting struggle against each other.

The war took its toll on both sides. By 1620, the number of rebellious Araucanians had declined about 75 percent through diseases and constant warfare. Meanwhile, about 30,000 Spanish soldiers and settlers died fighting the Araucanians at an official cost of 17,000,000 gold pesos. Constant warfare made Chile a poor ward of the Viceroyalty of Peru.

After 1700, relations between the Spanish and Araucanians became more peaceful, but Araucanians continued dwindling in numbers because of harsh labor, malnourishment, smallpox epidemics, and miscegenation. This was especially true in the southern bishopric of Santiago, where indigenous peoples dropped from almost half the population in 1700 to less than 10 percent only seventy years later. In the later part of the century, the Crown finally abolished two institutions hated by Indians—slavery and the *encomienda* system. Abolition coincided with a declining need for Indian labor as a large and growing mestizo working class appeared throughout Chile.

Meanwhile, centuries of bloody wars had created an Araucanian diaspora in the eastern Andes and Argentine Pampa. On the other side of the Cordillera, the Araucanians and their Indian allies fought the Spanish to the outskirts of Buenos Aires. Chile's Arauco was gradually colonized by Spanish and foreign immigration, and the last Araucanian uprising ended in 1883.

Today, there are about 300,000 Mapuches in Chile. About two-thirds of them still live in Araucania, where they proudly retain their distinct identity, religion, and language. They consider all indigenous people Mapuches, which means "people of the land." All non-indigenous peoples, in contrast, are called *winka*, which means plunderer or raider.[4]

Demographic Recovery in the Ecuadoran Highlands

After the Spanish destroyed the Inca empire, over the next century 90 percent of the native population died, mostly from diseases imported by Europeans. Although mortality rates remained very high for hundreds of years, during the seventeenth century the population actually increased in the highlands of colonial Ecuador. In the face of so many disasters, some Indians learned to survive under their new masters.

In the early seventeenth century, European diseases continued to devastate Indian communities. In 1645, measles and diphtheria struck the region with great virulence. Throughout the rest of the century, dysentery and fever remained major threats in the highlands, and the area around Quito was plagued by malaria during the hot summer months. Periodic droughts, heavy rains, and major earthquakes added to the misery.

Nevertheless, in Quito and other places Indians doubled their numbers during the seventeenth century. There were many reasons for this unexpected upturn. Favorable economic conditions, especially the low cost of living and the lack of a mining *mita*, kept most native highland Ecuadorans in the region while attracting many Indians from other areas. From 1598 to 1626, the native population in the Quito area rose from 105,000 to 425,000, and the number of Indian tributaries tripled to 85,000. In Riobamba, the tributary population also made impressive gains from 5,625 in 1590 to over 17,000 by 1678. The Ecuadoran highlands acted like a geographical magnet, attracting Indians searching for healthier living conditions and economic opportunities.

Many of them fled their native *ayllus* because of deadly epidemics, abuse by royal officials, dangerous *mita* work in the silver mines, and natural disasters. Some Andean peoples also abandoned their communities as fertile lands owned by *ayllus* fell under Spanish control. They came to Quito and neighboring communities to labor as artisans, domestic servants, and textile workers. *Haciendas* [large estates] attracted their share of Indians looking for steady work and better living conditions.

Increased mobility helped Andean peoples survive the conquest and disruption of their society, but at a heavy price. By the end of the seventeenth century, less than half of Andean peoples lived in their communities of birth and could no longer count on being granted land or receiving assistance from kin.

127

As a result of migration and European diseases, the native demographic profile changed in the northern Andes. Under Inca rule, most Indians had lived in extended families comprising several generations, and *curacas* often had several wives. By the seventeenth century, Indian households were usually nuclear in composition, and few Indians practiced polygamy. Disease and infertility had drastically reduced the size of families. Most couples had no more than two living children, and in some Indian villages up to 75 percent of families had no children at all.

Indian men had precipitously declined to one-third of the native population, one-quarter of whom were unmarried. As a result, many Indian women had to marry outside their *ayllus*, which further increased the residential mobility of the population. Indians found ways to survive under Spanish rule, but families became smaller and less rooted to their traditional communities.

As death and infertility stalked Ecuador's peoples, native men and women desperately searched for ways to evade the harshness of Spanish rule. Families fled to the anonymity of Quito's native *barrios* [neighborhoods], established new *ayllus* where they could at least live among other Indians, and migrated into the inaccessible mountains away from the watchful eyes of prying priests and grasping royal officials. In the high sierras they could worship the guardian spirits of the land and the burial sites of their ancestors while shielding their children from the contaminating influence of Spaniards. In the Ecuadorian highlands, mobility and physical retreat were often their best defense against oppression.

At the end of the seventeenth century, however, life became more precarious for Indians in the northern Andes. The Spanish created new *mita* mining regulations as silver production declined, and deadly epidemics of smallpox, measles, diphtheria, influenza, and typhus appeared again. In 1687, a series of earthquakes devastated Lima and the central coast of Peru. Survivors fled the wrecked city, which lost half its population. Along the coast, the destruction of ancient irrigation systems led to a decline in agricultural production. Inland, the once flourishing Quito textile market declined in the face of international competition. Throughout the eighteenth century, highlands Ecuador was no longer a prosperous or populous region.[5]

The Yaruros and Horses

According to the Yaruros of southwestern Venezuela, the differences between themselves and the Creoles were due to the acquisition of horses. In one Yaruro story, the "First Ones," the original Yaruros, and the Creoles were together when a large, mean horse appeared. The leader of the Yaruros was afraid to mount the horse because it was so big. But the leader of the Creoles jumped on the horse and disappeared. Two weeks later, he returned still mounted on his horse. This is why the Creoles are more talented than the Yaruros. "They know how to study and read, and they are not afraid."

In another Yaruro story, in the beginning the creator made a horse for the Yaruros, but they were too timid to mount it. The creator told one frightened man to "get on the horse. I am not making this for the others," the Creoles. But the man refused. Then the creator told a Creole, "You get on the horse. It shall be yours if you do." Immediately, the Creole mounted the horse. "To fill a need, the creator brought about the horse. But because the Yaruro failed to mount it, we were left out. If he had mounted up, we would now be the owners of horses."

Note: Johannes Wilbert and Karin Simoneau, eds., *Folk Literature of the Yaruro Indians* (Los Angeles: UCLA Latin American Center Publications, 1990), pp. 49–50.

Pachacuti: Andean Contraries

When the Spanish invaded Peru, Andean peoples naturally thought of *pachacuti* [a "turning of time and space"] when the traditional social order became radically altered amid chaos and uncertainty. Popular legends quickly arose about the tragic death of Emperor Atahualpa and the end of Inca rule.

What rainbow is this black rainbow that rises?
The horrible thunderbolt of Cuzco's enemy flashes,
And everywhere a sinister hailstorm strikes.

In the seventeenth century, when Andean communities performed the "Tragedy of the Death of Atahualpa" at Christian festivals, audiences wept openly at the Spanish military triumph.

A Village Shaman

About 1645, the Peruvian villagers of San Pedro de Hacas claimed the lands of the abandoned community of Cochillas. After receiving title, they decided to build a new irrigation canal. Each household gave the village shaman one guinea pig to sacrifice, and every inhabitant contributed one Spanish coin so the village could purchase a sacrificial llama for the *mallquis* [mummified bodies] of Cochillas's ancestors. Although San Pedro de Hacas was a nominally Christian community, villagers feared that unless the *mallquis* were treated properly, they "would be angry and the villagers would not be able to construct the irrigation canal or sow the fields."

These traditional ceremonies were carried out by Hernando Hacaspoma, who was in charge of communicating with the *mallqui* "Guamancama," a powerful mountain god and the son of "Lightening." According to him, Guamancama "raised men and increased them and gave the Indians money and possessions and told them what they had to do." After Hacaspoma made the sacrifices, he "heard within himself that the mallqui spoke to him and told him if it was going to be an abundant year or not and if there was going to be plague or disease."

San Pedro de Hacas recognized Hacaspoma as its shaman because he was well trained and had successfully interceded with the village's ancestors. On one occasion, villagers asked Hacaspoma for assistance because they wanted to get rid of their parish priest, avoid repairing a bridge, and sue a lawyer they hated. Hacaspoma told the villagers to fast for two days. He also made sacrifices to Guamancama, who "came down into his heart and told him what had to be done regarding the matters on which they had consulted him." Thanks to Hacaspoma's intervention and the power of Guamancama, the village's wishes came true.

In 1658, Hacaspoma was discovered by the Spanish and tortured to death for practicing shamanism. Other male and female shamans in the region met the same fate. The Spanish authorities also destroyed *huacas* and *mallquis* and confiscated any property used to support what they considered devil worship.

Diego Vasicuio

In 1671, Diego Vasicuio, an elderly man from the *ayllu* of Salamanca, was summoned before a tribunal in southern Peru. According to his accuser, Catalina Paicaua, he was secretly worshipping a stone *huaca* named "Saramama." Paicaua had denounced Vasicuio to her parish priest after she admitted casting a spell to help a woman entangle her boyfriend.

When Vasicuio and other residents of Salamanca appeared before Father Bernardino de Prado, they confessed to organizing the worship of Saramama. After the Catholic holiday of Corpus Christi in the late spring, Vasicuio and his followers would go to a nearby cave where he would bath Saramama in *chicha* [native corn beer] and then offer her sacrifices. After quietly conversing with Saramama, Vasicuio would utter the following prayer: "You are the only one who gives, the Creator of the Earth. Look at me. I am poor.

Give me strength, give me food. Have pity on me. Give me corn. I have nothing. Help me."

The Catholic priest was outraged by this sacrilege and demanded that Vasiciuo produce the *huaca*. After some delay, he produced a stone wrapped in white cloth that supposedly was Saramama. Vasiciuo and his followers loudly confessed their sins and swore by the cross that they would stop being heretics and idol worshippers. Once back in Salamanca, however, they began worshipping the real Saramama again.

An Andean Saint

In the Iberian peninsula and the New World, the Spanish military's patron saint was Santiago, or St. James the Apostle. According to Spanish lore, Jesus had named Santiago the "Son of Thunder" because of his violent temper. Santiago Mata-moros (Santiago the Moor killer) had led Christians to victory in Spain, and soldiers shouted his name before discharging their firearms.

In Peru, Santiago inspired the Spanish to victory and became the patron saint of Cuzco because he fought so bravely against the Indians. In Cuzco's main cathedral, there was a painting of Santiago "seated on top of a white horse grasping his leather shield in one hand and his sword in the other, and many Indians, wounded and dead, were thrown down head long at his feet." Guaman Poma claimed that during the siege of Cuzco, Santiago came down from the sky preceded by an enormous clap of thunder to "chastise the Indians and lend support to the Spanish." Both Spaniards and Indians admired his great power.

When Andean peoples converted to Christianity, they naturally associated Santiago with their own "Illapa," a powerful mountain deity who represented thunder and lightening. He ruled the heavens, guarded the livestock, and watered the crops. Because Andean mountain gods were able to change their appearance and to speak to Indians through images, Illapa could be fused with Santiago without any sense of religious contradiction. Santiago, the Spanish patron saint of conquest and colonial domination, became Santiago-Illapa, who protected the Indians as an enduring Andean mountain god.

Andean peoples associated James with his brother John, twins who had been called "the thunderbolts" by Jesus; and some Peruvian parents named one of their twin boys Santiago instead of the Son of Thunder. The Church was so outraged at this native form of biblical exegesis that they ordered local priests not to name any male twin Santiago or Diego (James) because it was a "great superstition."

Santiago-Illapa now was partly Hispanized, but Andean peoples still per-

131

formed sacrifices to him, worshipped him at secret shrines, and addressed him respectfully as "Apuhuayna," or young lord. As the lord of thunder and lightening, he retained his indigenous authority and character. If Santiago could terrify and defeat the Indians, his miraculous strength could also ensure their well-being.[6]

Mesoamerica and the Caribbean

Nahuatl in New Spain

Until about 1550, Nahuatl—the major language of New Spain's Valley of Mexico—changed very little. Probably the only Nahuas who frequently spoke to Spaniards were servants and the aides of conquistadors, royal officials, the clergy, and those privileged young Indians from noble families who were studying Spanish reading and writing with friars. Nahuatl documents using the Latin alphabet began to appear, but the only linguistic changes that occurred involved nouns. When the Nahuas could not identify a Spanish object or concept, they used a Nahuatl noun with another word to modify it. A pirate was described as an *acalco tenamoyani*, "one who robs people on a boat," while the law became *tlamelahuacachihualiztli*, "doing things straight."

By the mid-sixteenth century, Nahuas were using hundreds of Spanish-noun loan words in their documents. Many described animals, plants, objects, functions, and new social identities. A *caja* was a wooden chest, while *puerta* meant a swinging door. In Nahuatl, figs became *habas* and a church was called a *santa iglesia*. Nahua speakers had considerably more contact with Spaniards, yet the basic linguistic structure of Nahuatl did not really change for over a century. The Nahuas continued seeing the world through their own eyes and incorporated only new nouns into their language.

After 1650, Nahua speakers liberally modified their language with Spanish nouns, verbs, particles, prepositions, and conjunctions. Spanish idioms were translated freely. They also changed their rules for creating plurals to conform to Spanish usage and added new Spanish sounds to Nahuatl. Loan verbs, especially legal, religious, and economic terms, added the Nahuatl -oa ending to Spanish infinitives. *Notificar*, "to notify," turned into *notificaroa*, and *pasearoa* meant "to take a stroll or parade about." Calques, or native words used to express Spanish idioms, also appeared.

Nahua speakers freely incorporated Spanish into their language because some of them had learned it from priests. According to one educator's account, Spanish religious school language immersion techniques could be quite brutal. On one occasion, Spanish priests locked up 1,000 children and forbade them to speak Nahuatl so that "they might neglect their excessive idolatries and their excessive sacrifices from which the devil had secured countless souls." Priests concentrated their pedagogical zeal on the sons of the dwindling Aztec nobility, the Nahua community's future leaders.

In Peru, Spanish officials and priests were always ambivalent about Quechua, the official language of the Inca empire. Some wanted to eradicate Quechua while others believed that the language would promote missionary work and more effective political control. In colonial Mexico, the Spanish had no ambivalence about preserving and using what they called classical Nahuatl. They believed that Nahuatl would enable them to communicate more effectively with the pre-conquest nobility and to impose Spanish colonization more firmly on their Indian subjects. By learning to speak Nahuatl, Spaniards also flattered themselves that they understood the culture of the people they had vanquished.

Although Nahuatl changed its structure and vocabulary under the impact of Spanish colonization, the language still retained its suppleness, oratorical quality, and rootedness in Nahua culture. Flexible and yet still tied to traditional Aztec poetry, songs, and ceremonial occasions, Nahuatl even successfully adapted itself to classical European literature without losing its sense of place.

In the sixteenth century, there appeared a Nahuatl translation of forty-seven Aesop's fables from a 1479 Latin edition. The Latin edition was brief and straightforward, but the Nahuatl translation transplanted the fables into a Mexican environment, incorporated Aztec concepts and rituals into the stories, and made them rhetorically more subtle. In "The Old Man and Death," the Latin text plainly states that the Old Man "asked death to come." In Nahuatl, this passage became:

O death
wherever you may be
come now destroy me
do away with me
take away all the evil
that I suffer.

Similarly startling changes took place in "The Lion and the Frog." The Latin text says that a "lion once heard a frog croaking; he turned towards the noise thinking it was some great beast; when he saw the frog by the pond he went up and squashed it." Transposed into Nahuatl, the story retains its theme but becomes localized and describes the beast's psychology. "A jaguar once heard a frog, screaming and croaking a great deal." The jaguar was frightened and thought that it was a large four-footed animal.

"To quiet his heart, he looked around him in all directions." When he came to the water's edge, the jaguar was very angry and ashamed of being frightened by such a small creature. "He squashed him and killed him." Despite the Spanish conquest, Nahuatl remained anchored in Aztec conversation and culture.

Throughout the Valley of Mexico, Nahuatl continued as the indigenous language, but it was transformed as a result of its speakers' growing exposure to Spanish. This occurred everywhere and affected everyone, from Aztec nobility to farmers and industrial workers. As the Nahuas drastically declined over 90 percent in just a century, a mestizo or Spanish/Indian culture appeared in Central Mexico. Mestizos were especially valuable as mediators between Spaniards and Mexico's shrinking Indian population, serving as interpreters and stewards on *haciendas*, officials in their own communities, and even as priests after 1588.

Expanding economic activities and widespread miscegenation in Mexico City led to the partial acculturation of many Nahuas into Spanish culture and subsequent changes in their language. Increasing numbers of Nahuas lived and worked outside their traditional villages and had more prolonged contact with Spaniards in artisanal shops, *haciendas*, bars and gambling dens, apartment buildings, and bedrooms. A growing number of mestizos (from 2,437 in 1570 to 249,368 by 1742) found themselves between two languages and two worlds. By the end of the seventeenth century, the Nahuas had become a bicultural and bilingual society.[7]

Mayan Resistance in the Guatemala Highlands

Throughout the colonial period, forced Indian labor, which the Crown considered "a just token of the vassalage owed by Natives to the Sovereign," formed the backbone of Spain's New World economy. In the rugged Cuchumatán highlands of northwest Guatemala, over three centuries the Crown modified the structure of Indian labor in response to changing political goals, evolving economic enterprises, and native population decline in order to benefit itself, the Church, and Spanish settlers.

While the Crown was creating *encomiendas* in the Guatemalan highlands in the sixteenth century, native peoples were resettled in *congregaciónes* [Indian towns] so they could be more easily converted to Christianity and harnessed as a labor force. These new settlements were designed with a church, central plaza, a priest's residence, and streets organized in a geometrical grid pattern. Each village received about 6.5 square miles of inalienable common land, which was administered by local Mayan officials. Ironically, by granting the defeated Mayas jurisdiction over their farmland

and local political affairs, the Crown enabled them to retain critically important elements of their cultures.

According to Spanish law, all married Indian males between the ages of eighteen and fifty were liable for periodic tribute payments. Mayans who had been forcibly resettled near large Spanish settlements were subject to another form of forced labor, the *repartimiento*, that involved rotating personal services for individuals and municipalities. By the early seventeenth century, a combination of European diseases, Crown reform legislation, the geographical isolation of the highlands, and persistent complaints by some clergy had combined to diminish the more brutal forms of forced labor. In response, Spanish landowners and town dwellers turned to patriarchal rural estates and peonage as powerful weapons to insure a permanent supply of inexpensive Indian workers.

There was always a wide gap, however, between Spanish imperial ideals and the determination of the Mayas to resist their alien oppressors, especially in the highlands where there were few Spaniards. Mayas avoided tribute labor by fleeing their confining *congregaciónes* for dispersed settlements away from officials and priests. Wherever they lived, few of them imitated Spaniards. Led by their women, they proudly spoke local languages, dressed distinctively, and seldom married outside their communities.

Highland Mayas divided their lands into *chinamitales* [collectively owned land]. Before the Spanish arrived, the Mayan kingdoms of the Guatemalan highlands consisted of *chinamitales* with nobles and commoners. The nobles were a sacred lineage, received tribute, owned slaves, and lived in magnificent palaces. Commoners paid tribute and were farmers, warriors, merchants, and artisans. As a result of the Spanish conquest, the Mayans fundamentally altered the composition and structure of the *chinamit* but continued using it to anchor their social world.

In each *chinamit*, membership, based on birth, confirmed certain rights and obligations. The collective membership of the *chinamit*, and not its individual members, controlled land and its natural resources. Although individuals received the right to farm or use portions of the land to farm, they could not give away or sell their land. Each member assumed collective responsibility for the individual behavior of his or her fellow members, and members of the *chinamit* usually engaged in specialized economic activities that were defined by their group. The *chinamitales*, which existed into the twentieth century, helped define the distinctive contours of Mayan life and enabled them to maintain their identity under colonial rule.

The Mayas used the Latin alphabet to produce such texts as the *Popol Vuh, The Annals of The Cakchiquels*, and the *Title of the Lords of Totonicapán* to preserve their own understanding of history and religion. In 1554, for example, the *Title of the Lords of Totonicapán* traced Quiché history from their origins to Quikab, their great ruler of the late fifteenth century, by imaginatively combining the reign of Quiché kings with Bible stories to demonstrate that the Quichés were descended from the ten tribes of ancient Israel.

According to the Quichés, the Wise Men and the three great peoples who followed them extended "their sight over the four parts of the world and over all that is beneath the sky, and finding no obstacle, came from the other part of the ocean, from where the sun rises, a place called *Pa Tulán, Pa Civan.*" These were the three nations of Quichés, who "came from where the sun rises, descendants of Israel, of the same language and the same customs." When they arrived at the edge of the sea, their leader Balam-Qitzé "touched it with his staff and at once a path opened, which then closed up again, for thus the great God wished it to be done, because they were the sons of Abraham and Jacob."

Some Mayans learned Spanish to acquire land, deed it to their families, and bring law suits against Spaniards who wanted their property, specifically memorializing their ancestral rights so that it would not fall under Spanish control. Others used alphabetic writing to defend the authenticity of acquired rights or to claim new ones. The Mayas, like other subject peoples, became adept at using the official rhetoric of the Spanish government to protect themselves, preserve their communal identity, and manufacture and manipulate documents to their advantage.

In 1619, almost a century after the conquest, one priest claimed that if "after baptism an Indian began to steal, swear, lie, kill, and steal women, he would say, 'I am getting to be a little like a Christian.'" In 1770, over two centuries after the conquest, another Spanish priest in the highlands "seized an old women kneeling with a smoking clay censer on an artificial mound raised on a small hill, and there were several eggs broken open with much chicken blood on the ground." When the astonished priest asked her why she was burning incense, the woman replied that she was asking God for health like the others who visited the place. The priest sadly concluded that the Mayas had practically no respect for the holy sacraments based on "the tedium and repugnance with which they receive them."

Four years later, an archbishop who had visited the highland parishes came to an even more pessimistic conclusion. The Indians, he observed, "take the Spanish . . . for foreigners and usurpers of these lands. For this reason they view them with implacable hatred, and those that obey them do so only out of pure, servile fear." He concluded that "the Indians want nothing from the Spanish—neither religion, nor doctrine, nor customs." In the highlands of Guatemala, Spain's control over its Indian subjects was formally acknowledged but never uncontested.[8]

Europe

Spain and Europe's Price Revolution

In the sixteenth century, the influx of New World gold and silver dramatically transformed Europe's economy and society. Over 20,000 tons of silver, worth more than $3 billion in today's prices, entered Seville, and from 1537 to 1731 over 700,000,000 gold and silver pesos were minted just in New Spain.

In Andalucia, prices increased more than fivefold in less than a century. Across the border in France, mid-seventeenth century prices more than doubled. Across the channel, English prices soared threefold from 1500 to 1550 and kept increasing. At the same time, however, wages lagged far behind price inflation, especially in England, France, and the German states.

As a result of the price revolution, large amounts of capital became available for governments, businessmen, and merchants to invest. By 1585, one quarter of the Spanish crown's total revenue consisted of silver and gold from the New World. This represented a historical reversal of the flow of European specie. Until the discovery of the New World, European gold and silver had moved to the Middle East, Africa, and Asia to purchase spices and luxury goods. But by the early sixteenth century, New World silver and gold were flooding Europe and contributing to the rise of a monetized economy.

The price revolution affected countries differently. Ironically, many Spaniards probably became poorer after the conquest. The influx of precious metals mostly went to pay debts, foreign wars, foreign bankers and merchants ("our Spain is the Indies of the Genoese," sardonically wrote one Spaniard), and conspicuous consumption by the Crown and nobility—new monasteries, private chapels, works of art, dowries for daughters to live comfortably as nuns, country estates and sumptuous palaces, titles of nobility, and gambling.

Meanwhile, the price of corn skyrocketed, famines and plagues ravaged Castile, and thousands migrated abroad in search of a better life. When Philip II came to the throne in 1556, most of his gold and silver was leaving Spain to cover the Crown's debts. Seville became known as the "Great Babylon of Spain" as it became overrun with thieves, beggars, prostitutes, and a criminal underworld that developed profitable relations with the city's venal public officials.

Throughout Spain, little was invested or produced except raw materials for export. As one exasperated Spaniard complained in 1600, "wealth has not sent its roots deep because it has never come down to earth, remaining in the form of papers, bills of exchange, and gold and silver coin—and not in the form of goods capable of yield or of attracting foreign wealth through interior strength." By the early seventeenth century, imperial Spain was mired in debt and dreams of past glory.[9]

Potatoes and the Conquest

When Columbus established Europe's first New World colony in 1493, Europe was in the grip of a little ice age. Beginning around 800 CE and continuing for five centuries, warmer air and sea surface temperatures led to high summer temperatures and mild winters across Europe. During this period, Europe's population rapidly expanded as farmers increased their cereal harvests, grew crops on once marginal soils, and expanded their acreage into higher altitudes. From the eleventh to the fourteenth century, England's population increased from 1.4 to 5 million while France boomed from 6.2 to almost 18 million inhabitants.

Beginning in the early fourteenth century, however, Europe's climate became cooler, stormier, wetter, and more unpredictable for the next five centuries. The little ice age began with a terrible famine that devastated Europe in 1315. One out of ten people in the great Flemish cloth city of Ypres succumbed to starvation in just six months, and some people even consumed the dead. Travel to Greenland and Newfoundland became more difficult as heavy pack ice blocked Viking ships. All over Europe, crops failed, cattle died, and epidemic diseases ravaged the land. Only in the mid-nineteenth century did Europe's weather become milder.

In this precarious environment, Columbus's discovery of the New World dramatically changed the health and diet of Europe. Perhaps the New World's most precious gift to the Old World has been plants first domesticated by Indians. New World agriculture provided Europeans with maize, beans, peanuts, manioc, potatoes, sweet potatoes, squashes, papayas, guava, avocados, pineapples, tomatoes, chile peppers, and coca. Manioc, which could thrive in poor soils, produced three times the caloric yield of maize and became the mainstay of colonial Brazil's diet.

Of all these foods, maize and the potato have had the most beneficial impact north of the Mediterranean because they produced far more calories per acre than Europe's cereal mainstays. On one acre of land, the average caloric yield of potatoes (3 million) and maize (2.92 million) was far in excess of oats (2.2 million), barley (2.04 million), and wheat (1.68 million). In addition, maize and potatoes could be grown on lands that had been considered marginal or left fallow.

The Andean potato was domesticated many thousands of years ago and grown above the 8,000–foot elevation limit of maize cultivation. When the Spanish conquered the Incas, they began feeding potatoes to their slaves and sailors, many of whom were Basques. By 1576, potatoes were being eaten at a hospital in Seville, and around the same time the Basques of northern Spain became the first Europeans to begin planting potatoes in their gardens. The potato spread to Belgium in the seventeenth century and then to Germany, Poland, Hungary, and Russia over the next hundred years.

The potato, however, at first was considered an inferior food because it grew underground and was likened to other foods gathered by New World peoples—roots, berries, and nuts. Only in the mid-seventeenth century was the potato recognized across Europe for its high nutritional value, but it was always valued as an aphrodisiac because of its shape.

The potato, of course, is closely associated with Ireland. In just twenty years, half of Ireland's seventeenth-century population probably disappeared through a combination of English military defeats, deportation to North America and the West Indies, and outright starvation due to the deliberate destruction of livestock. The Irish would not have survived the brutal conquest of their island over the next three centuries without the potato.

Ireland's climate and soil were perfect for potatoes. Except for the Dublin area, most of the cool island received between sixty and eighty inches of rain each year, and its rich, powdery soil and bogs were well suited to the cultivation of tubers, such as potatoes. The Irish grew their potatoes in plots called "lazy-beds" just as they had been cultivated for millennia in Peru and Bolivia. With just a spade, a half acre of potatoes could feed a family for one year, and once planted, the aptly named lazy-bed needed little attention until harvest time. And when hostile clans or the English attacked farms, potatoes could be easily concealed in dry, underground ditches for a year without damage.

The success of the Irish potato was repeated all over Europe. The cultivation of New World plants helped lead Europe to world domination by greatly increasing its population, general health, and standard of living. Europe benefited more from New World foods than any other continent because its climate and rainfall were well suited for potatoes and maize.

Only when potatoes were fully incorporated into the Europe's diet could its inhabitants avoid the famines and periodic cycles of hunger that had stalked them since the little ice age began in the early fourteenth century. Ironically, as indigenous peoples succumbed by the tens of millions to European diseases, warfare, and adverse conditions, Europeans became healthier and more numerous by consuming potatoes and other foods from the New World.[10]

➤ 6 ◀

License My Roving Hands

Spain, Portugal, Britain, and France developed different justifications for their New World empires. Spain and Portugal used medieval religious doctrines to wage "just wars" against heathen and infidel peoples so they could become part of the "congregation of the faithful." Catholic France and Protestant England, however, considered Spain's global religious claims absurd and based their New World empires on the ancient Roman law principle of *terra nullius* [lands unoccupied by a sovereign state] or *vacuum domicilium* [vacant land]. Unoccupied territories, they argued, were the common property of humanity until properly put to use. Indians had migrated into uninhabited or uncultivated lands and could legitimately settle there because they were empty. But over the centuries, they had done little to improve their lands. Consequently, the New World was still unoccupied territory and open to European settlement. Although Britain and France rejected Spain's religious claims to the New World, their imperial philosophies were honed in debates with Spanish diplomats and their intensive study of Spanish texts on colonization. Not surprisingly, they came to similar conclusions about their right of conquest.

According to the influential seventeenth-century English philosopher John Locke, America was a "vacant place" and in a political "state of nature." Its indigenous peoples had property rights only to the products of their own labor and not to land they claimed as their own. As a result, Europeans could settle and acquire property by cultivation without the consent of the local inhabitants. If Indians objected, they were violating nature's laws and should be punished as "savage beasts" by those who were capable of transforming the land. In the pithy words of Locke, a strong proponent of English colonization, only by the "negation of Nature" could Europeans find "the way toward happiness."

140

The French also believed they had the right to possess regions "uninhabited and not possessed or ruled by any other Christian princes." The laws of nature permitted European countries to settle unoccupied pagan territories and establish their authority abroad, "by means of friendship and amicable agreements, if that can be done, or by force of arms, strong handed and all other hostile means" if necessary. The "consent and tuition of the said countries" was not a requirement, for France had the God-given authority to claim the territories of infidel nations.

Britain and France made these aggressive arguments because the New World's indigenous peoples had not yet been incorporated into Christian society. In Roanoke, Jamestown, and the Massachusetts Bay Colony, Indians were "the devil's minions," "beastly," and the "refuse of the world." This "rude, barbarous, and naked people" were "aliens to the holy covenant of God." Because they lived in "wastelands and woods," they were naked, ferocious, and uncivilized.

French descriptions of Canada's Indians were equally uncomplimentary. These "infidels" and "savages" enjoyed the "liberty of wild ass colts." Native communities had no laws or government. No one listened to the chiefs, children disobeyed their parents, and women were impudent and promiscuous. Especially from the Jesuits' perspective, Canada's Indian peoples were a frightening inversion of Christianity.

New France, which included the St. Lawrence River Valley, Acadia, the lower Mississippi River Valley, and the Ohio River Valley, was a commercial empire based on deerskins and furs. Since few French men and women migrated to Canada—New France had only 3,000 inhabitants in 1663—French settlements hugged the St. Lawrence River and a few strategic trading posts in the interior of North America. The French were completely reliant on native peoples, for Indians hunted deer, prepared furs, and performed many day-to-day tasks that enabled settlers to survive. The small number of French settlers and their dependence on Indian commodities made New France unique in the Western Hemisphere.

Although they made similar arguments in defense of colonization, Britain and France governed their colonies very differently. In the British empire, authority was never centralized and many British agencies had overlapping jurisdictions. The Board of Trade and Plantations, Treasury, Admiralty, War Office, and Parliament all had some control over the administration of the colonies. On the local level, colonial authority was also divided between elected and appointed officials and bicameral legislatures that represented both the aristocracy and local, popular interests. Britain's imperial administration developed out of England's economic growth, not as an extension of her monarchy.

France's New World colonies, in contrast, after 1663 were an extension of centralized monarchical power. The king appointed a military governor general, a civil administrator called an intendent, and a Catholic bishop to govern New France. Overseeing the colonies was an appointive sovereign council, which combined executive, legislative, and judicial functions. It was composed of the governor general, intendent, bishop, and five to seven siegneurs, who were aristocrats of great financial means charged with promoting immigration and governing French Canada. There were no elective assemblies in New France. Officials governed by command, just as did the French monarch.

Britain's North American colonies were quite different from the French and Spanish empires because they grew quickly as a result of European migration and from the beginning were oriented around agriculture and trade. For the English, access to what they saw as virginal, untamed land and not native labor was the focus of their colonization efforts. As the English poet John Donne rhapsodized:

> License my roving hands, and let them go,
> Behind, before, between, below.
> O my America! my new-found-land.

North America, in the eyes of the English, was ripe for conquest. The only barrier was indigenous peoples, who perversely would not readily submit to English sovereignty.

Unlike the Aztec and Inca empires, the conquest of North America took a long time. There were three basic reasons for this long, slow process of colonial incorporation. First, North American Indians had no knowledge of precious metals, and as a result, many of their lands at first seemed unprofitable to Europeans. Second, the Indians' low population densities in comparison to Mexico and Peru and the unwillingness of native peoples to submit to foreign rule meant that Britain and France could not establish *encomiendas* and other forms of forced Indian labor. And third, because indigenous peoples did not live in highly stratified states like the Aztec and Inca empires, Britain and France could not use existing economic and political structures like the Andean *ayllu* to exploit the land and its native peoples. In North America, Britain and France would have liked to establish tributary colonies like Spain, but the kinds of Indian societies they encountered necessitated different imperial strategies.

From the English perspective, the New World was a place for their own redemption, not the redemption of its current inhabitants. The English believed they had a providential role to play throughout North America in spreading the true gospel, but they were puzzled and angered that the Indians of Virginia and New England refused to abandon their own cultures for one so obviously superior. They quickly concluded that missionary work would succeed only after their colonies were firmly established.

With the founding of Jamestown and the Massachusetts Bay Colony, native peoples were given four stark choices: move out of the way; become slaves like most African Americans; survive within English society as despised, dependent, and dwindling peoples; or be killed. By displacing Indians and then rapidly modifying their environments, the English developed the most prosperous colonies in the New World. They failed, however, to convert many native peoples to Protestantism or English ways.

Despite different colonization patterns, the New World empires of Britain, France, Spain, and Portugal were based on strikingly similar attitudes about indigenous peoples. All European powers believed they were divinely charged to spread themselves into the barbaric parts of the globe. Colonialism would increase their glory and wealth while civilizing millions of heathenish savages living outside the Christian realm. Conquest would defeat the forces of darkness, hasten the redemption of humanity, and enable Europeans to acquire more wealth, which would further promote their colonization efforts.

Since the triumph of Christianity, Europeans had believed that their civilization with its earthy capital of Jerusalem was the *axis mundi* [the center of the world] where the sacred was manifested. The New World, in stark contrast, was a savage land lacking any moral purpose. Its pitiful inhabitants were human, but they dwelled outside the boundaries of civilized life. European powers had no doubt about their right to acquire non-Christian lands. Sovereignty was a concept asserted only against their rivals since indigenous peoples paradoxically lived in unoccupied territories. As an eminent English jurist said, all infidels were "perpetual enemies" because "between them, as with devils, whose subjects they be, and the Christians, there is perpetual hostility, and can be no peace."[1]

North America

Jamestown

About eight centuries ago, Algonquian-speaking Indians from the Great Lakes region migrated into the Potomac Valley and the Chesapeake Bay. Eventually, many small chiefdoms along Virginia's York and James Rivers and the eastern shore united into a larger chiefdom to protect itself from their enemies to the West. By the early seventeenth century, the Powhatans comprised about 15,000 people covering 6,000 square miles of territory.

The chiefdom was under the control of a powerful *mamanatowick* who had male *werowances* and female *werowansquas* to assist him. They controlled the production and distribution of large amounts of maize through tribute payments, community labor, and the domestic production of their wives. The *mananatowick* was constantly attended by servants, shamans, and personal bodyguards, and when he died his remains were preserved in distinctive mortuary temples.

In April 1607, three English ships with over 300 soldiers and settlers appeared at the mouth of Virginia's James River. The Jamestown colony had developed out of the failure of Walter Ralegh's Roanoke venture. After Ralegh was convicted of high treason in 1603, his Virginia patent reverted to the English Crown. Three years later, James I gave eager London and West County merchants a charter to establish another colony in Virginia.

The Virginia Company was patterned after commercial companies that had been chartered by the English Crown during the Middle Ages to promote trade in the Low Countries, the Baltic region, Russia, and the Levant. Like the Templars and Teutonic Knights, these trading companies were self-governing corporations with extremely broad powers. To attract settlers, the Virginia Company promised them free passage abroad, a share of the company's profits, and the opportunity to own land.

The new monarch hoped that "the true word, the service of God and Christian faith" would be preached in the New World to "beastly *Indians*, slaves to the Spaniards, refuse of the world, and as yet aliens to the holy covenant of God." The Virginia Company agreed, stating that one of its major goals was to propagate the "Christian religion to such People, as yet live in Darkness and miserable Ignorance of the true Knowledge and Worship of God." After all, as one minister argued, "the time was when wee were as savage and uncivill, and worshipped the divill, as now they do, then God sent some to make us civill, and others to make us christians." Just as outsiders had brought Christianity and civilization to a barbarous England, so the English would now uplift the Indians.

The Virginia Company's colonization plan came from men who had carefully studied Spain's legal and theological justifications for conquest while debating Spanish diplomats at the English court. Although the English did not use the Catholic doctrines to defend their New World colonial venture, their arguments were remarkably similar to the Spanish. Because the Indians were naked, ignorant, and heathenish savages, the English had the right to conquer them.

Just as the "rude and barbarous" Irish were being bludgeoned into an acknowledgment of "their duty to God and to us," so Indians would be taught to obey their proper masters. The Roanoke colony had failed to establish plantations in North Carolina, which were England's equivalent of the Spanish *encomienda*. Perhaps the Virginia Company would be more successful. They hoped to find gold and expected the Indians to feed them.

To his chagrin, the Spanish ambassador concluded that the merchants backing the Virginia Company had "actually made the ministers in their sermons dwell upon the importance of filling the world with their religion." He was wrong. No convincing by merchants was necessary. The Virginia Company was founded by nationalistic Protestants who wanted their colonial enterprise to be both a successful religious experiment and a profitable commercial plantation. Achieving both goals depended on securing the support of the Indians.

Around Jamestown, the Indian tidewater tribes were under the rule of an elderly *mamanatowick* named Powhatan, who wore a deerskin mantle ornamented with thirty-four shell circles surrounding a figure representing himself. The Powhatans wanted European technology but feared that the English would ally themselves with other Algonquian groups living west of the fall line of the Potomac River. Powhatan was especially worried about the Susquehanocks, who claimed the upper reaches of the Chesapeake Bay and regularly attacked his allies on the Patuxent and Potomac Rivers. As the English established themselves at Jamestown, the Susquehanocks moved southward along the bay to trade and intensify their raiding parties along the fringe of Powhatan's chiefdom.

Only twelve days after Jamestown was founded, hundreds of Powhatan's warriors attacked the colonists. When deadly English firepower repelled them, Powhatan, whom the English considered a "subtell owlde foxe," decided to give them maize in exchange for copper, beads, metal hoes, and metal utensils. His generosity, though, had its limits. For five years, Powhatan fought a bloody war to check the expansionist Virginia Company because he understood that the English coveted his land for mining and agriculture. He also knew that four years before the arrival of Virginia Company, English ships in the Chesapeake had kidnapped several of his people. To the day he died, Powhatan refused to become an English vassal and denied that England had sovereignty over his land.

The English also pursued a dual strategy in Virginia. While they hoped that a combination of trade and grim determination would win the friendship of Powhatan, they also forged alliances with his enemies and frequently used violence to intimidate him and other Indians. In the summer of 1610, for example, the English attacked a local village; killed over sixty men, women, and children; and burned their houses and corn fields. They captured a female village leader, her children, and a man and then cut off his head; killed the children by "Throweinge them overboard and shoteinge owtt their Braynes in the water," and stabbed the woman to death. When Pocahontas, the daughter of Powhatan, was kidnapped by the English to induce the *mamanatowick's* cooperation, the first phase of the Anglo-Powhatan War concluded in 1614 with her marriage to John Rolfe.

Although the English remained heavily dependent on Virginia's Indians for food as drought ravaged the Virginia coast, relations deteriorated steadily as both sides became involved in "vengeful perpetual warre." Smith never trusted Powhatan, especially after the *mananatowick* hinted that he had killed all the survivors of Ralegh's Roanoke Colony.

Besides, Smith fancied himself an English Cortés and looked forward to Powhatan's military defeat. Smith routinely kidnapped young Indian children before his arrival in local villages to conduct negotiations and behaved as if all Indians were savage, treacherous people whose "cheife God they worship is the Diuill."

As Jamestown slowly grew to almost 1,600 settlers by 1622, the Virginia Company escalated its demands against Opechancanough, Powhatan's brother and successor. Because they needed land to grow food and tobacco, colonists began arbitrarily annexing prime Powhatan farmland along the coast. Colonial expansion deprived the Powhatans of corn and restricted their access to valuable hunting and foraging areas.

On March 22, 1622, Opechancanough and his warriors attacked the struggling colony with English muskets and killed 347 settlers. Once the Indians were repulsed, the English concluded that "the way of conquering them is much more easy than of civilizing them by fair means, for they are a rude, barbarous, and naked people." They had to expel the Indians because it was "infinitely better to have no heathen among us, who at best were but a thorn in our sides, then to be at peace and league with them." The English were puzzled that "so cursed a nation" could be so "ungratefull to all benefitts."

The uprising of 1622 was a turning point in Jamestown's history, for it demonstrated to the English that they were still too weak to dominate the Indians surrounding them. In the wake of the attack, the English initiated a brutal policy of terrorism to rid the colony of Indians. By 1629, the English were strong enough to begin removing all Indians along the James and York River's southern peninsula.

On April 18, 1644, a desperate Opechancanough and his warriors again attacked the settlers with English firearms and killed about 400 colonists. The English retaliated, and two years later native peoples were so "rowted, slayne and dispersed" by the now populous settlers that the Powhatan chiefdom no longer existed. Formerly indigenous lands were divided into private property to be bought, sold, or used by settlers as investments. Without sufficient territory of their own, the Powhatans could no longer hunt, fish, grow crops, or maintain their independence. Reduced greatly in number by warfare, diseases, and dislocation, Indian survivors were forced to become tributaries of the royal colony of Virginia. The English even began choosing their *werowances*.

Although the Jamestown colonists did not find gold, John Rolfe taught the colonists how to raise tobacco, which thrived in Virginia's long, hot, and humid summers. In 1624, the colony raised 200,000 pounds of tobacco. Just a little more than ten years later, production had increased to 3 million pounds. As tobacco plantations began to dominate the Chesapeake landscape, Indians either vacated the region, lived on English plantations, or survived on small reservations. The native population precipitously declined from about 15,000 in 1607 to just 2,000 about sixty years later. By 1675, there were 44,000 English settlers and slaves.

Some warriors hunted and fished for the English. Others became indentured servants or were enslaved by settlers to labor next to recently imported African slaves, who comprised a small but growing number of laborers. At Jamestown, the English successfully transplanted the plantation system into the New World that they had originally developed in Ireland. Based on African slave labor, the plantation system would become the economic mainstay of the South until the Civil War. As did the Portuguese in Brazil, England turned to Africa as its major source of coerced plantation labor in North America and the Caribbean because too many native peoples perished from European diseases, made poor slaves in comparison to Africans, and violently resisted becoming wards of the English.

At Jamestown, the English had articulated a compelling justification for colonization that would carry them throughout North America. If Indians were depraved enough to resist their rightful masters, then force would make them reasonable. God's means would always be inscrutable, but the English thought it was their manifest destiny to plant colonies in North America. "So then here," said Smith with great pride, is a "nurse for souldiers, a practice for marriners, a trade for marchants, a reward for the good, and that which is most of all, a businesse (most acceptable to God) to bring such poore infidels to the true knowledge of God and his holy Gospell."

Smith was right about everything except conversion. As a result of vicious warfare, the English concluded that Virginia's Indians would forever remain "poore infidels" because they were savage "Outlaws of Humanity." For reasons only He knew, God had hardened their treacherous hearts against His loyal servants and inexplicably closed their ears to the sweet sounds of Protestantism.

War was brutal and costly, but as one Jamestown colonist happily noted, it was also very moral and rewarding. "We, who hitherto have had possession of no more ground then their waste, and our purchase . . . may now by right of Warre, and law of Nations, invade the Country, and destroy them who sought to destroy us; whereby we shall enjoy their cultivated places." Before, the English had grubbed in the woods. Now, however, "all their villages (which are situate in the fruitfullest places of the land) shall be inhabited by us."

This object lesson in colonial relations was not lost on England's Puritans. Even before they left for the New World in 1630, Puritans had concluded that their neighbors would be "barbarous, inhumane, insolent, and bloody." The Jamestown venture had convinced them that only violence would transform North American Indians from the savage state to civility.[2]

The Erotic New World

Beginning with Christopher Columbus, who depicted paradise in the New World as a "round ball, on part of which is something like a woman's nipple," European males often described the Western Hemisphere as a virginal woman ready for seduction and possession by virile men like themselves. The English waxed the most amorous when they considered the bountiful treasures awaiting them abroad. In 1587, Richard Hakluyt, one of Elizabethan England's most influential proponents of empire, encouraged Walter Ralegh in his Virginian colonization efforts with these words: "If you persevere only a little longer in your constancy, your bride will shortly bring forth new and most abundant offspring, such as will delight you and yours, and cover with disgrace and shame those who have so often dared rashly and impudently to charge her with barrenness."

Several years later, Ralegh described Guiana with a similar ardor. Guiana, he wrote, "is a country that hath yet her maidenhead, never sacked, turned, nor wrought, the face of the earth hath not been torn, nor the virtue and salt of the soil spent by manurance, the graves have not been opened for gold, the mines not broken with sledges, nor their images pulled down out of their temples. It hath never been entered by any army of strength, and never conquered by any Christian prince."

The most poetic description of the New World as a woman ready for European penetration, however, came from the poet John Donne in his "Elegie: Going to Bed":

> License my roving hands, and let them go,
> Behind, before, between, below.
> O my America! my new-found-land,

148

My kingdome, safeliest when with one man man'd,
My Myne of precious stones: My Emperie,
How blest am I in this discovering thee!
To enter in these bonds, is to be free;
Then where my hand is set, my seal shall be.

As the witty Donne understood, European colonization could never be separated from male sexual fantasies of ravishment, possession, and domination.

Note: Christopher Columbus, *The Four Voyages*, trans. J.M. Cohen (New York: Penguin Books, 1969), p. 218; Louis Montrose, "The Work of Gender in the Discourse of Discovery," *Representations* 33 (1991): 1–41; Annette Kolodny, *The Land Before Her: Fantasy and Experience of the American Frontiers, 1630–1860* (Chapel Hill: University of North Carolina Press, 1984), pp. 3–4; Richard Hakluyt, *Voyages and Discoveries: The Principal Navigations, Voyages, Traffiques, and Discoveries of the English Nation*, ed. Jack Beeching (Harmondsworth, UK: Penguin Books, 1972), pp. 408–409; John T. Shawcross, ed., *The Complete Poetry of John Donne* (Garden City, NY: Anchor Books, 1967), p. 58.

Canada's Fur Trading Frontier

The fur trade between Canada's Indians and Europe began informally on the Atlantic coast when European ships visited Newfoundland's Grand Banks during the early sixteenth century in search of cod. When the French explorer Jacques Cartier entered the St. Lawrence River in 1534, the Micmacs literally traded the furs off their backs for French merchandise.

In 1588, two of Cartier's nephews petitioned their sovereign for a monopoly on the fur trade in the St. Lawrence Gulf, and by 1678 the French were shipping almost 80,000 beaver pelts a year from Quebec to be made into hats. Furs gradually replaced fish and timber as the foundation of New France's economy because the trade was extremely beneficial both to Indians and French merchants. From France's perspective, furs seemed an ideal item to export. They were completely unavailable in Europe, light in weight, easy and inexpensive to transport by water, and existed in abundant quantities along eastern Canada's many creeks and rivers. The French also could carry on a thriving trade with few permanent settlers or debilitating wars of conquest.

For thousands of years, Canada's Indians had hunted and trapped animals during the winter when their fur was thickest. Beaver was by far their most important source, but they also killed muskrat, otter, mink, fisher, marten, deer, antelope, bison, elk, moose, and caribou. By wearing and sleeping in the skinned pelts for about 15 months, they loosened the long outer "guard hairs" and left the soft underfur and a malleable leather. They also created "parchment" beaver from skins that were dried in the sun once a beaver had been skinned.

Canadian natives were as enthusiastic about the fur trade as their French counterparts. "The beaver," the Montagnais amusingly observed, "does everything perfectly well, it makes kettles, hatchets, swords, knives, bread." The Hurons called the French *gens du fer* [iron people] and thought that only the king and the greatest warriors of France had the power to fashion such marvelous items as pots, axes, and knives.

For the French, the fur trade was a highly profitable trading venture. Chiefs, in contrast, led fur trading expeditions lasting three or four months to undertake exciting adventures, display their prowess, raise their social status, and demonstrate their generosity by redistributing attractive French goods to their followers. Other Indians acted similarly, sharing European goods or using them in burial ceremonies. Trading European goods for furs also cemented military alliances, promoted intermarriage among French and Indians, and established peaceful social relationships in a volatile environment where commerce and violence often were intertwined. In the beginning, the fur trade did not turn Indians into capitalists.

In fact, both the French and English were puzzled by the seemingly irrational economic behavior of Canada's eastern Indians. Native peoples tried to get the best price for their furs in order to purchase European goods with the least amount of effort. They had no desire to hoard or accumulate goods but instead redistributed them to kin and clans or simply gave them away. Eastern Canada was not London or Paris, and native communities were not places where anonymous buyers and sellers exchanged money for goods. Throughout the sixteenth and seventeenth centuries, most eastern Canadian Indians lived outside a market economy, and their reasons for acquiring goods were very different from their European trading partners.

New France's fur trading empire relied on Indian trappers and middlemen and French *voyageurs,* who transported European items to Indian villages in exchange for furs. England's Canadian fur trading empire, in contrast, emerged in 1670 under the direction of a monopolistic joint-stock trading enterprise called the Hudson's Bay Company (HBC) that answered only to the Crown. Before 1763, the HBC built permanent trading posts at the mouths of rivers emptying into James and Hudson Bay to exchange furs for liquor, guns, and metal tools.

Although the furs exchanged with the HBC were calculated in British sterling, Indians neither used nor understood the value of currency. Consequently, the English created a system of measurement that they applied both to furs and goods called "made beaver," which was set by the company's directors in London. The company made handsome profits by using inaccurate measuring standards for tobacco and by watering down the large quantities of brandy consumed by Indians.

When Indians arrived at a trading post with furs, an elaborate gift-giving ceremony preceded any transactions. Both parties welcomed each other with long speeches before the English provided brandy, clothing, guns, and other gifts to Indian leaders as a reward for patronizing their post. Then they exchanged a pipe of peace and friendship and began their bargaining speeches in English. Indian leaders emphasized their loyalty and desire to be treated fairly.

HBC officials, in turn, thanked the Indians for their furs and exhorted them to avoid the French, whose merchandise they claimed was inferior. After the rate of exchange was accepted, individual Indians bartered with the English using a combination of pity, pleas to bargain fairly, and thinly veiled threats to go elsewhere if the transaction was unsatisfactory. Once the bargaining ended, the Indians left the trading post and were given most of the gifts their leaders had received.

On the surface, the fur trade between indigenous peoples and Europeans benefited both parties. But there was also a darker side to the process of exchange. As the fur trade intensified, deadly diseases, alcoholic consumption, warfare, economic dependency, and the degradation of the native ecosystem gradually weakened the Indians of Canada. Over time, the fur trade forever changed the Indians' traditional world.

The introduction of lethal European diseases was the first and most destructive result of the fur trade. To the east, the Micmacs believed that since the French "mingle with and carry on trade with them, they are dying fast." Fur-trading networks rapidly spread contagious diseases throughout Canada, decimating Indian peoples who had never been exposed to deadly Old World microbes. Many chiefs and elders died, taking with them their traditional religious knowledge and hard-won ways of coping with disasters.

Although the Indians of eastern Canada may have been ravaged by European diseases in the sixteenth century, the first recorded epidemic occurred in 1634. It probably began in the St. Lawrence Valley when French ships arrived in June. By the next month, large numbers of Montagnais were dying from either measles, smallpox, or influenza. The French recovered quickly from this outbreak, but Canada's Indians were not as fortunate. In August of 1636, an influenza epidemic first appeared in the St. Lawrence Valley and reached the Hurons one month later. Over the next 400 years, the Hurons were buffeted further by scarlet fever and smallpox epidemics.

Before the arrival of the French, a typical Huron family had between five and eight members. After the epidemics, usually only three family members survived. From 1634 to 1640, the Hurons lost about 10,000 men, women, and children to European diseases, or half their population.

Alcohol, another by-product of the fur trade, also had a pernicious effect on Indian life. At first, visiting fishing fleets bartered alcohol for fur pelts. Later, New France provided 20,000 pints of brandy each year in exchange for furs. The English also distributed generous amounts of rum and brandy from their HBC trading posts. As one Frenchman sadly observed about Canada's eastern Indians in 1632, "at first it needed only a little wine or brandy to make them drunk. But at present, and since they have frequented the fishing vessels, they drink in quite another fashion." Because liquor was a costly, bulky item to transport, most Indians did not use ardent spirits regularly. But as the fur trade intensified and merchants found ways to bring large quantities of liquor into the back country, alcohol helped lead to the disintegration of native societies. Liquor introduced another unsettling element into Indian societies already under great stress.

While disease and alcohol were buffeting Indians in eastern Canada, warfare became more frequent and deadly as a result of the fur trade. The growing availability of European flintlock and matchlock muskets, pistols, explosives, metal hatchets and knives, swords, and brass and iron arrowheads made fighting more destructive. Increasingly, native peoples began fighting with each other to expand their hunting territories.

As casualty rates increased from warfare and European diseases, northeastern Indians fought more "mourning wars" to replace deceased men, women, and children in their communities. At the same time, native peoples, especially the Iroquois, started deadly wars with their rivals to control fur trade routes, for without furs they could not acquire European goods.

Even scalping increased as both the French and English offered attractive bounties for the deaths of their enemies. When Cartier visited the Stadaconans in 1535, they proudly showed him Micmac "skins of five men's heads, stretched on hoops, like parchment." By 1688, Canada's governor was offering ten beaver skins for each enemy Indian scalp while the English made similar proposals.

In the eighteenth century, liberal scalp bounties brought perpetual warfare to the fur-trading frontier. English bounties for one Abenaki scalp increased from 50 pounds sterling in the late seventeenth century to 300 pounds by 1757. Steel knives acquired through the fur trade also made scalping easier and more profitable.

As the fur trade intensified, Indians became more dependent on European goods. Indigenous peoples had less time to hunt, fish, and gather wild plants because they increased the length of their winter beaver hunting and summer trading with Europeans. Although their traditional subsistence patterns did not disappear, the fur trade led to periodic food shortages in many native communities, especially during the winter. Local foods were replaced with less nutritious foreign items such as biscuits, flour meal, dried peas, and liquor, which Indians purchased by exchanging furs for foodstuffs.

As Canada's Indians were exposed to European diseases, alcohol, international warfare, and an international market economy, they began behaving in new and more aggressive ways toward their environment. Among the indigenous societies of eastern Canada, there had always been strong sanctions against excessive hunting. Because humans and animals were involved in a symbiotic and beneficial relationship, animals had to be propitiated with prayers and ceremonies before they allowed themselves to be killed by hunters.

Soon after the arrival of Europeans on the Atlantic coast, however, Indians began slaughtering furbearing animals in great numbers in complete violation of the ancient spiritual compact. Wherever the French and English established Canadian trading posts, Indians, not Europeans, destroyed most of game.

European technology probably played a role in this transformation of traditional hunting practices. With guns and metal fish hooks, knives, swords, arrowheads, and harpoons, Indians became better hunters. European digging tools, axes, and ice chisels also enabled Indians to supply more furs for the international market.

Attractive European goods such as textiles and kettles, which could only be obtained with furs, might also have spurred them to kill the plentiful wildlife around them. As gift giving soon turned into a straightforward market transaction, Indians hunted animals to extinction to obtain foreign commodities. This occurred from the eastern woodlands of Canada to the lower Mississippi Valley.

Finally, disease may have played a role in changing Indian attitudes towards animals. As native peoples mysteriously died in great numbers, and their shamans, rituals, and medicines proved powerless to protect them, their traditional place in nature changed. The natural environment inexplicably became more hostile, and as a result, they may have become less respectful toward the animals they once had honored and supplicated with prayers.[3]

Deserted Shores

In the winter of 1620, Pilgrim colonists led by William Bradford landed on the Massachusetts coast and to their surprise encountered an English-speaking Patuxet named Squanto. He had probably met European explorers on their New England voyages before being kidnapped by the English in 1605. After he returned home in 1614, he was captured again by the English and sold into Spanish slavery before escaping to England. When Squanto returned home, almost all his people had been decimated by European diseases. From the Penobscot Bay in Maine to Cape Cod, almost 90 percent of New England's coastal Indians had died, probably from plague and hepatitis.

Squanto's village fields were covered with weeds, and unburied bodies lay everywhere. The Indians, wrote one astonished Englishman in 1622, "died on heapes, as they lay in their houses." Their bones "made such a spectacle after my coming into those partes, that, as I travailed in the forrest nere the Massachusetts, it seemed to me a new found Golgotha."

Note: Neal Salisbury, "Squanto: Last of the Patuxets," in *Struggle and Survival in Colonial America,* eds. David G. Sweet and Gary B. Nash (Berkeley: University of California Press, 1981), pp. 231–236; Alfred W. Crosby, Jr., *The Columbian Exchange: Biological and Cultural Consequences of 1492* (Westport, CT: Greenwood Press, 1972), p. 42; Dean Snow and Kim M. Lanphear, "European Contact and Indian Depopulation in the Northeast: The Timing of the First Epidemics," *Ethnohistory* 35, no. 1 (1988): 15–33.

Land, Sovereignty, and the Pequot War

When the Puritans landed on the Massachusetts coast in 1630, they saw themselves as England's righteous vanguard abroad. These religious nonconformists, who yearned to purge the Anglican Church of its Catholic influences, left England to create a model Christian commonwealth that would compel other colonists to "say of succeeding plantations: 'The Lord make it like that of New England.'"

From the beginning of their venture, Puritans had an ambivalent attitude toward New England's Indians. The early seal of the Massachusetts Bay Company (MBC) optimistically pictured a stoic, scantily clothed Indian male armed with a bow and arrow framed by two trees saying "Come over and help us." The Puritans' charter also claimed that one of its goals was to "wynn and incite the Natives . . . to the Knowledg and Obedience of the onlie true God and Savior of Mankinde, and the Christian Fayth."

They were prepared to undertake missionary activities, but Puritans fully expected that the example of a righteous Christian community would be sufficient to rescue the Indians from their barbarism. As one minister confidently predicted, commerce and the example of our "course of living cannot but in time breed civility among them."

With Jamestown in mind, however, the Puritans were unwilling to wait years and to sacrifice their lives trying to convince Indians that they should emulate their betters. From the moment Puritans landed in Massachusetts, they argued that Massachusetts was a virgin wilderness, a *vacuum domicilium*, and thus open to settlement. The present inhabitants, Puritans contended, possessed no titles, deeds, fences, civil government, and institutions of private property.

Because the native population had not improved the land, they had no natural right to it, and because they possessed no government like that of European nations, they had no sovereignty over it either. Eventually, Puritans would claim that the Indians had no real property except through grants issued by the MBC. The land belonged to those who could use it best, as defined by the English.

Underlying these arguments was a barely concealed contempt for native peoples. Even before the Puritans landed in New England, their leader John Winthrop already was dispossessing the Indians. Contemplating the Puritan's New Canaan, he asked himself and his supporters by "what warrant have we to take that land, which is and hath been of long time possessed of others the sons of Adam?" He supplied four reassuring answers.

First, Christians should "have liberty to go and dwell amongst them in their wastelands and woods (leaving them such places as they have manured for their corn) as lawfully as Abraham did among the Sodomites." Indians once had a natural right to their lands when "men held the earth in common," but this natural right had long been superseded by a civil right to property, which Puritans and not the Indians possessed because of their Christian culture.

Winthrop's other three reasons were so obvious that he felt no need to explain them. "There is more than enough for them and us. . . . God hath consumed the natives with a miraculous plague, whereby the greater part of the country is left void of inhabitants. . . . We shall come in with good leave of the natives." With this kind of reasoning, Puritans concluded that the Indians were "the veriest ruins of mankind" who blocked the "passing to the Promised Land."

Abroad the flagship *Arbella* on the voyage to Massachusetts Bay, Winthrop lectured his followers about the task before them. To become "a city upon a hill," they would have to understand the Lord's conception of the ideal society. "God Almighty, in His most holy and wise providence, hath so disposed of the condition of mankind, as in all times some must be rich, some poor, some high and eminent in power and dignity, others mean and in subjection."

Puritan New England, according to Winthrop, would be a land bounded by private property, a rigid class structure sharply dividing rich and poor, and ruled by the most powerful. Even before the *Arbella* landed, conflict between Indians and Puritans was inevitable because they had diametrically opposite understandings about the proper organization and ends of society.

In the MBC, land was treated as a private commodity that could be sold in a market economy, preferably after it had been "improved." The Indians also recognized property, but they limited its acquisition and administered it quite differently than the English. Individuals might possess their own clothes and tools, but the community controlled its carefully delineated land.

As the prominent English colonist Roger Williams observed, the "*Natives* are very exact and punctuall in the bounds of their Lands, belonging to this or that Prince or People." Families by common agreement used land for hunting, fishing, and farming, but they could not alienate it from community control. New England's native population resolutely refused to treat land as a commodity.

Puritan settlers introduced a radically new ecology that started with the clearing of New England's bountiful forests for farmlands, buildings, fences, ships, barrels, tanning operations, and especially fuel, which required an acre of forest each year for a typical English household. In fact, the prosperity of the MBC depended on timber seized from Indian lands. The timber trade to Barbados, Newfoundland, the Canary Islands, Madiera, the Azores, Portugal, and Spain quickly became New England's most profitable industry, providing about half of the colony's total exports.

Native peoples often told Williams that the English must have come to their land looking for fuel. "It is because you want *firing*," they said, and "are faine to follow the *wood*; and so to remove to a fresh new place for the *woods* sake." By the 1680s, over a half million acres of forests had been cleared by English settlers for farmland, pastures, industry, and exports. In a remarkably brief period of time, settlers recreated the treeless landscape of their homeland in New England.

As a result of deforestation, many animal and plant species disappeared, water runoff, flooding, and erosion increased, streams dried up, and the region became colder during the winter and hotter and drier in the summer. The traditional food chain was rapidly modified. English sawmills blocked fish runs and clogged rivers with floating and sunken logs. As standing water replaced forests, the anopheles mosquito found new breeding grounds. By the late seventeenth century, many New Englanders began suffering from malaria—the "ague," "fever," and "chills" of colonial America.

Once the forest was cleared, the English began bounding their property with fences to grow maize and grain and raise domesticated animals such as sheep, horses, oxen, pigs, and cows. Livestock required up to ten times the acreage as farm land and soon came to dominate the new landscape. Grazing animals crowded out the human population and made the land seem cramped and inadequate.

At first, the Puritans imitated the farming techniques of New England's

Indians. They really had no other choice. As in Virginia, the MBC had unreliable supply lines to England, and their settlers could not at first grow enough food for themselves. Fortunately for them, neighboring Indians were very willing to trade food for European goods and to teach them how to grow maize. Even more fortunately, many fertile corn fields fell under English control because numerous Indian communities had been wiped out by diseases before the Puritans arrived in Massachusetts Bay.

The colonial New England system of farming combined indigenous and European agricultural techniques through a four-step process: clearing woodlands by girdling trees like the Indians; growing Indian corn, squash, and beans together; using a traditional European three-field crop rotation for grains; and converting uplands into pasture. Although this was a profitable synthesis of New World and European techniques, it was an ecological disaster for Indians.

Once New England's natural resources became marketable goods, traditional native subsistence patterns were severely disrupted. As the forests quickly disappeared, so did many plants and wildlife. Marauding livestock destroyed Indian corn and clogged Indian animal traps, and fenced fields made hunting, fishing, and gathering impossible. New England maps reflected the growing power of the settlers on the land as traditional Indian names and boundaries were replaced by English place names and new jurisdictions.

The MBC even passed an ordinance making it illegal to shoot a gun "on any unnecessary occasion, or at any game except an Indian or a wolf." Like the region's wildlife, native New Englanders were quickly becoming an endangered species.

This situation was clearly understood by the Indians. As Miantonomo, a Narragansett sachem allied with the English, pointed out, when the English arrived "our fathers had plenty of deer and skins, our plains were full of deer, as also our woods, and of turkies, and our coves full of fish and fowl. But these English having gotten our land, they with scythes cut down the grass, and with axes fell the trees; their cows and horses eat the grass, and their hogs spoil our clam banks, and we shall all be starved." One year after making this statement, the English arranged his murder by a rival tribe. In New England, Indians rapidly became superfluous once the fur trade declined along the coast. They were disposable, just like the environment.

The first major military conflict between New England's native population and the Puritans came in 1637. The Pequot War stemmed from a combination of Indian belligerence and the Bay Colony's desire for complete sovereignty over the lower Connecticut River Valley. In 1632, the Dutch West India Company purchased a parcel of land from the Pequots for a trading post on the Connecticut River. The Dutch wanted to trade European goods for shell beads [wampum] produced in southern New England and then trade the wampum for Iroquois and Mahican furs in Albany. A Dutch trading post alarmed the English, who coveted the land for themselves and wanted to dominate the region's fur and wampum trade.

The Pequots, however, quickly violated their agreement by attacking the Dutch and the Narragansetts, a nearby rival visiting the trading post. They also kidnapped English colonists and tortured them to death. Pequot pugnacity frightened not only the MBC, but also the native peoples of southern New England, who looked to the Dutch and English for protective alliances against their bellicose neighbor.

As hostilities increased between the Dutch and Pequots, they decided to ally themselves with the MBC, hoping that they could trade wampum and other goods with the Puritans and convince them to mediate their dispute with the Narragansetts. After lengthy negotiations, in 1634 the Pequots agreed to a treaty that promoted trade and generously allowed the MBC to establish settlements along the Connecticut River. The Pequots, like the Powhatans of Virginia, were in a terrible bind. In less than a decade, they had been devastated by a smallpox epidemic that reduced their numbers by almost 80 percent. The survivors wanted European goods, but they fully understood that the English intended to subjugate them.

Relations between the Pequots and Puritans were never amicable. In July 1636, the Puritans accused the Pequots of murdering a settler named John Oldham on Block Island. Although the Naragansetts actually committed the crime, Winthrop and his council decided to punish both the Narragansetts, who had already revenged Oldham's death, and the Pequots, who had shocked the Bay Colony by killing almost a dozen English settlers. The Bay Colony's goals were very clear. Boston wanted to control Block Island and make "that insolent and barbarous nation, called the Pequots" their tributaries.

Troops attacked Block Island and then moved into Connecticut. In two major battles, the Puritans and their southern New England Indian allies slaughtered the Pequots, who had been besieging a Connecticut fort. On May 26, 1637, about ninety English soldiers and their Mohegan and Narragansett allies attacked a palisaded Pequot fort near the Mystic River. First the soldiers fired a deadly volley of gunfire, and then they burned the fort to the ground. Pequot men, women, and children who escaped the inferno were cut down by soldiers surrounding the structure. About 500 Pequots died. Only twenty-two English soldiers were killed or wounded.

The Naragansetts were so horrified at the killing of hundreds of defenseless Pequot women and children that they withdrew from the war. A week before the battle, they had asked the MBC "that women and children be spared," and during the slaughter they begged the English to show mercy.

The Puritans, however, felt no guilt about their military tactics and saw the hand of God in their great victory. The "devil's minions" had been vanquished.

"When a people is grown to such a height of blood," said one of the victorious commanders, "and sin against God and man, and all confederates in the action, there he hath no respect to persons." Sometimes Scripture demonstrated that "women and children must perish with their parents. Sometimes the case alters; but we will not dispute it now. We have sufficient light from the Word of God for our proceedings."

According to John Mason, another military leader, it pleased God "to give us their Land for an Inheritance." William Bradford, leader of the nearby Plymouth Colony, made similarly effusive comments about the slaughter of the Pequots. In the British colonies, God would always be an avenging real estate agent.

Armed conflict with the Pequots introduced a new military concept into New England that had first been used in Virginia—total warfare. Until 1637, violent clashes among New England's Indians were frequent but brief because their military aims were quite limited. Once they claimed victory, warriors usually returned to their villages with a few scalps and captives, for they lacked the will or ability to keep large numbers of warriors in the field. As one Puritan leader scornfully said, Indian combat seemed "more for pastime than to conquer and subdue enemies," for "they might fight seven years and not kill seven men."

The English, however, were not interested in simple acts of revenge against individuals. They wanted complete victory over their enemies and even felt insulted because the Pequots refused to engage them in open field battles. The Puritan response was a calculated campaign of extermination and terror. Because Puritan military objectives were so broad—the annihilation of their enemies—they killed large numbers of men, women, and children and destroyed whole villages.

By the end of the conflict, almost half the Pequots—about 1,500 men, women, and children—had died. Less than one-quarter of their sachems lived through the war. The survivors gradually rebuilt their communities in southern New England, and the Mohegans and Narragansetts eagerly adopted Pequot women and children into their communities. They were delighted that the Pequots were no longer a threat to them and used the war to augment their populations.

The Puritans discouraged the adoption of survivors, but they could not prevent it. According to the 1638 Treaty of Hartford, the Pequots ceased to exist as a people. The English indentured some young Pequot boys as servants and sold others as slaves to the West Indies. Most Pequot land was annexed by the colonies of Connecticut and Massachusetts.

Despite their losses, the Pequots managed to survive as a people with a distinct identity. As they slowly reconstituted themselves, the Pequots became loyal to the English and fought with them four decades later against their Indian enemies. In 1983, the Pequots became a federally recognized tribe and today possess reservation land in eastern Connecticut. Despite their crushing military defeat in 1637, they have maintained their communal identity for over three centuries.

The brief and bloody war of extermination had served its purpose. The MBC emerged as the most powerful English colony in New England, the Pequots were silenced, and southern New England Indians were awed into submission. To survive, they sold much of their ancestral domains, paid the English tribute in wampum, and formally recognized the sovereignty of their new masters. The Puritans exchanged the roughly 7 million wampum beads in tribute payments they received over the next thirty years for furs in northern New England, which helped make Massachusetts Bay a profitable colony.

Now the Puritans could create special Indian courts to attack Indian behavior that did not conform to their beliefs. Because New England's Indians were "brutish men, which range up and down little otherwise than wild beasts," the English had a solemn responsibility to use fines, whippings, and hangings to teach them Protestant manners. In the wake of the Pequot War, the steady enlargement of colonial legal jurisdiction over once sovereign native peoples signified the triumph of the English in southern New England.[4]

Montagnais Women and the Jesuits

When the Society of Jesus, or the Jesuits, came to New France in 1632, they had a well-deserved reputation as the shock troops of Roman Catholicism, the Church's "soldiers of God beneath the banner of the cross" in the words of Pope Julius III. In China, India, and Tibet, the Jesuits spent many decades futilely trying to convert the ruling elites. In the New World, their goal was equally bold and ambitious. Jesuit priests intended to live among the Indians and convert them to Catholicism.

After the Jesuits reached Quebec, they concentrated on the Montagnais-Naskapsis, a mobile hunting and foraging people who lived in the southern Labrador peninsula. Although they sometimes clashed with the French, the Montagnais wanted European goods and military protection against hostile Iroquois. As a result, they agreed to support Jesuit missionaries in their villages as a visible sign of their alliance and friendship with France.

When the Jesuits began proselytizing among the Indians, they encountered an intellectual obstacle unknown in their Asian missionary activities. According to them, all the words for "piety, devotion, virtue; all terms that are used to express things of the other life, the language of Theologians, Philosophers, Mathematicians and Physicians, in a word, of all learned men; all words which refer to the regulation and governance of a city, Province or Empire; all that concerns justice, reward and punishment; the names of an infinite number of arts which are in Europe . . . are never found in the thought or upon the lips of the savages."

Once Jesuit priests moved into Montagnais communities, they also complained about another serious problem. Their hosts did not believe in hierarchy and obedience. "They imagine," said Father Paul Le Jeune, "that they ought by right of birth, to enjoy the liberty of wild ass colts, rendering no homage to anyone whatsoever, except when they like. They have reproached me a hundred times because we fear our Captains, while they laugh at and make sport of theirs. All the authority of their chief is in his tongue's end; for he is powerful insofar as he is eloquent; and, even if he kills himself talking and haranguing, he will not be obeyed unless he pleases the Savages." From the Jesuits' perspective, anarchy reigned in Montagnais villages.

Fathers had very little authority, children happily disobeyed their parents, and no one was punished for their misdeeds. The French saved their severest condemnations for Montagnais women, whom they considered "firebrands of Hell" because of their haughty independence and sexual freedom. The Jesuits were shocked that Montagnais women did not conform to the subordinate role Aristotle, Thomas Aquinas, and God had chosen for them. Montagnais women were the allies of Satan because they would not act meekly and obey their fathers and husbands.

To eliminate these evil habits, the Jesuits developed an ambitious four-part missionary program. First, the Jesuits wanted Montagnais communities to end their seasonal migrations and establish permanent agricultural villages under the direction of a powerful chief. Second, the Jesuits tried to make the Montagnais feel guilty about their frequent misbehavior. Third, Le Jeune and his colleagues dreamed of separating malleable children from their indulgent parents for training in strict Jesuit boarding schools.

And last, the Jesuits wanted to subordinate Montagnais women. Under their stern but benevolent direction, Christian husbands would learn to rule their wives and children, reject divorce, and enforce chastity before marriage and sexual monogamy afterwards. "Heaven and a little grace," they predicted, "are stronger and more powerful than the cannons and arms of kings and monarchs, which could not subdue them." Because the Montagnais possessed the ability to reason, the Jesuits optimistically believed they could be weaned from their mistaken beliefs and customs.

In their frequent reports home, the Jesuits candidly described their struggles with the Montagnais. At first, they encountered a great deal of resistance.

But as the Jesuits began making conversions, some Montagnais began treating their women differently. Once Le Jeune asked a convert why he permitted his baptized wife to live separately from him. The man responded that "he had tried all sorts of means to make her return to her duty," but had failed. Le Jeune convinced the husband and his supporters that the erring wife should be taken by canoe to Quebec and thrown into prison for her disobedience.

When he attempted to capture the young woman, "some Pagan young men, observing this violence . . . made use of threats, declaring that they would kill any one who laid a hand on the woman." But the Christian Montagnais told them "there was nothing that they would not do or endure, in order to secure obedience to God," which "silenced the infidels." When the woman realized her hopeless situation, she humbly begged for forgiveness and promised to be obedient. "The Infidels," Le Jeune concluded, were finally learning "the importance of exercising justice."

The Jesuits recorded plenty of deathbed baptisms, indifference, aggressive hostility, and backsliding, but in just a few decades they convinced many Montagnais to adopt a very restrictive Christian code of personal conduct emphasizing sin, guilt, and submission to Crown and Church. Perhaps most important for the Jesuits, they succeeded in making Montagnais women into objects of male fear and aggression. This radically new culture represented a dramatic rupture in the once egalitarian life of the Montagnais.

When the French first arrived in Canada, the Montagnais and other native peoples had a very low opinion of them because they seemed such poor hunters, trappers, and canoeists. Native peoples also rejected French political and social behavior and were contemptuous of the way Frenchmen treated their wives. As the Montagnais became more involved in the international fur trade, however, French and Jesuit influence increased. By about 1625, the Montagnais wore French woolen clothing, used French cooper kettles and iron axes, purchased French longboats to travel on the St. Lawrence River, hunted with French guns, and bought French crackers, biscuits, maize, and dried foods. Since the Jesuits functioned as fur traders and distributors of guns and food in New France, the Montagnais had to rely on them.

At the same time, virulent epidemic diseases brought by the French heightened warfare over the control of fur trading routes, and alcohol weakened the Montagnais. As their elders and traditional ways of life disappeared, they lost their sense of confidence and communal ethos. As one Jesuit happily noted in 1646, "this little people was very proud; but God, wishing to incline it to receive his Son, has humbled it by diseases which have almost entirely exterminated it. These blows, nevertheless, are beneficent. . . . They have given themselves up to Jesus Christ."

European diseases helped change the Montagnais kinship structure to the detriment of women. As many of their relatives died or converted to Catholicism, women lost the support of male relatives and the ability to augment their families by adopting war captives. Once women became more isolated in dwindling Montagnais communities, Jesuit priests and their converts could force them to conform to French notions about proper behavior. By contrast, Montagnais in isolated northern Labrador maintained their traditional kinship structures, and their women continued to exercise great independence.

The Montagnais also became a more fractious society after the Jesuits began making conversions. As they became divided between a militant minority Christian faction and a majority of traditionalists, Montagnais solidarity was broken, and collective action became more difficult. When converts placed the spiritual salvation of their souls above the good of the community, the Montagnais became more distrustful of each other. The inability to act collectively greatly strengthened the missionaries and their new allies.

Catholicism also became acceptable to growing numbers of Montagnais because the Jesuits wisely allowed them to blend their new religion with traditional practices. Indians still consulted shamans for illnesses, used amulets and charms to ward off evils spirits and diseases, believed in the power of dreams, and celebrated traditional festivals. When the priests were not looking, Montagnais performed libations when they ate or drank and sacrificed animals before going to war. In the forests outside their villages, deer and moose were still hunted using age-old prayers and rituals. Many Montagnais who sincerely converted to Catholicism still honored their ancestors' ways.

But these Jesuits were not simply French priests. Among the Montagnais and other eastern Canadian peoples, Father Le Jeune and his colleagues were considered magicians and conjurers with great spiritual powers. As Montagnais died from smallpox and measles, their shamans could neither cure nor explain these frightening illnesses. When the Montagnais lost their power to heal, some converted to Christianity because they believed that "all our ill-luck comes to us because we do not pray to God." In Montagnais society, only spiritually powerful men had the power to kill and survive sorcery.

When European diseases began decimating the Montagnais, they accused the Jesuits of using witchcraft to spread the epidemics. To the Montagnais, the evidence seemed incontrovertible. The arrival of the Jesuits in their villages coincided with the appearance of new and baffling diseases. The Jesuits quickly recovered from diseases that were killing the Montagnais and their neighbors. In addition, the Jesuits behaved more like witches than normal people. They were celibate, mordantly talked about death and the afterlife, and used strange paintings, crosses, and food, such as communion wafers. Sometimes they covertly baptized seriously ill Montagnais children, who then died. And they openly scorned Montagnais shamans and loudly prayed for their demise.

Devastating European diseases and a growing dependence on French goods weakened Montagnais society and magnified the power of the Jesuits, who seemed the linchpin of Montagnais survival. The price of survival, however, was very steep. In exchange for the Jesuits' goods, Montagnais fathers and husbands had to discipline their daughters and wives. Only when their women became chaste and submissive would the Montagnais be saved from damnation. Montagnais aggression, which had formerly been directed outward toward their enemies, now began to focus inwardly on themselves and especially their women.[5]

The Handkerchief and Civilization

"Politeness and propriety," noted a Frenchman in seventeenth-century Canada, "have taught us to carry handkerchiefs. In this matter the savages charge us with filthiness—because, they say, we place what is unclean on a white piece of linen, and put it away in our pockets as something very precious, while they throw it on the ground." After seeing a Frenchman blow his nose into a handkerchief, one Indian laughed and said, "If thou likest that filth, give me thy handkerchief and I will soon fill it."

Note: Reuben Gold Thwaites, ed., *The Jesuit Relations and Allied Documents* (Cleveland: Burrow Brothers, 1896–1901), vol. 44, p. 297.

Europe

England and Europe's Price Revolution

Beginning in the sixteenth century, Europe was transformed by the influx of gold and silver from the New World. Spain profited the most from its mining ventures, but New World bullion mostly went to pay debts, foreign wars, foreign bankers, and lavish consumption by the Crown, Church, and nobility. Throughout Spain, little was invested or produced except raw materials for export.

The situation was quite different in England. At the beginning of the sixteenth century, England was economically weaker than its continental rivals—

164

Spain, Italy, the Netherlands, Germany, and France. By the English Civil War in 1642, however, England had become the greatest industrial power in Europe. In sharp contrast to Spain, there was an impressive increase in population, urban growth, shipbuilding, agricultural output, and the manufacture of salt, soap, gunpowder, and metal goods. New enterprises such as paper mills, glass factories, and alum plants dotted the once bucolic countryside. Coal production, which fueled the industrial revolution, ballooned from 35,000 tons in 1560 to 200,000 tons by 1700.

Across the English realm, there was a rapid expansion in the use of machinery driven by water and horses. Manufacturers concentrated on reducing the cost of labor to bolster production and using labor-saving machinery, cheaper raw materials, and cheaper forms of transportation. Utility was replacing quality as the engine of production, and private investment focused on producing basic consumer goods.

The early industrial revolution in England was propelled by two other critical forces. As a result of the Protestant Reformation, one-quarter of England's land changed hands from the Catholic Church to merchants, farmers, and manufacturers. Far more than their clerical predecessors, these individuals wanted to make profits from their investments.

In addition, traditions of absolute government were not as firmly established in England as they were on the continent. English kings had trouble imposing taxes without the consent of Parliament, and private enterprise was less regulated in England than elsewhere. There was a greater spirit of individual freedom in England, which in turn led to a novel emphasis on private investment, private enterprise, and the creation of a national consumer market.

In England, profits surged ahead of wages, and capitalists invested surplus funds in agriculture, mines, and industrial enterprises as bullion from the New World helped keep down the cost of labor and land. England rapidly became a powerful industrial nation, thanks partly to the growing availability of American gold and silver from its favorable balance of trade.[6]

➤ 7 ◄

Unacquainted with the Laws of the Civilized World

If Felipe Guaman Poma de Ayala's *El primer nueva corónica y buen gobierno* was the seventeenth century's greatest literary subversion of Spanish colonialism, the eighteenth-century prize for the most rebellious book on native history belongs to a Milenese nobleman, Lorenzo Boturini Benaducci. After leaving a war-torn Italy in 1733, Boturini visited England, Portugal, and Spain, where he went on a long pilgrimage and decided to visit Mexico to learn more about the cult of the Virgin of Guadalupe.

In Mexico, Boturini concentrated on two activities. He used his papal connections in Rome to have the Catholic Church declare the Virgin of Guadalupe "the sworn patron of this vast empire." With the help of the Jesuits and through his own diligent research, he also traveled throughout Mexico collecting over 500 maps, letters, and indigenous documents. After the Viceroy of New Spain arrested and then expelled him in 1743 for his intellectual curiosity, he went to Madrid and published a brilliant, idiosyncratic book, the *Idea de una nueva historia general de la América Septentrional* [Idea for a New General History of Northern America] (1746).

Heavily influenced by his contemporary, the Neopolitan philosopher Giambattista Vico, Boturini divided Mexican history into the age of gods, the age of heroes, and the age of men. Unlike his contemporaries, Boturini marveled at the eloquence and sophistication of indigenous thought. Mexican "Figures, Symbols, Characters, and Hieroglyphs," "poems full of exquisite metaphors and noble conceits," "manuscripts in both languages, Indian and Castilian," and a precise chronology that "surpasses in its elegance that of the Egyptians and the Chaldeans" were a monumental cultural achievement in the eyes of Boturini.

According to him, the Mexican people, though pagans, had developed through the "natural law of all people." Although Boturini believed that St. Thomas the Apostle had preached the gospel in ancient Mexico, he argued that the Mexicans' hieroglyphics and calendar "does not belong to a people whom Europeans depict as ignorant and incapable of reason, but who are a most subtle and perspicacious intelligence." By using Vico's "new science" of human society, Boturini offered an evolutionary and naturalistic explanation of Mexican religion that did not rely on the Devil or the migration of Jews to explain the origins of native culture.

Boturini grandly claimed that his subject, "never having been written about before, is my exclusive privilege, and such an enjoyable one, and of such use to the public, that it would be foolish to claim otherwise," but there is no evidence that his contemporaries found the book convincing, despite the backing of several powerful Spanish patrons. Some nationalistic Mexican Creole intellectuals admired his work, but Boturini's defense of indigenous Mexican culture either was ignored or dismissed by other thinkers. He received praise for collecting precious documents but not for his interpretations. One Spaniard considered his historical explanations "somewhat fantastic." Another writer, the great Scots historian William Robertson, thought Borturini was a "whimsical, credulous man" because he could not see that the Aztecs were a childish and barbaric people with a "gloomy and atrocious religion."

Although Borturini's book was difficult to understand, his reliance on the controversial Vico or his often perplexing organization and terminology were not the main problems readers faced. Borturini was an erudite revolutionary. In an age characterized by studied indifference or profound contempt for indigenous cultures on both sides of the Atlantic, Borturini had the courage and temerity to suggest that the ancient Mexicans were a profound, accomplished people who deserved serious and sympathetic study. This was the real problem with his book. If readers took Borturini seriously, they would have to question the basic assumptions that were rooted in every European colony in the New World. Not one of his commentators was able to follow Borturini to the startling conclusion of his remarkable intellectual journey.

As Boturini was celebrating Mexico's indigenous cultures, Spain, Portugal, France, and Britain were trying to alter traditional indigenous patterns of land ownership, labor, and production to accumulate new sources of wealth. Throughout the New World from the Great Lakes to Brazil's Sertaô, settlements were established to bring Indian lands under European control. In every colony, a dynamic extractive economy arose to channel New World resources from the periphery of Europe's possessions to metropolitan centers such as Seville, Lisbon, London, and Paris. In the global division of labor, the New World's task was to provide European countries with profitable raw materials and light manufactured products.

Within this expanding imperial system, New World colonies had three common structural characteristics. First, metropolitan European centers aggressively generated enormous profits for themselves in the form of gold, silver, furs, fish, timber, and other raw materials from their colonies. Second, New World revenues hinged on the control of indigenous lands and labor. Without mines, forests, and rich agricultural lands and Indian trade, tribute, and coerced labor, colonies would have had little value to their new owners. And without radically unequal exchange relationships between indigenous peoples and Europeans, New World colonies could not have produced such huge profits. The Indians' very marginalization and dependency were the foundation of Europe's success in the New World.

And third, this international economic system was polarized into a radically asymmetrical relationship between the metropolitan center and its peripheral satellites. In fact, within Europe's imperial structure there was a quadruple polarization between the metropolises and the New World periphery. Resources and profits moved from the periphery to the center; from the countryside to places like Charleston, South Carolina, and then abroad; from the poor to the middle and upper classes; and from indigenous peoples to Europeans.

Although economic relations between the metropolises and hinterlands changed over time, the colonies never ceased playing the critical role that had been established at the beginning of the conquest—enriching the colonial and international metropolises through their labor and natural resources. As the Viceroy of Peru observed in 1736, "the commerce of this Kingdom is a paradox of trade and a contradiction of riches not known until its discovery, thriving on what ruins others and being ruined by what makes others thrive." While the metropolises waxed, the indigenous hinterlands waned.

Native peoples found ways accommodate themselves to European rule, but accommodation was very difficult in the face of devastating diseases, aggressive settlers, and a changing political and ecological environment that favored European settlers. To survive, Indians did not just rebel against colonial domination. They also developed new ways of life that combined their own traditions with those of other Indians, Europeans, and Africans. Native strategies of adaptation faced daunting challenges, however, because most Europeans believed that indigenous peoples were "unacquainted with the laws of the civilized world." With few exceptions, in their daily behavior settlers, ministers, and government officials acted in ways that loudly refuted everything Boturini had defended.[1]

North America

Pennsylvania and the Expanding British Frontier

When King Charles II in 1680 made William Penn the proprietor of a huge colony the size of England, Penn immediately began applying his Quaker religious principles to the colony's Indian inhabitants. In liberality "they excell," he wrote after meeting the Lenni Lenapes, whom the English called the Delawares. "Nothing is too good for their friend; give them a fine Gun, Coat, or other thing, it may pass twenty hands, before it sticks." In contrast to many English settlers, Penn never thought that Indians were savages.

Because "this great God hath written his law in our hearts, by which we are taught and commanded to love," he insisted that the colony's Indians be treated with justice, "for we have their good in our eye, equall with our own interest." Penn insisted on good relations with his colony's Indians because he was "very sensible of the unkindness and injustice that has been too much exercised towards you by the people of these parts of the world, who have sought themselves, and to make great advantages by you, rather than be examples and goodness unto you."

He respected their way of life and insisted that the colony purchase lands from Indians without bribes, alcohol, or force. Penn's attempt to deal fairly with the Indians was an integral component of what he called his "holy experiment." This task was made difficult, however, by the rapidly changing settlement patterns of both indigenous peoples and Europeans.

The Delawares were gradually moving westward from New Jersey into Pennsylvania in search of furs and territory unclaimed by European settlers. Meanwhile, the powerful Iroquois Confederacy wanted to protect its homeland in the colony of New York from European encroachment and French attacks by encouraging friendly Indians to relocate on their southern flank in Penn's colony. They invited the Delawares and the Mahicans of the Hudson River Valley to settle the strategic Wyoming Valley in northeastern Pennsylvania. Around 1692, the Shawnees settled along Pennsylvania's Susquehanna River in the southeast. Nine years later, with Penn's permission Indians from Virginia and southern Maryland also moved into the Susquehanna River Valley. They were joined by the Tuscaroras, Tutelos, Nanticokes, and other indigenous peoples.

At the same time, European settlers also began pouring into Pennsylvania, which was fast becoming known as the "best poor man's country." Dutch, Swedes, Welsh and English Quakers, Finns, and Scots-Irish immigrants rapidly boosted its population from 8,800 in 1690 to 175,000 by 1760. On the eve of the American Revolution, Pennsylvania was the most heterogeneous of Britain's North American colonies with a population evenly divided among the English, Germans, and Scots-Irish.

To accommodate European settlers, Penn and his successors purchased large tracks of native land, primarily from the Delawares. By 1754, Indians had ceded their rights over almost all of eastern and central Pennsylvania. In these transactions, the Pennsylvania government thought it was acting in the best interests of both parties. Neither side, however, saw the Penn family's efforts in this light. From the beginning, European settlers criticized the government's Indian policy for its excessive generosity, although Penn's heirs were more interested in land speculation than in justice for the Delawares. Settlers constantly demanded more native land and repeatedly clashed with Indians in the Susquehanna and Wyoming Valleys and along the westward frontier.

For the Delawares, the founding of Pennsylvania culminated a disastrous process that had begun with Dutch, Swedish, and English settlements along the eastern seaboard. After over a century of exposure to Europeans, they had became dependent on the English for guns, gunpowder, cloth, clothing, brandy, axes, and even shoes. Meanwhile, recurring famines and epidemics had reduced, weakened, and demoralized them.

In Pennsylvania as in other British colonies, the Delawares were displaced by the transformation of land from a public resource to a private commodity. There were four key elements in this process. First, British law and notions of property rights made land a commodity that could be owned, bought, and sold in the marketplace. Second, as most of Pennsylvania's land was transferred from public to private ownership, many Delawares could no longer hunt, fish, and farm in Pennsylvania because they owned no property. Third, the laws of inheritance and land tenure arrangements promoted increasing disparities in wealth. And fourth, European settlers rapidly changed Pennsylvania's ecological environment to produce products for a global world economy. As common land disappeared, the Delawares could only survive as individuals, not collectively as a people. There was literally no place left for them in Pennsylvania.

As the Delawares lost their independence, they began killing wildlife in ways that shocked both European setters and other Indians. Throughout Pennsylvania and the Ohio River Valley, the Delawares developed an unenviable reputation as the most wasteful of Indian hunters. The Miamis even prohibited them from hunting on their lands because they "shoot the deer for the sake of the skins and leave the flesh lying in the bush." Similar complaints were heard from the Ottawas and the Chippawas as the Delawares desperately expanded their hunting territory in search of more fur.

The Delawares once believed that the rattlesnake was their grandfather and had been placed here "on purpose to guard us, and to give notice of impending danger by his rattle." In the mid-eighteenth century, a Delaware man told a German missionary that his people would not kill any rattlesnakes because "if we were to kill one of those, the others would soon know it, and the whole race would rise upon us and bite us." He warned the missionary that "they are a very dangerous enemy; take care you do not irritate them in *our* country; they and their grandchildren are on good terms, and neither will hurt the other."

According to the missionary, "these ancient notions have, however in a great measure died away with the last generation, and the Indians at present kill their grandfather the rattle-snake without ceremony, whenever they meet with him." The Delawares had once "considered themselves in a manner connected with certain animals." Now they lived in a broken and disenchanted world.

Incoming settlers killed their game, cleared their forests, dammed their streams for sawmills, and turned a seemingly unlimited natural order into private property. As Pennsylvania's fur and deer trade declined in importance, the Delawares became an impediment to the colony's prosperity. They were caught between European settlers and the Iroquois, but they could not accommodate themselves to either culture. By the end of the eighteenth century, many Delawares had simply become part of Pennsylvania's working poor.

The Delawares also recognized that Quaker benevolence did not always include them, for Indian slavery legally existed in Pennsylvania. In the absence of war captives, Indians were purchased as slaves from other colonies or kidnapped into slavery by hostile settlers. In Chester County outside Philadelphia, Delawares complained that their children and young men were abducted when they played outdoors or hunted. Although growing numbers of Quakers criticized slavery, it remained legal until the state of Pennsylvania passed a gradual abolition law in 1782.

A greater threat to Pennsylvania's Indians came from frontier settlers who rejected Quaker notions of benevolence. By the mid-eighteenth century, Indians were constantly clashing with aggressive colonists from Britain's borderlands who hated "any Thing that Savours of the Name of an Indian." During the seventeenth century, lowland Scots had migrated to Ulster where they vanquished the Irish. After moving to the Pennsylvania frontier along with fellow Highland Scots who had been displaced by failed political rebellions and backbreaking poverty, they again fought over access to land. Violence escalated during the Great War for Empire (1754–1763), when the Delawares of the Ohio River Valley, who were allied with the French, terrorized western Pennsylvania.

Hostilities continued even after the war ended. In 1763, a group of about fifty armed Lancaster County vigilantes called "the Paxton Boys" killed twenty unarmed, friendly Indians and then marched on Philadelphia to slaughter more. "The only object of the rioters," one Pennsylvanian observed, "was the destruction of all the Indians, under the idea that they were descendants of the Canaanites, who, by God's commandment, were to be cut off from the face of the earth." Among the remains of the murdered Indians was a 1701 peace treaty with William Penn stating that both parties "shall forever hereafter be as one Head & One Heart, & live in true Friendship & Amity as one People."

The Paxton Boys were never identified or punished for their murders. As Benjamin Franklin lamented, "the Outrages committed by the Frontier People are really amazing. . . . Rising in Arms to destroy Property publick and private, and insulting the King's Troops and forts, is going great lengths indeed!" In the decades before the American Revolution, settlers and Indian hunters constantly threatened the colony's native peoples, whom they considered "faithless Barbarians." Quakers and Crown officials condemned the violence, but they could not enforce law and justice along Pennsylvania's volatile western frontier. Settlers literally got away with murder as violence escalated against Indians, who seldom received justice in local courts for the outrages perpetrated against them.

By the mid-eighteenth century, many Delawares believed that the colony of Pennsylvania had betrayed them. Teedyuscung, a Delaware leader who was nominally Christian, fluent in English, and closely acquainted with the colony's leaders, argued that land had been stolen from his people. "When one Man had formerly Liberty to purchase Lands, and he took the Deed from the Indians for it, and then dies; after his Death, the Children forge a Deed, like the true One, with the same Indian Names on it, and thereby take Lands from the Indians which they never sold—this is Fraud." After almost two centuries of contact with English settlers, the Delawares still had difficulty understanding the ultimate goal of many settlers—the removal of Indians from Pennsylvania.

In 1763, Teedyuscung became yet another Indian victim of frontier violence when he was killed in an arson attack in the disputed Wyoming Valley. The perpetrators were probably from Connecticut's Susquehannah Company. Their Puritan ancestors had slaughtered Pequots to settle the Connecticut River Valley, and now they grandly claimed the distant Wyoming Valley by virtue of their expansive colonial charter. Despite the Penn family's best intentions, in his colony the Delawares could never feel very secure.

The American backwoods frontier in Pennsylvania and the British colonies was unique in the New World because it expanded so rapidly in the eighteenth century. England's earliest settlers clung to the coast and river valleys of North America for almost a century because they could not survive in a woodland environment. The English eagerly cut down forests for fuel and export, but they liked treeless environments for their farming and herding.

This changed in the eighteenth century as settlers learned to live in a forested environment beyond the coast and the lower reaches of navigable rivers. In the first half of the eighteenth century, the population of English settlements multiplied from about 300,000 in 1700 to 2 million in 1754 as immigrants from England, Scotland, Ireland, and Germany moved into the interior of the continent. America's backwoods pioneer culture originated in the lower Delaware Valley of Pennsylvania among the Finnish settlers of New Sweden, who created a superbly adaptive frontier culture by melding their own heritage with that of their neighbors, the Delawares.

Nya Sverige, or New Sweden, was founded in 1638 on the banks of the lower Delaware River between present-day New Castle, Delaware, and Philadelphia. In 1655, Holland seized the colony, but nine years later the English ousted the Dutch. When William Penn arrived, he discovered that half of New Sweden's settlers were actually eastern Finns from Savo and Karelia who had migrated to central Sweden in search of open land before coming to America.

Unlike the English, the Savo-Karelians were well prepared for frontier life in a woodland environment. For almost 1,000 years, they had lived an independent, mobile life in northern Europe by hunting large animals, gathering wild plants, fishing, raising cattle, and cultivating rye. Swedes and Norwegians settled Scandinavia's fertile stream valleys, but migratory Savo-Karelians rapidly turned their forested environment into open farmland with log cabins and split-rail zigzag fences.

In Finland, the Savo-Karelians had lived among the Lapps for over eight centuries as fur trading and marriage partners. In America, they quickly established good relations with the Delawares. Finns traded liquor, firearms, livestock, and textiles for corn, furs, land, and herbal medicines. Some Finns became bilingual and served as interpreters while others married Delaware women.

Relations were so close among the two peoples that the Delawares called Finns and Swedes "fellow tribesmen" and "those who are like us." By the end of the seventeenth century, new immigrants to the Delaware Valley thought "the savages and our Swedes are like one people." These Swedes were "accursed," settlers claimed, because they were "already half Indians."

Out of the mixing of Savo-Karelian and Delaware cultures came a new way of life suited to a forested frontier environment. In the Delaware Valley, settlers learned to clear homesteads with iron axes, kill large animals for meat, grow maize through slash and burn agriculture, gather edible plants, keep open range hogs and cattle, and create versatile buildings made of notched, horizontal logs.

Some of these traits were distinctly Savo-Karelian in origin, such as felling trees with iron axes, hunting animals with rifles, and building log cabins. Others were clearly Delaware or Algonquian, especially the reliance on corn, vegetable, and fruit sources, slash and burn farming, and the use of local herbal remedies.

Corn was the mainstay of the Savo-Karelian diet because it was easier to sow and harvest than grain and produced far more food per acre than wheat or rye. Finns cleared their farm plots like the Delawares by girdling trees, burning the ground cover to clear brush and fertilize the soil, and then building low mounds of soil to grow intermixed corn, squash, beans, and watermelons. Since the Savo-Karelians were already familiar with bread made from rye and grits made from barley and oats, they readily took to Delaware corn bread, corn grits, and corn pone. They even made beer from "Injun corn."

Savo-Karelians learned about new sources of meat such as skunk, raccoon, and opossum (Algonquian names) from their indigenous neighbors. Expert deer and bear stalkers, they integrated the Delaware techniques of trap hunting and encirclement with fire torches into their own hunting traditions. Finns even dressed in deerskin, fur, and moccasins (another Algonquian word), which resembled their traditional clothing in northern Europe.

The Delawares also taught the Finns how to identify Pennsylvania's edible wild fruits, vegetables and nuts, and medicinal plants. Walnuts, sassafras, ginseng, maple sugar, honey, plums, blueberries, raspberries, strawberries, and pokeberry, pecan, and pawpaw (Algonquian names) became part of the Finns' diet. Ginseng root, which the Delawares thought extremely potent and called Grandmother and Grandfather, became a popular Finnish panacea for headaches, wounds, cramps, stomach troubles, and fevers. Because the Savo-Karelians had been gatherers of plants and medicinal herbs in Scandinavia, they eagerly incorporated Delaware wild foods and plants into their own culture. Probably much of their knowledge came directly from Delaware male and female herbalists.

By the early eighteenth century, the Finns had reached the limits of their geographical expansion into Pennsylvania, New Jersey, Delaware, and Maryland. When the Scots-Irish and Germans arrived in the lower Delaware Valley and began intermarrying with them, America's backwoods culture was ready to expand. As settlers flooded into eastern North America, Savo-Karelians disappeared as a distinct ethnic group. Ironically, the Delawares lost their remaining land in New Jersey and Pennsylvania to Europeans who had learned all too well from them how to live in a woodland environment.[2]

174

An Afro-Indian Br'er Rabbit

During the seventeenth century, Indian slavery appeared in the American Southeast as the region became part of a global export economy that included deerskins and human chattel. Especially in Virginia, the Carolinas, and Georgia, British settlers enslaved indigenous peoples, exported them to other colonies and the West Indies, and encouraged southeastern tribes to sell their enemies into bondage.

The slave trade in the South developed out of the struggle for control over the Southern Appalachians by the British along the Atlantic coast, the French in the lower Mississippi Valley, and the Spanish in Florida. European powers understood that whomever could establish alliances with the Cherokees and Creeks would successfully shore up their weak frontier defenses, control a strategic region, deter runaway African slaves and slave insurrections, and promote trade. Establishing good trade relations with the indigenous peoples was the cement that would make successful alliances.

Beginning in the late seventeenth century, Indians in the southern Appalachians gradually became traders in deerskins and leather, which they eagerly exchanged for European manufactured goods and especially rifles and ammunition. By 1700, South Carolina exported more than 50,000 deerskins annually, and this number more than doubled by 1730. In the early years of South Carolina, the deerskin trade was a major commercial activity for the struggling colony. In a good year, trading companies might realize profits of 500 percent.

Cherokee society was transformed by the deerskin trade in two significant ways. First, the trade brought with it deadly European diseases, especially smallpox, and intensified warfare with Indian trading rivals and the British. In 1685, the Cherokees numbered about 32,000. By 1790, the first federal census, they had declined to 7,500, and many of their villages had disappeared.

And second, as the British colonies grew the Cherokees lost over half of their traditional lands—over 43 million acres. Through illegal settlements in the Appalachian Mountains, the building of forts, stores, and settler towns, the constant redrawing of boundaries, and the frequent exchange of land in payment for debts, land became privatized in ways that excluded the Cherokees. For example, the Cherokees lost over 7 million acres in treaties of 1721 and 1755 in exchange for colonial stores and good trade relations with the British government. From 1765 to 1777, the Cherokees surrendered a further 2 million acres to extinguish their trading debts with the colonies of Georgia, South Carolina, and Virginia. The Cherokees complained that British encroachment would ruin their hunting grounds, but they were in a weak position to protest because of their growing dependence on the deerskin trade.

In the early southern triangular trade, the British colonies received African slaves and European manufactured goods in exchange for Cherokee deerskins and Indian slaves. Although slavery encountered periodic opposition from government officials, colonies such as South Carolina became heavily dependent on both Indian and African slavery. Like the Portuguese in Brazil, South Carolina's government rewarded Indians who bartered war captives into English slavery. When numbers lagged, Carolinians and their Indian allies went on slave raids into Spanish Florida and the Mississippi Valley in search of native prey.

As early as 1681, the British were trading in Indian slaves. Two years later, a Cherokee delegation visited Charleston to plea for the cessation of slave raids, but to no avail. By the early eighteenth century, the Cherokees were no longer interested in stopping the slave trade. To purchase more rifles, metal tools, utensils, and liquor, they too had become slave traders. Before Europeans arrived, the Cherokees had frequently fought with their enemies for revenge. Now, armed with British rifles and ammunition, they fought to capture Indians and exchange them for European goods and liquor.

In November of 1702, South Carolina raiders captured 500 Indians in northern Florida. Two years later, South Carolina settlers and their Creek, Yamasee, and Savannah allies destroyed thirteen Spanish missions, many Indian villages under Spanish control, and captured 325 adults and children who were enslaved. By 1710, Spain's other Florida missions completely collapsed as over 10,000 Indians were seized by South Carolina slave raiders. Raiders also destroyed over thirty Indian villages, burned churches, and tortured priests to death. With these brutal attacks, South Carolina became the leading Indian slave trading colony in British North America.

Most Indian captives went to the British West Indies, where two Indians were exchanged for one African slave to work on the Carolina rice plantations. Some Indians, however, labored closer to home. In 1708, South Carolina had 9,580 inhabitants, including 4,100 black and 1,400 Indian slaves. Almost twenty years later, there were 2,000 Indian slaves in South Carolina —900 women, 600 men, and 500 children. Settlers thought that women and children would adapt more successfully to slavery than Indian men.

Native slave labor, however, became less important in South Carolina during the eighteenth century. When Europeans and Africans arrived in South Carolina's swampy lowlands, they brought with them smallpox, malaria, and other deadly diseases that decimated indigenous peoples. Numbers, however, were not the only problem. British settlers feared that Indian slaves might ally themselves with Spanish and French colonists or African runaways to wreak havoc on the colony.

Indian slavery also declined in South Carolina because an "Indian Man or Woman may cost 18 or 20 pound, but a good Negro is worth more than twice that Sum." In 1719, the colony taxed its slaves equally "save that an Indian slave being reputed of much less value than a negroe, all persons possessed of Indian slaves shall pay for each Indian in proportion to half the value of what shall be rated and imposed for each negroe." Colonists valued Indians as hunters, fishermen, guides, household servants, and even soldiers, but not as plantation slaves. By 1745, there were twice as many African slaves as free colonists in South Carolina.

Despite the decline of Indian slavery, throughout the eighteenth century South Carolina newspapers frequently advertised for runaway Indian and Afro-Indian slaves. In 1746, one slaveowner was looking for a "tall, lusty young Wench, can speak good English, Chickasaw, and perhaps French, the Chickasaws having taken her from the French settlements on Mississippi." She was accompanied by her husband, who was black. And in 1773, another slaveowner advertised for a "Mulatto or half-Indian Man, named Frank, well made, about nineteen or twenty years old."

As a result of Indians and African Americans sharing the same plantation quarters into the mid-eighteenth century, an ethnically mixed slave population appeared throughout South Carolina. Because there were many more African male than female slaves and many more Indian female than male slaves, Africans and Indians had little choice but to intermarry. The peculiar demography of the African and Indian slave trade led to the creation of a large new racial group in South Carolina, Afro-Indians, who were frequently classified by whites as mulattoes.

Especially on rice plantations in the wet lowlands of South Carolina, southeastern Indian knowledge and skills quietly became part of the slave culture. Native corn, tobacco, clay tobacco pipes, pottery, baskets, mats, and wooden bowls, yaupon tea, canoes, various folk medicines such as snakeroot and sassafras, and agricultural and fishing techniques all contributed to the development of an Afro-Indian culture in colonial South Carolina.

Perhaps the most unusual result of protracted contact between Southeastern Indians and European settlers was the development of African slavery among the Cherokee, Creek, Choctaw, Chickasaw, and Seminole peoples. When the Spanish explorer Hernando de Soto's expedition encountered Cherokees in 1540, Spaniards met war captives called *atsi nahsa'i* [one who is owned], but they were not slaves in the European or African sense. They had no significant economic functions, but probably served to remind the highly individualistic Cherokees that they had no identity outside their clans and kin.

By the early eighteenth century, the Cherokees stopped killing or adopting their enemies and started selling them to the English. Several decades later, they bought, sold, kidnapped, and owned African slaves. As Cherokee women and European settlers intermarried along the southern trading frontier, slavery became more attractive to Cherokees of mixed extraction, who broke with their traditions by tracing descent through their fathers rather than their mothers, converting to Protestantism, entering the market economy through cotton farming, and measuring their wealth and status by the number of slaves they owned. By the American Revolution, some of these families lived in individual log cabins and farmed their own plots of land.

As Cherokee culture changed, Africans became associated with the plantation economy of slavery. As one Cherokee explained, "Black was a stigma fixed upon a man for crime; and all his descendants ever since had been born black." It was "marked by the signal of God's displeasure. Some said it was for murder, some cowardice, and some said it was lying." Like their white neighbors, the Cherokees developed an elaborate religious and social justification for the enslavement of African peoples.

For the first time in their history, skin color now helped determine status in Cherokee society. While many Cherokees condemned slavery as a divisive and alien institution, they were able to outlaw slavery only at the end of the Civil War. In 1867, freed slaves were given Cherokee citizenship and the right to vote and hold office in the Cherokee nation.

Although the Cherokees and other Southeastern Indians practiced slavery for over a century, they never fully succeeded in completely separating themselves from African Americans because there had been too many centuries of intermarriage and close relations between the two peoples. In 1881, William O. Tuggle, a close friend of the writer Joel Chandler Harris, heard a fascinating story from a Creek Indian living in Oklahoma that vividly illustrated this point.

After a man discovered that someone was stealing his garden peas, he "made a tar-person & put it in the garden near the peas." The rabbit who was stealing the peas encountered the tar-person. "Who's that, What's your name?" he asked. When he heard no reply, he hopped close to the figure and threatened to hit him if he did not speak. When the tar-person failed to respond, the rabbit hit him four times, and each time his foot stuck to the tar-person. "The rabbit than struck with his head & it stuck." At the end of the story the rabbit was scolded with hot water by an angry farmer after he tricked a wolf into taking his place. Harris, who read Tuggle's collection of Indian tales, turned Br'er Rabbit and Br'er Fox into the "Wonderful Tar Baby Story."

According to Harris, Uncle Remus told this story as he sat by the fire smoking a corn-cob pipe. The tobacco and pipe are Indian, and probably so

178

is the story. Tales about elephants, gorillas, and spiders were clearly African in origin, but Southeastern Indians had stories about a rabbit trickster figure whom the Cherokees identified as "the leader of them all in mischief." Perhaps even Uncle Remus was part Indian. Br'er Rabbit and Br'er Fox, like so many other aspects of southern culture, emerged out of the region's Afro-Indian heritage.[3]

William Tapp's Inventory

In 1719, William Taptico, or Tapp as he was known to the English, died. He was the last *werowance* of the Wicomocos, who had occupied land along the Potomac River in Virginia's Northern Neck when Jamestown was founded. After the defeat of Powhatan's chiefdom, the colony of Virginia had given each tributary Indian warrior fifty acres, but they continued losing their ancestral lands to English settlers.

William Tapp and his wife Elizabeth lived quite well by early eighteenth-century Virginia standards. They owned an English frame house with a hearth, and their goods and livestock were worth over £100. They possessed table linen, over thirty pewter plates, four feather beds, some old books, a canoe, boat rigging, fish hooks and other maritime equipment along with iron wedges and axes. Tapp's wife owned three pair of wool cards, knitting needles, a spinning wheel, three hoes, cooking utensils, and pottery described as "4 English milkpanns and 3 Indian." These were the only purely Indian possessions in their house.

Although the Tapp family was comfortable, William Tapp lacked the attributes of a traditional Wicomoco *werowance*. In 1696, Tapp's father sold the last Wicomoco property to the English. Six years later, a Virginian noted that the Wicomocos had only three warriors left, "which yet keep up their Kingdom, and retain their fashion; they live by themselves, separate from all other Indians, and from the English."

A century earlier, the Powhatan chiefdom had controlled 6,000 square miles of territory and 15,000 people. By William Tapp's death in 1719, the Wicomocos and other Powhatan peoples were landless and almost extinct.

Note: Stephen R. Potter, *Commoners, Tribute, and Chiefs: The Development of Algoquian Culture in the Potomac Valley* (Charlottesville: University Press of Virginia, 1993), pp. 195, 223–229; Peter Nabokov and Robert Easton, *Native American Architecture* (New York: Oxford University Press, 1989), pp. 52–55; Helen C. Rountree, *Pocahontas's People: The Powhatan Indians of Virginia Through Four Centuries* (Norman: University of Oklahoma Press, 1990), pp. 158–159.

A New People on the Great Lakes

Beginning in late seventeenth century, a large community of Métis—people of mixed French and Indian backgrounds—appeared in the present states of Michigan, Illinois, and Wisconsin. In villages such as Green Bay, Prairie du Chien, Sheboygan, Michilimackinac, River Rouge, Milwaukee, and Fort Pontchartrain (Detroit), male fur traders of French origin settled and freely intermarried among the Huron, Ottawa, Potawatomi, Peoria, Chippewa, Miami, and Menominee peoples; because very few French women lived in the Old Northwest, the newcomers had few alternatives.

French military commanders especially were interested in promoting intermarriage. According to one, it would "strengthen the friendship of these tribes, as the alliances of the Romans perpetuated peace with the Sabines through the intervention of the women, whom the former had taken from the others." Eventually, the Jesuits performed French/Indian marriage ceremonies if they could baptize the bride. From 1680 to 1702, the French government even provided dowries for Indian and French women.

According to a contemporary observer, "when a Frenchman trades with them, he takes into his services one of their Daughters, the one, presumably, who is most to his taste; he asks the Father for her, & under certain conditions, it is arranged; he promises to give the father some blankets, a few shirts, a Musket, Powder & Shot, Tobacco & Tools; they come to an agreement at last, & the exchange is made." The bride, in turn, agreed to serve her husband, dress his fur pelts, and sell his merchandise. This was marriage *á la façon du pays* [according to the custom of the country].

These bicultural marriages were based on the pragmatic needs of both peoples. The Indians in the Old Northwest wanted access to European goods, reliable trading partners, and protection against the Iroquois, who constantly attacked them. The French wanted wives, furs, and Indian allies in their frequent wars with the British. The combination of trade and intermarriage helped to reduce French-Indian violence (in 1684, thirty-nine French traders in the Old Northwest were murdered by Indians) and to create bonds of friendship where once conflict had existed.

As sparse French settlements turned into permanent villages and forts, they were dominated neither by French nor Indians but by their mixed offspring. Métis traders exchanged European clothing, vermilion, glass and porcelain beads, metal traps, metal tools, guns, metal swords, bayonets and daggers, iron fishhooks and spears, brass rings, iron kettles, liquor, and ammunition for furs, corn, dried fish, birchbark canoes, and meat. In the first half of the eighteenth century, most of the trade involved furs and clothing, blankets, brandy, and gunpowder.

In Michilimackinac, Michigan, from 1698 to 1765 almost 50 percent of the settlement's marriages were between French and Indians, French and Métis, and among Métis. Almost 40 percent of Michilimackinac's births were Métis while another 30 percent were Indian. From 1765 to 1797, the percentage of births to Métis increased to 71 percent. During this period, only 6 percent of Michilimackinac's births were French.

In Green Bay, Wisconsin, there was a similar demographic pattern. From 1740 to 1816, over 80 percent of the town's households were Métis. By the early nineteenth century, there were about 15,000 residents in Métis communities along the Great Lakes who spoke a combination of French, local Indian languages, and a Métis creole speech called "Michif" that used French nouns, articles, and adjectives with Cree syntax.

When the Old Northwest passed into American control after the Revolution, arriving settlers were disturbed by the presence of Métis. As one surprised American noted in Fort Wayne, Indiana, "the inhabitants are . . . all more or less imbued with Indian blood" that it was "almost impossible to fancy ourselves still within the same territorial limits" of the United States. Americans had little respect for the Métis because they seemed "unacquainted with the laws of the civilized world." Unlike the French, American settlers were uninterested in the fur trade or in accommodating themselves to Indian and Métis life. They only wanted land for their agricultural settlements.

When an American soldier entered Vincennes, Indiana, in 1811, he described the residents as a "rabble whose appearance caused us to doubt whether we had not actually landed among the savages themselves." The Métis had too many strikes against them. They were Catholic, were culturally as much Indian as French, were mobile traders and not sedentary farmers; they spoke no English; and they had supported the French and then the British in the eighteenth century.

Americans offered the Métis two stark choices: Either they could live in a Protestant and agricultural English community and lose their cultural identities or they could leave. Some Métis converted to Protestantism and settled down on farms, while others migrated northward to the Red River Valley near Winnipeg or westward into Montana. Within a few decades, Métis communities completely disappeared from the United States side of the Great Lakes region. Today, there are about 1 million people of Métis descent living in Canada and the United States.

The Métis also declined in the Great Lakes region because the fur trade collapsed and the French trading population aged. In the early nineteenth century, one visitor noted that most of Green Bay's household heads were "worn out voyageurs or boatman, who having become unfit for the hardships of the Indian trade, had taken wives generally among the Menomonee

181

tribe and settled down on a piece of land," pretending to "cultivate the soil." Once France lost Canada and the Old Northwest to Britain in 1763, Métis communities gradually became aliens among the English.

As American settlers poured into the Old Northwest, any people of Indian or Métis ancestry became a despised and hapless minority. At Sault Saint Marie, once a thriving Métis community, Americans derisively referred to people of mixed Indian and French descent as "Negroes."[4]

The French-Choctaw Trade in the Lower Mississippi Valley

Throughout most of the eighteenth century, the French controlled the lower Mississippi Valley and depended on trade with its native peoples. In exchange for over 100,000 deerskins, the French annually supplied the Choctaws with the following items around 1750:

- 6,000 meters of blue and red cloth;
- 1,200 white blankets;
- 500 striped blankets;
- 2,500 men's shirts;
- 150 muskets;
- 4,000 pounds of gunpowder;
- 300 pieces of scarlet ribbon;
- 400 pounds of vermilion;
- 200 pounds of blue and white drinking glasses;
- 4,320 woodcutter knives;
- 18,000 musket flints;
- 576 pairs of scissors;
- 432 rifle flint locks;
- 432 awls; and
- 400 mirrors in cases.

The French focused on guns and ammunition for two reasons. First, they wanted the Choctaws to hunt deer and other fur bearing animals with rifles and not native bows and arrows. And second, well-armed and loyal Choctaws would be better able to protect themselves and their French allies from the British and hostile Indians. Unofficially, almost 80 percent of the import-export trade with the Choctaws involved liquor, especially brandy and rum.

Note: Daniel H. Usher, Jr., *Indians, Settlers, and Slaves in a Frontier Exchange Economy: The Lower Mississippi Valley Before 1783* (Chapel Hill: University of North Carolina Press, 1992), pp. 259–268.

South America

Rebellion in the Backlands

If Brazil, in the words of one writer, was "an inferno for Negroes, purgatory for Whites, and paradise for Mulattoes and Mulattas," what was it for its native peoples? In the Sertaô of Brazil's Northeast, it was a running battle between Tapuias and Portuguese settlers, who coveted the Sertaô's arid lands for profitable cattle ranches. Ultimately, the Tapuias, who had successfully resisted the Portuguese for two centuries, were defeated by a combination of Portuguese homesteaders and slave hunters, cattle, and hostile Indians.

When the Portuguese began exploring the Brazilian interior south of the Amazon River in the early sixteenth century, they encountered the Tapuias, whom they unfavorably compared to the Tupinambás. Related to the Gê peoples of the central Brazilian savannah, the Tapuias were a mobile hunting and gathering people who subsisted on roots, berries, honey, and game, which they chased on foot and clubbed to death.

When the Tapuias moved from the coastal forest into Brazil's inhospitable Sertaô to escape first the Tupís and then European invaders, they thought that the Portuguese would never follow them. The Sertaô, which literally means "the Backlands," is a huge area in Brazil's Northeast parched by the sun. In the words of its most famous chronicler, Euclides de Cunha, "here are shrubs with scarcely any roots in the scant earth and with intertwining branches, with solitary cacti here and there standing stiff and silent, giving to the region the appearance of the edge of a desert."

Although the Sertaô seemed inhospitable, the Portuguese learned that it could supply the Bahía and Pernambuco coasts with meat, for cattle could survive by roaming freely across its arid land. In the seventeenth century, Portuguese settlers built ranches on the alluvial plains bordering the Sertaô's rivers and moved their scrawny cattle weighing less than 200 pounds on overland drives to sugar plantations, where they supplied table meat, fat to grease machinery, hides for clothing, and they served as beasts of burden.

Cattle ranching was critical to Brazil's prosperity because in the early eighteenth century the sugar trade between Portugal and its South American colony was so large and profitable. In 1710, Brazil shipped about 328 million pounds of refined sugar to Portugal. The Sertaô produced 800,000 head of cattle to support the coastal sugar plantations.

At first the Tapuias welcomed the cattle ranchers. Some of them even intermarried with the local cowboys and became excellent ranch hands. Others enjoyed hunting cattle on foot, for they were easier to catch than mice and small animals. Soon, however, the Tapuias realized that the growing number of Portuguese settlers were driving them out of the Sertaô.

Portuguese priests and settlers treated the Tapuias like vermin. Native women were raped by marauding soldiers, their lands were invaded by cattle ranchers, and Jesuit missions forced the Tapuias to participate in cattle drives. Peaceful Tapuias were killed with impunity, while soldiers captured and sold them into slavery, "three or four redskins being bartered for one Negro from Angola." If a Portuguese settler harmed an Indian, he could be fined and even deported, "but, as with all orders favorable to Indians, this had no effect."

According to one famous Bahía slave hunter who had seven Indian mistresses and needed an interpreter to speak Portuguese, waging war on the Tapuias was part of Brazil's cultural mission. He told the king that his irregular militia entered the Sertaô "not to enslave (as some hypochondriacs would have Your Majesty believe), but to acquire Tapuia (a fierce people who eat human flesh) to domesticate them to the knowledge of civilized life and human association and rational commerce." By enslaving the Tapuias, they would "come to have the light of God and the mysteries of the Catholic faith which is necessary for their salvation. . . . If we later use them in our fields we do them no injustice, for this is to support them and their children as much as to support us and ours." This was not really slavery, for "we render them a gratuitous service by teaching them to till, plant, harvest and work for their livelihood—something they do not know until the whites teach them."

In 1712, the Tapuias responded to decades of abuse by attacking the Portuguese throughout the Sertaô. Led by Mandú Ladino, an Indian educated by the Jesuits, the Tapuias and their allies used stolen firearms and ammunition to keep the Portuguese at bay. They assaulted troop detachments, ambushed cattle drives, and killed hundreds of settlers. Although they destroyed many churches, the Tapuias killed only one priest and carefully removed any religious images before burning churches to the ground. In just several years, the Tapuias had plundered almost 100 cattle ranches, and nervous Lisbon officials fretted that "all care is necessary if those regions are not to be lost."

In 1716, Ladino was killed by the Tobajaras, allies of the Jesuits who fought "without any whites whatsoever, who were only an embarrassment to them." After Ladino's death, the revolt ebbed, and the Sertaô again became safe for cattle ranchers. Barely one decade later, other Indian peoples began fighting Portuguese settlers as their cattle empire expanded westward.

The war against the Tapuias altered the Sertaô's landscape. A 1724 census listed 8,000 residents, but in 1759 the government counted more than 75,000 inhabitants. As the Tapuias disappeared, cattle ranches expanded to hundreds of square kilometers and became self-contained kingdoms with their own armies, retainers, and courts of justice.

The growing prosperity of the Sertaô was based on the successful war against the Tapuias. If Brazil was "an inferno for Negroes, purgatory for Whites, and paradise for Mulattoes and Mulattas," it was death for many indigenous peoples.[5]

The Wakuénais Explain Christian Behavior

According to the Wakuénais, who live at the headwaters of the Río Negro in Colombia, Brazil, and Venezuela, humans first appeared from a hole beneath the rapids near the village of Hipana on the Aiary River. At the "navel of the world," Iñápirríkuli the creator gave them one name and a tobacco spirit. "Later we will go search for the names of these people," he said. Next, Iñápirríkuli gave almost all the Wakuénais names and a pair of tobacco spirits, but because "there were too many people" he stopped naming them.

The Wakuénai creation story helps explain why Christians behave so oddly and destructively. The Wakuénais are human beings who are closely related to the natural species and environment around the headwaters of the Río Negro. They have been fully created. Christians, in contrast, are only semi-human and incomplete cultural beings because they are still searching for their names and thus must form their souls from inanimate objects—books and papers. At night, the missionary's soul becomes a Bible and traders turn into financial statements. The Wakuénais admire European skills, but they are not surprised by the violent and unpredictable behavior of Christians. Without names and individual spirits, they are incapable of living harmoniously among themselves or with others.

Note: Jonathan D. Hill and Robin M. Wright, "Time, Narrative, and Ritual: Historical Interpretations from an Amazonian Society," in *Rethinking History and Myth: Indigenous South American Perspectives on the Past*, ed. Jonathan D. Hill (Urbana: University of Illinois Press, 1988), pp. 81–93.

Quechua and Colonialism

Europeans always recognized the special relationship between language and conquest. On the heels of the Moorish conquest and just fifteen days after Columbus set sail for the Orient, Elio Antonio de Nebrija wrote in his preface to the first grammatical study of Castilian that language "was always the companion of empire." When the Bishop of Avila presented a copy of Nebrija's *Gramática de la lengua castellana* to Queen Isabella, she bluntly asked the prelate about its usefulness.

"Soon Your Majesty will have placed her yoke upon many barbarians who speak outlandish tongues," the bishop politely responded. "By this, your victory, these people shall stand in a new need; the need for laws the victor owes to the vanquished, and the need for the language we shall bring with us." Nebrija agreed. Now that "the enemies of the Faith have been subdued by our arms," Castilian should be standardized and propagated abroad. Through a combination of "armas y letras," Spain could establish a universal empire.

The Spanish brought this linguistic philosophy to their administration of former Inca lands, but they realized that Castilian could not immediately replace indigenous languages. Southern Peruvian Quechua, the Incas' official language, had no proper name. Instead, Quechua speakers referred to themselves as users of *runa simi* [human speech]. Outsiders' languages were frequently called *hawa simi*, the speech of the puna (high plateau) or non-Cuzco speech. *Hawa* and *ukhu* [outside and inside] were important distinctions in Inca politics and marriage, and so insider language referred to a Quechua speaker or to the Inca nobility in Cuzco.

Although the Spanish first used Quechua to designate a variety of Andean languages, they decided by 1560 that *qheswa simi* [Quechua speech] was the name of "the lingua franca of all the natives and inhabitants. The ones who had it for their own . . . are the Quichuas, just as Castilian is called that because it is the mother tongue that we, Castilians, speak." The Quechua language, the Spanish believed, would help integrate Andean ethnic groups into the new Spanish state, convert the native population to Catholicism, and continue serving as the basic language of communication among the region's varied language groups.

In 1560, the Spanish produced their first Quechua lexicon and grammar book, and priests were ordered to pass a proficiency examination in the language. About twenty years later, the Church prepared an official Quechua catechism and confessional, and academic chairs for the study of Quechua were created in Lima and Quito.

In religious matters, language and empire intersected most clearly. The Third Provincial Council of Lima (1581–1583) recommended that priests use the word *ruray* rather than *kamay* to describe the biblical creation because Andean peoples might understand *kamay* not as a reference to a distant creator god, but to one who was the soul of the world. Religious texts about Quechua grammatical usage made clear the explicit social contrasts between Christian insiders and idol-worshipping outsiders—the saved and the damned. "Exclusion is when we exclude the person or persons with whom we speak in the matter, as if we were speaking to pagans we might say, 'We Christians worship one god' as *Zocaycu christianocuna huc Hapay*

Diosllactam muchaycu." This approach to Quechua grammar was based on the 1551 Conciliar Council of Lima, which declared that all Andean peoples who had lived before the conquest were burning in Hell.

Opponents of Quechua argued that the language helped maintain a separate ethnic and cultural identity for Andean peoples. After the Spanish defeated the Moors in Spain, they pointed out, Muslims were forbidden to use their language and literature. Similarly, Castilian should be promoted as the exclusive language in the Andes. Opponents also thought that the language contained too much pagan vocabulary and could not express such key Christian words as "God," "faith," "angel," "virtue," "matrimony," and "virginity." After many arguments and petitions, a royal decree in 1634 ended the promotion of Quechua as a religious language, and throughout the remainder of century no new Quechua religious and linguistic works were published.

But this policy failed in colonial Peru. Even after a century of Spanish rule, few Andean peoples learned Castilian. The *curacas* who served as mediators between Andean ethnic groups and the Spanish usually became the most Hispanized element of the native population. They learned Castilian, sometimes married Spaniards and mestizos, dressed in Spanish clothing, rode horses, and took on the imperial attitudes of their employers. But most of their subjects, whether they lived in traditional *ayllus* or forced resettlements, spoke their native language exclusively.

Quechua had become the language of the dominated in the same ways it had functioned as an elite language during Inca rule. Quechua speakers still referred to themselves as users of *runa simi*, but their language had been transformed from *ukhu simi* to *hawa simi*. Quechua was no longer the language of the capital or its governing elite. As Peru's lowland Indians were decimated by European diseases, Quechua dominated the high plateau and the growing Indian *barrios* of Spanish towns.

Ruled by new masters who spoke Castilian, Quechua speakers occupied the poorest and most exploited ecological niches of the Andes. The language could no longer be identified with a single ethnic group or geographical location, but with a culture of resistance. As the conquest collectively turned many distinctive Andean ethnic groups into generic Indians who spoke Quechua, it became associated with indigenous peoples who withstood assimilation. Castilian opponents of Quechua had been right. Quechua continued as a living language primarily because many Andean peoples had no desire to become Spaniards.

The regime also failed to eradicate Quechua because Hispanic society was divided about its vernacular and cultural value. While many officials and priests believed that Quechua had no future in the Andes, other Hispanics found Quechua a valuable political tool. The most ardent supporters of

Quechua language and culture were often the most exploitative rural land-owners. Along with local priests, they used Quechua as one more means of consolidating their control over the countryside.

In the eighteenth century, Quechua became darkly associated with revolts against the Crown. In the most densely populated Quechua-speaking region of southern Peru, there were dozens of revolts between 1730 and 1783. The largest—the Tupac Amaru rebellion—coincided with new taxes and a de-pressed economy. The leader of the revolt was a wealthy *curaca* with a mes-tiza wife who had changed his name to Tupac Amaru II, the last Inca emperor and his distant ancestor.

After Tupac Amaru II was tortured and executed in 1781, the administra-tion decided that "in order that these Indians remove the hatred of Spaniards which they had conceived . . . they are to dress in our Spanish clothing and speak the Castilian language." Quechua literature was banned along with the quipus that Tupac Amaru's followers had used to communicate with each other. The chair of Quechua at the University of San Marcos disappeared, and official policy became "the extirpation of the Indian language." Priests were ordered to give sermons only in Spanish, and administrators predicted that in just four years Spanish would become the common language of com-munications throughout the Andes.

The colonial regime, however, once again failed to eradicate Quechua. Compulsory education was too costly and reached only small numbers of Indians. Spaniards also realized that Quechua served as an effective disen-franchising linguistic barrier between themselves and their subjects. By re-lying on priests, *curacas*, and official interpreters to represent them, Indians consigned themselves to marginality. Although Quechua speakers knew they were at a serious disadvantage, they refused to learn Spanish because it threat-ened the core of their culture and identity. In colonial Peru, too many Quechua and Spanish speakers, for widely different reasons, wanted to maintain sepa-rate societies.

Little has changed in modern Peru. Spanish is still the language of the rulers, and Quechua remains the language of the dominated. A Quechua trans-lation of the bible, jointly sponsored by the Catholic Church and Protestant groups, appeared only in 1988. Even then the Church had grave misgivings about the translation because it rightly feared biblical verses would become part of indigenous religious practices.

There is still only one way Quechua speakers can overcome their alleged inferiority—by abandoning the Quechua language and the culture associ-ated with it. Even today, Quechua-speaking Indians refer to their language as *runa simi* or human speech. Spanish, on the other hand, is considered *alqo simi* or dog speech.[6]

188

Mesoamerica and the Caribbean

The Cost of Survival in Spanish Central America

During the colonial period, the Audiencia de Guatemala included Chiapa, Soconusco, Guatemala, Honduras, Nicaragua, and Costa Rica, which today make up part of southern Mexico and all of Central America. In Spanish Central America, the Indian population suffered a drastic decline in the early sixteenth century, continued dropping until the early or mid-eighteenth century, and then very slowly began increasing. By this time, however, Central America's demographic profile had changed dramatically since the conquest.

At the time of the conquest, Central America had a population of almost 6 million people. Guatemala had the largest population (2,000,000), followed by Panama (1,000,000), Nicaragua (800,000), Honduras and Belize (800,000), El Salvador (700,000), and Costa Rica (400,000). As the Spanish entered Mexico and Central America, most Indians died because they had no immunity to European viral infections (such as smallpox, measles, chicken pox, and influenza). Indians also succumbed to malaria and yellow fever, which came from Africa. The most severe death rates occurred in the first twenty-five years of the conquest. In addition, slavery and harsh encomienda labor led to the deaths of many Indians.

There is little disagreement about rates of decline and when they halted. Everywhere, European diseases killed about 80–90 percent of the native population. In 1524, for example, there were between 19,800 and 48,000 Quiché Mayans in nine highland Guatemalan towns. By about 1550, they had declined to just 4,950. Only in 1893 did the Quiché Mayan population finally surpass its pre-contact level.

Nicaragua had similar demographic variations over the centuries. The approximately 826,248 indigenous peoples in Nicaragua in 1524 declined in twenty-five years about 75 percent to 191,029. By the end of the seventeenth century, the Indian population had dropped to about 61,106, which represented a further reduction of 68 percent. But by the beginning of the nineteenth century, Nicaragua's Indian population began reversing its decline and now stood at around 83,059. This represented a 36 percent increase from the end of the seventeenth to the beginning of the nineteenth centuries.

Honduras went through a comparable demographic cycle. By 1550, the native population of Honduras has drastically fallen from an estimated 800,000 to 132,000. Disease mortality rates were highest in western and central Honduras, where the Indian population declined about 95 percent. In 1700, the Indian population was about 47,544, but by 1800 the native population had risen to almost 63,000.

Once Indian populations drastically dropped after the conquest, it took them two centuries to begin increasing because of the frequency of epidemics and the demography of the survivors. Throughout the colonial period, Indians were buffeted by regional and local epidemics. In the Cuchumatán Highlands of Guatemala, there were six local disease outbreaks during the eighteenth century, some of them lasting over a year. In Guatemala, there were smallpox epidemics in 1752, 1761, 1780, and 1789. From 1768 to 1770, there was a measles epidemic that left "stiff cadavers lying about streets and royal roads." In the town of Alotenango, almost 75 percent of all infants died.

As diseases ravaged Central America's Indians, the native demographic structure changed. In 1683, the average Indian family size in two Honduran villages was less than three. Among the Quiché Mayans in the Rabinal region of Guatemala in 1769, families averaged less than two children in nuclear and single-parent families. In the same region, Spanish families on average were more than double the size of their Mayan counterparts while families of mixed ethnic backgrounds had on average fewer children than the Spanish but more than the Indians.

Throughout Spanish Central America, the Indian population kept dropping for two centuries because families had small numbers of children and could not reproduce their numbers. Among the survivors, there was an increase in sterility and infant mortality. Put simply, Indian death rates were far higher than birth and survival rates.

This demographic trend finally began changing in the early eighteenth century. For example, in the Quiché Mayan village of Momostenango, the population increased 250 percent from 1714 to 1813. In another Quiché Mayan area, between 1776 and 1816 the Indian population rose from 25,334 to 73,960. Petén, the ancient heartland of the Mayas, showed a similar trend. In this densely forested northernmost province of Guatemala, the total urban and rural population was 3,027 in 1714. It later dipped and rose, and by 1839 the population stood at 6,327.

All over Spanish Central America, Indian women were having more children and more of them were surviving into adulthood. There were fewer unmarried males and females in Indian villages and a higher ratio of children to adults in comparison to earlier periods. After 1750, the Indian population increased rapidly and has continued to accelerate in the twentieth century.

When Central America became independent from Spain in 1821, it had a dramatically different demographic profile than at the time of the conquest. The population had declined to about one million people. There now were about 580,000 Indians, 375,000 mestizos and other castes, and only 45,000 Spaniards. Guatemala still had the largest population in Central America and the highest percentage of Indians, 84 percent.

Native population dynamics varied throughout Spanish Central America, but over two centuries the results were very similar. The large highland sedentary Indian kingdoms along the Pacific coast were hardest hit by the conquest because the Spanish coveted their labor and resources. Where there were few attractive resources such as gold and less concentrated populations, more Indians survived the conquest. Everywhere, however, Indian populations drastically declined into the eighteenth century. By 1821, there were about 80 percent fewer Indians in Central America than when the Spanish first appeared.[7]

The Backbone of Spanish Central America

Until the mid-eighteenth century Indian tribute was the backbone of the Central American economy. Throughout the region, married male Indians between the ages of sixteen or eighteen and fifty had to make an annual tribute payment of two pesos in commodities that went directly to the Crown. Maize was the most common form of tribute. Unmarried adults were considered half-tributaries. As the number of tributaries declined, the Spanish government addressed the problem of declining revenue in two imaginative ways.

First, local government officials were forbidden to take an accurate census of the actual number of Indians within their jurisdiction and instead had to use the old numbers of tributaries. And second, beginning in the late sixteenth century single Indian women were identified as special tributaries and had to pay a half peso annually in commodities. Within several decades, they had to pay two pesos annually. Despite numerous complaints, this practice ended only in 1759.

In 1735, 71 percent of Nicaragua's total taxes came from Indian tributaries. Only 7 percent came from non-Indian levies. Most Indian taxes were used to support the Catholic Church, the salaries and pensions of government officials, and especially the military.

The situation was no different in neighboring Guatemala. From 1731 to 1735, Indian tribute made up 81 percent of the colony's taxes. Although the Crown collected more nontribute taxes in the second half of the eighteenth century and tribute declined as a proportion of tax revenue, throughout the colonial era Indians provided most of the financial support for Central America's church and government.

Note: Miles L. Wortman, *Government and Society in Central America, 1680–1840* (New York: Columbia University Press, 1982), pp. 89–104, 146; W. George Lovell, *Conquest and Survival in Colonial Guatemala: A Historical Geography of the Cuchumatá Highlands, 1500–1821* (Montreal: McGill-Queen's University Press, 1992), pp. 101–104; Christopher H. Lutz, *Santiago de Guatemala, 1541–1773: City, Caste, and the Colonial Experience* (Norman: University of Oklahoma Press, 1994, pp. 56, 65–78, 147–148).

➤ 8 ◄

Beware of the
Long Knives

———————
====

The eighteenth century was the great age of global maritime empires. Britain, France, Spain, Portugal, and Holland used "industry and audacity," in the evocative words of Voltaire, to further extend their imperial reach. The British, who tripled their shipping tonnage in the eighteenth century while reducing insurance and freight costs, made the most spectacular gains. From 1700 to 1780, about 2 million people migrated to British America. Almost 67 percent of them were African slaves, most of whom were shipped to the West Indies. At the beginning of the century, Britain's gross domestic product was 96 percent larger than the thirteen American colonies. By 1770, this figure had declined to 60 percent, and the standard of living of nonindentured white colonists was probably higher than their counterparts in Britain. During the same period, the British colonial consumption of the mother country's total exports rose from 10 to 37 percent.

The Caribbean island of Hispaniola provided a dramatic example of the New World's power to generate enormous wealth for Europe. After Columbus established Christendom's first New World colony at Isabella, the Spanish rapidly worked the Taínos to death in their feverish pursuit of tribute and gold. Once the gold mines were exhausted, Europeans disappeared from western Hispaniola. About 1650, French settlers arrived and began growing tobacco. In 1697, Hispaniola officially had became St. Domingue.

On the eve of the French Revolution in 1789, St. Domingue had become the most prosperous European colony in the Caribbean. With over one million African slaves savagely controlled by about 70,000 French and mulattos, St. Domingue accounted for two-thirds of France's total overseas trade.

It produced over half of the world's coffee and more refined sugar than all the British colonies in the Caribbean put together. Almost one-fifth of France's population owed their livelihoods to St. Domingue's incredible tropical plantation wealth. All of it had been generated from seized Taíno land and the coerced labor of many millions of people—first the Taínos, then indentured servants, convicts, and the kidnapped urban poor from Europe, and finally a massive influx of slaves from West Africa.

These staggering financial figures were not unique among the maritime empires. During the eighteenth century, the profits from the French slave trade were about 500 million French gold pounds. Profits from slave labor in the British West Indies were close to 300 million English gold pounds. By the end of the eighteenth century, the Spanish mines of Potosí had produced almost 1 billion pesos worth of silver, or about half of all the silver mined in the entire New World. At the same time, in southeastern Brazil the Portuguese mined about 2 million kilograms of gold and 2.4 million carats in diamonds.

Elsewhere in the world, imperial profits were equally high. Between 1650 and 1780, the Dutch Company of the East Indies pillaged Indonesia of about 600 million gold florins while the British plundered at least 100 million gold pounds from India. Not surprisingly, the Hindustani word "loot" entered the English language at the same time.

By the eighteenth century, 200 years of European exploration, conquests, and settlement had drastically altered many New World indigenous societies. Since Columbus, Christendom had not just colonized space in the Western hemisphere. Indian thought and culture had also been colonized as their religious and moral systems, languages, histories, and ways of understanding the world were modified substantially by conquest and European settlement. Against their will, most native societies gradually had been incorporated into the Western world.

Survival, however, was a constant struggle because after 200 years of contact and supposedly close study, most Europeans still judged indigenous peoples to be brutish, cruel, superstitious, devoid of culture, and governed by the most basic lusts and desires. As the great eighteenth-century philosopher Jean-Jacques Rousseau lamented, although we Europeans have "inundated the other parts of the world, and continuously published new collections of voyages and reports, I am convinced that we know no other men except the Europeans." Worse, under the "pompous name of the study of man everyone does hardly anything except study the men of his own country. In vain do individuals come and go; it seems that philosophy does not travel."

Rousseau may have been referring to the intellectuals he heard talking about the New World in chic Parisian salons. Some European philosophers admired Indian societies for their liberty and generosity, but most could not

193

grant them much dignity or respect. Indians were still described, in the words of that great work of the French Enlightenment, the *Encyclopédie*, as ferocious and nomadic cannibals who lived without any laws or religion.

By the eighteenth century, few European thinkers described Indians using theological language. Instead, they focused on questions of human origins and development. In England and France, intellectuals constructed a four-stage typology of human development that began with hunting and progressed through pasturage, agriculture, and finally commerce. Each stage also corresponded to varying morals, customs, governments, laws, and systems of property. In this typology, the New World's indigenous peoples were consigned to the hunting stage, despite the fact that Europeans knew that almost the overwhelming majority of them also farmed and engaged in trade.

Indians were not only in the earliest stage of human development. Their societies also represented the mental childhood of humanity. Especially in the second half of the eighteenth century, writers frequently compared the minds of children with the minds of Indians. As one Frenchman wrote, Indians lived in a state of infancy "similar to that of individuals of our own continent who have not reached the age of puberty." This meant that there was a tremendous intellectual distance between "a stupid Huron, or a Hottentot, and a profound philosopher." According to many Enlightenment thinkers, a savage stood in the same relationship to a civilized person as did a child to an adult. Previously, Indians had been considered devilish and barbaric because they were non-Christians. Now, the fashionable new Enlightenment social sciences—economics, sociology, and anthropology—placed them in similarly benighted categories but for ostensibly secular and objective reasons.

Europeans considered indigenous peoples at the bottom of human development because they stubbornly refused to become darker versions of their masters. Part of Christendom's condemnation stemmed from the problem of having peoples within their own colonies who stubbornly tried to maintain their independence and their own ways of life. Since they disgusted and frightened Christians so much, native cultures had to be radically devalued and then transformed or else they would forever remain threatening.

In the late eighteenth century, Indians were confronted with a new challenge as two projects of the Enlightenment, Bourbon Spanish reforms and the American Revolution, heralded even more drastic changes. As Pachgantschihilas, a Delaware war chief, told his followers in 1787, "I admit that there are good white men, but they bear no proportion to the bad; the bad must be strongest, for they rule. . . . I know the *long knives*; they are not to be trusted." He understood that the conquest was not a single event but a process, and thus it never ended.[1]

194

North America

The Custom of the Country

After France began colonizing eastern Canada, fur traders started marrying Indian women "after the custom of the country" because both peoples understood the economic and personal benefits of these unions. When the Hudson Bay Company (HBC) was established in 1670, it tried prohibiting "converse" between native women and the British, but by the end of the eighteenth century officials had intermarried extensively with Ojibwa, Cree, and Chippewa women. These relationships had been initiated by Indian women with the consent of their husbands and communities.

Unofficial and sometimes clandestine marriages occurred soon after HBC forts were established in Canada. In the late seventeenth century, for example, the HBC ordered young Henry Kelsey, "a very active Lad, delighting much in Indians Company, being never better pleased than when he is travelling amongst them," to undertake several long exploring expeditions. On one of his trips, he returned dressed like an Indian "and attended by a wife, who wanted to follow him into the factory." Kelsey told his superiors that "he would not go in himself if his wife was not suffered to go in," and both were allowed to enter.

In 1732, James Isham was hired as a bookkeeper by the HBC and eventually became chief of the York and Churchill forts. On his arrival in Canada, he thought Indian women were "very frisky when Young," "well shap'd," and "very Bewitchen." When the company confirmed him as chief of the York Factory almost twenty years later, he was admonished not to allow Indian women into his fort and serve as an example to his men. After Isham's death in 1761, the company instructed his successor to "send home Charles . . . an Indian Lad said to be the Natural Son of Mr. James Isham deceased." Charles lived with his English uncle and then returned to the HBC as an apprentice.

When the HBC set up its trading forts around Hudson Bay, it discovered that most of the region's Indians practiced wife-lending with the approval of the women's husbands. Wife-lending was a gift, and Indians initiated it to establish bonds of friendship and peace with other peoples. Wives and daughters were offered as tokens of hospitality, and wife-lending provided Indians with English consumer goods, trading opportunities, support for their families in times of hardship, and employment for themselves and their mixed offspring in Company posts.

With an uncomplicated native marriage ceremony, a couple wed and were expected to be loyal to each other. Company men had to obtain permission from the bride's parents and offer them presents, such as blankets, metal utensils, liquor, clothing, and guns. Henry Kelsey probably gave his in-laws a horse. After these presents were accepted, the trader and his new relatives might smoke a long-stemmed pipe and hear a lecture from community elders about the importance of the bride's being "chaste, obedient, industrious, and silent." Finally, the newly married couple would be happily escorted by the bride's family to the husband's fort. If the union was not satisfactory, either partner could end the relationship simply by leaving the other.

When Indian women entered marriages after the custom of the country, they did not take on all the values and functions of eighteenth-century British wives. Indian women were not treated as minors or considered their husband's property. Instead, they continued acting within the norms of their own cultures. Wife-lending, after all, was an institution devised by Indians, not colonists.

What Indians heartily detested were forced sexual relations or unions that were advantageous only to one party. In the early eighteenth century, Cree women held against their will at a French fort decided to revenge themselves against their captors. The women wet the French fuses with their urine and then their husbands attacked the fort. When the fighting ended, eight Frenchmen had been "Kill'd for their prefidiousness." And in 1775, Indians attacked Henley House because the British lived with their women but denied them access to the trading post.

Wife-lending became an acceptable HBC institution by the end of the eighteenth century. At first the British found it shocking and compared it to London prostitution, but they soon learned that Indians "were a sensible People, and agree their women should be made use of." Besides providing social companionship and sex, wife-lending served the British in other ways. Native women acted as guides, interpreters, trading emissaries, and teachers of local customs and languages. Company Indian women cleaned and prepared furs, sewed moccasins, and threaded leather snowshoes. In 1800, the Indian women at York Factory made 650 pairs of moccasins just for summer use. Since Indian women traditionally played important roles in the fur trade, native wives helped make company posts more profitable.

These unions often became more than utilitarian conveniences. Couples frequently developed close, affectionate ties and even spoiled their children. One reason for the growth of affectionate ties was a soaring Indian birth rate. Indian women at HBC posts often gave birth to double the number of children (eight to twelve) than women living in native communities. They became more fertile because their diet and living conditions improved, and they nursed their babies for much shorter periods of time. In addition, Company men abstained from sexual relations with their wives less often than did Indian husbands. Not surprisingly, Canadians Indians were shocked that HBC men would father so many children.

By the late eighteenth century, the British openly acknowledged their relationships with Indian women and established their sons and daughters in company posts. In casual conversations, diary entries, and official correspondence, company men began describing their partners as wives rather than "my woman" or the "mother of my children." New company recruits commonly formed country marriages with the daughters of mixed unions. These women made even better wives than their mothers because they were already integrated into Company society, spoke English along with their native languages, were skilled in the preparation of furs, and supplied important trading contacts with their mothers' peoples.

In just over a century, Indians and settlers had created a completely new subculture in Canada composed of native women who had married after the custom of the country, their British husbands, and their offspring. Because the British learned to love, respect, and cherish their native wives, wife-lending commonly evolved into a permanent relationship.[2]

Seminole Traders

From the Amazon to Hudson Bay, the introduction of European trade and consumer goods profoundly changed many native societies. When Indians living in relatively unstratified communities began exchanging products such as deerskins and beaver pelts for foreign items, they became integral parts of a global market economy that originated in Europe and ended at their homes. At first, New World peoples used European goods to intensify ceremonial exchanges and maintain traditional patterns of community redistribution. Eventually, however, the intrusion of the market system disrupted traditional clan and group relationships by encouraging individuals to differentiate themselves materially from their kin and neighbors. Despite the growing importance of European goods in native societies, however, most Indians continued maintaining their cultural identity and a sense of separateness within colonial society.

The Seminoles, who lived in the north Florida peninsula and the panhandle around Tallahassee during the eighteenth century, are descended from the Lower Creek Indians who once lived in Georgia and Alabama. After the British and the Lower Creeks destroyed Florida's northern Spanish missions, bands of Lower Creeks living in what is now eastern Alabama and western Georgia began migrating into Florida around 1710 to trade with settlers. As Creeks bartered deerskins, they divided into almost self-sufficient nuclear families. Creek clans gradually relinquished the power to organize subsistence activities, and chiefs no longer redistributed goods or carried out sacred ceremonies.

The Seminoles prospered in northern Florida. In the late eighteenth century, Seminole hunters prepared more than 300,000 pounds of deerskins each year for French, Spanish, and English saddles, shoes, gloves, harnesses, whips, and clothing. Men also raised cattle and pigs and drove them to markets in St. Augustine, Savannah, Pensacola, and Mobile. Some Seminoles even settled near Ft. Myers in South Florida to trade animal skins and furs with Cuban fishermen who regularly visited nearby beaches to cure and salt their catch.

Seminole women also increased their wealth and status as they became involved in Florida's international economy. Traditionally, Lower Creek men and women had very different roles in their communities. Men hunted animals and took enemy scalps, while women raised children, planted and harvested, wove, and made pottery and baskets. In North Florida, however, women began to produce such commercial crops as oranges, corn, rice, and peaches and to sell them in St. Augustine, Apalachee, and St. John.

Some even married English merchants. According to one traveler, these marriages were not always mutually beneficial. One North Carolina trader had "made a little fortune by traffic with the Seminoles." When he married a beautiful Seminole woman, however, his situation changed. According to one British observer, "he loves her sincerely, as she possesses every perfection in her person to render a man happy . . . and these powerful graces she has so artfully played upon her beguiled and vanquished lover, and unhappy slave, as to have already drained him of all his possessions, which she dishonestly distributes amongst her savage relations. He is now poor, emaciated, and half distracted, often threatening to shoot her, and afterwards put an end to his own life."

In exchange for their cattle, fruits and vegetables, and skins, the Seminoles received Spanish olive jars, English ceramics, buttons, knives, razors, gun parts, and blankets, glass beads, metal tools, fabrics, handkerchiefs, looking glasses, silver buckles, riding saddles, and cash. Guns and gunpowder were the warriors' most valued European objects. As individual wealth became more important in Seminole society, matrilineal inheritance declined so that sons could inherit their fathers' African slaves, land, cattle, and horses.

Seminole warfare and religion also changed by the late eighteenth century. Lower Creek and early Seminole villages once had two kinds of civil offices. Town chiefs representing the white clan organized village affairs, while war leaders from the red clan supervised formal warfare, raiding, and ball games between rival communities. In Florida, however, leadership ceased being collective as it became closely tied to material success. War leaders from the red clan could no longer restrain young fighters. By the end of the century, the Seminoles had developed a culture that was highly receptive to innovation and showed a deep respect for individual rights as opposed to communal obligations.

Male Creek society had always stressed the acquisition of prestige through successful scalping parties, punitive raids, and hunting. After the British moved into the Southeast, fighting continued to be a major source of male prestige, but it was augmented by the deerskin trade and the herding of cattle and pigs. British trade provided the Seminoles with rewarding opportunities to demonstrate their prowess and acquire prestigious items. The Seminoles found ways to retain their independence and incorporate European goods into their culture by changing their society in directions their ancestors would have recognized, if not approved.

Close contact with the British encouraged the Seminoles to borrow new ideas and new ways of living that were consistent with their own culture. At the same time, the growing power of the British colonies stimulated them into defining and asserting a distinct ethnic identity to avoid being assimilated into colonial society. The Seminole/British frontier was always fluid. It encouraged both the development of a shared commercial culture in the Southeast and a strong sense of separateness.

As American settlers poured into northern Florida and claimed native lands, the Seminoles fought one war with the United States in 1812, another from 1835 to 1842, and a third from 1855 to 1858. Of all the Southeastern Indians, the U.S. government had the most difficulty subduing Florida's Seminoles.[3]

"I Once Owned All This Land"

In 1782, a man living in the cypress swamps on the border of Maryland and Delaware met Will Andrew, an elderly Indian who might have been a Nanticoke. According to the man, Andrew told him that "I once owned all this land about here. Come, said he, I will shew you where my father lived; I walked with him about two hundred paces to an eminence about three hundred yards from a creek, where I saw a large quantity of shells. Here said he, stamping with his foot is the very spot where my father lived. But white people gave him rum and took it away, and I am not so well off as a Ratcoon."

Note: C.A. Weslager, The Nanticoke Indians—Past and Present (Newark: University of Delaware Press, 1983), p. 197.

Pueblo Marriage Under the Spanish

For almost three centuries, Spain controlled a huge empire in North America that stretched from California across Arizona, New Mexico, and Texas to Florida. In California and Florida, there was widespread racial mixing between indigenous peoples and Spaniards, but the Pueblo Indians of New Mexico preserved their racial homogeneity by severely limiting intermarriage and sexual relations with Spaniards.

There were three reasons why there was little miscegenation between Pueblo Indians and Spaniards despite conquest, nominal Pueblo conversion to Catholicism, and demanding tribute and *repartimiento* labor. First, the Spanish resettled the Pueblo population in New Mexico, defined their lands and political boundaries, and used vagrancy laws to isolate each community. As a result, Pueblo men and women periodically labored in Spanish towns but lived primarily in their own communities. In this environment, sexual relations and intermarriage were less likely to occur.

The decline in the number of Pueblo Indians and communities made spatial segregation more likely. When the Spanish first entered the Southwest, there were over 100,000 Pueblo Indians living in more than 100 pueblos. By the early eighteenth century, disease and warfare had greatly reduced their numbers. There were now less than 7,000 Indians occupying only eighteen pueblos.

Second, throughout the eighteenth century, the Spanish fought the "barbarous and ferocious heathen" surrounding them—the Navajos, Utes, and especially the Apaches—whom the Pueblos also feared and loathed. As a result of these conflicts, which the Spanish considered just wars, thousands of prisoners of war became slaves in Spanish households if they were not sent to Mexico's silver mines or Cuba's tobacco plantations. Since female household slaves often became mistresses and produced mestizo offspring, Spanish males never needed Pueblo women for sex. The presence of Indian slaves in colonial households made Pueblo women less likely targets of Spanish sexual aggression.

And third, Pueblo communities took drastic social steps to discourage intimacy with Spaniards. Women accused of having sexual relations with Spaniards were stigmatized as outcasts and expelled from their communities along with their light-skinned children. Especially after the Pueblo revolt of 1680, the Pueblos demanded that their women be chaste while laboring in Spanish villages. Twenty years later, the Hopis even destroyed one of their own villages, Awatobi, because it had become too Spanish. Strict penalties for sexual relations with Spaniards, along with disease, helped lead to a drastic decline in the Pueblo population, but they also preserved the homogeneity of Pueblo communities. Unlike Indian communities to the south, the Pueblos never developed a mestizo population.

The Pueblos were not adverse to adopting some aspects of Spanish culture, such as using metal tools; growing European crops; and raising horses, cattle, sheep, pigs, and chickens. Some of them even switched from matrilineal to patrilineal forms of kinship and residence patterns under pressure from priests and government officials. None of them, however, tolerated sexual relations with Spaniards, for only degraded female slaves and outcasts would stoop so low.[4]

The First Families of Los Angeles (1781)

Felix Antonio Villavicencio, Spaniard, 45, married to María de los Santos Sobernia, Indian, 30, one daughter.

Antonio Mesa, African American, 36, married to Ana Gertrudes López, mulatto, 27, two daughters.

José Lara, Spaniard, 50, married to María Antonia Campos, Indian, 20, one son and two daughters.

José Vanegas, Indian, 28, married to Mariana Agular, Indian, 20, one son.

Pablo Rodríguez, Indian, 25, married to María Rosario Noriega, Indian, 26, one daughter.

Manuel Camero, mulatto, 30, married to María Tomosa, mulatto, 24, no children.

José Navarro, mestizo, 42, married to María Guadalupe, mulatto, 47, two sons and one daughter.

Basilio Rosas, Indian, 67, married to María Manuela Calistra, mulatto, 43, five sons and one daughter.

Alejandro Rosas, Indian, 19, married to Juana Rodríguez, coyote, 20, no children.

Antonio Rodríguez, Chinese, 50, a widower with one daughter.

Luís Quintero, African American, 65, married to Petra Rubio, mulatto, 40, two sons and three daughters.

Note: Jack D. Forbes, *The Indian in America's Past* (Englewood Cliffs, NJ: Prentice-Hall, 1964), pp. 148–149.

Cayuse Horses

The Cayuses of western Oregon called themselves "Waiilatpu," or "the Superior People," but their origins were quite modest. Along with the Mollalahs, the Cayuses lived west of Mount Hood where they hunted, fished, and gathered wild roots and vegetables. After quarreling with the Cayuses, the Mollalahs abandoned their ancestral lands for the Willamette Valley. The Cayuses began fighting the peoples to the south collectively known as the Snakes—the Shoshone, Banneck, and Paiute peoples.

Around 1750, an incident fundamentally altered Cayuse life. While the Cayuses were stalking the Snakes, spies reported astonishing news: their enemies were riding elk or deer. The Cayuses arranged a truce with them and received as gifts two horses whose ancestors had come from northern Mexico. Through careful breeding and frequent raids, the Cayuses quickly produced their own large herds.

When Columbus brought horses with him on his voyage to Hispaniola in 1493, the dog's life as a beast of burden slowly ended for Indians. Although many horses died in the Gulf of Mares between the Canaries and the Caribbean, by 1503 there were at least sixty horses in Hispaniola. Horses helped Cortés conquer Mexico, and they dazzled the Incas two decades later. "After God, we owe the victory to the horses" became a common statement in Spanish battle accounts. By the end of the sixteenth century, horses were found throughout Spanish settlements and especially in the grassy plains of Argentina and Uruguay, the fertile plains of Venezuela and Columbia, and the vast prairies north of Mexico City.

At first, indigenous peoples were awed by the horse. When the Spanish entered a Hopi village in 1583, cotton scarves were placed on the ground for their horses to walk over. In some Indian stories, the horse originated from the sun and the earth. Only a sacred origin could explain its amazing power and usefulness.

With horses, the Cayuses became an aggressive and expansionist people. They stopped hunting on foot and trained their horses to stalk large animals. Mounted Cayuses left their homeland and moved north until they reached the Grande Ronde, a tributary of the Snake River. There they found plentiful fish, game, and grass for their horses. Along with the Nez Perces, who shared the Grande Ronde Valley, Shoshonean peoples appeared in the summer and fall at great trading fairs. The highly mobile Cayuses became prosperous middlemen in this trade.

From the Pacific Northwest, the Cayuses obtained dried salmon, shells, and captives, which they traded to the Snakes for buffalo meat, animal robes, and fur. They also supplied horses to the Salishan and Nez Perce peoples. The Cayuses became such friendly and reliable trading partners with the Nez Perces that they even started speaking the Nez Perce language.

When the Cayuses were not trading, their young men eagerly enjoyed going on war parties. The horse helped proud Cayuse males prove their valor in deadly raids. To become a war chief was the greatest Cayuse honor. Males lived for adventure and measured their success by the number of prisoners and horses they accumulated.

The Cayuse horse—unattractive but exceptionally hardy and swift—completely changed the lives of its owners. By the end of the eighteenth century, the Cayuses were the imperious trading masters of a great domain covering thousands of square miles. The horse had helped make them bold, fearless, and eager to meet new challengers.[5]

The First Cold War

After Vitus Bering explored the Alaskan coast in 1741 on behalf of Russia, Russian merchant ships entered the North Pacific Ocean searching for sea otters, whose fur were even more valuable than Siberian sables. In Siberia, armed Russian fur traders had forced the native peoples to hunt for sables. If they refused or could not meet their annual quotas, they were beaten or killed. Traders quickly established a similar tribute system on the Alaskan coast among the Aleut people, who probably numbered about 15,000.

Until the late eighteenth century, Russian fur traders attacked Aleut villages and routinely kidnapped women and children. From 1799 to 1867, the Russian American Company forced all healthy Aleut males between the ages of fifteen and fifty to hunt sea otters in exchange for the return of their women and children along with the payment of food, tobacco, and clothing. While the men hunted otters for several months, Russians traders moved into their villages, ate their food, had sexual relations with their women, and spread their deadly diseases. After fifty years of contact, the Aleut population had declined to only 2,000.

After the Aleuts, the maritime Kodiaks to the east were the next victims. Again, Russian fur traders attacked villages and held women and children hostage to force Kodiak men into hunting sea otters. Many harpooners died in hunting accidents supplying Russians with food, and smallpox and venereal disease decimated the Kodiaks. Forty years after the Russians appeared, the Kodiaks had lost two-thirds of their people.

Note: Hector Chevigny, *Russian America: The Great Alaskan Venture, 1741–1867* (New York: Viking Press, 1965), pp. 31–124; Benson Bobrick, *East of the Sun: The Epic Conquest and Tragic History of Siberia* (New York: Poseidon Press, 1972), pp. 111–133, 211–253; James R. Gibson, "Russian Dependence Upon the Natives of Alaska," in *Russia's American Colony*, ed. S. Frederick Starr (Durham, NC: Duke University Press, 1987), pp. 77–104; R.G. Liapunova, "Relations with the Natives of Russian America," in *Russia's American Colony*, pp. 108–21; Henry Aaron Coppock, *Interactions Between Russians and Native Americans in Alaska, 1741–1840* (Ann Arbor, MI: University Microfilms, 1973), pp. 76–129.

The Alcoholic Global Economy

With the arrival of European explorers and settlers, the New World became awash in alcohol. In 1770, British settlers produced and imported 8.6 million gallons of rum, and the average colonist annually imbibed almost four gallons of hard liquor. Especially in British and French North America, liquor was an important part of global commerce and a major source of profits for both the Crown and colonists.

European liquor affected native peoples differently. In the Pueblo Southwest, Mexico, and Central and South America, Indians traditionally had consumed alcoholic beverages in carefully defined social situations and religious ceremonies. Native consumption of liquor increased after the conquest because of the commercialization of alcohol production and the appearance of numerous Catholic holidays, but relatively small numbers of indigenous peoples became drunkards.

In Spanish Florida, New France, and British North America, however, the response to alcohol was very different and much more devastating. Native peoples in these areas had no previous exposure to alcohol, but after the appearance of Europeans, increasing numbers of them became binge drinkers and alcoholics. They used rum and brandy in gift exchanges, dances, marriages, and in welcoming and mourning ceremonies. Hard liquor cemented alliances and friendships, lowered inhibitions to violence and sexual relations, and enabled Indians to temporarily forget the problems that assailed them.

In many native communities, alcohol increased tensions, violence, and individual indebtedness to liquor and fur traders. Drunken Indians neglected their hunting and agricultural responsibilities, and even exchanged precious corn for rum. In the Southeast, the Choctaws traded deerskins for liquor.

Native peoples realized that "rum is the thing that makes us poor & foolish," but proponents of temperance failed in their crusade to end the hated liquor trade because they faced two insurmountable problems. First, too many Indians had become dependent on alcohol for prohibition to succeed. Although there were eighteenth-century temperance movements among the Choctaws, Miamis, Shawnees, Iroquois, and other indigenous peoples ("Rot Your grain in Tubs," one Catawba leader tartly told North Carolina officials), no Indian communities successfully banned liquor from their lands. As one Choctaw lamented, when "the Clattering of the Packhorse Bells are heard at a Distance our Town is Immediately deserted young and old run out to meet them joyfully crying Rum Rum; they get Drunk, Distraction Mischief Confusion and Disorder are the Consequences and this the Ruin of our Nation."

Second, despite periodic colonial protests from priests and government officials, the British and French governments could never stop the sale of liquor to Indians because it was so profitable. Brandy was a key ingredient in New France's fur trade, and the same was true of rum in British North America. The liquor trade was most brisk along the backwoods frontier where Indians exchanged furs and deerskins for European goods and watered-down alcohol. Throughout the British and French colonies, liquor was a powerful, profitable lubricant in the burgeoning Atlantic market economy.[6]

Indians and the American Revolution

As a result of the Great War for the Empire between France and England from 1756 to 1763, Great Britain became the dominant colonial power in eastern North America. The British now controlled all lands once held by the French in Canada and the Ohio River Valley, but native peoples told the Crown that they still had their sovereignty. As a Chippewa leader named Minivavana warned, "Englishman, although you have conquered the French, you have not yet conquered us. We are not your slaves. These lakes, these woods and mountains, were left to us by our ancestors. They are our inheritance; and we will part with them to none."

In both the South and the North, Indians wanted the British to acknowledge their sovereignty and demanded that they create an effective boundary between themselves and encroaching white settlers. While some dreamed of ridding their communities of alien corrupting influences, others decried British economic measures that reduced their access to European goods. All of them, however, wanted to limit the acquisition of Indian land by settlers.

When the Great War for the Empire began, Indians allied with the French had attacked settlers in Virginia, Maryland, and Pennsylvania. Without the assistance of indigenous peoples, France could never have held off the more numerous and better equipped British soldiers in the early years of the conflict. Britain triumphed only when many Indians abandoned the French, aided British troops, or chose neutrality.

But in 1761 as fighting subsided, the British stopped distributing gifts of food and military supplies to their Indian allies and began erecting forts in the Ohio River Valley. Two years later, Ottawa, Delaware, Seneca, Ojibwa,

205

Potawatomi, and Shawnee attacked communities from Detroit to western Pennsylvania. About 2,000 settlers lost their lives before the uprising ended. With the rebellion of Pontiac, which the British named after one of the revolt's Ottawa chiefs, Great Britain realized that its victory over the French had made Indians west of the Appalachians fearful and mistrustful.

Native conflicts and complaints led King George III to issue the Proclamation of 1763, which established a boundary running down the crest of the Alleghenies dividing Indian lands from British settlements. There were precedents for this dramatic response to Indian-settler conflicts on the frontier. In the 1758 Treaty of Easton, white settlement was prohibited west of the Alleghenies, and in 1761 the Privy Council had stated that royal colonies could neither make land grants nor encourage settlements on Indian lands.

Through the Proclamation of 1763, the British government hoped to promote interracial peace, friendship, and imperial trade by establishing a clearly defined boundary beyond which white settlers could not live. The British Crown understood that it could not establish stronger rule in North America while settlers and Indians clashed along the western frontier.

Indians were delighted with the Proclamation. From 1763 to 1768, the Creek, Choctaw, Cherokee, and Chickasaw peoples signed eight treaties with the British establishing a boundary line south of the Ohio River. The Cherokees even helped the British locate and mark the boundary in the Carolinas with blazes on trees. In the North, with the strong encouragement of the Iroquois Confederacy, over twenty Indian peoples signed treaties of peace between 1763 and 1766, and the British gave over 10,000 English pounds of gifts to Indians who ceded some of their lands. In 1767, fourteen Iroquois and an interpreter helped Charles Mason and Jeremiah Dixon run a boundary line along the Maryland-Pennsylvania border that went no further than the "Top of the Great Dividing Ridge" of the Allegheny Mountains. This is commonly known as the Mason-Dixon line.

As a result of the Great War for the Empire, Great Britain's national debt had skyrocketed from 73 million to 137 million pounds. With an annual interest rate of 5 million pounds a year, the war debt alone consumed more than 60 percent of the national budget. To finance its new imperial responsibilities and maintain a standing army and more forts to enforce the Proclamation, Parliament passed the Stamp Act in 1764, which levied a tax on documents and newspapers.

Many American colonists responded to the Proclamation of 1763 and the Stamp Act with outrage. As the royal governor of Virginia recognized, colonists denied that any government had the right to "forbid their taking possessions of a Vast tract of country . . . which serves only as a Shelter for a few scattered Tribes of Indians . . . whom they consider but little removed from the brute Creation." Beginning with Jamestown, colonial prosperity had been predicated on easy access to land, and wealth and status in American society was founded on intense real estate speculation. As George Washington, whose legal and illegal land grants in the Ohio River Valley had been abrogated by the Proclamation of 1763, candidly admitted, "I can never look upon that proclamation . . . than as a temporary expedient to quiet the minds of the Indians." Since indigenous peoples, in Washington's words, had "nothing human except the shape," why should the Crown placate them by inhibiting colonial expansion and prosperity?

The Proclamation of 1763 seemed to affect all Americans, not just wealthy landowners like Washington. North Carolina's population increased sixfold between 1750 and 1775. During the same period, Georgia ballooned from just 2,300 inhabitants to more than 30,000. In Pennsylvania, twenty-two new towns appeared during the same period, and in just one decade, New York's population expanded from 80,000 to over 150,000. In the throes of a growing land mania, American colonists would not accept the Crown's decision that the huge territory between the Appalachians and the Mississippi was reserved for native peoples.

After the British took over the Northwest from the French, they were powerless to stop their own settlers from invading Indian lands in open violation of the Proclamation. Unlike French fur traders, British colonists were repelled by the notion of living among Indians. They simply wanted to dispossess them, and too often murdered, raped, or robbed Indians who stood in their way. According to one exasperated Crown official, they were a "Sett of People . . . near as wild as the country they go in, or the People they deal with, & by far more vicious & wicked." They loathed all Indians, and were "too Numerous, too Lawless and Licentious ever to be restrained." Another official was even blunter. "The country beyond the Alleghenies talks of nothing but killing Indians and taking possession of their lands."

Colonists objected to Parliament's assertion of imperial authority, claiming that the Proclamation of 1763 and the Stamp Act reduced traditional British liberties in America by limiting colonial rights to property and self-government. The King, they argued, could not divest them of rights "consistent with the law of God and nature." Only the colonists, who had occupied North America by the hallowed right of conquest, had the authority to dispose of lands in the West.

The Proclamation of 1763 began the legal and political disputes that led to the Declaration of Independence thirteen years later. The furor over the Proclamation meant that the American Revolution would actually be two wars—a war against England for independence, and a war for control over Indian lands beyond the Appalachian Mountains.

The opening salvo of the war against indigenous peoples appeared in the Declaration of Independence. To prove that the "history of the present King of Great Britain is a history of repeated injuries and usurpations," among many other reasons the signers claimed that the king "has endeavored to bring on the inhabitants of our frontiers, the merciless Indian savages, whose known rule of warfare, is an undistinguished destruction of all ages, sexes and conditions." All Indians officially were branded as vicious killers and supporters of British tyranny in 1776. They could have no role in the new nation's future. In America's birth certificate, Thomas Jefferson and the Founding Fathers solemnly declared all Indians to be orphans.

As a result of the American Revolution and later the Napoleonic wars in Europe, Americans forcefully could assert the laws of God and nature because France, Spain, and Britain could no longer support effectively their former Indian allies in the new nation's territory. Native peoples, weakened by bitter fighting from 1754 through 1781 and the abandonment of their European supporters, were now at the mercy of an expansive nation that considered them a barrier to future settlement. In just a few decades, the military power and diplomatic position of Indians in eastern North America had been eroded seriously over millions of square miles.

The changing position of the Iroquois signaled this new relationship between native peoples and the United States. Until the late eighteenth century, the Iroquois Confederacy had been a major power in the Northeast because of its military prowess, diplomatic skills, and its strategic location between the French and British. By the end of the Revolution, however, the Iroquois found themselves in a perilous position precisely at the time when New York State's land-hungry settlers were becoming more ruthless and demanding.

Since the early eighteenth century, settlers fraudulently had acquired hundreds of thousands of acres of Mohawk land near Albany. Dispossession accelerated after the Revolution as a result of Iroquois internal divisions (the Tuscaroras and Oneidas had sided with the Americans, while other members of the Confederacy supported the British), disease and starvation, and the destruction of villages and crops by both British and American soldiers. Between 1783 and 1796 the Iroquois signed seventeen treaties with the United States, Pennsylvania, New York, and private individuals selling or ceding over 2 million acres of their ancestral lands. They were gradually confined to small reservations surrounded by a growing and hostile white population.

"Brothers," one Mohawk leader told New York officials, "formerly we enjoyed the privilege we expect now is called freedom and liberty; but since our acquaintance with our brother white people, that which we call freedom and liberty, becomes an entire stranger to us." His pleas that "every brother might have their rights throughout the continent" fell on deaf ears.

No longer did Americans have to accommodate peoples they considered savages and impediments to their destiny. By the end of the eighteenth century, treaties became very thinly disguised ways of transferring land ownership from Indian communities to the United States. A new era in ethnic relations had dawned in North America that Indians clearly recognized. They understood that the American Revolution had given birth to a new republic eager to enlarge itself at the expense of the remaining indigenous peoples within its borders.

The new era was reflected in the fiscal policy of the United States. In the last decade of the eighteenth century, over 80 percent of the total federal budget was spent fighting Indian wars beyond the Appalachians. The goal of the new nation was very straightforward: Coerce once sovereign Indian peoples into ceding their lands so they could quickly and cheaply be sold to incoming land companies and settlers.

As Pachgantschihilas, a Delaware war chief, told his followers in 1787, "I admit that there are good white men, but they bear no proportion to the bad; the bad must be strongest, for they rule. . . . They would make slaves of us if they could, but as they cannot do it, they kill us! There is no faith to be placed in their words. They are not like the Indians, who are only enemies, while at war, and are friends in peace. . . . Remember! that this day I have warned you to beware of such friends as these. I know the *long knives*; they are not to be trusted."[7]

From First Majority to Last Minority

In 1685, about four-fifths of the South's 250,000 inhabitants were Indians. By 1790, the year of the first federal census, these numbers had drastically changed. There were now over 1.6 million people in the South. At least 1 million of them were white, almost 600,000 were African Americans, and only 55,900 identified themselves as Indians. Indigenous peoples had been the overwhelming majority of the South's population in 1685, but a century later they had precipitously dwindled to less than 4 percent of the total population.

Note: Marvin T. Smith, *Archaeology of Aboriginal Culture Change in the Interior Southeast: Depopulation During the Early Historic Period* (Gainesville: University Presses of Florida, 1987), pp. 54–85; Peter H. Wood, "The Changing Population of the Colonial South: An Overview by Race and Region, 1685–1790," in *Powhatan's Mantle: Indians in the Colonial Southeast*, ed. Peter H. Wood, Gregory A. Waselkov, and M. Thomas Bailey (Lincoln: University of Nebraska Press, 1989), pp. 35–103.

Mesoamerica and the Caribbean

Hacienda Labor in Guadalajara

When the Spanish invaded Mexico, conquistadors eagerly looked forward to acquiring estates and tribute labor as they had done in Granada, the Canary Islands, and the Caribbean. The Crown reluctantly complied by granting them *encomiendas* throughout the most heavily populated areas of Mexico. As *encomienda* lands gradually reverted to the Crown, new estate owners multiplied as government officials granted or sold Indian lands to settlers. The great *hacienda* or rural estate, one of Latin America's most important institutions, made its appearance.

The *hacienda* was hardly a unique institution. It had deep roots in the Roman Iberian peninsula, and was used for centuries by the Spanish to repopulate territory seized from the Moors. In Spain's New World possessions, the *hacienda* emerged once again, this time among a recently conquered Indian population.

In the region around Guadalajara, which is about 350 kilometers northwest of Mexico City, the *hacienda* blossomed in the eighteenth century. From 1542 to 1803, this municipality grew from just sixty-eight Spaniards to over 30,000, making it the fourth largest city in Mexico. As Guadalajara expanded, its inhabitants constantly needed more wheat, maize, and beef, which fueled the development of the region's agriculture. None of this growth would have occurred without a remarkable demographic surge of the indigenous population. After precipitously declining until the mid-seventeenth century, the number of Indians increased by about 1 percent a year in the late seventeenth century and doubled over the next century. As Indian villages became overcrowded, they could no longer provide adequate farmland for all their inhabitants.

The potent combination of urban demand and native population growth had profound economic consequences for Guadalajara. Land became more valuable and scarcer, especially in Indian villages. *Haciendas* stopped specializing in livestock ranching and grew more cereals, which required intensive labor for sowing, plowing, and harvesting. To take advantage of the region's growing Indian labor supply, the Spanish created a new kind of semi-free labor. Called *peones*, *indios laboríos*, and *gañanes*, these *hacienda* laborers were tied to their places of work by indebtedness. On many Guadalajara *haciendas*, they constituted half the labor force.

Debt peonage served two significant purposes in eighteenth-century Guadalajara. First, the region had a chronic scarcity of money because the economy was tied to the agricultural cycle and Guadalajara's major trade

210

fairs. When *haciendas* extended credit to rural laborers, they immediately received needed cash and goods. And second, debt peonage enabled *hacienda* owners to control an increasingly mobile and independent labor force. By granting credit advances, they insured that many workers could not seek employment elsewhere until they had paid their debts, which might take years.

This was definitely a buyer's market. As the rural population increased and native pueblos no longer had enough land for their residents, real wages declined (prices increased while wages hardly changed) as did many Indians' already precarious standards of living. Successful *hacienda* owners earned about a 5 percent annual profit while many of their Indian employees slid further down the economic ladder.

Advancing credit to rural laborers in Guadalajara took different forms. In 1732, Efigenio Antonio, a *hacienda* herder, received an advance which he could erase in eighteen months. The *hacienda* gave him twenty Spanish reales to cover his tribute payment and a little over nine pesos in cash. Antonio also obtained 87.5 pesos worth of cloth (serge, wool, linen, cotton, silk, blankets, ponchos, jackets, thread, ribbon, two sombreros, and one pair of women's stockings), and 18.5 pesos in food (two pounds of chocolate, sugar, salt, and soap).

In 1785, an Indian vaquero received an advance of almost 102 pesos. His wages included 41 pesos in cash and clothing worth 30.5 pesos. Thirteen pesos—almost 13 percent of the total—went to the local priest for the burial of two children.

From the beginning of colonial rule, the economic deck had been stacked against Mexico's native population. In the sixteenth and seventeenth centuries, native labor became scarce because so many Indians succumbed to smallpox, measles, and other European diseases. Some Indians benefited from this labor market in the form of higher wages, but *encomiendas* and *repartimiento* labor insured that Spaniards had a steady supply of coerced, inexpensive workers. As Indian villages shrank or disappeared, estate owners often seized their unused land.

When the Indian population increased throughout the eighteenth century, indigenous peoples were forced to enter a semi-free labor market at a competitive disadvantage. They had no other choice. There was not enough land to farm in their own villages because of population growth and the expansion of *hacienda* acreage in the wake of the earlier Indian population decline. Throughout Guadalajara and the rest of Mexico, Indians became progressively more impoverished as *hacienda* owners prospered. The two economic trends were closely interrelated.[8]

Race Mixing in Oaxaca

Before 1519, the Valley of Oaxaca with its 350,000 people was the most ethnically diverse region of central Mexico. By 1568, however, disease, dislocation, and harsh *encomienda* labor had reduced their population over 50 percent, and a century later fewer than 50,000 Indians survived. Despite the precipitous decline in population, by the end of the century an urban Indian culture had appeared in Antequera as indigenous peoples fled the countryside to escape epidemics, the destruction of their crops by marauding Spanish livestock, tribute, and demanding government officials. The cultivation of cochineal insects by Indians became the foundation of the city's prosperity. Cochineal, a widely used red dye, was Mexico's second most valuable export, and Antequera produced millions of pesos worth of the insects.

Throughout the colonial period, almost all positions of wealth and power in Antequera were monopolized by two groups of males—peninsular Spaniards and Creoles, or people designated as Spaniards born in Mexico. Nevertheless, by the late eighteenth century a great deal of racial mixing had occurred in Antequera. About 32 percent of the Creole population married mestizos, mulattos, and Indians. The intermarriage rates were even higher for mestizos (60 percent) and mulattos (66 percent).

Indians had the lowest rate of intermarriage, but 11 percent wed Creoles, while almost 16 percent chose mestizos as their spouses. By the end of the eighteenth century, increasing numbers of Antequera's mestizo, mulatto, and Indian women were marrying upward, while more Creoles were choosing wives outside their own social group. Light-skinned mestizos and mulattos marrying Creoles were often classified as Creoles in parish registers, and thus their children were considered Spanish. Despite wide differences in wealth and status, all of the city's neighborhoods were racially mixed.

Intermarriage and miscegenation blurred racial lines in Antequera for over two centuries. Except for the peninsulares, by the late eighteenth century most Antequera Spaniards were part mestizo, mulatto, and Indian, no matter what they called themselves. In the Valley of Oaxaca, intermarriage whitened.[9]

"This Cannibal Lie"

On Christopher Columbus's first voyage to the New World in 1492, the Admiral thought that the Taínos he met on the island of Hispaniola were warning him about their deadly enemies, the Caribs. According to him, there was an island at the "entrance into the Indies, which is inhabited by a people who are regarded in all the islands as very ferocious, who eat human flesh. They have many canoes with which they range through all the islands of India, rob and take whatever they can." Columbus was skeptical about labeling these Indians eaters of human flesh because he believed the Caribs might actually be the Great Khan's soldiers.

On his second voyage in 1493, however, Columbus became convinced that they were actually cannibals. His surgeon agreed and provided Europeans with the first detailed account of this "bestial" people and "their evil custom of eating the flesh of man." He wrote that the Caribs incessantly raided the surrounding islands for captives. The youngest and most beautiful women were spared to become concubines while male prisoners suffered a far crueler fate, for "those who are alive they bring to their houses to butcher for meat." Columbus's voyages made the word Carib synonymous with cannibalism. They were considered the most ignoble savages in the entire New World.

In 1492, there were three indigenous cultures in the Caribbean—the Ciboney, the Arawak, and the Island Carib. The Ciboneys may have arrived in the Greater Antilles about 9,000 years ago and lived in western Cuba and southwestern Hispaniola. About 2,300 years ago, the Arawaks migrated from South America's Orinoco River basin into the Great and Lesser Antilles and the Bahamas. The origin of the Island Caribs is shrouded in mystery, and they may actually be an Arawak people who came to the Windward Islands of the Lesser Antilles a thousand years ago. Their cultural and linguistic connections with mainland Caribs in South America may have come through trade and political alliances. When Columbus arrived, there may have been about 2 million Indians living in the Caribbean, half of them on Hispaniola.

Once Columbus returned to Spain, he argued that the Caribs should be enslaved because they would always resist Spanish efforts to civilize them. In 1503, Queen Isabella agreed and authorized their capture. A decade later, many thousands of Caribs began disappearing from the Lesser Antilles from a combination of European epidemic diseases and Spanish raids.

Despite their awful experiences with the Spanish, the Caribs avidly traded with the French, English, Dutch and sometimes even the Spanish. As long as Europeans did not attack them, trample their gardens, or violate their women, they maintained friendly relations and even allowed outsiders to visit their islands. As trade relations intensified, Carib words such as "canoe," "hurricane," "barbecue," "hammock," "cacique," and "cassava" entered the English and Spanish languages.

During the seventeenth century, the Caribs in the Lesser Antilles faced two new challenges to their independence: French and English colonization and the emergence of the Black Caribs. In 1625, the French and English occupied part of St. Christopher. Three years later, the English tried to take over Nevis, Montserrat, and Antiqua. Soon afterward, the English, French and Dutch began settling Dominica, Martinque, Guadeloupe, Tobago, Grenada, St. Lucia, Barbuda, Maria Galante, St. Martins, and other neighboring islands. Europeans hoped to mount privateering expeditions against the Spanish and grow tobacco, a native crop. Later, European agriculture expanded to include indigo, cacao, and especially sugar cane. Although the Carib economy combined fishing, long-distance trading, and agriculture (manioc and sweet potatoes), Europeans considered the Lesser Antilles unimproved, uninhabited, and thus available for settlement.

Throughout the seventeenth century, the Caribs pursued a dual policy with their European rivals. They made their islands a living hell for Europeans by ambushing ships in their swift canoes and attacking settlements. At the same time, they continued to exchange food for muskets, pistols, and swords in order to bolster their military strength. The English fared the worse with the Caribs, for they clearly wanted to take their lands. English prosperity in the West Indies depended on large sugar cane plantations and the importation of hundreds of thousands of African slaves, not coexistence with the Caribs. The French fared the best, despite the presence of evangelizing Jesuit missionaries, because they believed that gifts and "good treatment" would win over their enemies. Often, the Caribs allied themselves with the French and Dutch to keep the more aggressive English off their islands.

Island Caribs, who had no hereditary chiefs, were "jealous of their liberty" and resented "more actively & more impatiently the least affront that might be given them." A Jesuit missionary living in Dominica reported that the Caribs mocked the French "when they see that we respect & obey our superiors. They say that we must be the slaves of those whom we obey, since they give themselves the liberty to command us, & we are cowardly enough to execute their orders." The Caribs admired European technology but saw no advantages in submitting to foreign rule.

While the Island Caribs fought to maintain their independence, they faced a second challenge. In the 1580s, the Caribs raided Puerto Rico and "carried away a great quantity of negroes and left some in Dominica and distributed the rest among the Indians of these islands, which they take to their lands in order to serve them." Further raids, shipwrecked slave ships, and escaped fugitive slaves greatly increased the number of Africans in the Lesser Antilles at a time when the Caribs were declining in numbers. In St. Vincent, the Caribs eventually divided into two separate groups, Black and Yellow Caribs. By 1763, there were five Blacks for every one Yellow Carib.

Several decades later, the Yellow Caribs concluded that their struggle was doomed. They could no longer attack European ships or destroy European settlements and were now heavily outnumbered by Black Caribs, English settlers, and their African slaves. While a few thousand Island Caribs remained on the islands of Dominica and St. Vincent, most abandoned the Lesser Antilles and returned to their ancient homeland at the mouth of the Orinoco River. Today, about 15,000 Caribs live in small communities along the Atlantic coast of Venezuela and Guyana.

In 1763, the British received St. Vincent through the Treaty of Paris and immediately began establishing large sugarcane plantations as they had already done on Barbados and the surrounding islands. The Black Caribs, who controlled much of the island's most fertile land, claimed an "exemption from all civil jurisdiction or subordination whatsoever." At first the British preceded cautiously because the Black Caribs were "jealous of their property" and were "sufficiently numerous to defeat any settlements attempted to be made without their consent."

From 1763 to 1795, the Black Caribs alternated between fighting the British and working for them transporting sugar in canoes. The Black Caribs, who may have numbered about 8,000, gradually sold or lost most of their most fertile lands as the British West Indies became the most lucrative English colonies in the New World. Sugarcane thrived in the Lesser Antilles, producing about 2 tons an acre.

In 1786, St. Vincent's Black Caribs helped the French recapture the island, but France returned it to Britain in 1789. Inspired by the French Revolution and bolstered by French military support from Guadeloupe, Black Caribs again revolted against the British in 1795. The next year, the British pacified St. Vincent and deported about 4,000 Black and 100 Yellow Caribs to a small island off the coast of Honduras. Over half of them died from typhus or yellow fever. Later, the British returned the Yellow Caribs to St. Vincent and pardoned them.

Soon afterward, the Spanish persuaded the Black Caribs to settle in Honduras. Today, there are over fifty thriving Black Carib communities along the Atlantic littoral in Belize (15,000), Guatemala (6,000), and Honduras (200,000). There are several thousand more Black Caribs scattered in Nicaragua and the Lesser Antilles. The Garifunas, as they call themselves, are a unique ethnic group in Central America. Their language is an unusual combination of Arawak, French, Yuroba, Banti, and Swahili and their Afro-Carib religion centers around ancestor worship. Although Black Caribs have lived in Spanish Central America for 200 years, their language, music, rituals, and matriarchal families dramatically set them apart from their neighbors.

Hostilities died out on St. Vincent in 1805. In Dominica, the British established a Carib reserve of 3,700 acres in 1903. Today, about 3,000 Caribs of mixed Black and Yellow ancestry live in the northeast corner of Dominica.

Although much has changed since their last revolt against British rule, they still hold all of their land in common, build beautiful boats, and maintain a distinct ethnic identity that links them to other Island Caribs. They have been undergoing an indigenous revival since the 1970s when the Black Power movement heightened racial sensibilities in Caribbean countries like Trinidad and Tobago.

In 1990, José Barreiro visited the Carib reserve in Dominica to find out what they thought about the upcoming celebration of the Columbus quincentenary. According to their chief, Irvince Auguiste, the Caribs still laugh about Columbus's description of them as bloodthirsty cannibals. "They even claim that we had a preference for French meat," Auguiste told Barreiro. They "claimed that we ranked French, British, Spanish, and so forth. I think maybe the Dutch were supposed to be the worst tasting."

"This cannibal lie," he argued, "goes back to the Spaniards, to the English. Columbus came to the new world looking for gold. . . . And the Carib people had enjoyed centuries of freedom, making their cassava bread and catching fish. Naturally they would retaliate against anyone trying to enslave them." Because the Spanish could not conquer the Caribs, they slandered them. With a smile, Auguiste said that humans were never a dietary staple because "we have too many good things to eat."

Later that day, a young Carib took Barreiro to the snake's staircase, a lava extension that extends into the ocean. As they walked through the woods to the top of the staircase, Barreiro learned that this is the place where "Master Snake," a sacred creature, would come out of the ocean to answer the questions of old people in their dreams. "When the Caribs disappear, the old people said, the Master Snake has vowed to return to the underbelly of the ocean. And the world will end."

Five hundred years after Columbus, the Caribs still live.[10]

South America

The Absent Indian in the Río de Plate Region

In 1681, a Spanish government official made a remarkable statement about the Río de Plate region, which today is the modern state of Uruguay. He hoped to establish good relations with the indigenous population, for "if they do not want to subject themselves to us but accept our friendship and trade, you have to treat them well and regale them, so that, by these means, you are able to profit from that deserted land." About fifty years later, a Portuguese historian made a similar comment about the struggle between his countryman and the Spanish for control of the Río de Plate. According to him, the

216

region was a bizarre place because a "land like that, without a Christian population, is like a body without a soul or a sky without stars."

These statements were not unusual in the history of the Río de Plate. From the moment Europeans appeared in the mouth of the river around 1516 to look for precious metals and a passage linking the Atlantic and Pacific oceans, they believed that the area was simultaneously populated and deserted. It was an inhabited but uncivilized land. Over three centuries, the Spanish finally resolved this paradox by eliminating all Indians from Uruguay.

In the second decade of the sixteenth century, Juan Díaz de Solís appeared on the north shore of the Río de Plate. He was followed by other Spanish explorers, who produced accounts of their voyages that were used to paint a frightening picture of the native population. At the Spanish court, the great Milanese humanist Pietro Martire d'Anghiera wrote about the hostile Indians who attacked Solís. He called them Caribs, whom Columbus had identified as cannibals on his second Caribbean voyage. According to the Italian chronicler, the Caribs of the Río de Plate "in the manner of sly foxes, feigned peace signs but were, in actuality, planning a sumptuous banquet. When they saw their guests from afar, they drooled like customers at a cheap diner." After attacking Solís and several of his hapless crew, the Indians "cut them into pieces and prepared for the future banquet at the beach." Subsequent accounts echoed him. Treacherous Indians had attacked an innocent Solís and "killed him and ate all the Spaniards who landed with him."

By using the Caribs as an ethnographic label for the Indians of the Río de Plate, Spanish writers were not confusing widely separated Indian peoples. They were making a very direct analogy between the supposed barbarism of the Caribs and the inhabitants of the Río de Plate. Both peoples lived outside the boundaries of civilized society because they could not distinguish between what was natural and unnatural. According to Spanish writers, all Indians' shared interest in cannibalism was a disgusting sign of their savagery.

Eventually, the Spanish identified three distinct Indian groups living in the Río de Plate—the Guaranís, Chaná-Beguas, and the Charrúas—all of whom had probably entered the region about 4,000 years ago. From the Spanish perspective, any group differences were overshadowed by one common characteristic: They were Caribs who ate human flesh. Not surprisingly, the early maps of the Río de Plate region showed a very distinct coastline but a blank interior. The Spanish knew that Indians inhabited the region, but they could not bring themselves to portray cannibals exercising sovereignty over themselves and controlling a demarcated geographical space.

Spanish writers praised the native peoples for their ability to swim and their prowess as warriors, but they were usually described in negative terms.

The Indians lacked writing, cities, proper clothing, and just about everything else associated with civilization. Put simply, they were barbarians.

The Spanish, in common with other Europeans, could only conceive of human societies that were authoritarian, hierarchical, and based on relations of command and obedience, coercion and subordination. The Guaranís, Chaná-Beguas, and the Charrúas horrified them because they were societies without a state. Power did not reside in a chief but was dispersed throughout the community. Except temporarily in war, chiefs could not give orders or compel obedience but could only plan and persuade. Political compulsion was completely alien to Uruguay's Indians.

Europeans understood that Indian societies were organized very differently than their own but interpreted this difference as a sign of bestiality. Like the Indians they encountered, the Spanish were ethnocentric and considered their culture superior to all others. Unlike the Indians, however, the Spanish never considered these differences benign. Instead, their rage led to the production of a huge body of speeches and texts that justified domination over Uruguay's Indians.

Portuguese slave raiders were never troubled by the supposed barbarism of the Indians, but the Spanish faced a more serious problem. In the early eighteenth century, when Argentines from Buenos Aires decided to introduce cattle ranching into Uruguay's fertile prairies, they were repelled by the locals. "We also heard," wrote one Spaniard, "that the neighbors of this city could not cross to the other shore or exploit the wealth of that land, of which they have a great need." A once unwanted land had now become economically and strategically valuable in the struggle against the Portuguese.

The Spanish prevailed over the Portuguese by 1776, but they could never completely subdue the native population, which probably numbered about 10,000 at the time. Throughout their struggle, they were genuinely puzzled why indigenous peoples would want to defend their lands against foreign intruders or preserve their way of life. For inexplicable reasons, Indians had not only "resisted true religion" but also "manifested an immeasurable hatred against the people who populate Montevideo."

As they slowly gained the upper hand around Montevideo, Spaniards began forcing treaties on Indians that treated both parties very differently. In one treaty, Indians agreed not to harm any cattle ranches, farms, and cattle. If they were caught "robbing or performing other evils," any Spaniard could "punish them without taking them prisoners." On the other hand, if Spaniards disturbed the "peace of their tents" or robbed Indians, they had to take the malefactor prisoner, transport him to Montevideo, and let Spanish law decide his fate.

Throughout the Age of Enlightenment, the Spanish continued treating the Indians of the Río de Plate as an irrational, unpredictable, and promiscuous people. As one hostile commentator wrote, the "wild Indian" cannot write, "speaks very little in an unknown language," and only does "what his few needs dictate." Although the Spanish had lived among indigenous peoples for over two centuries, their descriptions of them had hardly changed from the time of Pietro Martire d'Anghiera. They could never understand the strangers who dwelled in their midst because they divided the peoples of Río de Plate into two opposing types: the Creole male who defines and commands and the Indian who meekly listens and obeys. How could the Spanish cede any human agency to peoples "who live like beasts in the countryside or the woods, without house or roof" and "walk nude under the rain and sun" while never combing their hair? With their bronze skin and ugly faces, they were little more than beasts. Their unwillingness to become Catholics and enter Jesuit missions was an affront to Spaniards. Although the Charrúas became outstanding horsemen and cattle herders on the Uruguayan prairies, the Spanish still considered them outside the boundaries of civilization.

By the late eighteenth century, the Viceroyalty of the Río de Plate with its capital of Buenos Aires became a very prosperous region as cattle ranchers and merchants exchanged salted beef and leather hides for African slaves. Uruguay achieved its independence in 1828 following a debilitating war between Brazil and Uruguayan patriots supported by Britain. Uruguay's first constitutional president slaughtered many of the new republic's remaining Indians and then sent four Charrúas in the cargo hold of a ship, bound like African slaves, to the Natural Sciences Academy in Paris. Scientists eagerly studied them as curious Parisians flocked to stare at the strange collection of humans. In two months, three of them died, but a father and his newborn daughter escaped and mysteriously vanished forever.

Today, Uruguay's national soccer team players pride themselves on their "Charrúa" valor, local archaeologists excavate indigenous sites, and Uruguayan intellectuals openly discuss their country's long and troubled relationship with its indigenous peoples. This will entail a great act of historical recovery, for ever since Solís was allegedly devoured by cannibals, the most respected travel accounts, histories, and public documents of the Río de Plate have devoured the Guaranís, Chaná-Beguas, and the Charrúas. Until very recently, Indians have been a factor in Uruguayan culture mostly by their absence or opposition. What were their names? What did they think about the gradual erosion of their independence? These Indians speak to us in muted voices and with muted identities, and almost always from the pens of those who loathed them.[11]

The Last Inca

In September of 1572, Tupac Amaru I, the last Inca emperor, was captured by the Spanish, tortured, and hung in Cuzco. A little more than two centuries later, José Gabriel Condorcanqui, who called himself Tupac Amaru II, was also tortured and executed in Cuzco for leading the greatest of all insurrections against Spain in the colonial period. There were many violent rebellions against Spanish rule in eighteenth-century Peru, but the Tupac Amaru revolt was the most threatening because it was an independence movement, an attempt to revive the ancient Inca empire, and a political reform movement that claimed to act in the name of the Spanish Crown.

Eighteenth-century Peru was the nursery of insurrection in South America. From 1750 to Tupac Amaru's rebellion in November of 1780, there were ninety-six revolts in what is now Peru and northern Bolivia. Many of them were small, but others were armed uprisings involving thousands of people. These rebellions were directly related to the Bourbon monarchy's political and financial reforms in the Andes.

When Carlos III became the last Bourbon king of Spain in 1759, he realized that his New World empire was in serious trouble. Tax revenues were declining, trade between Spain and its possessions was anemic, and the British were threatening Cuba and other Spanish colonies. France earned more from her colony of Martinique, and England profited more from Barbados than did Spain from her entire New World possessions put together. Carlos III's Bourbon predecessors, who had come to the Spanish throne in 1700, had begun the process of reform by centralizing power, stimulating commerce and trade, developing a more efficient fiscal system, and strengthening the military and bureaucracy.

Using French Enlightenment absolutist principles as a guide, Carlos III and his ministers attempted to restore Spain's worldwide power and bolster its imperial wealth through a series of actions known as "the Bourbon Reforms." In the New World, he expelled the Jesuits from all Spanish possessions in 1767 and confiscated their wealthy properties. The Crown also imposed severe restrictions on the building of new monasteries and expelled all friars from their parishes. At the same time, the king destroyed the special corporate privileges of the nobility, the Church, the Inquisition, guilds, and the *mestas*, powerful associations of stockmen. To gain more revenue, Spain raised taxes, tightened its system of revenue collection, and tried to stimulate international trade. Carlos III also reorganized the imperial army and built new fortifications to repel his European rivals.

Bourbon reforms fueled an imperial revival in Peru but at a heavy price. In 1776, Cuzco lost economic and political power when it became part of the newly created Viceroyalty of Río de Plate with its capital in distant Buenos Aires. In the same year, the sales tax increased from 2 percent to 6 percent. Indians lost their exemption from certain taxes while the legalization of the *repartimiento de comercio* [the forced distribution of European merchandise] and other fiscal duties suddenly increased. At the same time that economic competition was increasing throughout the empire, the imposition of higher taxes hurt many indigenous communities because they were compelled to produce local goods and purchase merchandise at inflated prices. By 1780, the once prosperous Cuzco region was groaning under heavy taxes and stagnating production.

José Gabriel Condorcanqui was born in 1738, a fifth-generation lineal descendant of the last Inca emperor. His father was a prominent *curaca* of three towns southeast of Cuzco. After an excellent education at a Jesuit school in Cuzco, José Gabriel married a mestiza named Micaela Bastidas Puyucahua, became a successful trader between Cuzco and Potosí after inheriting his father's 350 mules, and in 1766 was given the position of *curaca* once held by his father and older brother.

He was also a deeply frustrated man. In 1769, José Gabriel lost his *curaca* position but regained it two years later. In 1776, he filed a suit to be officially declared the legitimate descendant of Tupac Amaru I and petitioned the Viceroy of Lima to have his communities exempted from the terrible Potosí *mita*. As riots broke out around Cuzco in response to the distress caused by the Bourbon reforms, José Gabriel decided to take matters into his own hands and declared his own revolt in November of 1780.

José Gabriel began by calling himself "Don José the First, by the Grace of God Inca King of Peru, Duke of the Most High, Lord of the Caesars and Amazons and over the realm of Great Paititi, Commissary Officer and Distributor of Divine Piety, and Exalted Bursar" and announced that "the clamoring for justice on the part of the Peruvians has reached heaven." He and his followers captured a local government official, whom Tupac Amaru considered "harmful and tyrannical," forced him to give them money and weapons, and then executed him in front of thousands of awed Indians. This man had once opposed José Gabriel's bid to succeed his father as *curaca*.

Afterwards, thousands of Quechua-speaking Indians eagerly joined Tupac Amaru's revolt. Using stones, spears, and sling shots, they attacked local officials; destroyed churches, *haciendas*, and textile mills; repulsed well-armed troops; and killed priests who opposed them. They also desecrated Catholic religious objects. In one town, Indian women tore the robes off an image of a Virgin and pushed pins into her body. In another, angry Indians drank from a chalice filled with corn beer. According to one surprised commentator, the rebel forces grew "by the minute, its courage increasing in light of its triumphs." Tupac Amaru was excommunicated by the bishop of Cuzco, but this only enhanced his reputation and enlarged his ranks.

His rebel army was the most unusual fighting force ever assembled in the Americas. Micaela Bastidas, the wife of Tupac Amaru, was the logistical commander of operations. She coordinated the movement of provisions and soldiers and constantly urged her husband to act more aggressively. On one occasion, she complained to him that "I am capable of turning myself over to the enemy so they kill me, because I see your lack of enthusiasm about such a grave affair, thus putting everyone's life in danger." Micaela Bastidas was not alone. Many women fought in the ranks and some commanded troops. They often gathered rocks for slings and used sharpened animal bones to fend off Spanish troops.

Although most of the Tupac Amaru's forces were tributary Indians or Indians who had recently migrated to *ayllus*, troop leaders came from a wide range of Peruvian society. After the rebellion had been crushed, the government brought charges against nineteen Spaniards, twenty-nine mestizos, seventeen Indians, and four Africans or mulattos. Their occupations were also varied. Most of them were farmers, tradesman, artisans, muleteers like Tupac Amaru, secretaries, *curacas*, and a few professionals. Tupac Amaru's army was an alliance of many different groups who had one perspective in common—a hatred of Bourbon reforms.

As his rebel army swelled to over 20,000 men and women, Tupac Amaru began issuing edicts to explain his actions. Throughout the rebellion, Tupac Amaru announced that he was a loyal subject of the Spanish crown and a practicing Catholic. He claimed that his quarrel was with corrupt royal officials and bad laws such as the *repartimiento de comercio*, not with the Bourbon king. He had no desire to overthrow the social order, just reform Peruvian society and help people truly understand God's will.

But Tupac Amaru also spoke in strong messianic and apocalyptic terms about his struggle, claiming that he was carrying out divine edicts against those who rebelled against God's laws. He compared himself to King David and Moses and described himself as an avenging prophet. In common with several other eighteenth-century Andean rebel leaders, he wanted to reestablish the Inca dynasty with himself as the head. After his revolt began, Tupac Amaru started wearing Inca clothing and commissioned a painting of himself and his wife as the Inca emperor and empress.

Carlos III had brought chaos and ruin to the Andes. This was a period of *pachacuti* when the traditional order was torn asunder. Now was the time "for the prophecies of Saint Rose of Lima to be fulfilled upon us, the time when it will be necessary to return the kingdom to its former rulers." This is why Tupac Amaru and his wife singled out *haciendas*, textile mills, and churches for destruction. They represented the demonic rule of the *puka kunkas* [rednecks], as the Quechua-speaking Indians contemptuously called the Spaniards.

The authorities and the frightened citizens of Cuzco, however, did not see Tupac Amaru and his troops as saviors but as blasphemous rebels. Claimed one, "they cruelly killed every male and female Spaniard they came upon . . . and, what is even more horrible, they lewdly took advantage of all the attractive women, killing them afterwards and going on to the greater impiety of having sex with the cadavers of other women." There could be no compromise with such savage enemies. Many Indians in the Cuzco region agreed and supported the royal government in its struggle against Tupac Amaru.

On April 6, 1781, Tupac Amaru was seized after failing to capture Cuzco. Soon afterwards, he was tortured and executed. As he died, Tupac Amaru told his executioner, "here there are no accomplices but you and me. You as oppressor, I as liberator, both of us deserve death." Spanish officials forced Tupac Amaru's nine-year-old son to watch the gradual dismemberment of his father, mother, and older brother. A first cousin, Diego Cristóbal, continued the rebellion but he was executed two years later after being promised a pardon. The Spanish government justified its treachery by arguing that "it is not fitting either for the King or for the State that any seed or race of this or any Túpac Amaru should remain."[12]

After Columbus

Living in an Age of Missing Information

A Seneca Chief Speaks

In 1805, the Evangelical Missionary Society of Massachusetts sent a minister to convert the Senecas to Christianity. Missionaries were hardly unknown to the Senecas. For centuries both Catholic priests and Protestants ministers had tried, but failed, to convert them. This minister told his Seneca audience that "there is only one religion, and only one way to serve God, and if you do not embrace the right way, you cannot be happy hereafter. You have never worshipped the Great Spirit in a manner acceptable to him; but have all your lives been in great errors and darkness."

After respectfully discussing the missionary's damning sermon for two hours, a chief named Sa-Go-Ye-Wat-Ha responded. He politely thanked the missionary for journeying so far to meet them and then explained "what our fathers have told us, and what we have heard from the white people." There was a time when the Senecas' forefathers owned this land. The "Great Spirit" had provided buffalo, bear, and deer, and the earth produced corn. "But one evil day came upon us. Your forefathers crossed the great waters and landed on this continent. Their numbers were small. They found friends and not enemies. They told us they had fled from wicked men in their own country and had come here to enjoy their religion. They asked for a small seat."

The Senecas responded by giving them corn and meat. In return they received rum. "They called us brothers. We believed them and gave them a

225

large seat. At length their numbers greatly increased. They wanted more lands. They wanted our country. Our eyes were opened, and our minds became uneasy." Now, after years of fighting and strong liquor, whites have "now become a great people, and we hardly have a place left to spread our blankets. You have our country, but you are not yet satisfied. Now you want to force your religion on us."

The Senecas were puzzled by the white man's religion. If it had been written in a book, why did the Great Spirit never give it to them? And if there was only one true religion, why did white people argue so much over it? Sa-Go-Ye-Wat-Ha told the missionary that the Seneca religion had also been handed down from their forefathers. The Great Spirit was pleased that the Senecas faithfully followed their traditions, and in return gave them "abundance, and strength and vigor for the hunt." The Senecas went to sleep content and woke up with gratitude.

Since the Great Spirit made the Senecas and whites with different colors and customs, "why shouldn't we conclude that he has given us a different religion, according to our understanding?" Although their worship differed, Sa-Go-Ye-Wat-Ha thought it did not matter to the Great Spirit, for "what pleases him is the offering of a sincere heart, and this is how we worship him. We do not want to destroy your religion or to take it from you. We only want to enjoy our own."

Sa-Go-Ye-Wat-Ha said his people knew that this missionary had been preaching to their white neighbors and suggested a practical way of testing the truths of his religion. "We will wait a little while, and see what effect your preaching has on them. If we find that it does them good and makes them honest and less disposed to cheat the red man, we will consider again what you have said." At the conclusion of his speech, Sa-Go-Ye-Wat-Ha stepped toward the missionary to shake his hand, but the missionary angrily refused since there could be "no fellowship between the religion of God and the devil." The chief smiled and walking away.[1]

Sa-Go-Ye-Wat-Ha's words were prophetic. In the first half of the nineteenth century, New Yorkers worked unrelentingly to dispossess the Senecas and other Iroquois of their lands because they believed that they were an impediment to the development of their state. During this period, the Senecas were forced to sell almost all their property for pennies an acre, and they became confined to small reservations as wards of the state. With Iroquois land cessions, New York was able to build the Erie Canal, develop Buffalo as one of the great inland ports in the United States, and open up fertile western New York to rapid settlement. By 1850, New York State led the nation in population; the number and value of its farms; and in the production of wheat, maple sugar, milk, hay, potatoes, butter, and cheese. In that same year, the Erie Canal carried about 23 million bushels of wheat and flour, almost one-fourth of all the grain produced in the United States. The inexpensive purchase of over 10 million acres of Iroquois land was the foundation of New York's phenomenal antebellum economic growth.[2]

As Sa-Go-Ye-Wat-Ha recognized, with the European invasion of the New World came a momentous loss from which we are still suffering along with the Western Hemisphere's indigenous peoples: the deliberate destruction of precious wisdom and age-old cultures; the rout of life-affirming redemptive visions; the spiritual impoverishment of the past and future; and a reign of mass death that lasted four centuries. From 1492 to 1650, probably 90 percent of the New World's indigenous peoples died from European diseases, warfare, slavery, cruelty, starvation, and dislocation. In the United States, Indians steadily declined in numbers until the late nineteenth century. This may be roughly the same number of people that died during World War II, about 50 million. Many millions of Indians also disappeared as they were absorbed into colonial society through racial intermixing.

A Demographic and Cultural Disaster

This cultural and demographic disaster is unmatched in world history. In our own brutal century, tyrannical governments have tried to destroy Jews, Armenians, and many other peoples. None of these slaughters, however, comes close in duration or intensity to the carnage that occurred in the New World. No comparable ethnic groups have lost as many people as the indigenous inhabitants of the Western Hemisphere. No other group has had such a great percentage of their people die over such an extended period of time.

This has been one of the greatest failures of Europe's fragile humanism. From 1492 to the late eighteenth century, there were many magnificent European accomplishments in the humanities, arts, and sciences. European humanism, however, spectacularly failed to save indigenous peoples from conquest and colonization. Worse, many great humanists in both Europe and the Americas abetted the conquest by enthusiastically promoting it or by remaining silent in the face of the tragedy they witnessed.

European humanism failed to respond to the challenge of the New World in another significant way. Although many humanists incorporated ethnographic information about indigenous cultures into their writings, only a few of them used this new knowledge to raise fundamental questions about their own societies. Too many thinkers, like the English philosopher John Locke, argued that Europeans could settle Indian lands without the consent of the local inhabitants.

Despite the huge amount of ethnographic material about native societies that became available after 1492, most humanists failed to pursue important political, social, and cultural questions about the New World. In the centuries after Columbus, more Europeans should have asked themselves how it was possible to create societies that:

- Share widely accepted rules and a sense of justice without laws, courts, police, and armies.
- Function smoothly without a state.
- Educate and train everyone broadly without formal schooling.
- Respect manual labor.
- Lack class conflict and exploitation.
- Depend on a social compact rather than coercion.
- Enable adults to have equal access to essential resources.
- Enable adults to engage in a wide variety of daily tasks.
- Produce few misfits or superfluous people.
- Enable women to have important spiritual, economic, and political functions.
- Allow people to have plenty of time for leisurely activities.
- Manifest a strong sense of solidarity and common purpose that also encourages individuality.
- Connect people spiritually to each other and to the natural world around them.

There were many native societies with at least some of these characteristics in the New World, but they were systematically disparaged and ignored by Europe's best thinkers.[3]

Ironically, for hundreds of years Europeans and Americans complained that Indian culture and thought were childish, inflexible, and based on bizarre sacred narratives that lacked profundity and defied common sense. Yet after Columbus, indigenous peoples were considerably more pragmatic and intellectually flexible in their response to the invaders than were Europeans to them. Most European and American interpreters of native cultures rarely moved beyond crude stereotypes and facile generalizations.

The modern age—the age of huge state-sanctioned projects of mass murder and conquest—began in Hispaniola when Columbus established Europe's first New World colony in 1493. In the New World, the empires of Spain, Portugal, France, and Britain created the roots of our own times, which the brave Czech intellectual Vaciav Havel has accurately identified as the "irrational momentum of anonymous, impersonal, and inhuman power."[4] The deadly combination of imperial bureaucracy, relentless military expansion, the deliberate modification of the environment on an enormous scale, and the calculated destruction of whole peoples and nations did not suddenly appear in the twentieth century.

The Conquest of the Western Hemisphere

It is not the world wars or the Holocaust that mark a moral turning point in the history of the West, but the discovery, conquest, and settlement of the Western Hemisphere. In the New World, the West's laws, religion, and morality did not simply fail to protect millions of innocent people, but they actively sanctioned their degradation and destruction. Beginning with the Renaissance, most legal and moral inhibitions against wholesale violence were eroded throughout the New World in a three-stage process.

First, legitimate and widely respected authorities—the church and the state—authorized violence against indigenous peoples on a scale unknown in their own societies. Explorers and settlers were not expected to deny traditional moral values but only their application to peoples different from themselves. Second, indigenous peoples were dehumanized by being labeled barbarians. Once they were placed outside the European moral universe, explorers and settlers did not have the same human obligations toward them that they had to each other. And third, the repeated and successful use of violence against native peoples became routine. Soon, any moral qualms were overcome and forgotten. The terror directed at indigenous peoples was not a breakdown of European culture but its systematic expression.[5]

Europeans could not treat indigenous peoples as equals or even as legitimate enemies because they were "wild men and women"—barbaric, brutal, treacherous, completely lawless, and governed by their basest passions. Indians faced the full fury of conquest reserved for infidels and savages by peoples who confidently asserted that they were carrying out God's will. By the late Middle Ages, a consensus had emerged among popes and political rulers about territorial expansion beyond Europe. Because the rest of the world was not as fully human as Christendom, infidels, heathens, and savages had to be conquered to redeem humanity and God's name. When Columbus arrived in the Bahamas, the Indians' fate had already been sealed because Europeans had placed them outside the realm of normal moral duty or obligations.

Partly as a result of the conquest of the New World, we are now living in what writer Bill McKibben has called "the age of missing information." Perhaps this is the greatest loss suffered in our encounter with native peoples. This is a "moment of deep ignorance, when vital knowledge that humans have always possessed about who we are and where we live seems beyond our reach." According to McKibben, we are missing the idea that human beings "are not all-important, not at the center of the world. That is the one essential piece of information, the one great secret, offered by any encounter with the woods or the mountains or the ocean or any wilderness or chunk of nature or patch of sky."[6]

This perspective has been at the core of the fundamental difference between the Old and New Worlds since 1492. Indigenous peoples believed they were just a small, modest part of an interconnected universe. They understood, in the words of a contemporary Lacandon Maya, that "the root of all living things are tied together. When a mighty tree is felled, a star falls from the sky; before you cut down a mahogany you should ask permission of the keeper of the forest, and you should ask permission of the keeper of the star."[7]

In the sacred narratives and daily lives of native peoples, the past was a living part of the present, time and space were not treated as separate dimensions, and the entire cosmos functioned as a living, unified whole. Native peoples did not conserve the environment; the environment conserved them. The indigenous view of the world was benevolent, for it had the power to nurture and fulfill its inhabitants. Reciprocity was the glue that bound their spiritual and social worlds together.

Christians, in bold contrast, thought and acted as if the world revolved around them. They believed that there were no limits to what they could do to change other peoples and cultures because in the beginning, they had been given dominion over the entire world. In their sacred narratives and daily lives, they sharply separated themselves from the rest of creation and did not see any deep kinship between themselves and the trees and stars. The universe was not a fundamentally benevolent place, and both earthly fulfillment and heavenly salvation did not depend on propitiating the natural order.

Since Columbus's arrival, Europeans have been estranged from native peoples. For over five centuries, Christians have worked tirelessly to overcome this estrangement in two ways, both of which have intensified the problem and made lasting solutions less likely. Europeans tried to save Indians' souls and improve their lives by forcing them to become Christians and abandoning what was most precious in their lives. At the same time, Europeans rarely hesitated to overcome estrangement through ruthless violence.

The War Against Indigenous Peoples

But as indigenous peoples have always recognized, diversity is a gift of the gods. It is part of the primordial condition of existence because of the earth's fertility and the cyclical nature of life. To recognize diversity as the underlying principle of creation is to choose and honor the mystery of life, as indigenous peoples have always done. To reduce diversity to such static, inane dualisms such as civilization versus savagery or Christianity versus heathenism leads only to perpetual crusades against those labeled "outsiders."

Europeans tried to establish a single religion and culture in the New World by rejecting its amazing pluralism and trying to destroy its many rich cultures. Sadly, this effort has partially succeeded but at the cost of mutilating the victor. What is the cause of the West's perpetual restlessness, its proud alienation from its earthy origins, its aggressive desire to dissolve differences and diversity in favor of itself? Hugo of St. Victor, a twelfth century Saxon monk, may have explained its roots the most beautifully. "It is a source of great virtue for the practiced mind to learn, bit by bit, first to change about in the visible and transitory things, so that afterwards it may be able to leave them behind altogether. The person who finds his homeland sweet is still a tender beginner; he to whom every soil is as his native one is already strong; but he is perfect to whom the entire world is a foreign place. The tender soul has fixed his love on one spot in the world; the strong person has extended his love to all places; the perfect man has extinguished his."[8]

Since at least the triumph of Christianity, the West has deeply distrusted human nature, the natural world, and the existence of peoples different from itself. As a result, Christendom has used a large part of its talents and creative energies to feverishly change itself and other peoples to fulfill its historic destiny. This aggressive approach to peoples labeled infidels and heathens began with Europe's treatment of the Jews, intensified during the First Crusade, and then spread to other parts of Europe and the Canary Islands before landing in the Caribbean with Columbus. In the name of the West's highest values, Europeans systematically tried to eradicate the diversity and wisdom of countless New World cultures simply because they did not see anything civilized about them.

The West has long acted as if there is only one story to tell which can only be heard and believed if all others are excluded. Despite Christendom's very diverse religious and cultural foundations, until recently Western culture has had great difficulty acknowledging the validity of other spiritual paths. Instead, Christendom created adversarial relations between itself and others that were used to justify the conquest and settlement of the New World.

Today, this aggression continues unabated throughout the Americas. Native societies are still besieged by missionaries and self-proclaimed reformers who want to wipe out the last vestiges of native beliefs. Mormons and Protestant fundamentalists are spending extraordinary amounts of time, energy, and money trying to extinguish indigenous cultures. And although on his trips to Latin America Pope John Paul II is fond of describing the Catholic Church as the historic protector of the Indians, the Catholic Church has never wavered in its belief that indigenous peoples must be converted to achieve redemption.

Meanwhile, land developers, squatters, national governments, military forces, and corporations relentlessly chip away at native homelands and cultures from northern Canada through Guatemala to the Amazon. Their determination to dispossess indigenous peoples of their lands and cultures has never flagged. They believe that native peoples are inferior, obsolete, and impediments to progress. For their own good, they must be taught to become eager consumers of western goods, happily participate in a cash economy, and surrender their communal and distinctive ways of life.

Today's war against indigenous peoples is based on exactly the same premises that animated Columbus and his successors. These indigenous peoples possess only what we once had in the dim and benighted past. Their history begins with our discovery of them. And they can progress only by alienating themselves from their most cherished beliefs and life ways and becoming more like us.[9]

Estrangement—from the natural world and other peoples—is the most powerful psychic and cultural device in the global triumph of the West. All societies, of course, are wary of outsiders, and many of them have conquered and forcibly assimilated other peoples in ways no different from Europe. In the history of cross-cultural contacts and colonization, however, the assault on native societies is unique, for Europeans and their New World descendants have been battling Indians for 500 years. The ultimate goal has never changed: to destroy the value and meaning of indigenous cultures while simultaneously benefiting from native lands, labor, resources, and knowledge.

This aggressive form of estrangement on the part of the West has been well understood by indigenous peoples. It remains obscured, however, to most westerners because estrangement is the very foundation of our culture. A restlessness, an impatience with traditions, and a desire to dominate our planet in the name of God and human progress have long characterized Christendom. In this sense, Columbus and his successors cannot be condemned for their actions, at least not within the traditional norms of western culture.

The Europeans who helped create the New World were neither demented nor cruel by the contemporary standards of Christendom. They behaved no differently than Christians in the Baltic region, the Iberian peninsula, Ireland, the Canary Islands, and in their treatment of Jews. Europeans were only being themselves, not monsters, and in their behavior toward indigenous peoples they embodied the highest religious and cultural ideals of the West. Most of their deadliest beliefs (enshrined in standard American textbooks as "the conquest of the wilderness" and the "transit of civilization") have been considered virtues that helped spread a superior culture around the world. We should not condemn our ancestors but do something far more difficult—try to understand them because their heritage has become our modern world.[10]

There is also another piece of missing information that contributes to our estrangement: our inability to acknowledge and understand native peoples' profoundly important role in shaping the history and development of the Americas. Spain, Portugal, France, and Britain failed to recreate their traditional societies in the New World because of the thousands of native societies they encountered. The New World became different from Europe as a result of tobacco, corn, potatoes, gold and silver, Indian knowledge, medicine, and free labor, Indian and Afro-Indian slavery, the fur trade, European/ Indian politics and warfare, and the widespread mixing of indigenous peoples, Europeans, and Africans.

The Twenty-first Century

At the beginning of the twenty-first century, our biggest challenge is to find ways to remember, understand, and reclaim our earliest heritage. Remembrance will not succeed, however, if it is undertaken in the name of a trendy multiculturalism or what Robert Hughes has aptly called the "culture of complaint" where everyone claims status as a victim.[11] It must be done in the name of something far more important: our collective sanity and survival.

This means first recognizing what native peoples have always believed— the world around us is not cursed but sacred. As indigenous peoples have always recognized, almost everything on earth, from the trees to the stars, is potentially our ally, friend, and mentor. Our environment is a living force that has the power to sustain us spiritually if treated wisely.

When Columbus and other Europeans came to the New World, they did not enter a land where every warrior was a noble savage and a sage and every woman a healer and font of ancestral wisdom. Europeans were not intruders in paradise. Native societies had their full share of greedy, violent, and uncooperative members. While some societies were relatively egalitarian, many were hierarchical and stratified. Others practiced slavery. Warfare between native peoples was endemic and often deadly. And the Aztec, Inca, and Mayan empires, like contemporary European states, frequently used violence to expand their boundaries and control their subjects.

But if indigenous peoples were merely human, they also had accumulated an incredible wealth of knowledge and insights over thousands of years— knowledge and insights as broad and deep as Christendom's—that were there for the sharing. Most Christians, however, resisted the New World. They chose not to listen or learn, and assimilated into their own cultures only the most material and superficial aspects of indigenous life. What was most profound and lasting they ignored or systematically tried to destroy in their attempts to overcome estrangement.

By denying or trying to obliterate the indigenous spiritual legacy, we have only succeeded in impoverishing many indigenous peoples and making it even more difficult for us to become wiser. Nevertheless, native wisdom still exists along with its possessors, and it has never been far from us. This bequest waits to wake and revive us to our land and its ancient heritage.

At the beginning of the twenty-first century, only the blindest person can continue ignoring the frightening warning signs. As the six nations of the Iroquois stated in 1978, today we face the question "of the very survival of the species. The way of life known as Western Civilization is on a death path on which their own culture has no viable answers. . . . We think even the systems of weather are changing. Our ancient teachings warned us that if Man interfered with the Natural laws, these things would come to be. When the last of the Natural Way of Life is gone, all hope for human survival will be gone with it."[12]

This is our contemporary challenge—to work cooperatively and humbly with Indians to find new ways to learn from our past and to use the New World's precious inheritance to give our communities the attention and resources they require. Try as we may, we can never forget or completely obliterate the world of indigenous peoples because our conflicts with them have shaped the modern world and our own identities. Once we recognize our interdependence, we might be able to use this principle to our advantage without excluding entire peoples.

A good start would be to listen. As Joseph Conrad wrote in one of his short stories:

> There are those who say that a native will not speak to a white man. Error. No man will speak to his master; but to a wanderer and a friend, to him who does not come to teach or to rule, to him who asks for nothing and accepts all things, words are spoken by the campfires, in the shared solitude of the sea, in riverside villages, in resting-places surrounded by forests—words are spoken that take no account of race or colour. One heart speaks—another one listens; and the earth, the sea, the sky, the passing wind and the stirring leaf, hear also the futile tale of the burden of life.[13]

Listening is very difficult, however, because from elementary school through college, indigenous peoples have been airbrushed out of the study of mainstream American history, literature, and culture. Even a cursory reading of standard high school and college American history texts, written by chaired professors and Pulitzer prize winners, indicates how successfully we have ignored our most valuable inheritance by making believe Europeans created the New World by themselves.

Despite several decades of brilliant scholarship about New World peoples and Indian/European relations, most history textbooks, primary and secondary social studies teachers, and college professors continue treating indigenous peoples very superficially. They are often rapidly dismissed from the historical stage in a few pages, or North America is described as a vacant, virgin wilderness eagerly awaiting European settlement. Missing from most classroom accounts are thoughtful descriptions of indigenous societies and their profound impact on the development of the Americas.[14]

To overcome this insidious form of intellectual and cultural amnesia, strong, dramatic measures are necessary. Jerome Rothenberg, who has immersed himself in indigenous texts for decades, had some interesting suggestions. In 1972, he recommended that for at least twenty-five years "take the great Greek epics out of the undergraduate curricula, & replace them with the great American epics. Study the *Popol Vuh* where you now study Homer, & study Homer where you now study the *Popol Vuh*." He also believed that we should teach courses in religion that begin, "This is the account of how all was in suspense, all calm, in silence; all motionless, still, & the expanse of the sky was empty—& use this as a norm with which to compare all other religious books, whether Greek or Hebrew."

He wanted poets to translate native American classics, but first they had to learn how to sing from young Indian poets. Rothenberg also argued that special chairs should be established in American literature and theology, and filled by people trained in the oral transmission of knowledge. By tapping into our native history and roots, perhaps we could finally discover where we live.[15]

Can we find ways to reconnect with our environment and ancestors? Are we prepared to accept indigenous cultures on their terms rather than our own? Are we capable of guaranteeing their existence rather than destroying them? And how do we find ways to do something profoundly new, unsettling, and visionary—listening to those who are left and to the environment that has spiritually sustained them? This is one of our greatest summons at the beginning of the twentieth-first century, and we cannot do it by ourselves.

As Queequeg, the harpooner from Fiji in Herman Melville's *Moby-Dick*, says: "It's a mutual, joint-stock world, in all meridians. We cannibals must help these Christians."[16]

Notes

_____

Introduction: Recovering Lost Worlds

1. William F. Keegan, *The People Who Discovered Columbus: The Prehistory of the Bahamas* (Gainsville: University Press of Florida, 1992).
2. David Murray, *Forked Tongues: Speech, Writing & Representation in North American Indian Texts* (Bloomington: Indiana University Press, 1991), pp. 1–13, 126–157; Dennis Tedlock, *The Spoken Word and the Work of Interpretation* (Philadelphia: University of Pennsylvania Press, 1983), pp. 31–61, 285–338; Dell Hymes, *"In Vain I Tried to Tell You": Essays in Native American Ethnopoetics* (Philadelphia: University of Pennsylvania Press, 1981), pp. 79–134, 309–55; Eric Cheyfitz, *The Poetics of Imperialism: Translation and Colonization from The Tempest to Tarzan* (New York: Oxford University Press, 1991), pp. 22–172; James Clifford, "Introduction: Partial Truths," in *Writing Culture: The Poetics and Politics of Ethnography*, eds. James Clifford and George E. Marcus (Berkeley: University of California Press, 1986), pp. 1–26; James Clifford, *The Predicament of Culture: Twentieth-Century Ethnography, Literature, and Art* (Cambridge: Harvard University Press, 1988), pp. 21–54, 255–276; Robert F. Berkhofer, Jr., *Beyond the Great Story: History as Text and Discourse* (Cambridge: Harvard University Press, 1995), pp. 170–201.
3. Jonathan Boyarin, *Storm from Paradise: The Politics of Jewish Memory* (Minneapolis: University of Minnesota Press, 1992), pp. 9–31, 72; Norman Daniel, *Islam and the West: The Making of an Image* (Edinburgh: Edinburgh University Press, 1980), pp. 163–194.
4. Joanne Rappaport, *The Politics of Memory: Native Historical Interpretation in the Columbian Andes* (Cambridge: Cambridge University Press, 1990), pp. 1, 10–17, 148–149, 164; Robert Young, *White Mythologies: Writing History and the West* (London: Routledge, 1990), pp. 1–20, 119–140.
5. Gary Urton, *The History of a Myth: Pacariqtambo and the Origin of the Inkas* (Austin: University of Texas Press, 1990), pp. 18–19; R. Tom Zuidema, *Inca Civilization in Cuzco*, trans. Jean-Jacques Decoster (Austin: University of Texas Press, 1990), pp. 3–10; Verónica Salles-Reese, *From Viracocha to the Virgin of Copacabana: Representations of the Sacred at Lake Titicaca* (Austin: University of Texas Press, 1997), pp. 100, 103.

237

6. *Popol Vuh*, trans. Dennis Tedlock (New York: Simon & Schuster, 1985), p. 71.

7. Peter Nabakov, "Native Views of History," in *The Cambridge History of the Native Peoples of the Americas*, eds. Bruce G. Trigger and Wilcomb E. Washburn (Cambridge: Cambridge University Press, 1996), Vol. I, pp. 1–53; Peter Nabakov, *A Forest of Time: American Indian Ways of History* (Cambridge: Cambridge University Press, 2002).

8. Keith H. Basso, *Wisdom Sits in Places: Landscape and Language Among the Western Apache* (Albuquerque: University of New Mexico Press, 1996), pp. 48–52.

9. T.J. Knab and Thelma D. Sullivan, eds. and trans. *A Scattering of Jades: Stories, Poems, and Prayers of the Aztecs* (New York: Simon & Schuster, 1994), p. 186.

10. Ioan P. Couliano, *The Tree of Gnosis: Gnostic Mythology from Early Christianity to Modern Nihilism* (San Francisco: HarperCollins, 1992), pp.121–127; David G. Roskies, *A Bridge of Longing: The Lost Art of Yiddish Storytelling* (Cambridge: Harvard University Press, 1995), pp. 5–7; George E. Marcus and Michael J. Fisher, *Anthropology as Cultural Critique: An Experimental Moment in the Human Sciences* (Chicago: University of Chicago Press, 1986), pp. 1–110; Clifford, *The Predicament of Culture*, pp. 1–17.

11. Eduardo H. Galeano, *Memory of Fire: Genesis*, trans. Cedric Belfrage (New York: Pantheon Books, 1985); Alan Taylor, *American Colonies* (New York: Viking Books, 2001); Daniel K. Richter, *Facing East from Indian Country: A Native History of Early America* (Cambridge: Harvard University Press, 2001); Ronald Wright, *Stolen Continents: The Americas Through Indian Eyes Since 1492* (Boston: Houghton Mifflin, 1992); Kerwin Lee Klein, *Frontiers of Historical Imagination: Narrating the European Conquest of Native America, 1890–1990* (Berkeley: University of California Press, 1997).

12. Geoffrey F. Hartman, ed. *The Selected Poetry and Prose of Wordsworth* (New York: New American Library, 1980), p. 320.

Chapter 1. Before the Wig and the Dress Coat

1. Pablo Neruda, *Canto General*, trans. Jack Schmitt (Berkeley: University of California Press, 1991), pp. 13–14.

2. Akë Hultkrantz, *The Religions of the American Indians*, trans. Monica Setterwell (Berkeley: University of California Press, 1979), pp. 15–65; Akë Hultkrantz, *Belief and Worship in Native North America*, ed. Christopher Vescey (Syracuse, NY: Syracuse University Press, 1981), pp. 3–27, 91–114, 135–146; Joseph Epes Brown, *The Spiritual Legacy of the American Indian* (New York: Crossroad, 1989), pp. 83–100; Anna Birgitta Rooth, "The Creation Myths of the North American Indians," in *Sacred Narratives: Readings in the Theory of Myth*, ed. Alan Dundes (Berkeley: University of California Press, 1984), pp. 166–181; Lawrence E. Sullivan, *Icanchu's Drum: An Orientation to Meaning in South American Religions* (New York: Macmillan, 1988), pp. 3–110, 615–672, 303–385; Alfredo López-Austin, *The Myths of the Possum: Pathways of Mesoamerican Mythology*, trans. Bernard R. Ortiz de Montellano and Thelma Ortiz de Montellano (Albuquerque: University of New Mexico Press, 1993), pp. 33–72, 274–299; Raffaele Pettazzoni, *Essays on the History of Religions*, trans. H.J. Rose (Leiden: E.J. Brill, 1967), pp. 11–36; Howard L. Harrod, *Renewing the World: Plains Indians Religion and Morality* (Tuscon: University of Arizona Press, 1987), pp. 38–156; Galeano, *Memory of Fire*, pp. 3–42; Michael F. Brown, *Tsewa's Gift: Magic and Meaning in an Amazonian Society* (Washington, DC: Smithsonian Institution Press,

1986), pp. 67–132; Richard Keeling, *Cry for Luck: Sacred Song and Speech among the Yurok, Hupa, and Karok Indians of Northwestern California* (Berkeley: University of California Press, 1992), pp. 39–57; William K. Powers, *Sacred Language: The Nature of Supernatural Discourse in Lakota* (Norman: University of Oklahoma Press, 1986), pp. 127–163; Davíd Carrasco, *Religions of Mesoamerica: Cosmovision and Ceremonial Centers* (New York: Harper & Row, 1990), pp. 24–91; Jeremy Rifkin, *Time Wars: The Primary Conflict in Human History* (New York: Simon & Schuster, 1987), pp. 228–243; Anthony F. Aveni, *Empires of Time: Calendars, Clocks, and Cultures* (New York: Basic Books, 1989), pp. 167–184; Mircea Eliade, *The Myth of the Eternal Return; or, Cosmos and History*, trans. Willard Trask (Princeton: Princeton University Press, 1965), pp. 3–92; Gary Urban, *A Discourse-Centered Approach to Culture: Native South American Myths and Rituals* (Austin: University of Texas Press, 1991), pp. 58–104; Jack Goody, *The Domestication of the Savage Mind* (Cambridge: Cambridge University Press, 1977), pp. 36–51; Nancy M. Farriss, "Remembering the Future, Anticipating the Past: History, Time, and Cosmology Among the Maya of Yucatan," *Comparative Studies in Society and History* 29, no. 3 (1987): 566–593.

3. Salles-Reese, *From Viracocha to the Virgin of Copacabana*, pp. 5–130; John Howland Rowe, "The Origins of Creator Worship Among the Incas," in *Culture in History: Essays in Honor of Paul Radin*, ed. Stanley Diamond (New York: Columbia University Press, 1960), pp. 408–429; John Howland Rowe, "Inca Culture at the Time of the Spanish Conquest," in *Handbook of South American Indians*, ed. Julian H. Steward (New York: Cooper Square Publishers, 1963), Vol. 2, pp. 293–314; John Bierhorst, ed. and trans., *Black Rainbow: Legends of the Incas and Myths of Ancient Peru* (New York: Farrar, Straus & Giroux, 1976), pp. 69–71; William Sullivan, *The Secret of the Incas: Myth, Astronomy, and the War Against Time* (New York: Crown, 1996), pp. 79–121, 306, 311; R. Tom Zuidema, "Una Interpretación alterna de la Historia Incaica," in *Ideología Mesiánica del Mundo Andino*, ed. Juan M. Ossio (Lima, Peru: Ignacio Prado Pastor, 1973), pp. 3–33; Manuel M. Marzel, "Andean Religion at the Time of the Conquest," in *South and Meso-American Spirituality: From the Cult of the Feathered Serpent to the Theology of Liberation*, ed. Gary H. Gossen (New York: Crossroad, 1993), pp. 86–92; R. Tom Zuidema, *Inca Civilization in Cuzco*, pp. 54–57, 61–78; Michael J. Sallnow, *Pilgrims of the Andes: Regional Cults in Cusco* (Washington, DC: Smithsonian Institution Press, 1987), pp. 38–39; Brian S. Bauer and David S.P. Dearborn, *Astronomy and Empire in the Ancient Andes: The Cultural Origins of Inca Skywatching* (Austin: University of Texas Press, 1995), pp. 14–16, 133, 135; Bernabe Cobo, *Inca Religion and Customs*, trans. and ed. Roland Hamilton (Austin: University of Texas Press, 1990), pp. 22–28, 34, 44–46, 47–84, 118–120, 172–174, 214; John Bierhorst, ed. and trans., *The Mythology of South America* (New York: William Morrow, 1988), pp. 199–208, 212–219; Thomas C. Patterson, "Andean Cosmologies and the Inca State," in *Civilization in Crisis: Anthropological Perspectives*, ed. Christine Ward Gailey (Gainesville: University Press of Florida, 1993), pp. 181–193; Susan A. Niles, *Callachaca: Style and Status in an Inca Community* (Iowa City: University of Iowa Press, 1987), pp. 53–54, 171–206, 231–232; Lawrence E. Sullivan, "Above, Below, or Far Away: Andean Cosmogony and Ethical Order," in *Cosmogony and Ethical Order: New Studies in Comparative Ethics*, eds. Robin W. Lovin and Frank E. Reynolds (Chicago: University of Chicago Press, 1985), pp. 98–129; Irene Silverblatt, *Moon, Sun, and Witches: Gender Ideologies and Class in Inca and Colonial Peru* (Princeton: Princeton University Press, 1987), pp. 3–108; R. Tom

Zuidema, "Inca Kinship," in *Andean Kinship and Marriage*, eds. Ralph Bolton and Enrique Mayer (Washington, DC: American Anthropological Association, 1977), pp. 240–281; R. Tom Zuidema, "Myth and History in Ancient Peru," in *The Logic of Culture: Advances in Structural Theory and Methods*, ed. Ino Rossi (South Hadley, MA: J.F. Bergin Publishers, 1982), pp. 150–156; Aveni, *Empires of Time*, pp. 284–304; Karen Spalding, *Huarochirí: An Andean Society Under Inca and Spanish Rule* (Stanford: Stanford University Press, 1984), pp. 42–105; Constance Classen, *Inca Cosmology and the Human Body* (Salt Lake City: University of Utah Press, 1993), pp. 11–25; Gary Urton, *The Social Life of Numbers: A Quechua Ontology of Numbers and Philosophy of Arithmetic* (Austin: University of Texas Press, 1997), pp. 44–81, 221; Charles Stanish, *Ancient Andean Political Economy* (Austin: University of Texas Press, 1992), pp. 1–28; Alfred Métraux, *The History of the Incas*, trans. George Ordish (New York: Schocken Books, 1970), pp. 91–120, 140–142; John V. Murra, "The *Mit'a* Obligations of Ethnic Groups to the Inka State," in *The Inca and Aztec States, 1400–1600: Anthropology and History*, eds. George A. Collier, Renato I. Rosaldo, and John D. Wirth (New York: Academic Press, 1982), pp. 239–262; Frank Salomon, *Native Lords of Quito in the Age of the Incas: The Political Economy of North Andean Chiefdoms* (Cambridge: Cambridge University Press, 1986), pp. 143–186.

4. Carlton S. Coon, *The Hunting Peoples* (New York: Nick Lyons Books, 1971), pp. 44, 215–216, 79–80; John M. Cooper, "The Ona," in *Handbook of South American Indians*, ed. Julian H. Steward (New York: Cooper Square Publishers, 1963), Vol. 1, pp.107–125; Martin Gusinde, *The Yamana: The Life and Thought of the Water Nomads of Cape Horn*, trans. Frieda Schütze (New Haven, CT: Human Relations Area Files, 1961), Vol. 1, pp. 146–155; Robert L. Kelly, *The Foraging Spectrum: Diversity in Hunter-Gatherer Lifeways* (Washington, DC: Smithsonian Institution Press, 1995), pp. 66, 112, 123–125.

5. Louis C. Faron, *Hawks of the Sun: Mapuche Morality and Its Ritual Attributes* (Pittsburgh: University of Pittsburgh Press, 1964), pp. 4–14, 49–79; Louis C. Faron, *The Mapuche Indians of Chile* (New York: Holt, Rinehart & Winston, 1968), pp. 63–71.

6. Michael E. Moseley, "Introduction: Human Exploitation and Organization on the North Andean Coast," in *Chan Chan: Andean Desert City*, eds. Michael E. Moseley and Kent C. Day (Albuquerque: University of New Mexico Press, 1982), pp. 1–24; Alan Louis Kolata, "Chronology and Settlement Growth at Chan Chan," in *Chan Chan*, pp. 67–85; Christopher B. Donnan, *Moche Art of Peru* (Los Angeles: UCLA Latin American Center, 1976), pp. 86–101; Michael Edward Moseley and Carol J. MacKay, *Twenty-four Architechtual Plans of Chan Chan, Peru: Structure and Form at the Capital of Chimor* (Campbridge, Mass: Peabody Museum Press, 1974).

7. Anna Curtenius Roosevelt, *Moundbuilders of the Amazon: Geophysical Archaeology on Marajo Island, Brazil* (San Diego, CA: Academic Press, 1991), pp. 1–97, 397–438; Anna Curtenius Roosevelt, *Parmana: Prehistoric Maize and Manioc Subsistence Along the Amazon and Orinoco* (New York: Academic Press, 1980), pp. 57–159.

8. Michael J. Harner, *The Jivaro* (Berkeley: University of California Press, 1972), pp. 134–143; Michael J. Harner, "The Sound of Rushing Water," in *Hallucinogens and Shamanism*, ed. Michael J. Harner (New York: Oxford University Press, 1973), pp. 15–27; Rafael Karsten, "Blood Revenge and War Among the Jibaro Indians of Eastern Ecuador," in *Law and Warfare: Studies in the Anthropology of Conflict*, ed. Paul Bohannan (Garden City, NY: Natural History Press, 1967), pp. 303–325.

9. Lydia M. Pulsipher, "Galways Plantation, Monserrat," in *Seeds of Change*, eds. Herman J. Viola and Carolyn Margolis (Washington, DC: Smithsonian Institution Press, 1991), pp. 140–141; David Watts, *The West Indies: Patterns of Development, Culture and Environmental Change Since 1492* (Cambridge: Cambridge University Press, 1987), pp. 44–77; Carl Ortin Sauer, *The Early Spanish Main* (Berkeley: University of California Press, 1968), pp. 37–69; Antonio M. Stevens-Arroyo, *Cave of the Jagua: The Mythological World of the Taínos* (Albuquerque: University of New Mexico Press, 1988), pp. 37–51, 53–69, 118–120, 239–240; Fred Olsen, *On the Trail of the Arawak* (Norman: University of Oklahoma Press, 1974), pp. 49–63, 89–120; Irving Rouse, *The Tainos: Rise & Decline of the People Who Greeted Columbus* (New Haven: Yale University Press, 1992), pp. 49–137; Irving Rouse, *Migrations in Prehistory: Inferring Population Movement from Cultural Remains* (New Haven: Yale University Press, 1986), pp. 106–156.

10. Mary W. Helms, *Ancient Panama: Chiefs in Search of Power* (Austin: University of Texas Press, 1979), pp. 70–143, 159–160; Mary W. Helms, *Craft and the Kingly Ideal: Art, Trade, and Power* (Austin: University of Texas Press, 1993), pp. 91–108, 160–170, 192–209; Vicente Restrepo, *Los Chibchas antes de la Conquista Española* (Bogota: La Luz, 1895), pp. 44–62.

11. Carrasco, *Religions of Mesoamerica*, pp. 92–123; Jill Leslie McKeever Furst, *The Natural History of the Soul in Ancient Mexico* (New Haven: Yale University Press, 1995), pp. 131–135; Linda Schele and Mary Miller, *The Blood of Kings: Dynasty and Ritual in Maya Art* (Fort Worth, TX: Kimball Art Museum, 1986), pp. 175–187; Linda Schele and David Freidel, *A Forest of Kings: The Untold Story of the Ancient Maya* (New York: William Morrow, 1990), pp. 266–270, 77–84; Munro S. Edmonson, *The Book of the Year: Middle American Calendrical Systems* (Salt Lake City: University of Utah Press, 1988), pp. 1–18, 97–178; Sylvanus Griswold Morley, *An Introduction to the Study of Maya Hieroglyphs* (New York: Dover, 1975), pp. 37–53; Miguel León-Portilla, *Endangered Cultures*, trans. Julie Goodson-Lawes (Dallas, TX: Southern Methodist University Press, 1990), pp. 35–112; David Freidel, Linda Schele, and Joy Parker, *Maya Cosmos: Three Thousand Years on the Shaman's Path* (New York: William Morrow, 1993), pp. 61–75; Vincent H. Malmström, *Cycles of the Sun, Mysteries of the Moon: The Calendar in Mesoamerican Civilization* (Austin: University of Texas, 1997), pp. 110–129; Dennis Tedlock, *Breath on the Mirror: Mythic Voices & Visions of the Living Maya* (San Francisco: HarperCollins, 1993), pp. 1–11, 234.

12. Nathaniel Altman, *Sacred Trees* (San Francisco: Sierra Club, 1994), pp. 35, 78, 202; Clyde E. Keller, *Apples of Immortality from the Cuna Tree of Life: The Study of a Most Ancient Ceremonial and a Belief that Survived 10,000 Years* (New York: Exposition Press, 1961), pp. 30–61; Joel Sherzer, *Verbal Art in San Blas: Kuna Culture Through its Discourse* (Cambridge: Cambridge University Press, 1990), pp. 67, 73.

13. Charles F. Carroll, *The Timber Economy of Puritan New England* (Providence, RI: Brown University Press, 1973), pp. 25–37; Neal Salisbury, *Manitou and Providence: Indians, Europeans, and the Making of New England, 1500–1643* (New York: Oxford University Press, 1982), pp. 13–49; William Cronon, *Changes in the Land: Indians, Colonists, and the Making of New England* (New York: Hill & Wang, 1983), pp. 19–65; Howard S. Russell, *Indian New England Before the Mayflower* (Hanover, NH: University Press of New England, 1985), pp. 96–103, 123–181; Carolyn Merchant, *Ecological Revolutions: Nature, Gender and Science in New England* (Chapel Hill: University of North Carolina Press, 1989), pp. 29–111; Barrie Kavasch, "Native Foods of New England," in *Enduring Traditions: The Natives Peoples of New England*,

ed. Laurie Weinstein and Russell Peters (Westport, CT: Bergin & Garvey, 1994), pp. 5–16; M.K. Bennett, "The Food Economy of the New England Indians, 1605–75," *Journal of Political Economy* LXIII, no. 5 (1955): 369–397; Mark Nathan Cohen, *Health and the Rise of Civilization* (New Haven: Yale University Press, 1989), pp. 105–129; Michael W. Flinn, *The European Demographic System, 1500–1820* (Baltimore: Johns Hopkins University Press, 1981), pp. 13–75; William A. Haviland and Marjory W. Power, *The Original Vermonters: Native Inhabitants Past and Present* (Hanover, NH: University Press of New England, 1981), pp. 160, 184–193.

14. James A. Tuck, "An Archaic Indian Cemetery in Newfoundland," *Scientific American* 222, no. 6 (1970): 112–121.

15. Ray A. Williamson, *Living the Sky: The Cosmos of the American Indian* (Boston: Houghton Mifflin, 1984), pp. 277–87; Travis Hudson and Ernest Underhay, *Crystals in the Sky: An Intellectual Odyssey Involving Chumash Astronomy, Cosmology and Rock Art* (Santa Barbara, CA: Ballena Press, 1978), pp. 27–38, 51–77, 141–148; Thomas C. Blackburn, ed., *December's Child: A Book of Chumash Oral Narratives* (Berkeley: University of California Press, 1975), pp. 63–74.

16. Paula Gunn Allen, *The Sacred Hoop: Recovering the Feminine in American Indian Traditions* (Boston: Beacon Press, 1986), pp. 13–42; Paula Gunn Allen, *Grandmothers of the Light: A Medicine Woman's Sourcebook* (Boston: Beacon Press, 1991), pp. 3–32; James H. Howard, *Shawnee! The Ceremonialism of a Native American Tribe and its Cultural Background* (Athens: Ohio University Press, 1981), pp. 163–164; Robert Steven Grumet, "Sunksquaws, Shamans, and Tradeswomen: Middle Atlantic Coastal Algonkian Women During the 17th and 18th Centuries," in *Women and Colonization: Anthropological Perspectives*, eds. Mona Etienne and Eleanor Leacock (New York: Praeger, 1980), pp. 43–62; Peggy R. Sanday, "Female Status in the Public Domain," in *Woman, Culture, and Society*, eds. Michelle Zimbalist Rosaldo and Louise Lamphere (Stanford: Stanford University Press, 1974), pp. 192–193; Louise Lamphere, "Strategies, Cooperation, and Conflict Among Women in Domestic Groups," in *Woman, Culture, and Society*, pp. 98–103, 108–112; Jordan Paper, "Through the Earth Darkly: The Female Spirit in Native American Religions," in *Religion in Native North America*, ed. Christopher Vescey (Moscow: University of Idaho Press, 1990), pp. 3–19; Marla Powers, "Mistress, Mother, Visionary Spirit: The Lakota Cultural Heroine," in *Religion in Native North America*, pp. 36–48; Priscilla A. Buffalohead, "Farmers, Warriors, Traders: A Fresh Look at Ojibway Women," in *The American Indian Past and Present*, ed. Roger L. Nichols (New York: Knopf, 1986), pp. 28–38.

Chapter 2. Toward a New World Order

1. Jerry H. Bentley, *Old World Encounters: Cross-Cultural Contacts and Exchanges in Pre-Modern Times* (New York: Oxford University Press, 1993), pp. 149–63, 176–84; William H. McNeill, *The Rise of the West: A History of the Human Community* (Chicago: University of Chicago Press, 1963), pp. 484–559; William H. McNeill, *The Pursuit of Power: Technology, Armed Force, and Society Since A.D. 1000* (Chicago: University of Chicago Press, 1982), pp. 63–102; Robert Bartlett, *The Making of Europe: Conquest, Colonization and Cultural Change, 950–1350* (Princeton: Princeton University Press, 1993), pp. 292–314; Michael Mann, *The Sources of Social Power* (Cambridge: Cambridge University Press, 1986), Vol. 1, pp. 373–446; Robert A. Williams, Jr. *The American Indian in Western Legal Thought: The Discourses of Conquest* (New York: Oxford University Press, 1990), pp. 3–8; James

*Muldoon, Popes, Lawyers, and Infidels: The Church and the Non-Christian World,
1250–1550* (Philadelphia: University of Pennsylvania Press, 1979), pp. 3–28; James
Muldoon, *The Americas in the Spanish World Order: The Justification for Conquest
in the Seventeenth Century* (Philadelphia: University of Pennsylvania Press, 1994),
pp. 15–65; Garth Fowden, *Empire to Commonwealth: Consequences of Monotheism
in Late Antiquity* (Princeton: Princeton University Press, 1993), pp. 80–93, 169–175;
L.C. Green and Olive Dickason, *The Law of Nations and the New World* (Edmonton:
University of Alberta Press, 1989), pp. 4–64, 143–214; Marc Shell, *The End of Kinship: 'Measure for Measure,' Incest, and the Ideal of Universal Siblinghood* (Stanford:
Stanford University Press, 1988), pp. 184–189; Charles H. Long, "Primitive/Civilized: The Locus of a Problem," *History of Religions* 20, nos. 1–2 (1980): 43–61;
Jacques Le Goff, *The Medieval Imagination*, trans. Arthur Goldhammer (Chicago:
University of Chicago Press, 1988), pp. 47–59.

2. Jean-Pierre Poly and Eric Bournazel, *The Feudal Transformation, 900–1200*,
trans. Caroline Higgit (New York: Holmes & Meier, 1991), pp. 9–140; Thomas F.
Glick, *From Muslim Fortress to Christian Castle: Social and Cultural Change in
Medieval Spain* (Manchester: Manchester University Press, 1995), pp. 92–124; Jeremy du Quesnay Adams, ed. *Patterns of Medieval Society* (Englewood Cliffs: Prentice-Hall, 1969), p. 233.

3. Fernand Braudel, *The Structures of Everyday Life: The Limits of the Possible*,
trans. Siân Reynolds (New York: Harper & Row, 1981), pp. 509–525; G.V. Scammell,
The World Encompassed: The First European Maritime Empires, c. 800–1650 (Berkeley: University of California Press, 1981), pp. 155–220; Robert S. Lopez, *The Commercial Revolution of the Middle Ages, 950–1350* (Cambridge: Cambridge University Press, 1976), pp. 139–141; Paul M. Hohenberg and Lynn Hollen Lees, *The Making of Urban Europe, 1000–1950* (Cambridge: Harvard University Press, 1985), pp.
22–73; Janet L. Abu-Lughod, *Before European Hegemony: The World System A.D.
1250–1350* (New York: Oxford University Press, 1989), pp. 102–134; Felipe
Fernández-Armesto, *Before Columbus: Exploration and Colonization from the Mediterranean to the Atlantic, 1229–1492* (London: MacMillan, 1987), pp. 96–120; Steven
A. Epstein, *Genoa & the Genoese, 958–1528* (Chapel Hill: University of North Carolina Press, 1996), pp. 140–146, 177–180; Joseph Gies and Frances Gies, *Merchants
and Moneymen: The Commercial Revolution, 1000–1500* (New York: Crowell, 1972),
pp. 98–113.

4. Archibald R. Lewis, "The Closing of the Medieval Frontier," *Speculum* XXXIII,
no. 4 (1958): 475–483; William H. TeBrake, *Medieval Frontier: Culture and Ecology
in Rijnland* (College Station: Texas A&M University Press, 1985), pp. 3–52, 107–
243; Johan Van Veen, *Dredge, Drain, Reclaim: The Art of a Nation* (Hague: Martinus
Nijhoff, 1962), pp. 11–73.

5. Elizabeth Kirk and Judith Anderson, eds., *Will's Version of Piers Plowman*, trans.
E. Talbot Richardson (New York: Norton, 1990), pp. 45–46; Martha C. Howell, *Women,
Production, and Patriarchy in Late Medieval Cities* (Chicago: University of Chicago
Press, 1986), pp. 9–46; Frances Gies and Joeseph Gies, *Women in the Middle Ages* (New
York: Harper & Row, 1978), pp. 143–183, 229–232; Richard H. Britwell, *The
Commercialisation of English Society, 1000–1500* (Manchester: Manchester University
Press, 1996), pp. 155–178; Alfred W. Crosby, *The Measure of Reality: Quantification
and Western Society, 1250–1600* (Cambridge: Cambridge University Press, 1997), pp.
69–74; Alan Macfarlane, *The Origins of English Individualism: The Family, Property
and Social Transition* (New York: Cambridge University Press, 1978), pp. 102–88.

6. Williams, *Indian in Western Legal Thought*, pp. 58–62; James Muldoon, ed., *The Expansion of Europe: The First Phase* (Philadelphia: University of Pennsylvania Press, 1977), pp. 105–107, 116–123; Nathaniel Altman, *Sacred Trees* (San Francisco: Sierra Club, 1994), pp. 51–52, 179; Desmond Seward, *The Monks of War: The Military Religious Orders* (New York: Penguin Books, 1995), pp. 17, 99; Anatol Lieven, *The Baltic Revolution: Estonia, Latvia, Lithuania and the Path to Independence* (New Haven: Yale University Press, 1993), pp. 42–45, 388, 398; William Urban, *The Baltic Crusade* (DeKalb: Northern Illinois University Press, 1975), pp. 33–45, 67–95; Eric Christiansen, *The Northern Crusades* (New York: Penguin Books, 1997), pp. 73–176, 199–262; Muldoon, *Popes, Lawyers, and Infidels*, pp. 86–88, 97–100, 107–19; Jaan Puhvel, *Comparative Mythology* (Baltimore: Johns Hopkins University Press, 1987), p. 223.

7. David Biale, *Power and Powerlessness in Jewish History* (New York: Schocken Books, 1986), pp. 58–86; Kenneth R. Stow, *Alienated Minority: The Jews of Medieval Latin Europe* (Cambridge: Harvard University Press, 1996), pp. 6–40, 102–120; Léon Poliakov, *The History of Anti-Semitism: From the Time of Christ to the Court Jews*, trans. Richard Howard (New York: Schocken Books, 1974), pp. 26–169; Sander L. Gilman, *Jewish Self-Hatred: Anti-Semitism and the Hidden Language of the Jews* (Baltimore: Johns Hopkins University Press, 1986), pp. 22–42; Rosemary Radford Ruether, *Faith and Fratricide: The Theological Roots of Anti-Semitism* (New York: Seabury, 1974), pp. 64–214; Joshua Trachtenberg, *The Devil and the Jews: The Medieval Conception of the Jew and its Relation to Modern Antisemitism* (1943, New York: Harper & Row, 1966); R. I. Moore, *The Formation of a Persecuting Society: Power and Deviance in Western Europe, 950–1250* (Oxford: Blackwell, 1987), pp. 27–45, 80–91; Elaine Pagels, *The Origin of Satan* (New York: Random House, 1995); Philippe Braunstein, "Toward Intimacy: The Fourteenth and Fifteenth Centuries," in *A History of Private Life: Revelations of the Medieval World*, ed. Georges Duby, trans. Arthur Goldhammer, (Cambridge: Harvard University Press, 1988), pp. 587–89, 514; Muldoon, *Popes, Lawyers, and Infidels*, pp. 3, 23–27; Howard Eilberg-Schwartz, *The Savage in Judaism: An Anthropology of Israelite Religion and Ancient Judaism* (Bloomington: Indiana University Press, 1990), pp. 37–38.

8. Eric J. Leed, *The Mind of the Traveler: From Gilgamesh to Global Tourism* (New York: Basic Books, 1991), pp. 25–41, 133–141; Gwyn Jones, *A History of the Vikings* (New York: Oxford University Press, 1973), pp. 1–13, 77, 145–311; Helge Ingstad, *Westward to Vineland: The Discovery of Pre-Columbian Norse House-sites in North America*, trans. Erik J. Friis (New York: Harper & Row, 1972), pp. 15, 39–69, 222–223; David B. Quinn, *North America from Earliest Discovery to First Settlements: The Norse Voyages to 1612* (New York: Harper & Row, 1977), pp. 20–40; Jack D. Forbes, *Africans and Native Americans: The Language of Race and the Evolution of Red-Black Peoples* (Urbana: University of Illinois Press, 1993), p. 19; J.R.S. Phillips, *The Medieval Expansion of Europe* (New York: Oxford University Press, 1988), pp. 164–184; Kirsten A. Seaver, *The Frozen Echo: Greenland and the Exploration of North America, ca. A.D. 1000–1500* (Stanford: Stanford University Press, 1996), pp. 14–43; William W. Fitzhugh, "Early Contacts North of Newfoundland Before A.D. 1600: A Review," in *Cultures in Contact: The Impact of European Contacts on Native American Cultural Institutions, A.D. 1000–1800*, ed. William H. Fitzhugh (Washington, DC: Smithsonian Institution Press, 1985), pp. 24–31.

9. Valerie I. J. Flint, *The Imaginative Landscape of Christopher Columbus* (Princeton: Princeton University Press, 1992), pp. 3–23; Robert L. Wilken, *The*

Land Called Holy: Palestine in Christian History & Thought (New Haven: Yale University Press, 1992), pp. 65–246; Eric J. Leed, *The Mind of the Traveler*, pp. 142–148; Mary B. Campbell, *The Witness and the Other World: Exotic European Travel Writing, 400–1600* (Ithaca, NY: Cornell University Press, 1988), pp. 4, 15–20; Carl Erdmann, *The Origin of the Idea of Crusade*, trans. Marshall W. Baldwin and Walter Goffart (1935, Princeton: Princeton University Press, 1977), pp. 57–117; Frederick H. Russell, *The Just War in the Middle Ages* (Cambridge: Cambridge University Press, 1975), pp. 195–212; Steve Runcimen, "The Pilgrimage to Palestine Before 1095," in *A History of the Crusades*, ed. Marshall W. Baldwin (Madison: University of Wisconsin Press, 1969), Vol. 1, pp. 68–78; Léon Poliakov, *The History of Anti-Semitism*, pp. 41–83, 242; Norman Cohn, *The Pursuit of the Millennium: Revolutionary Messianism in Medieval and Reformation Europe and its Bearing on Modern Totalitarian Movements* (New York: Harper & Row, 1961), pp. 40–52; Steve Runcimen, *The First Crusade* (Cambridge: Cambridge University Press, 1980), pp. 47–229; Robert Payne, *The Dream and the Tomb: A History of the Crusades* (New York: Stein & Day, 1984), pp. 18, 34–35, 38–46, 95–104, 261–289; Norman Daniel, *The Arabs and Mediaeval Europe* (London: Longman, 1975), pp. 111–139; Biale, *Power and Powerlessness in Jewish History*, pp. 73–74; Mircea Eliade, *A History of Religious Ideas: From Muhammed to the Age of Reforms*, trans. Alf Hiltebeitel and Diane Apostolos-Cappadona (Chicago: University of Chicago Press, 1985), Vol. 3, p. 96; Robert A. Williams, Jr., *The American Indian in Western Legal Thought*, pp. 13–50; Eric J. Leed, *Shores of Discovery: How Expeditionaries Have Constructed the World* (New York: Basic Books, 1995), pp. 62–83; Helen Nicholson, *Templars, Hospitallers, and Teutonic Knights: Images of the Military Orders*, 1128–1291 (Leicester: Leicester University Press, 1995), pp. 1–5, 15–34; Stephen Howarth, *The Knights Templar* (New York: Atheneum, 1982), pp. 233–248; Norman Housley, *The Later Crusades: From Lyons to Alcazar*, 1274–1580 (Oxford: Oxford University Press, 1992), pp. 204–420.

10. Alfred W. Crosby, *Ecological Imperialism: The Biological Expansion of Europe, 900–1900* (Cambridge: Cambridge University Press, 1986), pp. 80–100; J.H. Parry, *The Age of Reconnaissance* (Cleveland, OH: World Publishing, 1963), p. 36; John Mercer, *The Canary Islanders: Their Prehistory, Conquest, and Survival* (London: Rex Collins, 1980), pp. 17–65, 112–123, 155–227; Felipe Fernández-Armesto, *The Canary Islands After the Conquest: The Making of a Colonial Society in the Early Sixteenth Century* (Oxford: Clarendon Press, 1962), pp. 6–7, 11, 13–32, 67–92; Eduardo Aznar Vallejo, "The Conquests of the Canary Islands," in *Implicit Understandings: Observing, Reporting, and Reflecting on the Encounters Between Europeans and Other Peoples in the Early Modern Era*, ed. Stuart B. Schwartz (Cambridge: Cambridge University Press, 1994), pp. 134–56; Felipe Fernández-Armesto, *Before Columbus,* pp. 169–222; Williams, *Indian in Western Legal Thought*, pp. 68–72; Muldoon, *Popes, Lawyers, and Infidels*, pp. 104, 119–131; Seward, *Monks of War*, pp. 183–4; Russell, *Just War in the Middle Ages*, pp. 201–207, 251–257; David Gordon White, *Myths of the Dog-Man* (Chicago: University of Chicago Press, 1991), p. 59; Peter Mason, *Deconstructing America: Representations of the Other* (London: Routledge, 1990), pp. 71–94; W.R. Jones, "The Image of the Barbarian in Medieval Europe," *Comparative Studies in Society and History* 13, no. 4 (1971): 376–407; Hayden White, "The Forms of Wildness: Archaeology of an Idea," in *The Wild Man Within: An Image in Western Thought from the Renaissance to Romanticism*, ed. Edward Dudley and

Maximillian E. Novak (Pittsburgh: University of Pittsburgh Press, 1973), pp. 20–28; Richard Bernheimer, *Wild Men in the Middle Ages: A Study in Art, Sentiment, and Demonology* (New York: Octagon Books, 1970), pp. 21–48; John Block Friedman, *The Monstrous Races in Medieval Art and Thought* (Cambridge: Harvard University Press, 1981), pp. 37–58; Roger Bartra, *Wild Man in the Looking Glass: The Mythic Origins of European Otherness*, trans. Carl T. Berrisford (Ann Arbor: University of Michigan Press, 1994), pp. 85–125; Norbert Elias, *Power and Civility*, trans. Edmund Jephcott (New York: Pantheon, 1982); Peter Brown, *The Body and Society: Men, Women, and Sexual Renunciation in Early Christianity* (New York: Columbia University Press, 1988), pp. 33–64, 387–447; Braunstein, "Toward Intimacy," pp. 568–582; Ronald Sanders, *Lost Tribes and Promised Lands: The Origins of American Racism* (Boston: Little, Brown, 1978), pp. 35–9; J. Jorge Klor de Alva, "Sahagún and the Birth of Modern Ethnography: Representing, Confessing, and Inscribing the Native Other," in *The Work of Bernardino de Sahagún: Pioneer Ethnographer of Sixteenth-Century Aztec Mexico*, eds. J. Jorge Klor de Alva, H.B. Nicholson, and Eloise Quinones Keber (Austin: University of Texas Press, 1988), pp. 31–42.

11. Gianni Granzotto, *Christopher Columbus: The Dream & the Obsession*, trans. Stephen Sartarelli (London: Grafton Books, 1985); Felipe Fernández-Armesto, *Before Columbus*, pp. 11–150; Pierre Chaunu, *European Expansion in the Later Middle Ages*, trans. Katharine Bertram (Amsterdam: North Holland, 1979), pp. 93–197; Williams, *Indian in Western Legal Thought*, pp. 67–8; J.H. Elliott, *Imperial Spain, 1469–1716* (New York: New American Library, 1963), pp. 17–74; Muldoon, *Popes, Lawyers, and Infidels*, pp. 132–152; Forbes, *Africans and Native Americans*, p. 22; Pauline Moffitt Watts, "Prophecy and Discovery: On the Spiritual Origins of Christopher Columbus's 'Enterprise of the Indies,'" *American Historical Review* 90, no. 1 (1985): 73–102; Flint, *The Imaginative Landscape of Columbus*, pp. 115–214; Leonard I. Sweet, "Christopher Columbus and the Millennial Vision of the New World," *The Catholic Historical Review* LXXII, no. 3 (1986): 369–382; Mario Góngora, *Studies in the Colonial History of Spanish America*, trans. Richard Southern (London: Cambridge University Press, 1975), pp. 206–216; Sanders, *Lost Tribes*, p. 5; Delano C. West, "Wallowing in a Theological Stupor or a Steadfast and Consuming Faith: Scholarly Encounters with Columbus' *Libro de las Profecías*," in *Columbus and His World*, ed. Donald T. Gerace (Fort Lauderdale, FL: College Center of the Finger Lakes, 1987), pp. 45–56; Christopher Columbus, *The Life of Admiral Columbus by His Son Ferdinand*, trans. Benjamin Keen (New Brunswick, NJ: Rutgers University Press, 1959), p. 4; John Leddy Phelan, *The Millennial Kingdom of the Franciscans in the New World* (Berkeley: University of California Press, 1970), pp. 17–23, 134; Ferdinand Columbus, *The Four Voyages*, trans. J.M. Cohen (New York: Penguin Books, 1969), pp. 221–222; Deleno C. West and August King, eds. and trans., *The Libro de la Profecías of Christopher Columbus* (Gainsville: University Press of Florida, 1991), pp. 41–75, 101; Cristoforo Colombo, *Epistola de Insulis Nuper Inventis*, trans. Frank E. Robbins (Ann Arbor, MI: University Microfilms, 1966), p. 8; Paul Leicester Ford, ed., *Writings of Christopher Columbus* (New York: Charles L. Webster, 1892), pp. 28–30; Phillips, *Medieval Expansion*, pp. 227–252.

Chapter 3. Suffering a Great Misery

1. Jean de Léry, *History of a Voyage to the Land of Brazil, Otherwise Called America*, trans. and ed. by Janet Whatley (Berkeley: University of California Press, 1990), pp. lx–lxi.

2. Anthony Grafton, *New Worlds, Ancient Texts: The Power of Tradition and the Shock of Discovery* (Cambridge: Harvard University Press, 1992), pp. 59–256; Edmundo O'Gorman, *La Idea del descubrimiento de América: Historia de esa interpretación y crítica de sus fundamentos* (Mexico City: Universidad de Mexico, 1951), pp. 9–48; Margaret T. Hodgen, *Early Anthropology in the Sixteenth and Seventeenth Centuries* (Philadelphia: University of Pennsylvania Press, 1964), pp. 49–111; Stephen Greenblatt, *Marvelous Possessions: The Wonder of the New World* (Chicago: University of Chicago Press, 1991), pp. 1–25, 70–77, 108–110; J.H. Elliott, *The Old World and the New, 1492–1650* (Cambridge: Cambridge University Press, 1972), pp. 1–53; Johannes Fabian, *Time and the Other: How Anthropology Makes Its Object* (New York: Columbia University Press, 1983), pp. 11–35, 82, 95, 143–156, 191–206; Eric J. Leed, *The Mind of the Traveler: From Gilgamesh to Global Tourism* (New York: Basic Books, 1991), pp. 168–174; Michael Taussig, *Shamanism, Colonialism, and the Wild Man: A Study in Terror and Healing* (Chicago: University of Chicago Press, 1987), pp. 209–20; Daniel Defert, "The Collection of the World: Accounts of Voyages from the Sixteenth to the Eighteenth Centuries," *Dialectical Anthropology* 7, no. 1 (1982): 11–20; Angel Delgado-Gómez, "The Earliest European Views of New World Natives," in *Early Images of the Americas: Transfer and Invention*, eds. Jerry M. Williams and Robert E. Lewis (Tucson: University of Arizona Press, 1993), pp. 3–20; Anthony Pagden, *European Encounters with the New World: From the Renaissance to Romanticism* (New Haven: Yale University Press, 1993), pp. 17–87; Richard C. Trexler, *Sex and Conquest: Gendered Violence, Political Order, and the European Conquest of the Americas* (Ithaca, NY: Cornell University Press, 1995), pp. 141–172; W. Arens, *The Man-Eating Myth: Anthropology & Anthropophagy* (New York: Oxford University Press, 1979), pp. 18–31, 41–79; Philip P. Boucher, *Cannibal Encounters: Europeans and the Island Caribs, 1492–1763* (Baltimore: Johns Hopkins University Press, 1992), pp. 13–20; Gesa Mackenthun, *Metaphors of Dispossession: American Beginnings and the Translation of Empire, 1492–1637* (Norman: University of Oklahoma Press, 1997), pp. 48–70; Peter Mason, "Seduction from Afar: Europe's Inner Indians," *Anthropos* 82, nos. 4–6 (1987): 581–601; Peter Hulme, *Colonial Encounters: Europe and the Native Caribbean, 1492–1797* (London: Methuen, 1986), pp. 13–43; Alden T. Vaughan, *Roots of American Racism* (New York: Oxford University Press, 1995), pp. 34–54; Olive Patricia Dickason, *The Myth of the Savage and the Beginnings of French Colonialism in the Americas* (Edmonton: University of Alberta Press, 1984), pp. 29–84; Bernadette Bucher, *La sauvage aux seins pendents* (Paris: Hermann, 1977), pp. 3–35; Karen Ordahl Kupperman, *Settling with the Indians: The Meeting of English and Indian Cultures in America, 1580–1640* (Totowa, NJ: Rowman & Littlefield, 1980), pp. 33–140; Michel de Certeau, *The Writing of History*, trans. Tom Conley (New York: Columbia University Press, 1988), pp. 209–243; Eric J. Leed, *Shores of Discovery: How Expeditionaries Have Constructed the World* (New York: Basic Books, 1995), pp. 6, 21, 46; Mary W. Helms, *Ulysses' Sail: An Ethnographic Odyssey of Power, Knowledge, and Geographical Distance* (Princeton: Princeton University Press, 1988), pp. 172–210; Marshall Sahlins, *How "Natives" Think: About Captian Cook, for Example* (Chicago: University of Chicago Press, 1995), pp. 148–189; Bruce G. Trigger, "Early Native North American Responses to European Contact: Romantic Versus Rationalistic Interpretations," *Journal of American History* 77, no. 4 (1991): 1195–1215; James Axtell, *Beyond 1492: Encounters in Colonial North America* (New York: Oxford University Press, 1992), pp. 30–41; George R. Hammell, "Strawberries, Floating Islands, and Rabbit Captains: Mythical Realities and Euro-

pean Contact in the Northeast During the Sixteenth and Seventeenth Centuries," *Journal of Canadian Studies* 21, no. 4 (1986–87): 72–94; Christopher L. Miller and George R. Hamell, "A New Perspective on Indian-White Contact: Cultural Symbols and Colonial Trade," *Journal of American History* 73, no. 1 (1986): 311–328; Terence Turner, "Ethno-Ethnohistory: Myth and History in Native South American Representations of Contact with Western Society," in *Rethinking History and Myth: Indigenous South American Perspectives on the Past*, ed. Jonathan Hill (Urbana: University of Illinois Press, 1988), pp. 235–254; Richard Keeling, *Cry for Luck: Sacred Song and Speech Among the Yurok, Hupa, and Karok Indians of Northwestern California* (Berkeley: University of California Press, 1992), p. 20; Michael F. Brown, *Tsewa's Gift: Magic and Meaning in an Amazonian Society* (Washington, DC: Smithsonian Institution Press, 1986), p. 151; William K. Powers, *Oglala Religion* (Lincoln: University of Nebraska Press, 1977), p. 47.

3. Christopher Columbus, *The Four Voyages*, trans. J.M. Cohen (New York: Penguin, 1969), pp. 37–123; Anthony Pagden, *European Encounters*, pp. 17–21; Robert F. Berkhofer, Jr., *The White Man's Indian: Images of the American Indian from Columbus to the Present* (New York: Knopf, 1978), pp. 3–6; Lewis Hanke, *The Spanish Struggle for Justice in the Conquest of America* (Philadelphia: University of Pennsylvania Press, 1949), pp. 23–27; Mircea Eliade, *The Sacred and the Profane: The Nature of Religion*, trans. Willard R. Trask (New York: Harcourt Brace Jovanovich, 1959), pp. 20–54; William F. Keegan, *The People Who Discovered Columbus: The Prehistory of the Bahamas* (Gainsville: University Press of Florida, 1992), pp. 48–64, 175–206; J.H. Parry, *The Age of Reconnaissance* (Cleveland: World Publishing, 1963), pp. 19–37; J.H. Elliott, *Imperial Spain, 1469–1716* (New York: New American Library, 1963), pp. 44–74; Tzvetan Todorov, *The Conquest of America: The Question of the Other*, trans. Richard Howard (New York: Harper & Row, 1984), pp. 34–50; Beatriz Pastor Bodmer, *The Armature of Conquest: Spanish Accounts of the Discovery of America, 1492–1589*, trans. Lydia Longstreth Hunt (Stanford: Stanford University Press, 1992), pp. 9–49; Helen Tworkov, "Agent of Change: An Interview with Bell Hooks," *Tricycle* II, no. 5 (1992): 56.

4. Miguel León-Portilla, ed., *The Broken Spears: The Aztec Account of the Conquest of Mexico* (Boston: Beacon Press, 1962), pp. 14–31; Arthur J.O. Anderson and Charles E. Dibble, trans., *The War of Conquest: How It Was Waged Here in Mexico* (Salt Lake City: University of Utah Press, 1978), pp. 11–17.

5. Diego de Landa, *Yucatan Before and After the Conquest*, trans. William Gates, (New York: Dover, 1978), pp. 4–7; J.H. Elliott, *Spain and Its World, 1500–1700* (New Haven: Yale University Press, 1989), pp. 27–41; Dennis Tedlock, *Breath on the Mirror: Mythic Voices & Visions of the Living Maya* (San Francisco: HarperCollins, 1993), p. 40; Lesley Byrd Simpson, *Many Mexicos*, (1941, Berkeley: University of California Press, 1969), p. 33; Ida Altman, *Emigrants and Society: Extremadura and America in the Sixteenth Century* (Berkeley: University of California Press, 1989), pp. 165–209; Robert Ricard, *The Spiritual Conquest of Mexico: An Essay on the Apostolate and the Evangelizing Methods of the Mendicant Orders in New Spain: 1523–1572*, trans. Lesley Byrd Simpson (Berkeley: University of California, 1982), p. 15; Inga Clendinnen, "Fierce and Unnatural Cruelty: Cortés and the Conquest of Mexico," *Representations* 33 (1991): 65–100; Hernan Cortés, *Conquest: Dispatches from the New World*, ed. and trans. Irwin R. Blacker and Harry M. Rosen (New York: Grosset & Dunlap, 1962), pp. 2–15; Bernal Díaz, *The Conquest of New Spain*, trans. J. M. Cohen (New York: Penguin Books, 1963), pp. 59–65, 82, 88–94; Francisco López de

Gómara, *Córtes: The Life of the Conqueror by His Secretary*, trans. Leslie Byrd Simpson (Berkeley: University of California Press, 1965), pp. 28–32, 54–61.

6. H.B. Biggar, *The Precursors of Jacques Cartier, 1496–1534* (Ottawa: Canadian Archives Publications, 1911), pp. 35–36, 63–64, 66–67; Samuel Eliot Morison, *Portuguese Voyages to America in the Fifteenth Century* (New York: Octagon Books, 1965), pp. 68–70; L.T.S. Upton, "The Extermination of the Beothucks of Newfoundland," in *Sweet Promises: A Reader on Indian-White Relations*, ed. J.R. Miller (Toronto, Canada: University of Toronto Press, 1991), pp. 69–70; Jack D. Forbes, *Africans and Native Americans: The Language of Race and the Evolution of Red-Black Peoples* (Urbana: University of Illinois Press, 1993), pp. 29–30.

7. Samuel Eliot Morison, *The Great Explorers: The European Discovery of America* (New York: Oxford University Press, 1978), pp. 169–171; Bruce G. Trigger, *Natives and Newcomers: Canada's "Heroic Age" Reconsidered* (Kingston: McGill-Queen's University Press, 1985), pp. 124–130, 298–304; Carl Ortwin Sauer, *Sixteenth Century North America* (Berkeley: University of California Press, 1975), pp. 77–97; Henry S. Burrage, ed., *Early English and French Voyages, 1534–1608* (New York: Charles Scribner's Sons, 1930), pp. 11–24.

8. Samuel Eliot Morison, *The Great Explorers*, pp. 275–326; D.W. Meinig, *The Shaping of America: A Geographical Perspective on 500 Years of History. Volume 1: Atlantic America, 1492–1800* (New Haven: Yale University Press, 1986), pp. 28–35, 43–55; Fernand Braudel, *The Mediterranean and the Mediterranean World in the Age of Philip II*, trans. Siân Reynolds (1949, New York: Harper & Row, 1976), Vol. 1, pp. 612–613, 615, 627–629; A.L. Rowse, *The Expansion of Elizabethan England* (New York: Scribner, 1955), pp. 126–157, 415–438; William S. Maltby, *The Black Legend in England: The Development of Anti-Spanish Sentiment, 1558–1660* (Durham: Duke University Press, 1971), pp. 29–43, 61–75; David Beers Quinn, *England and the Discovery of America, 1481–1620* (New York: Knopf, 1974), pp. 264–281; Kenneth R. Andrews, *Trade, Plunder and Settlement: Maritime Enterprise and the Genesis of the British Empire, 1480–1630* (Cambridge: Cambridge University Press, 1984), pp. 41–63; Robert A. Williams, Jr., *The American Indian in Western Legal Thought: The Discourses of Conquest* (New York: Oxford University Press, 1990), pp. 119–147; Wilcomb E. Washburn, "The Moral and Legal Justifications for Dispossessing the Indians," in *Seventeenth Century America: Essays in Colonial History*, ed. James Morton Smith (Chapel Hill: University of North Carolina, 1959), p. 16; Nicholas P. Canny, *The Elizabethan Conquest of Ireland: A Pattern Established, 1565–76* (New York: Barnes & Noble, 1976), pp. 66–92, 117–36; David Beers Quinn, *The Elizabethans and the Irish* (Ithaca, NY: Cornell University Press, 1966), pp. 106–122; Richard Waswo, *From Virgil to Vietnam: The Founding Legend of Western Civilization* (Hanover, NH: University Press of New England, 1997), pp. 95–106; Michael Hechter, *Internal Colonialism: The Celtic Fringe in British National Development, 1536–1966* (Berkeley: University of California Press, 1977), pp. 47–123; Alden T. Vaughan, *Roots of American Racism*, p. 42; Ronald Sanders, *Lost Tribes and Promised Lands: The Origins of American Racism* (Boston: Little, Brown, 1978), pp. 225–229; Richard Hakluyt, *Voyages to the Virginia Colonies*, ed. A.L. Rowse (London: Century, 1986), pp. 63–76.

9. Walter James Hoffman, *The Menomini Indians* (New York: Johnson Reprint Corporation, 1970), pp. 214–216.

10. E. Bradford Burns, ed., *A Documentary History of Brazil* (New York: Knopf, 1965), pp. 20–29; John Hemming, *Red Gold: The Conquest of the Brazilian Indians*,

1500–1760 (Cambridge: Harvard University Press, 1978), pp. 1–6.

11. Wilbeforce Eames, "Description of a Wood Engraving Illustrating the South American Indians," *Bulletin of the New York Public Library* 26, no. 9 (1922): 755–760.

12. John Hemming, *The Conquest of the Incas* (New York: Harcourt Brace Jovanovich, 1970), pp. 22–33; Nathan Wachtel, *The Vision of the Vanquished: The Spanish Conquest of Peru Through Indian Eyes*, trans. Ben and Siân Reynolds (New York: Barnes & Noble, 1977), pp. 15–24; William Sullivan, *The Secret of the Incas: Myth, Astronomy, and the War Against Time* (New York: Crown, 1996), p. 321; Garcilasco de la Vega. *The Incas: The Royal Commentaries of the Incas*, trans. Maria Jolas (New York: Avon, 1961), pp. 339–79; Rolena Adorno, *Guaman Poma: Writing and Resistance in Colonial Peru* (Austin: University of Texas Press, 1986), pp. 147–148; Juan de Betanzos, *Narrative of the Incas*, trans. Roland Hamilton and Dana Buchanan (Austin: University of Texas Press, 1996), pp. 184, 235, 248–249, 254; Franklin G.Y. Pease, "Spanish and Andean Perceptions of the Other in the Conquest of the Andes," in *Violence, Resistance, and Survival in the Americas: Native Americans and the Legacy of Conquest*, eds. William B. Taylor and Franklin G.Y. Pease (Washington, DC: Smithsonian Institution Press, 1994), pp. 27–28; Huamán Poma, *Letter to a King: A Peruvian Chief's Account of Life Under the Incas and Under Spanish Rule*, trans. Christopher Dilke (New York: Dutton, 1978), p. 108.

Chapter 4. Rage Without Reason

1. Immanuel Wallerstein, *The Modern World-System: Capitalist Agriculture and the Origins of the European World-Economy in the Sixteenth Century* (New York: Academic Press, 1974), pp. 15–129; Eric R. Wolf, *Europe and the People without History* (Berkeley: University of California Press, 1982), pp. 129–194; G.V. Scammell, *The World Encompassed: The First European Maritime Empires, c. 800–1650* (Berkeley: University of California Press, 1981), pp. 225–298, 301–358; Steven J. Stern, "Feudalism, Capitalism, and the World-System in the Perspective of Latin America and the Caribbean," in *Confronting Historical Paradigms: Peasants, Labor, and the Capitalist World System in Africa and Latin America*, eds. Frederick Cooper, Allen F. Isaacman, Florencia E. Mallon, William Roseberg, and Steve J. Stern (Madison: University of Wisconsin Press, 1993), pp. 23–83; Gary C. Anders, "Theories of Underdevelopment and the American Indian," *Journal of Economic Issues* XIV, no. 3 (1980): 681–701; Claude Meillassoux, *Maidens, Meals, and Money: Capitalism and the Domestic Economy* (Cambridge: Cambridge University Press, 1981), pp. 91–123; Andre Gunder Frank, *Capitalism and Underdevelopment in Latin America: Historical Studies of Chile and Brazil* (New York: Monthly Review Press, 1969), pp. 1–33, 121–133, 145–155; Donald Denoon, *Settler Capitalism: The Dynamics of Dependent Development in the Southern Hemisphere* (Clarendon: Oxford University Press, 1983), pp. 16–42; Denys Delâge, *Bitter Feast: Amerindians and Europeans in Northeastern North America, 1600–64*, trans. Jabe Brierly (Vancouver: University of British Columbia Press, 1993), pp. 3–35, 78–162; C.B. MacPherson, *The Political Theory of Possessive Individualism* (Oxford: Oxford University Press, 1962), pp. 263–271; Kwame Anthony Appiah, *In My Father's House: Africa in the Philosophy of Culture* (New York: Oxford University Press, 1992), p. 145; Fernando Cervantes, *The Devil in the New World: The Impact of Diabolism in New Spain* (New Haven: Yale University Press, 1994), pp. 5–39; Richard Slotkin, *Regeneration Through Violence: The Mythology of the American Frontier, 1600–1860* (Middleton, CT: Wesleyan Univer-

sity Press, 1973), pp. 3–56; Enrique Florescano, *Memory, Myth, and Time in Mexico: From the Aztecs to Independence*, trans. Albert G. Bork and Kathryn R. Bork (Austin: University of Texas Press, 1994), pp. 65–99; Michael Harkin, "History, Narrative, and Temporality: Examples from the Northwest Coast," *Ethnohistory* 35, no. 2 (1988): 99–130; Jeremy Rifkin, *Time Wars: The Primary Conflict in Human History* (New York: Simon & Schuster, 1987), pp. 190–227; Marshall Sahlins, *Culture and Practical Reason* (Chicago: University of Chicago Press, 1976), pp. 166–221; Barbara E. Mundy, *The Mapping of New Spain: Indigenous Cartography and the Maps of the Relaciones Geográficas* (Chicago: University of Chicago Press, 1996), pp. 135–216; W.G.L. Randles, *De la terre plate au globe terrestre: Une mutation épistémologique rapid (1480–1520)* (Paris: Libraire Armand Colin, 1980); Walter D. Mignolo, The *Darker Side of the Renaissance: Literacy, Territoriality, & Colonization* (Ann Arbor: University of Michigan Press, 1995), pp. 259–313; *The Destruction of the Jaguar: Poems from the Books of Chilam Balam*, trans. Christopher Sawyer-Lauçanno (San Francisco: City Lights, 1987), p. 56.

2. Gianni Granzotto, *Christopher Columbus: The Dream & the Obsession*, trans. Stephen Sartarelli (London: Grafton Books, 1985), pp. 192–243; John Noble Wilford, *The Mysterious History of Columbus* (New York: Random House, 1991), pp. 161–180; Kirkpatrick Sale, *The Conquest of Paradise: Christopher Columbus and the Columbian Legacy* (New York: Penguin Books, 1990), pp. 123–161; Carl Ortin Sauer, *The Early Spanish Main* (Berkeley: University of California Press, 1968), pp. 70–103; Urs Bitterli, *Cultures in Conflict: Encounters Between European and Non-European Cultures, 1492–1800*, trans. Ritchie Robertson (Stanford: Stanford University Press, 1989), pp. 70–80; Valerie I.J. Flint, *The Imaginative Landscape of Christopher Columbus* (Princeton: Princeton University Press, 1992), pp. 125–126; Christopher Columbus, *The Four Voyages*, trans. J.M. Cohen (New York: Penguin Books, 1969), pp. 55–56; Bartolomé Las Casas, *The Devastation of the Indies: A Brief Account*, trans. Herma Briffault (Baltimore: Johns Hopkins University Press, 1992), pp. 32–43, 94–95, 107; Robert A. Williams, Jr., *The American Indian in Western Legal Thought: The Discourses of Conquest* (New York: Oxford University Press, 1990), pp. 78–81; Lewis Hanke, *The Spanish Struggle for Justice in the Conquest of America* (Philadelphia: University of Pennsylvania Press, 1949), p. 20; John H. Parry and Rovert G. Keith, eds., *New Iberian World: A Documentary History of the Discovery and Settlement of Latin America to the Early 17th Century* (New York: Times Books, 1984), Vol. 2, pp. 173–253; S. Lyman Tyler, *Two Worlds: The Indian Encounter with the European, 1492–1509* (Salt Lake City: University of Utah Press, 1988), pp. 70–206; Irving Rouse, *The Tainos: Rise & Decline of the People Who Greeted Columbus* (New Haven: Yale University Press, 1992), pp. 138–171; Michael Alexander, ed. *Discovering the New World, Based on the Works of Theodore de Bry* (New York: Harper & Row, 1976), p. 131; Jack D. Forbes, *Africans and Native Americans: The Language of Race and the Evolution of Red-Black Peoples* (Urbana: University of Illinois Press, 1993), pp. 24, 28, 32, 270; Philip P. Boucher, *Cannibal Encounters: Europeans and the Island Caribs, 1492–1763* (Baltimore: Johns Hopkins University Press, 1992), p. 16; David E. Stannard, *American Holocaust: Columbus and the Conquest of the New World* (New York: Oxford University Press, 1992), pp. 213–214.

3. Miguel León-Portilla, ed., *The Broken Spears: The Aztec Account of the Conquest of Mexico* (Boston: Beacon Press, 1962), pp. 32–149; Arthur J.O. Anderson and Charles E. Dibble, trans., *The War of Conquest: How It Was Waged Here in Mexico* (Salt Lake City: University of Utah Press, 1978), pp. 20–89.

4. Joseph Brodsky, "To Urania," in *To Urania* (New York: Farrar, Straus & Giroux, 1988), p. 22; William M. Denevan, "Native American Populations in 1492: Recent Research and a Revised Hemispheric Estimate," in *The Native Population of the Americas in 1492,* ed. William M. Denevan (Madison: University of Wisconsin Press, 1992), pp. xvii–xxxviii; David P. Henige, *Numbers from Nowhere: The American Indian Contact Population Debate* (Norman: University of Oklahoma Press, 1998); Alfred W. Crosby, Jr., *The Columbian Exchange: Biological and Cultural Consequences of 1492* (Westport, CT: Greenwood Press, 1972), pp. 35–63; Alfred W. Crosby, Jr., *Ecological Imperialism: The Biological Expansion of Europe, 900–1900* (Cambridge: Cambridge University Press, 1986), pp. 195–216; Alfred W. Crosby, Jr. *Germs, Seeds & Animals: Studies in Ecological History* (Armonk, NY: M.E. Sharpe, 1994), pp. 82–147; Russell Thornton, *American Indian Holocaust and Survival: A Population History Since 1492* (Norman: University of Oklahoma Press, 1987), pp. 15–77, 72; Nicolas Sánchez-Albornoz, *The Population of Latin America: A History* (Berkeley: University of California Press, 1974), pp. 37–76; Ann F. Ramenofsky, *Vectors of Death: The Archaeology of European Contact* (Albuquerque: University of New Mexico Press, 1987), pp. 137–176; Henry F. Dobyns, *Their Number Become Thinned: Native American Population Dynamics in Eastern North America* (Nashville: University of Tennessee Press, 1983), pp. 7–32, 247–335; Linda A. Newson, "Indian Population Patterns in Colonial Spanish America," *Latin American Research Review* 20, no. 3 (1985): 41–74 ; Nobel David Cook, *Born to Die: Disease and New World Conquest, 1492–1650* (Cambridge: Cambridge University Press, 1998), pp. 15–165; Michael Craton and Gail Saunders, *Islanders in the Stream: A History of the Bahamian People* (Athens: University of Georgia Press, 1992), pp. 43–59; Bernard R. Ortiz de Montellano, *Aztec Medicine, Health, and Nutrition* (New Brunswick, NJ: Rutgers University Press, 1990), pp. 72–119, 127–128, 181–192; Michael W. Flinn, *The European Demographic System, 1500–1820* (Baltimore: Johns Hopkins University Press, 1981), pp. 13–75; Mark Nathan Cohen, *Health and the Rise of Civilization* (New Haven: Yale University Press, 1989), pp. 130–142; John C. Super, *Food, Conquest, and Colonization in Sixteenth Century Spanish America* (Albuquerque: University of New Mexico Press, 1988), p. 4; Hanns J. Prem, "Disease Outbreaks in Central Mexico During the Sixteenth Century," in *"Secret Judgments of God": Old World Disease in Colonial Spanish America,* ed. Noble David Cook and W. George Lovell (Norman: University of Oklahoma Press, 1991), pp. 20–48; Thomas M. Whitmore, *Disease and Population in Early Colonial Mexico: Simulating Amerindian Depopulation* (Boulder, CO: Westview Press, 1992), pp. 201–218; Anderson and Dibble, *The War of Conquest,* p. 64; Serge Gruzinski, *The Conquest of Mexico: The Incorporation of Indian Societies into the Western World, 16th–18th Centuries,* trans. Eileen Corrigan (Cambridge: Polity Press, 1993), p. 97; Linda A. Newson, *Aboriginal and Spanish Trinidad: A Study in Culture Conflict* (New York: Academic Press, 1976), pp. 76–103; W. George Lovell and Christopher H. Lutz, *Demography and Empire: A Guide to the Population History of Spanish Central America, 1500–1821* (Boulder, CO: Westview Press, 1995), pp. 37, 52, 103, 124; W. George Lovell, "Surviving Conquest: The Maya of Guatemala in Historical Perspective," *Latin American Research Review* 23, no. 2 (1988): 25–57; Noble David Cook, *Demographic Collapse: Indian Peru, 1520–1620* (Cambridge: Cambridge University Press, 1981); Karen Vieira Powers, *Andean Journeys: Migration, Ethnogenesis, and the State in Colonial Quito* (Albuquerque: University of New Mexico Press, 1995), pp. 13–43; Henry F. Dobyns, "An Outline of Andean Epi-

demic History to 1720," *Bulletin of the History of Medicine* XXXVII, no. 6 (1963): 492–515; John Hemming, *The Conquest of the Incas* (New York: Harcourt Brace Jovanovich, 1970), pp. 347–348; *Destruction of the Jaguar*, p. 57; Henry F. Dobyns, "New Native World: Links between Demographic and Cultural Changes," in *Columbian Consequences*, ed. David Hurst Thomas (Washington, DC: Smithsonian Institution Press, 1991), Vol. 3, pp. 541–559; Vivian Nutton, "The Seeds of Disease: An Explanation of Contagion and Infection from the Greeks to the Renaissance," *Medical History* 27, no. 1 (1983): 19–34; David Herlihy, *The Black Death and the Transformation of the West* (Cambridge: Harvard University Press, 1997), pp. 71–72; David E. Stannard, "Disease and Infertility: A New Look at the Demographic Collapse of Native Populations in the Wake of Western Contact," *Journal of American Studies* 24, no. 3 (1990): 325–350.

5. Inga Clendinnen, *Ambivalent Conquests: Maya and Spaniard in Yucatan, 1517–1570* (Cambridge: Cambridge University Press, 1987), pp. 66–92, 139–192; Nancy M. Farriss, *Maya Society Under Colonial Rule: The Collective Enterprise of Survival* (Princeton: Princeton University Press, 1984), pp. 286–319; Frances Karttunen, *Between Worlds: Interpreters, Guides, and Survivors* (New Brunswick, NJ: Rutgers University Press, 1994), pp. 85–108; Ronald Wright, *Stolen Continents: The Americas Through Indian Eyes Since 1492* (Boston: Houghton Mifflin, 1992), pp. 161–174; Victoria Reifer Bricker, *The Indian Christ, the Indian King: The Historical Substrate of Maya Myth and Ritual* (Austin: University of Texas Press, 1981), pp. 13–28; Diego de Landa, *Yucatan Before and After the Conquest*, trans. William Gates (New York: Dover, 1978), pp. 24–29, 82, 111–112; Walter D. Mignolo, *The Darker Side of the Renaissance*, pp. 204–207; *Destruction of the Jaguar*, pp. 29, 33; Miguel Angel Asturas, *Men of Maize*, trans. and ed. Gerald Martin (Pittsburgh: University of Pittsburgh Press, 1993), p. 368; Matthew Restall, *The Maya World: Yucatec Culture and Society, 1550–1850* (Stanford: Stanford University Press, 1997), pp. 148–158, 276–281; Grant D. Jones, *Maya Resistance to Spanish Rule: Time and History on a Colonial Frontier* (Albuquerque: University of New Mexico Press, 1989), pp. 1–24, 93–123; Enrique Florescano, *Memory, Myth, and Time in Mexico*, pp. 108–110; Victor Perera and Robert D. Bruce, *The Last Lords of Palenque: The Lacandon Mayas of the Mexican Rain Forest* (Berkeley: University of California Press, 1982), p. 8; Manuel Gutiérrez Estévez, "The Christian Era of the Yucatec Maya," in *South and Meso-American Native Spirituality: From the Cult of the Feathered Serpent to the Theology of Liberation*, ed. Gary H. Gossen (New York: Crossroad, 1993), pp. 251–278; Dennis Tedlock, "Torture in the Archives: Mayans Meet Europeans," *American Anthropologist* 95, no. 1 (1993): 138–151; Cecil Roth, *The Spanish Inquisition* (New York: Norton, 1964), p. 95; Nancy M. Farriss, "Remembering the Future, Anticipating the Past: History, Time, and Cosmology Among the Maya of Yucatan," *Comparative Studies in Society and History* 29, no. 3 (1987): 566–593; Linda Schele and David Freidel, *A Forest of Kings: The Untold Story of the Ancient Maya* (New York: Morrow, 1990), pp. 346–347, 396–397; David Freidel, Linda Schele and Joy Parker, *Maya Cosmos: Three Thousand Years on the Shaman's Path* (New York: Morrow, 1993), pp. 251–256, 405, 457.

6. Stuart B. Schwartz, *Sugar Plantations in the Formation of Brazilian Society: Bahía, 1550–1835* (Cambridge: Cambridge University Press, 1989), pp. 3–72; Stuart B. Schwartz, *Sovereignty and Society in Colonial Brazil: The High Court of Bahía and Its Judges, 1609–1751* (Berkeley: University of California Press, 1973), pp. 115–116, 122–139; Bernadette Bucher, *La sauvage aux seins pendents* (Paris:

Hermann, 1977), pp. 55–68; Annette Rosentiel, *Red & White: Indian Views of the White Man, 1492–1982* (New York: Universe Books, 1983), p. 27; Hemming, *Red Gold: The Conquest of the Brazilian Indians, 1500–1760* (Cambridge: Harvard University Press), pp. 24–44, 97–118, 139–160. Alexander Marchant, *From Barter to Slavery: The Economic Relations of Portuguese and Indians in the Settlement of Brazil, 1500–1580* (Gloucester, MA: Peter Smith, 1966), pp. 13–47; Warren Dean, "Deforestation in Southeastern Brazil," in *Global Deforestation and the Nineteenth-Century World Economy*, eds. Richard P. Tucker and J. F. Richards (Durham, NC: Duke University Press, 1983), pp. 50–61; Warren Dean, *With Broadax and Firebrand: The Destruction of the Brazilian Atlantic Forest* (Berkeley: University of California Press, 1995), pp. 20–94, 152–155; Dauril Alden, "Indian Versus Black Slavery in the State of Maranhao During the Seventeenth and Eighteenth Centuries," in *Iberian Colonies, New World Societies: Essays in Memory of Charles Gibson*, eds. Richard L. Garner and William B. Taylor (n.p.: Private Printing, 1986), pp. 71–102; Dauril Alden, "Black Robes Versus White Settlers: The Struggle for 'Freedom of the Indians' in Colonial Brazil," in *Attitudes of Colonial Powers Toward the American Indians*, eds. Howard Peckham and Charles Gibson (Salt Lake City: University of Utah Press, 1969), pp. 19–46; Colin MacLachlan, "The Indian Labor Structure in the Portuguese Amazon, 1700–1800," in *Colonial Roots of Modern Brazil*, ed. Dauril Alden (Berkeley: University of California Press, 1973), pp. 199–230; Philip D. Curtin, *The Rise and Fall of the Plantation Complex: Essays in Atlantic History* (Cambridge: Cambridge University Press, 1991), pp. 46–57; Stuart B. Schwartz, *Slaves, Peasants, and Rebels: Reconsidering Brazilian Slavery* (Urbana: University of Illinois Press, 1996), pp. 41, 107, 110–111, 144–145, 159; Forbes, *Africans and African Americans*, pp. 243, 245, 247; Anthony Pagden, *The Fall of Natural Man: The American Indian and the Origins of Comparative Ethnology* (Cambridge: Cambridge University Press, 1982), pp. 157, 175; Lawrence E. Sullivan, *Icanchu's Drum: An Orientation to Meaning in South American Religions* (New York: Macmillan, 1988), p. 515.

7. Anthony Pagden, *Spanish Imperialism and the Political Imagination: Studies in European and Spanish-American Social and Political Theory, 1513–1830* (New Haven: Yale University Press, 1990), pp. 13–36; Pagden, *Fall of Natural Man*, pp. 1–108, 119–145; Lewis Hanke, *Aristotle and the American Indians: A Study in Race Prejudice in the Modern World* (London: Hollis & Carter, 1959), pp. 12–27, 74–96; J.H. Elliott, *The Old World and the New, 1492–1650* (Cambridge: Cambridge University Press, 1972), p. 44; William R. Taylor, *Drinking, Homicide and Rebellion in Colonial Mexican Villages* (Stanford: Stanford University Press, 1979), p. 42; Williams, *Indian in Western Legal Thought*, pp. 94; Brooke Larson, *Colonialism and Agrarian Transformation in Bolivia: Cochabamba, 1550–1900* (Princeton: Princeton University Press, 1988), pp. 13–91; Steven J. Stern, *Peru's Indian Peoples and the Challenge of the Spanish Conquest: Huamanga to 1640* (Madison: University of Wisconsin Press, 1982), pp. 35–113; Karen Spalding, *Huarochirí: An Andean Society Under Inca and Spanish Rule* (Stanford: Stanford University Press, 1984), pp. 106–208; Susan E. Ramírez, *Provincial Patriarchs: Land Tenure and the Economics of Power in Colonial Peru* (Albuquerque: University of New Mexico Press, 1986), pp. 1–105; Michael T. Taussig, *The Devil and Commodity Fetishism in South America* (Chapel Hill: University of North Carolina Press, 1980), pp. 199–201; Garcilasco de la Vega, *The Incas: The Royal Commentaries of the Incas*, trans. Maria Jolas (1617, New York: Avon, 1961), pp. 161–2; Jean Berthelot, "L'exploitation des métaux précieux au temps des incas," *Annales: Économies, Sociétés, Civilisations* 33, nos.

5–6 (1978): 948–66; Karen Spalding, "Exploitation as an Economic System: The State and the Extraction of Surplus in Colonial Peru," in *The Inca and Aztec States, 1400–1800,* eds. George A. Collier, Renato I. Rosaldo, and John D. Wirth (New York: Academic Press, 1982), pp. 321–342; Nicacnor Jácome and Inés Llumiquinga, "Ecuador: The Indigenous Tribute System as a Mechanism of Exploitation During the Colonial Period and the First Years of Independence," in *Western Expansion and Indigenous Peoples: The Heritage of Las Casas, ed. Elias Sevilla-Casas* (The Hague: Mouton, 1977), pp. 87–111; Luis F. Calero, *Chiefdoms Under Siege: Spain's Rule and Native Adaptation in the Southern Columbian Andes, 1535–1700* (Albuquerque: University New Mexico Press, 1997), pp. 103–161; Kenneth J. Andrien, "Spaniards, Andeans, and the Early Colonial State in Peru," in *Transatlantic Encounters: Europeans and Andeans in the Sixteenth Century,* eds. Kenneth J. Andrien and Rolena Adorno (Berkeley: University of California Press, 1991), pp. 121–148; D. A. Brading, *The First America: The Spanish Monarchy, Creole Patriots, and the Liberal State, 1492–1867* (Cambridge: Cambridge University Press, 1991), pp. 128–146; Thomas C. Patterson, *The Inca Empire: The Formation and Disintegration of a Pre-Capitalist State (New York: Berg, 1991), pp.* 136–156; *Peter John Bakewell, Miners of the Red Mountain: Indian Labor in Potosí, 1545–1650* (Albuquerque: University of New Mexico Press, 1984), pp. 61–80; Jeffrey A. Cole, *The Potosí Mita, 1573–1700: Compulsory Indian Labor in the Andes* (Stanford: Stanford University Press, 1985), pp. 1–45; Enrique Tandeter, *Coercion and Market: Silver Mining in Colonial Potosí, 1692–1826* (Albuquerque: University of New Mexico Press, 1992), pp. 15–71; Ann Zulawski, *They Eat from Their Labor: Work and Social Change in Colonial Bolivia* (Pittsburgh: University of Pittsburgh Press, 1995), pp. 37–84; Ann M. Wightman, *Indigenous Migration and Social Change: The Forasteros of Cuzco, 1570–1720* (Durham: Duke University Press, 1990), pp. 9–149; James Lockhart, "Letters and People to Spain," in *First Images of America: The Impact of the New World on the Old,* ed. Fredi Chiappelli (Berkeley: University of California Press, 1976), vol. 2, p. 788; Richard L. Garner, "Long-Term Silver Mining Trends in Spanish America: A Comparative Analysis of Peru and Mexico," *American Historical Review* 93, no. 4 (1988): 907.

8. David B. Quinn, *North America from Earliest Discovery to First Settlements: The Norse Voyages to 1612* (New York: Harper & Row, 1977), pp. 322–344; Alden T. Vaughan, *Roots of American Racism* (New York: Oxford University Press, 1995), p. 44; David Beers Quinn, *Set Fair for Roanoke: Voyages and Colonies, 1584–1606* (Chapel Hill: University of North Carolina Press, 1985), pp. 239–286; David Beers Quinn, *England and the Discovery of America, 1481–1620* (New York: Knopf, 1974), pp. 282–306; Karen Ordahl Kupperman, *Roanoke: The Abandoned Colony* (Totowa, NJ: Rowman & Allanfield, 1984), pp. 15–65, 115–118; Gesa Mackenthun, *Metaphors of Dispossession: American Beginnings and the Translation of Empire, 1492–1637* (Norman: University of Oklahoma Press, 1997), pp. 141–162; Bernard W. Sheehan, *Savagism and Civility: Indians and Englishmen in Colonial Virginia* (Cambridge: Cambridge University Press, 1980), p. 167; Kenneth R. Andrews, *Trade, Plunder and Settlement: Maritime Enterprise and the Genesis of the British Empire, 1480–1630* (Cambridge: Cambridge University Press, 1984), pp. 200–222; Carl Ortwin Sauer, *Sixteenth-Century North America* (Berkeley: University of California Press, 1975), pp. 250–265; Williams, *Indian in Western Legal Thought,* pp. 172–180, 183, 185; Richard Hakluyt, *Voyages to the Virginia Colonies,* ed. A.L. Rowse (London: Century, 1986), pp. 107–136, 81–82, 145–146.

Chapter 5. Black Rainbows and Sinister Hailstorms

1. J.H. Elliott, "A World United," in *Circa 1492: Art in the Age of Exploration*, ed. Jay A. Levenson (New Haven: Yale University Press, 1991), pp. 647–652; Anthony Pagden, *Lords of All the World: Ideologies of Empire in Spain, Britain and France c.1500–c.1800* (New Haven: Yale University Press, 1995), pp.11–73; Richard Koebner, *Empire* (Cambridge: Cambridge University Press, 1961), pp. 1–85; Charles Gibson, ed., *The Spanish Tradition in America* (New York: Harper & Row, 1968), p. 59; J.H. Parry, *The Establishment of the European Hegemony, 1415–1715* (New York: Harper & Row, 1961), pp. 60–75, 105–124, 185–194; G.V. Scammell, *The World Encompassed: The First European Maritime Empires, c. 800–1650* (Berkeley: University of California Press, 1981), pp. 301–369, 436–500; James Muldoon, *Popes, Lawyers, and Infidels: The Church and the Non-Christian World, 1250–1550* (Philadelphia: University of Pennsylvania Press, 1979), pp. 132–152; Patricia Seed, *Ceremonies of Possession in Europe's Conquest of the New World, 1492–1640* (Cambridge: Cambridge University Press, 1995), pp. 16–99; Robert A. Williams, Jr., *The American Indian in Western Legal Thought: The Discourses of Conquest* (New York: Oxford University Press, 1990), pp. 59–118; Bernard McGrane, *Beyond Anthropology: Society and the Other* (New York: Columbia University Press, 1989), pp. 7–19; Mary B. Campbell, *The Witness and the Other World: Exotic European Travel Writing, 400–1600* (Ithaca: Cornell University Press, 1988), pp. 165–209; Nathan Wachtel, "The Indian and the Spanish Conquest," in *The Cambridge History of Latin America*, ed. Leslie Bethell (Cambridge: Cambridge University Press, 1984), Vol. I, pp. 207–248; Colin M. MacLachlan, *Spain's Empire in the New World: The Role of Ideas in Institutional and Social Change* (Berkeley: University of California Press, 1988), pp. 21–66.

2. Alfred Métraux, "The Guarani," in *Handbook of South American Indians*, ed. Julian H. Steward (New York: Cooper Square Publishers, 1963), Vol. 3, pp. 69–94; Elman R. Service, *Spanish-Guarani Relations in Early Colonial Paraguay* (Westport, CT: Greenwood Press, 1971); Pierre Clastres, *Society Against the State: Essays in Political Anthropology*, trans. Robert Hurley (New York: Zone Books, 1987), pp. 87–97, 160–174; Mircea Eliade, *The Quest: History and Meaning in Religion* (Chicago: University of Chicago Press, 1969), pp. 101–111; Curt Nimuendajú, *Los Mitos de Creción y Destrucción del Mundo como Fundamentos de la Religión de los Apapokuna-Guaraní*, ed. Juergen Riester G. (Lima: Centro Amazonico de Antropología y Alicación Practica, 1978), pp. 29–39, 116–128; Alfred Métraux, *Religion y Magias Indigenas de America del Sur* (Madrid: Aguilar, 1973), pp. 7–24; Philip Caraman, *The Lost Paradise: The Jesuit Republic in South America* (New York: Seabury Press, 1975), pp. 51–234; Antonio Astrain, S.J., *Jesuitas, guaraníes y encomenderos: Historia de la compañía de Jesús en el Paraguay* (Asuncíon, Paraguay: Centro de Estudios Paraguayos, 1995), pp. 69–111, 365–403; Hélène Clastres, *The Land-Without-Evil: Tupí-Guaraní Prophetism*, trans. Jacqueline Grenez Brovender (1975, Urbana: University of Illinois Press, 1995), pp. 43–71.

3. Rolena Adorno, *Guaman Poma: Writing and Resistance in Colonial Peru* (Austin: University of Texas Press, 1986); Irene Silverblatt, *Moon, Sun, and Witches: Gender Ideologies and Class in Inca and Colonial Peru* (Princeton: Princeton University Press, 1987), pp. 125, 139, 143; Sabine MacCormack, *Religion in the Andes: Vision and Imagination in Early Colonial Peru* (Princeton: Princeton University Press, 1991), pp. 312–331; Juan M. Ossio, "Guaman Poma: Nueva Coronica o Carta al Rey. Un

Intento de Aproximación a las Categorías del Pensamiento del Mundo Andino," in *Ideología Mesiánica del Mundo Andino*, ed. Juan M. Ossio (Lima: Ignacio Prado Pastor, 1973), pp. 153–213; D.A. Brading, *The First America: The Spanish Monarchy, Creole Patriots, and the Liberal State, 1492–1867* (Cambridge: Cambridge University Press, 1991), pp. 147–165; Frances Karttunen, *Between Worlds: Interpreters, Guides, and Survivors* (New Brunswick, NJ: Rutgers University Press, 1994), p. 135; Kenneth J. Andrien, *Andean Worlds: Indigenous History, Culture, and Consciousness Under Spanish Rule, 1532–1825* (Albuquerque: University of New Mexico Press, 2001), pp. 121–139; Huamán Poma, *Letter to a King: A Peruvian Chief's Account of Life Under the Incas and Under Spanish Rule*, trans. Christopher Dilke (New York: Dutton, 1978), pp. 142–154, 166–169, 193–198, 228–231.

4. John M. Cooper, "The Araucanians," in *Handbook of South American Indians*, ed. Julian H. Steward (New York: Cooper Square Publishers, 1963), Vol. 2, pp. 996–998; Robert Charles Padden, "Cultural Change and Military Resistance in Araucanian Chile, 1550–1730," *Southwestern Journal of Anthropology* 13, no. 1 (1957): 103–21; Carlos Barella Iriarte, *Lautaro Guerrillero* (Santiago: Universidad Catolica de Chile, 1971), pp. 57–117; Henry F. Dobyns, "An Outline of Andean Epidemic History to 1720," *Bulletin of the History of Medicine* XXXVII (1963): 492–515; Lewis Hanke, *The Spanish Struggle for Justice in the Conquest of America* (Philadelphia: University of Pennsylvania Press, 1949), pp. 137–139; Eugene H. Korth, S.J., *Spanish Policy in Colonial Chile: The Struggle for Social Justice, 1535–1700* (Stanford: Stanford University Press, 1968); Brian Loveman, *Chile: The Legacy of Hispanic Capitalism* (New York: Oxford University Press, 1988), pp. 44–106; Kenneth J. Andrien, *Crisis and Decline: The Viceroyalty of Peru in the Seventeenth Century* (Albuquerque: University of New Mexico Press, 1985), pp. 69–70; Marcello Caramagnani, "Colonial Latin American Demography: Growth of Chilean Population, 1700–1800," *Journal of Social History* I, no. 1 (1967): 179–191; Fernando Casanueva, "Smallpox and War in Southern Chile in the Late Eighteenth Century," in *"Secret Judgments of God": Old World Disease in Colonial Spanish America*, ed. Noble David Cook and W. George Lovell (Norman: University of Oklahoma Press, 1991), pp. 183–212; L.C. Faron, *Hawks of the Sun: Mapauche Morality and Its Ritual Attributes* (Pittsburgh: University of Pittsburgh Press, 1964), pp. 77, 191–192.

5. Linda A. Newson, "Old World Epidemics in Early Colonial Ecuador," in *"Secret Judgments of God*," pp. 84–112; Linda A. Newson, *Life and Death in Early Colonial Ecuador* (Norman: University of Oklahoma Press, 1995), pp. 144–154, 337–352; Douglas H. Ubelaker, "The Biological Impact of European Contact in Ecuador," in *In the Wake of Contact: Biological Responses to Conquest*, eds. Clark Spencer Larsen and George R. Miller (New York: Wiley-LISS, 1994), pp. 147–160; Suzanne Austin Alchon, *Native Society and Disease in Colonial Ecuador* (Cambridge: Cambridge University Press, 1992), pp. 57–89, 130–133; Karen Vieira Powers, *Andean Journeys: Migration, Ethnogenesis, and the State in Colonial Quito* (Albuquerque: University of New Mexico Press, 1995), 45–80.

6. Mercedes López-Baralt, "The Quechua Elegy to the All-Powerful Inka Atawallpa: A Literary Rendition of the Inkarri Myth," *Latin American Indian Literatures* 4, no. 2 (1980): p. 83; Raquel Chang-Rodríguez, "Cultural Resistance in the Andes and Its Depiction in *Atau Wallpaj P'uchukakuyninpa Wankan* or *Tragedy of Atahualpa's Death*," in *Coded Encounters: Writing, Gender, and Ethnicity in Colonial Latin America*, eds. Francisco Javier Cevallos-Canau, Jeffrey A. Cole, Nina M. Scott, and Nicomedes Suárez-Araúz (Amherst: University of Massachusetts Press,

1994), pp. 115–134; Sabine MacCormack, "Pachacuti: Miracles, Punishments, and Last Judgment: Visionary Past and Prophetic Future in Early Colonial Peru," *American Historical Review* 94, no. 4 (1988): pp. 960–961, 984–985; MacCormack, *Religion in the Andes*, pp. 406–427; Nicholas Griffiths, *The Cross and the Serpent: Religious Repression and Resurgence in Colonial Peru* (Norman: University of Oklahoma Press, 1996), pp. 129, 192, 196, 199; Ann M. Wightman, "Diego Vasicuio: Native Priest," in *Struggle and Survival in Colonial America*, ed. David G. Sweet and Gary B. Nash (Berkeley: University of California Press, 1981), pp. 38–48; Irene Silverblatt, "Political Memories and Colonizing Symbols: Santiago and the Mountain Gods of Colonial Peru," in *Rethinking History and Myth: Indigenous South American Perspectives on the Past*, ed. Jonathan D. Hill (Urbana: University of Illinois Press, 1988), pp. 174–194; William Sullivan, *The Secret of the Incas: Myth, Astronomy, and the War Against Time* (New York: Crown, 1996), pp. 199–200; Louise M. Burkhart, "The Amanuenses Have Appropriated the Text: Interpreting a Nahautl Song of Santiago," in *On the Translation of Native American Literatures*, ed. Brian Swann (Washington, DC: Smithsonian Institution Press, 1992), pp. 342, 352.

7. James Lockhart, *The Nahuas After the Conquest: A Social and Cultural History of the Indians of Central Mexico, Sixteenth Through Eighteenth Centuries* (Stanford: Stanford University Press, 1992), pp. 261–325, 427–446; Frances Karttunen and James Lockhart, *Nahautl in the Middle Years: Language Contact Phenomena in the Texts of the Colonial Period* (Berkeley: University of California Press, 1976), pp. 1–51; Frances Karttunen, "Nahautl Literacy," in *The Inca and Aztec States, 1400–1800: Anthropology and History*, eds. George A. Collier, Renato I. Rosaldo, and John D. Wirth (New York: Academic Press, 1982), pp. 395–417; Serge Gruzinski, *The Conquest of Mexico: The Incorporation of Indian Societies into the Western World, 16th-18th Centuries*, trans. Eileen Corrigan (Cambridge: Polity, 1993), pp. 47, 59–60; Jorge Klor de Alva, "Language, Politics, and Translation: Colonial Discourse and Classical Nahautl in New Spain," in *The Art of Translation: Voices from the Field*, ed. Rosanna Warren (Boston: Northeastern University Press, 1989), pp. 143–162; James Lockhart, "Sightings: Initial Nahua Reactions to Spanish Culture," in *Implicit Understandings: Observing, Reporting, and Reflecting on the Encounters Between Europeans and Other Peoples in the Early Modern Era*, ed. Stuart B. Schwartz (Cambridge: Cambridge University Press, 1994), pp. 218–248; Walter D. Mignolo, "On the Colonization of Amerindian Languages and Memories: Renaissance Theories of Writing and the Discontinuity of the Classical Tradition," *Comparative Studies in Society and History* 34, no. 2 (1992): 325; Gordon Brotherston, *Book of the Fourth World: Reading the Native Americas Through Their Literatures* (Cambridge: Cambridge University Press, 1992), pp. 315–320; Charles Gibson, *The Aztecs Under Spanish Rule: A History of the Indians of the Valley of Mexico, 1519–1810* (Stanford: Stanford University Press, 1964), pp. 220–256, 300–367; Colin M. MacLachlan and Jaime E. Rodriguez, *The Forging of the Cosmic Race: A Reinterpretation of Colonial Mexico* (Berkeley: University of California Press, 1980), pp. 144–197; R. Douglas Cope, *The Limits of Racial Domination: Plebeian Society in Colonial Mexico City, 1660–1720* (Madison: University of Wisconsin Press, 1994), pp. 9–26, 68–85; Patricia Seed, *To Love, Honor, and Obey in Colonial Mexico: Conflicts over Marriage Choice, 1574–1821* (Stanford: Stanford University Press, 1988), pp. 145–156.

8. Anthony Pagden, *Spanish Imperialism and the Political Imagination: Studies in European and Spanish-American Social and Political Theory, 1513–1830* (New Haven: Yale University Press, 1990), pp. 13–36; W. George Lovell, *Conquest and*

Survival in Colonial Guatemala: A Historical Geography of the Cuchumatan Highlands, 1500–1821 (Montreal: McGill-Queen's University Press, 1992), pp. 37–198; Murdo MacLeod, *Spanish Central America: A Socioeconomic History, 1520–1720* (Berkeley: University of California Press, 1973), pp. 120–142; Murdo MacLeod, "Ethnic Relations and Indian Society in the Province of Guatemala, 1620–ca. 1800," in *Spaniards and Indians in Southeastern Mesoamerica: Essays on the History of Ethnic Relations*, eds. Murdo J. MacLeod and Robert Wasserstrom (Lincoln: University of Nebraska Press, 1983), pp. 189–214; W. George Lovell and William R. Sweazy, "Indian Migration and Community Formation: An Analysis of *Congregacíon* in Colonial Guatemala," in *Migration in Colonial Latin America*, ed. David J. Robinson (Cambridge: Cambridge University Press, 1990), pp. 18–40; Robert M. Hill II and John Monaghan, *Continuities in Highland Maya Social Organization: Ethnohistory in Sacapulas, Guatemala* (Philadelphia: University of Pennsylvania Press, 1987), pp. 63–89; Robert Hill II, "The Social Uses of Writing among the Colonial Cakchiquel Maya: Nativism, Resistance, and Innovation," in *Columbian Consequences: The Spanish Borderlands in Pan-American Perspective*, ed. David Hurst Thomas (Washington, DC: Smithsonian Institution Press, 1991), Vol. 3, pp. 283–299; *Title of the Lords of Totonicapán*, trans. Dionisio Jose Chonay and Delia Goetz (Norman: University of Oklahoma Press, 1953), pp. 163–165, 169–170; John M. Watanabe, *Maya Saints & Souls in a Changing World* (Austin: University of Texas Press, 1992), pp. 42–58, 217–225, 229.

9. Jack Weatherford, *Indian Givers: How the Indians of the Americas Transformed the World* (New York: Ballantine, 1988), pp. 5–20; Earl J. Hamilton, "What the New World Gave the Economy of the Old," in *First Images of America: The Impact of the New World on the Old*, ed. Fredi Chiappelli (Berkeley: University of California Press, 1976), Vol. 2, pp. 871–876; J.H. Elliott, *Imperial Spain 1469–1716* (New York: New American Library, 1963), pp. 109–123; J.H. Elliott, *Spain and Its World, 1500–1700* (New Haven: Yale University Press, 1989), pp. 217–240; Pierre Vilar, "The Age of Don Quixote," in *Essays in European Economic History, 1500–1800*, ed. Peter Earle (Oxford: Oxford University Press, 1974), pp. 100–112; John Lynch, *Spain 1516–1598: From Nation State to World Empire* (Oxford: Blackwell, 1991), pp. 174–184; John Hale, *The Civilization of Europe in the Renaissance* (New York: Atheneum, 1994), p. 150; Mary Elizabeth Perry, *Crime and Society in Early Modern Seville* (Hanover, NH: University Press of New England, 1980), pp. 1–11, 54–74.

10. Weatherford, *Indian Givers*, pp. 59–115; Fernand Braudel, *The Structures of Everyday Life: The Limits of the Possible*, trans. Siân Reynolds (New York: Harper & Row, 1981), pp. 31–51; Alfred W. Crosby, Jr., *The Columbian Exchange: Biological and Cultural Consequences of 1492* (Westport, CT: Greenwood Press, 1972), pp. 165–207; Alan Davidson, "Europeans' Wary Encounter with Tomatoes, Potatoes, and Other New World Foods," in *Chilies to Chocolate: Food the Americas Gave the World*, eds. Nelson Foster and Linda S. Cordell (Tuscon: University of Arizona Press, 1992), pp. 1–14; Henry Hobhouse, *Seeds of Change: Five Plants that Transformed Mankind* (New York: Harper & Row, 1987), pp. 191–206; Recliffe Salaman, *The History and Social Influence of the Potato* (Cambridge: Cambridge University Press, 1949), pp. 42–245; Ellen Messer, "Potatoes (White)," in *The Cambridge World History of Food*, ed. Kenneth F. Kiple and Kriemhild Coneè Ornelas (Cambridge: Cambridge University Press, 2000), pp. 187–194; Stuart B. Schwartz, *Slaves, Peasants, and Rebels: Reconsidering Brazilian Slavery* (Urbana: University of Illinois Press, 1996), p. 67; Alan Taylor, *American Colonies* (New York: Viking, 2001), p. 45; Berthold Laufer, *The American*

Plant Migration. Part I: The Potato (Chicago: Field Museum of Natural History, 1938), pp. 40–68; William H. McNeill, "American Food Crops in the Old World," in *Seeds of Change*, eds. Herman J. Viola and Carolyn Margolis (Washington, DC: Smithsonian Institution Press, 1991), pp. 43–59; Alfred W. Crosby, Jr., *Germs, Seeds & Animals: Studies in Ecological History* (Armonk, NY: M.E. Sharpe, 1994), pp. 148–166; William Langer, "American Foods and Europe's Population Growth, 1750–1850," *Journal of Social History* 8 (1975): 51–66.

Chapter 6. License My Roving Hands

1. Anthony Pagden, *Lords of All the World: Ideologies of Empire in Spain, Britain and France c.1500–c.1800* (New Haven: Yale University Press, 1995), pp. 63–102; Anthony Pagden, "The Struggle for Legitimacy and the Image of the Empire in the Atlantic to c. 1700," in *The Oxford History of the British Empire*, ed. Nicholas Canny (New York: Oxford University Press, 1998), Vol. I, pp. 34–54; Robert A. Williams, Jr., *The American Indian in Western Legal Thought: The Discourses of Conquest* (New York: Oxford University Press, 1990), pp. 121–192; Joanathan Hart, *Representing the New World: The English and French Uses of the Example of Spain* (New York: Palgrave Books, 2000), pp. 15–153; Alden T. Vaughan, *Roots of American Racism* (New York: Oxford University Press, 1995), pp. 3–54; James Tully, "Aboriginal Property and Western Theory: Recovering a Middle Ground," *Social Philosophy & Policy* 11, no. 2 (1994): 153–180; James Tully, *An Approach to Political Philosophy: Locke in Contexts* (Cambridge: Cambridge University Press, 1993), pp. 137–176; Jeremy Rifkin, *Time Wars: The Primary Conflict in Human History* (New York: Simon & Schuster, 1987), p. 165; Alfred A. Cave, "Canaanites in a Promised Land: The American Indian and the Providential Theory of Empire," *American Indian Quarterly* XII, no. 4 (1988): 277–298; Olive Patricia Dickason, *The Myth of the Savage and the Beginnings of French Colonialism in the Americas* (Edmonton: University of Alberta Press, 1984), pp. 29–132; Cornelius J. Jaenen, "French Sovereignty and Native Nationhood during the French Régime," in *Sweet Promises: A Reader on Indian-White Relations in Canada*, ed. J.R. Miller (Toronto: University of Toronto Press, 1991), pp. 19–42; Mircea Eliade, *The Quest: History and Meaning in Religion* (Chicago: University of Chicago Press, 1969), pp. 86–99; Mircea Eliade, *Images and Symbols: Studies in Religious Symbolism*, trans. Philip Mairet (London: Harvill, 1961), pp. 51–56; Mary W. Helms, *Ulysses' Sail: An Ethnographic Odyssey of Power, Knowledge, and Geographical Distance* (Princeton: Princeton University Press, 1988), 211–260; David Gordon White, *Myths of the Dog-Man* (Chicago: University of Chicago Press, 1991), pp. 60–67; Bernadette Bucher, *Icon and Conquest: A Structural Analysis of the Illustrations of de Bry's Great Voyages*, trans. Basia Miller Gulati (Chicago: University of Chicago Press, 1981), pp. 43–173; Roy Harvey Pearce, *Savagism and Civilization: A Study of the Indian and the American Mind* (Baltimore: Johns Hopkins University Press, 1965), pp. 3–49; John T. Shawcross, ed., *The Complete Poetry of John Donne* (Garden City, NY: Anchor Books, 1967), p. 58; Loren E. Pennington, "The Amerindian in English Promotional Literature, 1575–1625," in *The Westward Enterprise: English Activities in Ireland, the Atlantic, and America, 1480–1650*, eds. K.R. Andrews, N.P. Canny, and P.E.H. Hair (Detroit: Wayne State University Press, 1979), pp. 175–194; Bernard W. Sheehan, *Savagism and Civility: Indians and Englishmen in Colonial Virginia* (Cambridge: Cambridge University Press, 1980), pp. 37–88; Roderick Nash, *Wilderness and the American Mind* (New Haven: Yale Uni-

versity Press, 1967), pp. 25–36; Karen Ordahl Kupperman, *Settling with the Indians: The Meeting of English and Indian Cultures in America, 1580–1640* (Totowa, NJ: Rowman & Littlefield, 1980), pp. 159–188; James Axtell, *Beyond 1492: Encounters in Colonial North America* (New York: Oxford University Press, 1992), pp. 98–121.

2. James Axtell, *After Columbus: Essays in the Ethnohistory of Colonial North America* (New York: Oxford University Press, 1988), pp. 183–221; Williams, *Indian in Western Legal Thought*, pp. 146, 201–221; John Parker, "Religion and the Virginia Colony, 1609–10," in *The Westward Enterprise: English Activities in Ireland, the Atlantic, and America, 1480–1650*, pp. 245–270; Louis B. Wright, *Religion and Empire: The Alliance Between Piety and Commerce in English Expansion, 1558–1625* (Chapel Hill: University of North Carolina Press, 1943), pp. 150–166; Edmund S. Morgan, *American Slavery, American Freedom: The Ordeal of Colonial Virginia* (New York: Norton, 1975), pp. 44–130; Ian K. Steele, *Warpaths: Invasions of North America* (New York: Oxford University Press, 1994), pp. 37–50; Eric J. Leed, *Shores of Discovery: How Expeditionaries have Constructed the World* (New York: Basic Books, 1995), pp. 191–197; Perry Miller, *Errand into the Wilderness* (New York: Harper & Row, 1964), pp. 99–140; Francis Jennings, *The Invasion of America: Indians, Colonialism, and the Cant of Conquest* (New York: Norton, 1975), p. 80; Alex W. Barker, "Powhatan's Pursestrings: On the Meaning of Surplus in a Seventeenth Century Algonkian Chiefdom," in *Lords of the Southeast: Social Inequality and the Native Elites of Southeastern North America*, eds. Alex W. Barber and Timothy R. Pauketat (Washington, DC: American Anthropological Association, 1992), pp. 61–89; Stephen R. Potter, *Commoners, Tribute, and Chiefs: The Development of Algoquian Culture in the Potomac Valley* (Charlottesville: University Press of Virginia, 1993), pp. 7–47, 174–223; Stephen R. Potter, "Early English Effects on Virginia Algonquian Exchange and Tribute in the Tidewater Potomac," in *Powhatan's Mantle: Indians in the Colonial Southeast*, ed. Peter H. Wood, Gregory A. Waselkov, and M. Thomas Hatley (Lincoln: University of Nebraska Press, 1989), pp. 151–195; David Beers Quinn, *Set Fair for Roanoke: Voyages and Colonies, 1584–1606* (Chapel Hill: University of North Carolina Press, 1985), pp. 360–371; Jack D. Forbes, *Africans and Native Americans: The Language of Race and the Evolution of Red-Black Peoples* (Urbana: University of Illinois Press, 1993), p. 55; Kupperman, *Settling with Indians*, pp. 107–140; Gesa Mackenthun, *Metaphors of Dispossession: American Beginnings and the Translation of Empire, 1492–1637* (Norman: University of Oklahoma Press, 1997), pp. 193–264; Kenneth R. Andrews, *Trade, Plunder and Settlement: Maritime Enterprise and the Genesis of the British Empire, 1480–1630* (Cambridge: Cambridge University Press, 1984), pp. 304–326; Helen C. Rountree, *Pocahontas's People: The Powhatan Indians of Virginia Through Four Centuries* (Norman: University of Oklahoma Press, 1990), pp. 1–124; Sheehan, *Savagism and Civility*, pp. 43, 144–182; Vaughan, *American Racism*, pp. 12, 23, 48, 105–127; Edward T. Price, *Dividing the Land: Early American Beginnings of Our Private Property Mosaic* (Chicago: University of Chicago Press, 1995), pp. 89–98; Paul G.E. Clemens, *The Atlantic Economy and Colonial Maryland's Eastern Shore: From Tobacco to Grain* (Ithaca, NY: Cornell University Press, 1980), pp. 19–40; Allan Kulikoff, *Tobacco and Slaves: The Development of Southern Cultures in the Chesapeake, 1680–1800* (Chapel Hill: University of North Carolina Press, 1986), pp. 23–44.

3. Carl O. Sauer, *Seventeenth Century North America* (Berkeley: Turtle Island Press, 1980), pp. 69–85, 241; Eric R. Wolf, *Europe and the People Without History* (Berkeley: University of California Press, 1982), pp. 158–170; Philip D. Curtin, *Cross-*

Cultural Trade in World History (Cambridge: Cambridge University Press, 1984), pp. 207–229; W.J. Eccles, *The Canadian Frontier, 1534–1760* (Albuquerque: University of New Mexico Press, 1983), pp. 1–60, 103–131; Bruce G. Trigger, *Natives and Newcomers: Canada's "Heroic Age" Reconsidered* (Kingston: McGill-Queen's University Press, 1985), pp. 164–297; J.R. Miller, *Skyscrapers Hide the Heavens: A History of Indian-White Relations in Canada* (Toronto: University of Toronto Press, 1989), pp. 23–80; Arthur J. Ray and Donald Freeman *"Give Us Good Measure": An Economic Analysis of Relations Between the Indians and the Hudson's Bay Company Before 1763* (Toronto: University of Toronto Press, 1978), pp. 3–26, 39–75, 218–260; Daniel Richter, *The Ordeal of Longhouse: The Peoples of the Iroquois League in the Era of European Colonization* (Chapel Hill: University of North Carolina Press, 1992), pp. 50–74; Peter C. Mancall, *Deadly Medicine: Indians and Alcohol in Early America* (Ithaca, NY: Cornell University Press, 1995), pp. 29–79; Colin B. Calloway, *New Worlds for All: Indians, Europeans, and the Remaking of Early America* (Baltimore: Johns Hopkins University Press, 1997), pp. 92–114; Thomas S. Abler, "Beavers and Muskets: Iroquois Military Fortunes in the Face of European Colonization," in *War in the Tribal Zone: Expanding States and Indigenous Warfare*, eds. R. Brian Ferguson and Neil L. Whitehead (Santa Fe, NM: School of American Research, 1992), pp. 151–174; Susan Johnston, "Epidemics: The Forgotten Factor in Seventeenth Century Native Warfare in the St. Lawrence Region," in *Native People, Native Lands: Canadian Indians, Inuit, and Métis*, ed. Bruce Alden Fox (Ottawa: Carleton University Press, 1988), pp. 14–31; Bruce G. Trigger, "Ontario Native Peoples and the Epidemics of 1634–40," in *Indians, Animals, and the Fur Trade: A Critique of Keepers of the Game*, ed. Shepard Krech III (Athens: University of Georgia Press, 1981), pp. 21–38; Bunny McBride and Harald E.L. Prins, "Walking the Medicine Line: Molly Ockett, a Pigwacket Doctor," in *Northeastern Indian Lives, 1632–1816*, ed. Robert S. Grumet (Amherst: University of Massachusetts Press, 1996), pp. 324, 328–329; Charles A. Bishop, "Northeastern Indian Concepts of Conservation and the Fur Trade: A Critique of Calvin Martin's Thesis," in *Indians, Animals, and the Fur Trade*, pp. 41–58; Timothy Silver, *A New Face on the Countryside: Indians, Colonists, and Slaves in South Atlantic Forests, 1500–1800* (New York: Cambridge University Press, 1990), pp. 88–93; Richard White, *The Roots of Dependency: Subsistence, Environment, and Social Change Among the Choctaws, Pawnees, and Navajos* (Lincoln: University of Nebraska Press, 1983), pp. 69–101; Daniel Usner, Jr., *Indians, Settlers, & Slaves in a Frontier Exchange Economy: The Lower Mississippi Valley Before 1763* (Chapel Hill: University of North Carolina Press, 1992), pp. 244–275; Calvin Martin, *Keepers of the Game: Indian-Animal Relationships and the Fur Trade* (Berkeley: University of California Press, 1978), pp. 1–65, 113–156; Robert A. Brightman, "Conservation and Resource Depletion: The Case of the Boreal Forest Algonquians," in *The Question of the Commons: The Culture and Ecology of Communal Resources*, eds. Bonnie J. McCay and James M. Acheson (Tuscon: University of Arizona Press, 1987), pp. 121–33; James Axtell, *The European and the Indian: Essays in the Ethnohistory of Colonial North America* (New York: Oxford University Press, 1981), pp. 16–35, 207–241.

4. Paul F. Boller, Jr. and Ronald Story, eds. *A More Perfect Union: Documents in U.S. History*, (Boston: Houghton Mifflin Company, 1984) Vol. 1, p. 14; Elemire Zolla, *The Writer and the Shaman: A Morphology of the American Indian*, trans. Raymond Rosenthal (New York: Harcourt Brace Jovanovich, 1973), p. 16; Eric Cheyfitz, *The Poetics of Imperialism: Translation and Colonization from The Tempest to Tarzan* (New York: Oxford University Press, 1991), p. 140; Neal Salisbury, *Manitou and*

Providence: Indians, Europeans, and the Making of New England, 1500–1643 (New York: Oxford University Press, 1982), pp. 179, 178, 166–225; Alfred W. Crosby, Jr., *Germs, Seeds & Animals: Studies in Ecological History* (Armonk, NY: M.E. Sharpe, 1994), p. 74; Charles F. Carroll, *The Timber Economy of Puritan New England* (Providence: Brown University Press, 1973), pp. 41–97; Roger Williams, *A Key into the Language of America*, ed. John J. Teunissen and Evelyn J. Hinz (Detroit, MI: Wayne State University Press, 1973), pp. 167, 138; William Cronon, *Changes in the Land: Indians, Colonists, and the Making of New England* (New York: Hill & Wang, 1983), pp. 54–170; David E. Stannard, *American Holocaust: Columbus and the Conquest of the New World* (New York: Oxford University Press, 1992), p. 241; Carolyn Merchant, *Ecological Revolutions: Nature, Gender and Science in New England* (Chapel Hill: University of North Carolina Press, 1989), pp. 27–111; Price, *Dividing the Land*, pp. 29–56; J.B. Harley, "New England Cartography and the Native Americans," in *American Beginnings: Exploration, Culture, and Cartography in the Land of Norumbega*, ed. Emerson W. Baker (Lincoln: University of Nebraska Press, 1994), pp. 287–313; Brenda J. Baker, "Pilgrim's Progress and Praying Indians: The Biocultural Consequences of Contact in Southern New England," in *In the Wake of Contact: Biological Responses to Conquest*, eds. Clark Spencer Larsen and George R. Milner (New York: Wiley-Liss, 1994), pp. 35–46; Charles M. Segal and David C. Stineback, eds. *Puritans, Indians, & Manifest Destiny* (New York: G.P. Putnam, 1977), pp. 50–51, 49, 105–140; Francis Jennings, *The Invasion of America: Indians, Colonialism, and the Cant of Conquest* (New York: Norton, 1975), pp. 128–145, 186–227; Steele, *Warpaths*, pp. 179–225; Vaughan, *American Racism*, pp. 177–99; Richard Drinnon, *Facing West: The Metaphysics of Indian-Hating and Empire-Building* (Minneapolis: University of Minnesota Press, 1980), pp. 35–61; Alfred A. Cave, *The Pequot War* (Amherst: University of Massachusetts Press, 1996), pp. 1–48, 69–167; Mackenthun, *Metaphors of Dispossession*, pp. 265–298; Patrick M. Malone, *The Skulking Way of War: Technology and Tactics Among the New England Indians* (Lanham, MD: Madison Books, 1991), pp. 1, 23, 58–59, 75–79; Adam J. Hirsch, "The Collision of Military Cultures in Seventeenth-Century New England," *Journal of American History* 74, no. 4 (1988): 1187–1212; Ronald Dale Karr, ""Why Should You Be So Furious?": The Violence of the Pequot War," *Journal of American History* 85, no. 3 (1998): 876–909; Almon Wheeler Lauber, *Indian Slavery in Colonial Times within the Present Limits of the United States* (Williamstown, MA: Corner House), 1979, p. 124; Neal Salisbury, "Indians and Colonists in Southern New England after the Pequot War: An Uneasy Balance," in *The Pequots in Southern New England: The Fall and Rise of an American Indian Nation*, eds. Laurence M. Hauptman and James D. Wherry (Norman: University of Oklahoma Press, 1990), pp. 81–95; Kevin A. McBride, "The Legacy of Robin Cassacinamon: Mashantucket Pequot Leadership in the Historic Period," in *Northeastern Indian Lives*, 74–92; Axtell, *European and Indian*, pp. 131–167; Lyle Koehler, "Red-White Power Relations and Justice in the Courts of Seventeenth-Century New England," in *The American Indian Past and Present*, ed. Roger L. Nichols (New York: Knopf, 1986), pp. 89–104.

5. Cornelius J. Jaenen, *Friend and Foe: Aspects of French-Amerindian Cultural Contact in the Sixteenth and Seventeenth Centuries* (New York: Columbia University Press, 1976), pp. 41–83, 120–152; John Webster Grant, *Moon of Wintertime: Missionaries and the Indians of Canada in Encounter Since 1534* (Toronto: University of Toronto Press, 1984), pp. 26–46; James T. Moore, *Indian and Jesuit: A Seventeenth-*

Century Encounter (Chicago: Loyola University Press, 1982), pp. 51–97; Richard Waswo, *From Virgil to Vietnam: The Founding Legend of Western Civilization* (Hanover, NH: University Press of New England, 1997), pp.196–208; James Axtel, *The Invasion Within: The Contest of Cultures in Colonial North America* (New York: Oxford University Press, 1985), pp. 23–127; Leed, *Shores of Discovery*, pp. 84–124; Eleanor Leacock, "Montagnais Women and the Jesuit Program for Colonization," *in Women and Colonization: Anthropological Perspectives*, eds. Mona Etienne and Eleanor Leacock (New York: Praeger Books, 1980), pp. 25–41; Eleanor Burke Leacock, *Myths of Male Dominance* (New York: Monthly Review Press, 1981), pp. 33–81; Kenneth M. Morrison, "Montagnais Missionization in Early New France: The Syncretic Inperative," *American Indian Culture and Research Journal* 10, no. 1 (1986): 1–24; James P. Ronda, "European Indian: Jesuit Civilization Planning in New France," *Church History* 41, no. 3 (1972): 385–95; Reuben Gold Thwaites, ed., *The Jesuit Relations and Allied Documents* (Cleveland: Burrows Brothers, 1896–1901), Vol. 29, p. 123; Robert L. Kelly, *The Foraging Spectrum: Diversity in Hunter-Gatherer Lifeways* (Washington, DC: Smithsonian Institution Press, 1995), pp. 67, 112, 123, 125; Karen Anderson, *Chain Her by One Foot: The Subjugation of Women in Seventeenth-Century New France* (London: Routledge, 1991), pp. 1–100, 162–229; Carol Devens, "Separate Confrontations: Gender as a Factor in Indian Adaptation to European Colonization in New France," *American Quarterly* 38 (1986): 461–480; Axtell, *After Columbus*, pp. 106–121.

6. Fernand Braudel, *The Perspective of the World*, trans. Siân Reynolds (New York: Harper & Row, 1979), pp. 552–566; John U. Nef, *The Conquest of the Material World: Essays on the Coming of Industrialism* (Cleveland, OH: World Publishing, 1967), pp. 122–143, 169–212, 231–268, 336–337; G.N. Clark, *The Wealth of England from 1496 to 1760* (London: Oxford University Press, 1946), pp. 41–89; Andre Gunder Frank, *World Accumulation, 1492–1789* (New York: Monthly Review Press, 1978), pp. 25–64.

Chapter 7. Unacquainted with the Laws of the Civilized World

1. Walter D. Mignolo, *The Darker Side of the Renaissance: Literacy, Territoriality, & Colonization* (Ann Arbor: University of Michigan Press, 1995), pp. 143–163; D.A Brading, *The First America: The Spanish Monarchy, Creole Patriots, and the Liberal State, 1492–1867* (Cambridge: Cambridge University Press, 1991), pp. 381–386, 438–439, 455–456; Benjamin Keen, *The Aztec Image in Western Thought* (New Brunswick, NJ: Rutgers University Press, 1971), pp. 226–237; Andre Gunder Frank, *Capitalism and Underdevelopment in Latin America: Historical Studies of Chile and Brazil* (New York: Monthly Review Press, 1969), pp. 3–14, 54; Andre Gunder Frank, "The Development of Underdevelopment," in *Paradigms in Economic Development: Classic Perspectives, Critiques, and Reflections,* ed. Rajani Kanth (Armonk, NY: M. E. Sharpe, 1994), pp. 149–159; Fernand Braudel, *The Perspective of the World*, trans. Siân Reynolds (New York: Harper & Row, 1984), pp. 21–70, 386–429; Alan K. Smith, *Creating a World Economy: Merchant Capital, Colonialism, and World Trade, 1400–1825* (Boulder, CO: Westview Press, 1991), pp. 169–202; Stanley J. Stein and Barbara H. Stein, *The Colonial Heritage of Latin America: Essays on Economic Dependence in Perspective* (New York: Oxford University Press, 1970), pp. 3–106; Eric Wolf, *Sons of the Shaking Earth* (Chicago: University of Chicago Press, 1959), pp. 176–201; Enrique Semo, *The History of Capitalism in Mexico: Its Origins, 1521–1763,* trans. Lidia Lozano

(Austin: University of Texas Press, 1993), pp. 6–66; Ronald H. Chilcote and Joel C. Edelstein, *Latin America: Capitalist and Socialist Perspectives of Development and Underdevelopment* (Boulder, CO: Westview Press, 1986), pp. 1–39; Carol A. Smith, "Beyond Dependency Theory: National and Regional Patterns of Underdevelopment in Guatemala," *American Ethnologist* 5, no. 3 (1978): 574–617; June Nash, "Ethnographic Aspects of the World Capitalist System," *Annual Review of Anthropology* 10 (1981): 393–423; Christopher Lutz and W. George Lovell, "Core and Periphery in Colonial Guatemala," in *Guatemalan Indians and the State: 1540 to 1988*, ed. Carol A. Smith (Austin: University of Texas Press, 1990), pp. 35–51; Immanuel Wallerstein, *Historical Capitalism* (London: Verso, 1983), pp. 13–32, 47–72; R. David Edmunds, "'Unacquainted with the Laws of the Civilized World': American Attitudes Toward the Métis Communities in the Old Northwest," in *The New Peoples: Being and Becoming Métis in North America*, eds. Jacqueline Peterson and Jennifer S.H. Brown (Lincoln: University of Nebraska Press, 1985) p. 191.

2. Urs Bitterli, *Cultures in Conflict: Encounters Between European and Non-European Cultures, 1492–1800*, trans. Ritchie Robertson (Stanford: Stanford University Press, 1989), pp. 109–132; Paul A. W. Wallace, *Indians in Pennsylvania* (Harrisburg: Pennsylvania Historical and Museum Commission, 1981), pp. 9–19, 67–166; Thomas J. Sugrue, "The Peopling and Depeopling of Early Pennsylvania: Indians and Colonists, 1680–1720," *Pennsylvania Magazine of History and Biography* CXVI, no. 1 (1992): 3–31; C.A. Weslager, *The Delaware Indians: A History* (New Brunswick, NJ: Rutgers University Press, 1972, pp. 155–260; Beth Fowkes Tobin, "Native Land and Foreign Desire: William Penn's Treaty with the Indians," *American Indian Culture and Research Journal* 19, no. 3 (1995): 87–119; Lawrence Hauptman, "Refugee Havens: The Iroquois Villages of the Eighteenth Century," in *American Indian Environments: Ecological Issues in Native American History*, eds. Christopher Vecsey and Robert W. Venables (Syracuse: Syracuse University Press, 1980), pp. 128–139; Richard White, *The Middle Ground: Indians, Empires and Republics in the Great Lakes Region, 1650–1815* (Cambridge: Cambridge University Press, 1991), p. 490; Peter C. Mancall, *Valley of Opportunity: Economic Culture Along the Upper Susquehanna, 1700–1800* (Ithaca, NY: Cornell University Press, 1991), pp. 27–70; Almon Wheeler Lauber, *Indian Slavery in Colonial Times Within the Present Limits of the United States* (1913, Williamstown, MA: Corner House, 1979), pp. 115–116, 161–162; Wilma A. Dunaway, *The First American Frontier: Transition to Capitalism in Southern Appalachia, 1700–1860* (Chapel Hill: University of North Carolina Press, 1996), pp. 1–24; Calvin Luther Martin, *The Way of the Human Being* (New Haven: Yale University Press, 1999), pp. 57–58; Alden T. Vaughan, *Roots of American Racism* (New York: Oxford University Press, 1995), pp. 82–102; David Hackett Fischer, *Albion's Seed: Four British Folkways in America* (New York: Oxford University Press, 1989), pp. 605–639; Herbert C. Kraft, *The Lenepe: Archaeology, History, and Ethnography* (Newark: New Jersey Historical Society, 1986), pp. 180–181, 195–230; Marshall Becker, "Hannah Freeman: An Eighteenth-Century Lenape Living and Working Among Colonial Farmers," *Pennsylvania Magazine of History and Biography* CXIV, no. 2 (1990): 249–269; Anthony F. C. Wallace, *King of the Delawares: Teedyuscung, 1700–1763*, (1949, Syracuse: Syracuse University Press, 1990), pp. 2–17, 137–148; Francis Jennings, *Empire of Fortune: Crowns, Colonies & Tribes in the Seven Years War in America* (New York: Norton, 1988), pp. 100–108, 202, 434–436; James H. Merrell, *Into the American Woods: Negotiators on the Pennsylvania Frontier* (New York: Norton, 1999), pp. 19–41, 253–301; Charles F. Carroll, *The Timber Economy of Puritan New England* (Providence,

RI: Brown University Press, 1973), pp. 3–21; Terry G. Jordan and Matti Kaups, *The American Backwoods Frontier: An Ethnic and Ecological Interpretation* (Baltimore: Johns Hopkins University Press, 1989), pp. 38–246; C.A. Weslager, *New Sweden on the Delaware, 1638–1655* (Wilmington, DE: Middle Atlantic Press, 1988), pp. 11–55; John H. Wuorinen, *The Finns on the Delaware, 1638–1655: An Essay in American Colonial History* (New York: Columbia University Press, 1938), pp. 45–80; Virgil J. Vogel, *American Indian Medicine* (Norman: University of Oklahoma Press, 1970), pp. 307–310, 361–365; Gladys Tantaquidgeon, *Folk Medicine of the Delawares and Related Algonkian Indians* (Harrisburg: Pennsylvania Historical and Museum Commission, 1972), pp. 30, 32, 75, 98.

3. J. Leitch Wright, *The Only Land They Knew: The Tragic Story of the American Indians in the Old South* (New York: Free Press, 1981), pp. 102–147, 248–268; Wilma A. Dunaway, *The First American Frontier*, pp. 23–50; Verner W. Crane, *The Southern Frontier, 1670–1732* (Durham, NC: Duke University Press, 1928), pp. 112–115; Jerald T. Milanich, *Florida Indians and the Invasion from Europe* (Gainsville: University Press of Florida, 1995), pp. 222–227; Peter H. Wood, *Black Majority: Negroes in South Carolina from 1670 to the Stono Rebellion* (New York: Norton, 1974), pp. 13–53, 99–144, 305; Russell Thorton, *The Cherokees: A Population History* (Lincoln: University of Nebraska Press, 1990), pp. 19–46; Peter H. Wood, "The Changing Population of the Colonial South: An Overview by Race and Region, 1685–1790," in *Powhatan's Mantle: Indians in the Colonial Southeast*, ed. Peter H. Wood, Gregory A. Waselkov, and M. Thomas Bailey (Lincoln: University of Nebraska Press, 1989), pp. 61–66; Tom Hatley, *The Dividing Paths: Cherokees and South Carolineans Through the Era of Revolution* (New York: Oxford University Press, 1993), pp. 32–63; John Philip Reid, *A Better Kind of Hatchet: Law, Trade, and Diplomacy in the Cherokee Nation During the Early Years of European Contact* (University Park: Pennsylvania State University Press, 1976), pp. 23–31, 52–60, 189–196; Jack D. Forbes, *Africans and Native Americans: The Language of Race and the Evolution of Red-Black Peoples* (Urbana: University of Illinois Press, 1993), pp. 190–220; Theda Perdue, *Slavery and the Evolution of Cherokee Society, 1540–1866* (Knoxville: University of Tennessee Press, 1979), pp. 3–51, 119–145; William G. McLoughlin, *After the Trail of Tears: The Cherokees' Struggle for Sovereignty, 1839–1880* (Chapel Hill: University of North Carolina Press, 1993), pp. 201–254; Bitterli, *Cultures in Conflict*, pp. 26–27; Lauber, *Indian Slavery*, pp. 120–121, 137, 171, 178, 242–247, 249; James Mooney, *Myths of the Cherokees and Sacred Formulas of the Cherokees* (Nashville, TN: Charles and Randy Elder, 1982), pp. 232–234 (first pagination).

4. Olive Patricia Dickason, "From 'One Nation' in the Northeast to 'New Nation' in the Northwest: A Look at the Emergence of the Métis," in *The New Peoples*, pp. 19–36; Jacqueline Peterson, "Many Roads to Red River: Métis Genesis in the Great Lakes Region, 1680–1815," in *The New Peoples*, pp. 37–71; James E. Fitting, "Patterns of Acculturation at the Straits of Mackinac," in *Cultural Change and Continuity: Essays in Honor of James Bennett Griffin*, ed. Charles E. Cleland (New York: Academic Press, 1976), pp. 321–348; R. David Edmunds, "'Unacquainted with the Laws of the Civilized World': American Attitudes Toward the Métis Communities in the Old Northwest," in *The New Peoples*, pp. 185–193; White, *Middle Ground*, pp. 1–141, 366–517; Ian K. Steele, *Warpaths: Invasions of North America* (New York: Oxford University Press, 1994), pp. 179–225; George Irving Quimby, *Indian Culture and European Trade Goods: The Archaeology of the Historic Period in the Western Great Lakes Region* (Madison: University of Wisconsin, 1966), pp. 102–39; Robert E. Bieder, *Science En-

counters the Indian, 1820–1880: The Early Years of American Ethnology (Norman: University of Oklahoma Press, 1986), p. 166.

5. Stein and Stein, *Colonial Heritage*, p. 39; C.R. Boxer, *The Golden Age of Brazil, 1695–1750: Growing Pains of a Colonial Society* (Berkeley: University of California Press, 1962), pp. 236–237, 243; Caio Prado, *The Colonial Background of Modern Brazil*, trans. Suzette Macedo (Berkeley: University of California Press, 1969), pp. 182, 213–41; Frank, *Capitalism and Underdevelopment*, pp. 145–155; Euclides da Cunha, *Rebellion in the Backlands*, trans. Samuel Putnam (1902, Chicago: University of Chicago Press, 1975), p. 11; Robert H. Lowie, "The 'Tapuya,'" in *Handbook of South American Indians*, ed. Julian H. Steward (New York: Cooper Square Publishers, 1963), Vol. 1, pp. 553–556; John Hemming, *Red Gold: The Conquest of the Brazilian Indians, 1500–1760* (Cambridge: Harvard University Press, 1978), pp. 93–94, 298–299, 344–374; Stuart B. Schwartz, *Sugar Plantations in the Formation of Brazilian Society: Bahía, 1550–1835* (Cambridge: Cambridge University Press, 1989), pp. 90–91.

6. Stephen J. Greenblatt, *Learning to Curse: Essays in Early Modern Culture* (New York: Routledge, 1990), pp. 16–39; Ivan Illich, and Barry Sanders, *ABC: The Alphabetization of the Popular Mind* (New York: Vintage Books, 1988), pp. 65–70; John Howland Rowe, "Sixteenth and Seventeenth Century Grammars," in *Studies in the History of Linguistics*, ed. Dell Hymes (Bloomington: Indiana University Press, 1974), pp. 361–367; Walter D. Mignolo, *The Darker Side of the Renaissance*, pp. 29–52; Bruce Mannheim, *The Language of the Inka Since the European Invasion* (Austin: University of Texas Press, 1991); Shirley Brice Heath and Richard Laprade, "Castilian Colonization and Indigenous Languages: The Cases of Quechua and Aymara," in *Language Spread: Studies in Diffusion and Social Change*, ed. Robert L. Cooper (Bloomington: Indiana University Press, 1982), pp. 118–147; Regina Harrison, *Signs, Songs, and Memories in the Andes: Translating Quechua Language and Culture* (Austin: University of Texas Press, 1989), pp. 13–45; Brooke Larson, *Colonialism and Agrarian Transformation in Bolivia: Cochabamba, 1550–1900* (Princeton, NJ: Princeton University Press, 1988), pp. 133–170; Steven J. Stern, *Peru's Indian Peoples and the Challenge of the Spanish Conquest: Huamanga to 1640* (Madison: University of Wisconsin Press, 1982), pp. 138–157, 184–193; Steven J. Stern "The Age of Andean Insurrection, 1742–1782: A Reappraisal," in *Resistance, Rebellion, and Consciousness in the Andean Peasant World, 18th to 20th Centuries*, ed. Steven J. Stern (Madison: University of Wisconsin Press, 1987), pp. 34–93; Karen Spalding, *Huarochirí: An Andean Society Under Inca and Spanish Rule* (Stanford: Stanford University Press, 1984), pp. 270–293; Monica Barnes, "Catechisms and Confessionarios: Distorting Mirrors of Andean Societies," in *Andean Cosmologies Through Time: Persistence and Emergence*, eds. Robert V.H. Dover, Katharine E. Seibold, and John H. McDowell (Bloomington: Indiana University Press, 1992), pp. 67–94; Pierre Duviols, *La Destrucción de Las Religiones Andinas* (Conquista y Colonia), trans. Albor Maruenda (Mexico: Universidad Nacional Autónoma de México, 1977), p. 173; D.A. Brading, *The First America*, pp. 487–490; Fred Spier, *Religious Regimes in Peru: Religion and State Development in a Long-term Perspective and the Effects in the Andean Village of Zurite* (Amsterdam: Amsterdam University Press, 1994), p. 205.

7. William M. Denevan, "Native American Populations in 1492: Recent Research and a Revised Hemispheric Estimate," in *The Native Population of the Americas in 1492*, ed. William M. Denevan (Madison: University of Wisconsin Press, 1992), pp. xvii–xxxviii; Linda A. Newson, "Indian Population Patterns in Colonial Spanish America," *Latin America Research Review* 20, no. 3 (1985): 41–74; William H. Durham,

Scarcity and Survival in Central America: Ecological Origins of the Soccer War (Stanford: Stanford University Press, 1979), pp. 21–42; Peter Gerhard, *The Southeast Frontier of New Spain* (Norman: University of Oklahoma Press, 1993), pp. 23–30, 158–162, 169–171; David Browning, *El Salvador: Landscape and Society* (Oxford: Clarendon Press, 1971), pp. 41–45; Robert M. Carmack, *The Quiché Mayans of Utatlán: The Evolution of a Highland Guatemalan Kingdom* (Norman: University of Oklahoma Press, 1981), p. 106; Linda Newson, *Indian Survival in Colonial Nicaragua* (Norman: University of Oklahoma Press, 1987), pp. 110–124, 235–251, 336; Linda Newson, *The Cost of Conquest: Indian Decline in Honduras Under Spanish Rule* (Boulder, CO: Westview Press, 1986), pp. 3–8, 119–131, 285–336; Miles L. Wortman, *Government and Society in Central America, 1680–1840* (New York: Columbia University Press, 1982), pp.181–182; Sandra L. Orellana, *Indian Medicine in Highland Guatemala: The Pre-Hispanic and Colonial Periods* (Albuquerque: University of New Mexico Press, 1987), pp. 141–157; W. George Lovell, *Conquest and Survival in Colonial Guatemala: A Historical Geography of the Cuchumatán Highlands, 1500–1821* (Montreal: McGill-Queen's University Press, 1992), pp. 140–172; Norman B. Schwartz, *Forest Society: A Social History of Peten, Guatemala* (Philadelphia: University of Pennsylvania Press, 1990), p. 11; W. George Lovell and Christopher H. Lutz, *Demography and Empire: A Guide to the Population History of Spanish Central America, 1500–1821* (Boulder, CO: Westview Press, 1995), pp. 1–16, 37–38, 45, 67, 114–115.

Chapter 8. Beware of the Long Knives

1. J.H. Parry, *Trade & Dominion: The European Overseas Empires in the Eighteenth Century* (London: Phoenix Press, 1971), 3–219, 275; John M. Murrin, "The Beneficiaries of Catastrophe: The English Colonies in America," in *The New American History*, ed. Eric Foner (Philadelphia: Temple University Press, 1997), pp. 14–16; Jacob M. Price, "The Imperial Economy, 1700–1776," in *The Oxford History of the British Empire*, ed. P.J. Marshall (New York: Oxford University Press, 1998), Vol. II, pp. 78–104; James Horn, "British Diaspora: Emigration from Britain, 1680–1815," in *Oxford History of the British Empire*, vol. II, pp. 28–52; Enrique Semo, *The History of Capitalism in Mexico: Its Origins, 1521–1763*, trans. Lida Lozano (Austin: University of Texas Press, 1993), p. 50; Wade Davis, *Passage of Darkness: The Ethnobiology of the Hatian Zombie* (Chapel Hill: University of North Carolina Press, 1988), pp. 16–18, 215–216; Walter D. Mignolo, *The Darker Side of the Renaissance: Literacy, Territoriality, & Colonization* (Ann Arbor: University of Michigan Press, 1995), pp. 125–216, 315–334; Serge Gruzinski, *The Conquest of Mexico: The Incorporation of Indian Societies into the Western World, 16th-18th Centuries*, trans. Eileen Corrigan (Cambridge: Polity Press, 1993), pp. 229–281; Jean Jacques Rousseau, "Discourse on the Origin and Foundations of Inequality," in *The First and Second Discourses*, ed. Roger D. Masters and trans. Roger D. Masters and Judith R. Masters (New York: St. Martin's Press, 1964), p. 210; Jean David, "Voltaire et les Indiens D'Amerique," *Modern Language Quarterly* IX (1948): 90–103; Ronald L. Meek, *Social Science and the Ignoble Savage* (Cambridge: Cambridge University Press, 1976), pp. 68–176; P. J. Marshall and Glyndwr Williams, *The Great Map of Mankind: British Perceptions of the World in the Age of Enlightenment* (London: J. M. Dent & Sons, 1982), pp. 187–226; Colin B. Calloway, *New Worlds for All: Indians, Europeans, and the Remaking of Early America* (Baltimore: Johns Hopkins University Press, 1997), pp. 190–194; Jack Weatherford, *Indian Givers: How the Indians of the Americas Trans-*

formed the World (New York: Ballantine, 1988), pp. 117–131; Robert F. Berkhofer, Jr., *The White Man's Indian: Images of the American Indian from Columbus to the Present* (New York: Knopf, 1978), pp. 113–145; Michael Taussig, *Shamanism, Colonialism, and the Wild Man: A Study in Terror and Healing* (Chicago: University of Chicago Press, 1987), pp. 209–220; Alden T. Vaughan, *Roots of American Racism* (New York: Oxford University Press, 1995), pp. 3–33; Richard Waswo, *From Virgil to Vietnam: The Founding Legend of Western Civilization* (Hanover, NH: University Press of New England, 1997), pp. 186–195, 209–221; Philip P. Boucher, *Cannibal Encounters: Europeans and the Island Caribs, 1492–1763* (Baltimore: Johns Hopkins University Press, 1992), p. 123; Cornelius Jaenen, "'Les Sauvages Ameriquains': Persistence into the 18th Century of Traditional French Concepts and Constructs for Comprehending Amerindians," *Ethnohistory* 29, no. 1 (1982): 43–56; Gustav Jahoda, *Images of Savages: Ancient Roots of Modern Prejudice in Western Culture* (London: Routledge, 1999), pp. 15–25, 57, 132; Michèle Duchet, *Anthropologie et histoire au siècle des lumières: Buffon, Voltaire, Rousseau, Helèvtius, Diderot*(Paris: François Maspero, 1971), pp. 229–475.

2. W.J. Eccles, *The Canadian Frontier, 1534–1760* (Albuquerque: University of New Mexico Press, 1983), pp. 7–8, 110, 191; Jennifer S.H. Brown, *Strangers in Blood: Fur Trading Company Families in Indian Country* (Vancouver: University of British Columbia Press, 1980), pp. 51–80; Sylvia Van Kirk, *Many Tender Ties: Women in Fur-Trade Society, 1670–1870* (Norman: University of Oklahoma Press, 1980), pp. 9–96.

3. George Dalton, "The Impact of Colonization on Aboriginal Economies in State-less Societies," *Research in Economic Anthropology* 1, no. 1 (1978): 131–184; Brent Richards Weisman, *Like Beads on a String: A Culture History of the Seminole Indians in North Peninsular Florida* (Tuscaloosa: University of Alabama Press, 1989), pp. 14–148; James W. Covington, *The Seminoles of Florida* (Gainsville: University Press of Florida, 1993), pp. 3–49, 72–144; J. Leitch Wright, Jr., *Creeks and Seminoles: The Destruction and Regeneration of the Muscogulge People* (Lincoln: University of Nebraska Press, 1986), pp. 13–71, 185–215, 245–280; Richard A. Sattler, "Remnants, Renegades, and Runaways: Seminole Ethnogenesis Reconsidered," in *History, Power, and Identity: Ethnogenesis in the Americas, 1492–1992*, ed. Jonathan D. Hill (Iowa City: University of Iowa Press, 1996), pp. 36–51.

4. Ramón A. Gutiérrez, *When Jesus Came, the Corn Mothers Went Away: Marriage, Sexuality, and Power in New Mexico, 1500–1846* (Stanford: Stanford University Press, 1991), pp. 143–175; C.L. Sonnichsen, *The Mescalero Apaches* (Norman: University of Oklahoma Press, 1972), p. 43; Hamilton A. Tyler, *Pueblo Gods and Myths* (Norman: University of Oklahoma Press, 1964), p. 13.

5. Frank Gilbert Roe, *The Indian and the Horse* (Norman: University of Oklahoma Press, 1955), pp. 11–32, 72–73; Deb Bennet and Robert S. Hoffman, "Ranching in the New World," in *Seeds of Change*, eds. Herman J. Viola and Carolyn Margolis (Washington, DC: Smithsonian Institution Press, 1991), pp. 105–110; Gerald Hausman, *Turtle Island Alphabet: A Lexicon of Native American Symbols and Culture* (New York: St. Martin's Press, 1992), p. 59; Alfred W. Crosby, Jr., *The Columbian Exchange: Biological and Cultural Consequences of 1492* (Westport, CT: Greenwood Press, 1972), pp. 79–85; Robert H. Ruby and John A. Brown, *The Cayuse Indians: Imperial Tribesmen of Old Oregon* (Norman: University of Oklahoma Press, 1972), pp. 3–20; Peter Nabokov and Robert Easton, *Native American Architecture* (New York: Oxford University Press, 1989), pp. 176–181.

6. John C. Super, *Food, Conquest, and Colonization in Sixteenth Century Spanish America* (Albuquerque: University of New Mexico Press, 1988), pp. 72–78; Fernand

Braudel, *The Structures of Everyday Life: The Limits of the Possible*, trans. Siân Reynolds (New York: Harper & Row, 1981), pp. 231–47; Mark Edward Lender and James Kirby Martin, *Drinking in America: A History* (New York: Free Press, 1982), pp. 1–33; William R. Taylor, *Drinking, Homicide and Rebellion in Colonial Mexican Villages* (Stanford: Stanford University Press, 1979), pp. 28–72; W.J. Rorabaugh, *The Alcoholic Republic* (New York: Oxford University Press, 1979), pp. 7–9; Daniel K. Richter, *The Ordeal of the Longhouse: The Peoples of the Iroquois League in the Era of European Colonization* (Chapel Hill: University of North Carolina Press, 1992), pp. 266–267; Colin G. Calloway, *The American Revolution in Indian Country: Crisis and Diversity in Native American Communities* (New York: Cambridge University Press, 1995), p. 13; Peter C. Mancall, *Deadly Medicine: Indians and Alcohol in Early America* (Ithaca, NY: Cornell University, 1995).

7. Robert A. Williams, Jr., *The American Indian in Western Legal Thought: The Discourses of Conquest* (New York: Oxford University Press, 1990), pp. 233–307; Dorothy V. Jones, *License for Empire: Colonialism by Treaty in Early America* (Chicago: University of Chicago Press, 1982); Paula M. Strain, *The Blue Hills of Maryland: History Along the Appalachian Trail on South Mountain and the Catoctins* (Vienna, VA: Potomac Appalachian Trail Club, 1993), p. 252; Calloway, *American Revolution in Indian Country*, pp. 1–64, 108–157, 272–301; Gregory Evans Dowd, *A Spirited Resistance: The North American Indian Struggle for Unity, 1745–1815* (Baltimore: Johns Hopkins University Press, 1992), pp. 16–122; Joel W. Martin, *Sacred Revolt: The Muskogees' Struggle for a New World* (Boston: Beacon Press, 1991), pp. 87–113; Jack M. Sosin, *The Revolutionary Frontier, 1763–1783* (New York: Holt, Rinehart & Winston, 1967), pp. 20–92; Jack M. Sosin, *Whitehall and the Wilderness: The Middle West in British Colonial Policy, 1760–1775* (Lincoln: University of Nebraska Press, 1961), pp. 27–98; Gordon S. Wood, *The Radicalism of the American Revolution* (New York: Vintage Books, 1993), pp. 124–130; Daniel M. Friedenberg, *Life, Liberty, and the Pursuit of Land: The Plunder of Early America* (Buffalo, NY: Prometheus Books, 1992), pp. 99–176, 183, 249–260; Richard White, *The Middle Ground: Indians, Empires and Republics in the Great Lakes Region, 1650–1815* (Cambridge: Cambridge University Press, 1991), pp. 315–365; Francis Jennings, *Empire of Fortune: Crowns, Colonies & Tribes in the Seven Years War in America* (New York: Norton, 1988), pp. 63, 459–479; Bil Gilbert, *God Gave Us This Country: Tekamthi and the First American Civil War* (New York: Doubleday, 1989), pp. 57–58; Barbara Graymont, *The Iroquois in the American Revolution* (Syracuse, NY: Syracuse University Press, 1972), pp. 104–291; James H. Merrell, "Declarations of Independence: Indian-White Relations in the New Nation," in *The American Revolution: Its Character and Limits*, ed. Jack P. Greene (New York: New York University Press, 1987), pp. 197–223; Robert A. Williams, Jr., *Linking Arms Together: American Indian Treaty Visions of Law & Peace, 1600–1800* (New York: Oxford University Press, 1997), p. 121; Herbert C. Kraft, *The Lenepe: Archaeology, History, and Ethnography* (Newark: New Jersey Historical Society, 1986), pp. 235–236.

8. François Chevalier, *Land and Society in Colonial Mexico: The Great Hacienda*, trans. Alvin Eustis (Berkeley: University of California Press, 1963), pp. 7–83, 148–228, 263–307; Arthur Domen and Phillips Foster, *Iberian Antecedents of the Classical Hacienda of Latin America* (College Park: University of Maryland Press, 1977), pp. 57–71; Enrique Florescano, "The Hacienda in New Spain," in *Colonial Spanish America*, ed. Leslie Bethell (Cambridge: Cambridge University Press, 1987), pp. 250–285; Richard B. Lindley, *Haciendas and Economic Development: Guadalajara, Mexico, at*

Independence (Albuquerque: University of New Mexico Press, 1992), pp. 9–21, 28–34; Super, *Food, Conquest, and Colonization in Sixteenth Century Spanish America*, pp. 52–63; Cheryl English Martin, "Haciendas and Villages in Late Colonial Morelos," in *Readings in Latin American History: The Formative Centuries*, eds. Peter J. Bakewell, John J. Johnson, and Meredith D. Dodge (Durham: Duke University Press, 1985), Vol. 1, pp. 261–277; Eric Van Young, *Hacienda and Market in Eighteenth-Century Mexico: The Rural Economy of the Guadalajara Region, 1675–1820* (Berkeley: University of California Press, 1981), pp. 9–39, 105–113, 236–314.

9. William R. Taylor, *Landlord and Peasant in Colonial Oaxaca* (Stanford: Stanford University Press, 1972), pp. 17–18; John K. Chance, *Conquest of the Sierra: Spaniards and Indians in Colonial Oaxaca* (Norman: University of Oklahoma Press, 1989), pp. 89–122; John K. Chance, *Race & Class in Colonial Oaxaca* (Stanford: Stanford University Press, 1978), pp. 94–195; John K. Chance, "The Ecology of Race and Class in Late Colonial Oaxaca," in *Studies in Spanish American Population History*, ed. David J. Robinson (Boulder: Westview Press, 1981), pp. 93–117; Arthur D. Murphy and Alex Stepick, *Social Inequality in Oaxaca: A History of Resistance and Change* (Philadelphia: Temple University Press, 1991), pp. 9–26.

10. Philip P. Boucher, *Cannibal Encounters*, pp. 3–107; Franklin W. Knight, *The Caribbean: The Genesis of a Fragmented Nationalism* (New York: Oxford University Press, 1990), pp. 27–87; William F. Keegan, *The People Who Discovered Columbus: The Prehistory of the Bahamas* (Gainsville: University Press of Florida, 1992), pp. 3–11; Peter Hulme and Neil L. Whitehead, eds., *Wild Majesty: Encounters with Caribs from Columbus to the Present Day* (Oxford: Clarendon Press, 1992), pp. 15, 33, 40, 167, 345–354; Peter Hulme, "The Rhetoric of Description: The Amerindians of the Caribbean within Modern European Discourse," *Caribbean Studies* 23, no. 3–4 (1990): 35–50; Mary W. Helms, "The Indians of the Caribbean and Circum-Caribbean at the End of the Fifteenth Century," in *The Cambridge History of Latin America*, ed. Leslie Bethell (Cambridge: Cambridge University Press, 1984), Vol. I, pp. 37–58; Dave D. Davis and R. Christopher Goodwin, "Island Carib Origins: Evidence and Nonevidence," *American Antiquity* 55, no. 1 (1990): 37–48; Patricia L. Baker, "Ethnogensis: The Case of the Dominica Caribs," *América Indígena* 48, no. 2 (1988): 377–401; Bernard Marshall, "The Black Caribs—Native Resistance to British Penetration into the Windward Side of St. Vincent—1763–1773," *Caribbean Quarterly* 19, no. 4 (1973): 4–19; Nancy Gonzalez, *Sojourners of the Caribbean: Ethnogensies and Ethnohistory of the Garifuna* (Urbana: University of Illinois Press, 1988), pp. 15–34; Virginia Kerns, *Women and the Ancestors: Black Carib Kinship and Ritual* (Urbana: University of Illinois Press, 1997), pp. 17–39; Maximilian C. Forte, "The Contemporary Context of Carib 'Revival' in Trinidad and Tobago: Creolization, Developmentalism, and the State," *KACIIKE: Journal of Caribbean Amerindian History and Anthropology* 1, no. 1 (2000): 18–33.

11. Gustavo Verdesio, *Forgotten Conquests: Rereading New World History from the Margins* (Philadelphia: Temple University Press, 2001); Gustavo Verdisio, "Prehistoria de un imaginario: el territorio como escenario del drama de la diferencia," in *Uruguay: Imaginarios culturales desde las huellas indígenas a la modernidad*, ed. Hugo Achugor and Mabel Moraña (Montevideo: Ediciones Trilce, 2000), pp.11–36; Francisco Bustamente, "La implantación colonial y el nacimiento de una conciencia criolla," in *Uruguay*, pp. 37–66; Juan M. de la Sota, ed., *Historia del Teritorio Oriental del Uruguay* (Montevideo: Ministerio de Instrucción Pública y Previsión Social, 1965), Vol. I, pp. 11–19, 23–30; Jahoda, *Images of Savages*, pp. 97–112; Roger Bartra,

The Artificial Savage: Modern Myths of the Wild Man, trans. Christopher Follett (Ann Arbor: University of Michigan Press, 1997), pp. 113–126; J.B. Harley, "Silences and Secrecy: The Hidden Agenda of Cartography in Early Modern Europe," *Imago Mundi* 40 (1988): 57–76; Rolena Adorno, "El sujeto colonial y la construccion cultural de la alteridad," *Revista de Crítica Literaria Latinamericana* XIV, no. 28 (1988): 55–68; Pierre Clastres, *Society Against the State: Essays in Political Anthropology*, trans. Robert Hurley (New York: Zone Books, 1989), pp. 7–45; Eduardo Galeano, *Memory of Fire: Faces & Masks*, trans. Cedric Belfrage (New York: Pantheon Books, 1987), p. 144.

12. Kenneth J. Andrien, *Andean Worlds: Indigenous History, Culture, and Consciousness under Spanish Rule, 1532–1825* (Albuquerque: University of New Mexico Press, 2001), pp. 193–223; Steve J. Stern, "The Age of Andean Insurrection, 1742–1782: A Reappraisal," in *Resistance, Rebellion, and Consciousness in the Andean Peasant World, 18th to 20th Centuries*, ed. Steve J. Stern (Madison: University of Wisconsin Press, 1987), pp. 34–93; Charles F. Walker, *Smoldering Ashes: Cuzco and the Creation of Republican Peru, 1780–1840* (Durham, NC: Duke University Press, 1999), pp. 16–54; Daniel Valcárcel, *La Rebelión de Túpac Amaru* (Mexico City: Fondo de Cultura Económica, 1973), pp. 72–181; Jan Szeminski, "The Last Time the Inca Came Back: Messianism and Nationalism in the Great Rebellion of 1780–1783," in *South and Meso-American Native Spirituality: From the Cult of the Feathered Serpent to the Theology of Liberation*, ed. Garry H. Gossen (New York: Crossroad, 1993), pp. 279–299; Leon G. Campbell, "Social Structure of the Túpac Amaru Army in Cuzco, 1780–1781," *Hispanic American Historical Review* 61, no. 4 (1981): 675–693; Eduardo Galeano, *Memory of Fire*, pp. 53, 59, 65; D.A. Brading, "Bourbon Spain and its American Empire," in *Colonial Spanish America*, pp. 112–162; Anthony Pagden, "Heeding Heraclides: Empire and Its Discontents, 1619–1812," in *Spain, Europe, and the Atlantic World: Essays in Honor of John H. Elliott*, eds. Richard L. Kagan and Geoffrey Parker (Cambridge: Cambridge University Press, 1995), pp. 316–333; John Lynch, *Bourbon Spain, 1700–1808* (Oxford: Basil Blackwell, 1989), pp. 329–366; Colin M. MacLachlan, *Spain's Empire in the New World: The Role of Ideas in Institutional and Social Change* (Berkeley: University of California Press, 1988), pp. 67–111.

After Columbus: Living in an Age of Missing Information

1. Stephen Mitchell, ed. *The Enlightened Mind* (New York: HarperCollins, 1991), pp. 158–161.

2. Laurence M. Hauptman, *Conspiracy of Interests: Iroquois Dispossession and the Rise of New York State* (Syracuse, NY: Syracuse University Press, 1999); Ronald E. Shaw, *Canals for a Nation: The Canal Era in the United States, 1790–1860* (Lexington: University Press of Kentucky, 1990), pp. 30–49.

3. Stanley Diamond, *In Search of the Primitive: A Critique of Civilization* (New Brunswick, NJ: Transaction Books, 1974), pp. 100–171.

4. Paul Wilson, ed. *Open Letters: Selected Writings, 1965–1990, Václav Havel* (New York: Vintage, 1992), p. 267.

5. Stanley Cohen, *States of Denial: Knowing About Atrocities and Suffering* (Cambridge: Polity Press, 2001), pp. 76–101.

6. Bill McKibben, *The Age of Missing Information* (New York: Random House, 1992), p. 9.

7. Victor Perera and Robert D. Bruce. *The Last Lords of Palenque: The Lacandon Mayas of the Mexican Rain Forest* (Berkeley: University of California Press, 1982), p. 103.

8. Edward W. Said, *Culture and Imperialism* (New York: Random House, 1993), p. 335.

9. John H. Bodley, *Victims of Progress* (Menlo Park, CA: Mayfield, 1982); Peter Matthiessen, *Indian Country* (New York: Penguin, 1984).

10. J.H. Elliott, "Final Reflections: The Old World and the New Revisited," in *America in European Consciousness, 1493–1750*, ed. Karen Ordahl Kupperman (Chapel Hill: University of North Carolina Press, 1995), pp. 391–408.

11. Robert Hughes, *Culture of Compliant: The Fraying of America* (New York: Oxford University, 1993).

12. Arthur Versluis, *Native American Traditions* (Rockport, MA: Element, 1993), p. 102.

13. Joseph Conrad, "Karain: A Memory," in *The Complete Short Fiction of Joseph Conrad*, ed. Samuel Hynes (New York: Ecco Press, 1991), Vol. I, p. 78.

14. James Axtell, *Beyond 1492: Encounters in Colonial North America* (New York: Oxford University, 1992), pp. 197–216; James H. Merrell, "Some Thoughts on Colonial Historians and American Indians," *William and Mary Quarterly* XLVI, no. 1 (1989): 94–119; Daniel K. Richter, "Whose Indian History?" *William and Mary Quarterly* L, no. 2 (1993): 379–92; James A. Hijiya, "Why the West is Lost," *William and Mary Quarterly* LI, no. 2 (1994): 276–292; Robert A. Williams, Jr. *Linking Arms Together: American Indian Treaty Visions of Law & Peace, 1600–1800* (New York: Oxford University, 1997), pp. 14–39.

15. Jerome Rothenberg, *Pre-Faces and Other Writings* (New York: New Directions, 1981), p. 175.

16. Herman Melville, *Moby-Dick; or, the Whale* (Berkeley: University of California Press, 1979), p. 64.

Glossary

This glossary includes Spanish, Portuguese, Quechua, Mayan, Nahuatl, and Arawak words used in the text. Spanish terms are followed in parenthesis with an Sp; Portuguese with a P; Quechua with a Q; Mayan with an M; Nahuatl with an N; and Arawak with an A. Many indigenous terms became Spanish words. For example, the Spanish *huaca* comes from the Quechua *waqa*.

Aclla (Q)	Andean woman who served the Incas or worked in their state temples.
Alcabala (Sp)	Sales tax placed on certain Spanish commodities.
Audiencia (Sp)	A governing body of a region that judged criminal and civil cases and issued laws; also the region itself.
Ayllu (Q)	An Andean community whose residents claimed a common ancestry.
Ayni (Q)	Andean concept of balance and reciprocity.
Bandieras (P)	Brazilians who hunted Indians and sold them into slavery, especially around São Paulo.
Barrio (Sp)	Neighborhood.
Cacique (A)	Indigenous Indian ruler.
Cemíe (A)	Small Caribbean cone-shaped object made of stone, shells, or wood that could communicate with powerful spirits.
Ceque (Q)	Imaginary crooked lines that radiated outward from Cuzco's Temple of the Sun to include major Inca huacas.

275

Chica (Q)	Andean corn beer.
Chinamit (M)	Under the Spanish, land collectively owned by Mayans.
Congregación (Sp)	A town created by the forced resettlement of indigenous peoples.
Conuco (A)	Caribbean farm field.
Creole (Sp)	A Spaniard born in the Americas.
Curaca (Q)	Andean indigenous lord or ruler.
Encomienda (Sp)	Crown grant of indigenous land or towns to a Spaniard that entitled him to receive tribute from the Indians under his control.
Guamacama (Q)	An Andean mountain god.
Hacienda (Sp)	Large estate that usually combined ranching and agriculture.
Huaca (Q)	A sacred individual or a part of the landscape associated with the sacred in the Andes.
Huitzilopochti (N)	Patron god of the Mexica people.
Illapa (Q)	Andean god of rain and conquest; also used as an word for Spanish rifles because of their association with thunder and lightening.
Katun (M)	Twenty-year cycle in the Mayan calendar.
Kin (M)	Bundle of twenty days in the Mayan calendar.
Macehual (N)	Aztec commoner.
Mallqui (Q)	Andean mummified remains of an esteemed ancestor.
Mamacocha (Q)	Andean goddess of lakes and water.
Mestizo (Sp)	A person of mixed Spanish and Indian ancestry.
Mita (Sp)	Forced draft of indigenous laborers, primarily for silver mines.
Mitanyo (Sp)	A forced indigenous laborer.
Mulatto (Sp)	In Spanish America, a person of mixed black and white ancestry; in the British colonies, a person of mixed black and white or Indian ancestry.
Naboría (A)	Indigenous Caribbean commoner.
Nitaino (A)	Indigenous Caribbean noble or landlord.
Pachamama (Q)	Andean goddess of the earth.
Peninsular (Sp)	A person in the Americas who had been born in Spain.
Quetzalcoatl (N)	"Plumed Serpent," the god who founded Mexica culture.
Quinto (Sp)	Crown tax on mined silver.
Repartimiento (Sp)	Forced draft of indigenous laborers.

Repartimiento de comercio (Sp)	Forced distribution and sale of European merchandise at fixed prices to Andean communities.
Saramama (Q)	Andean goddess of corn.
Tributario (Sp)	An Indian, usually a male between the ages of eighteen and fifty, who was assessed annual tax payments in money or merchandise.
Wiraqocha (Q)	Andean creator god.

Index

About the Author

———————
————

Jayme A. Sokolow has a doctorate in history from New York University. He has taught at the secondary and university levels, and he has served as a senior program officer at the National Endowment for the Humanities. He has written about American and European reform movements and proposal management. Sokolow is the founding president of a proposal development services company. He and his family live in Silver Spring, Maryland.